WHITE'S POLITICAL DICTIONARY

WHITE'S
Political Dictionary

BY WILBUR W. WHITE

Professor of Political Science and Dean,
Graduate School, Western Reserve University

THE WORLD PUBLISHING COMPANY

CLEVELAND AND NEW YORK

Published by THE WORLD PUBLISHING COMPANY
2231 West 110th Street : Cleveland 2 : Ohio

First published August 1947

Preface

FOR some time there has existed a widespread consciousness of
the need for the interpretation of the current political scene to
the layman. The average reader is deluged continually with a
quantity of facts, current history, and comment in the field that
we loosely call politics. This material ranges widely from the
local community to world affairs, and problems of considerable
intricacy are hurled at him daily from the front pages, often in
terms that are not entirely clear.

A possible aid to the solution of this problem is the compilation of a political dictionary which endeavors to explain to the
ordinary reader terms which are new to him and which have not
yet become part of his general vocabulary. Existing contributions of the kind are either encyclopedic, or limited in scope to
some such field as American politics. This volume attempts in
brief compass to cover broadly the whole realm of political ter-
minology.

Such an attempt carries with it certain inherent difficulties. In
the first place, the definition of the field of politics is itself broad
enough to permit the inclusion of many terms not essentially political. In general, the effort herein has been to include only
terms of political content or interest. For example, the field of
law in general is omitted, but many terms in constitutional and
international law have been included; the field of economics is,
in general, excluded, but terms of public finance are, of course,
to a large extent within the political realm. Similarly an effort
has been made to avoid yielding to the great temptation to in-

clude military terms which have arisen in World War II. In general these have been included only where they are an object of political consideration. Most of the words in the volume were gleaned from the vocabularies of political parties and international relations, and from the mechanics of the governing processes. They are terms in wide current use found in the general reading on public affairs.

There is a problem also as to meanings. In most instances an effort has been made to give the meaning most generally in current use. When there is some disagreement as to meaning, or more than one accepted meaning, the policy has been made so to indicate.

It must be stated that this volume is not intended primarily for political scientists or specialists in the field of politics. The primary objective is to interpret the political world to the general reader.

Acknowledgment is due such a large list of colleagues and friends that it is impossible to mention them by name. Assistance has come primarily from persons at Western Reserve University in the social sciences and the Law School, but also from various individuals whose interest in politics is purely practical. They are in no way responsible for the shortcomings which may be found herein, but their help has been of inestimable value in avoiding many of the pitfalls that beset a work of this kind. The staff of the Western Reserve University Library has been unfailingly helpful. In the collection of material and revision of details of the manuscript I am indebted to Myrtle Horowitz, Kathryn Gorman, and Pauline Cash, and for continuous encouragement, assistance in the preparation of the manuscript, and help in reading the proofs I am particularly indebted to my wife.

WILBUR W. WHITE

WHITE'S POLITICAL DICTIONARY

A

A.A.A. See AGRICULTURAL ADJUST-
MENT ACT, AGRICULTURAL ADJUSTMENT
AGENCY.

abate. To bring to an end, as nuisances; to reduce, as taxes.

ABC powers. The three major states of South America: Argentina, Brazil, and Chile. In 1914 the United States accepted them as mediators when trouble threatened with Mexico. The ABC Treaty of May, 1915 provided for arbitration of disputes and set up a permanent mediation commission. The powers functioned jointly the same year in mediating a dispute between Colombia and Peru.

abdicate. To give up formally (a high office, throne, authority, etc.); surrender (a power or function). Despotic sovereigns may give up their powers at any time, but not so with a limited monarchy: for instance, the consent of both Houses of Parliament is necessary before the throne of Great Britain can be lawfully abdicated. Some famous abdications: Nicholas II (Russia) March 15, 1917; William II (Germany) November 9, 1918; Charles I (Austria-Hungary) November 12, 1918; Edward VIII (England) December 10, 1936.

ability theory. The theory that taxes for the general purposes and benefits of government should be levied on the taxpayer according to his ability to pay. No single index is adequate. One hundred fifty years ago the general property tax was considered the best tax for this theory. The problem of measuring ability today is more complex, but the income tax is the outstanding effort to meet the problem. See BENEFIT THEORY.

abolitionist. One who favored the abolition of slavery.

abrogate. To void or bring to an end, as treaties or contracts.

absent or **absentee voting.** Process of securing ballots and voting, usually considerably in advance, by a person who will not be able to vote in his own voting district on election day.

ABSIE. An abbreviation for the American Broadcasting Station in Europe, an American station set up in England which opened April 30, 1944 for sending propaganda in the form chiefly of news, comment, directions to the underground and instructions from Allied military commanders to the people of western continental Europe. It was a strong and complete station, transmitting its material in English, French, German, Norwegian, Danish and Dutch.

absolute majority. More than half the membership of a voting body. Sometimes such a majority is required to pass a measure although not all of the members may have voted.

absolute monarchy. A kingdom in which the king holds complete power.

absolutism. 1. The political doctrine that the rights and powers of the ruler

9

are unlimited even by natural law, or are absolute, not merely as against the people, but, especially in the 17th and 18th centuries, as against the Holy Roman Empire, the Church, and the nobles. 2. A government with practically unlimited power in the hands of the ruler.

A coupon. The basic gasoline coupon issued in the United States to every car owner during World War II. A number were issued in a small book, enough for several months' supply, depending on the rate of use. Each coupon permitted the purchase of from about two to five gallons per week, depending on local supplies.

Academy of Political Science. An organization in America of persons interested in the field of political science, which publishes the *Political Science Quarterly*. Although its membership is widespread, it is often thought of as primarily an organization of New York and vicinity, since its meetings are held in New York and its headquarters are there.

accession. The process of becoming a party to a treaty and being fully bound thereby after the original signing. See ADHESION, APPROBATION.

acclamation. A vote by voice; an enthusiastic approving vote without counting: as, elected by *acclamation*.

accretion. Process by which territory is slowly added to a state by the action of a boundary river or by silt deposited at a river's mouth. The boundary usually changes with this change in the course of the river. See AVULSION.

act. A law passed by a legislative body which begins with an "enacting" clause, i.e., "Be it enacted . . ."

Act of Chapultepec. A declaration of the Inter-American Conference at Mexico City, March 6, 1945. It reaffirmed the interest of the signatories in the peaceful settlement of disputes and consultation when peace is threatened, recognized that a threat to the peace was of common interest, and condemned intervention and acquisition of territory by conquest. It declared that the sovereign states are juridically equal and that an attack against one is an act of aggression against all, and provided for certain sanctions in case such aggression should occur.

Action Française (ahkts-YOHNG frahng-SEZ). Pro-monarchist organization in France. Before World War I it was also pro-Catholic, but in the 1920's it lost its religious complexion.

ad hoc. Literally, to this; that is, pertaining to a single case or situation.

ad valorem. A term used to describe a duty on goods or an assessment on property levied as a percentage value rather than as a fixed sum.

A.D.A. See AMERICANS FOR DEMOCRATIC ACTION.

Adamson Act. Law passed in 1916 limiting to eight hours the basic day of railroad employees on interstate work.

adhesion. The relationship of a state to a treaty to which it is not an original signatory but by whose terms it is willing to abide.

adjective law. The rules of legal procedure or the methods by which rights are protected, in contrast to *substantive law*, which names and defines rights and duties.

adjournment. The termination or suspension of a session of a legislative or judicial body or of a meeting of a committee.

adjudication. Settlement or attempted settlement of a dispute by a court on a basis of law. See ARBITRATION.

adjusted compensation. The soldiers' bonus granted by the United States Congress in 1924, which provided that those honorably discharged from the armed forces after service in World War I should be paid the additional amounts of one dollar per day for service in this country and a dollar twenty-five for overseas service. Those receiving less than fifty dollars were paid in cash; those receiving over that amount were paid in life insurance which in 1936 was made cashable. See BONUS.

administration. 1. Management, conduct, or application, as of law or an oath. See PUBLIC ADMINISTRATION. 2. The executive branch of government, or sometimes, the executive and judicial, as distinguished from the law-making branch. 3. The top executive officials, that is, those who change with a new president or prime minister. See GOVERNMENT. 4. The term of incumbency of the chief executive.

administrative court. One of a series of courts in European continental countries, particularly France, in which a person can sue the state for injury suffered at the hands of public officials. This is in contrast to the Anglo-American doctrine that the state is sovereign and cannot be sued.

administrative law. The law of the relation of public officials to private individuals, and of remedies to the latter for violation of their rights by the former.

administrative legislation. Rules and orders which are handed down by administrative agencies and which have the force of law. The binding quality of such rules and orders is often criticized on the ground that they are not the direct expression of the law-making part of the government.

administrative order. A rule issued by an administrative agency for the detailed regulation of some function covered by law in general terms only. Normally such orders extend the operation of, and have the force of, the original law.

administrative reorganization. A plan to rearrange the agencies of the executive branch of the government, particularly with a view to eliminating those that are unnecessary and of consolidating as many as possible of the independent agencies and commissions within the main cabinet offices.

administrative revenues. Income derived from the operation of government administrative bodies, as, for example, from licenses granted by such bodies.

administrator. 1. Any administrative official. 2. One who is appointed by a court to manage or settle the estate of a deceased person.

admiralty law. See MARITIME LAW.

admission of states to the Union. The Constitution of the United States says that new states may be admitted into the Union provided they are not formed of part or all of existing states, and seek statehood without the consent of the states concerned. Most of the states were formerly territories in which the inhabitants petitioned Congress for admission, and were empowered to draw up a Constitution. If the Constitution proved satisfactory, the state was admitted by a resolution of Congress.

adopt. To vote in a legislative body to pass a law or accept a report, as of a committee.

advisory commission. A group of experts whose function it is to provide information or suggestions for some official or agency which has the power to act. This latter power the commission does not have.

advisory opinion. Official statement by a court in answer to a request by the executive or legislative, interpreting the law but not having the binding force of a judicial decision. The United States Supreme Court has not considered this a judicial function and does not give such opinions. Some state courts do. In England the courts give such opinions which are called "consultative opinions."

A. E. F. American Expeditionary Force —United States Army troops sent to Europe 1917–18.

aeropolitics. The formulation of national policies in terms of both peacetime and war-time control of airways, the operation of air-transport systems, and aeronautical development. See AIR JURISDICTION; INNOCENT PASSAGE; CLOSED AIR DOCTRINE.

affiliation. The association of a union of public employees with a large national labor organization such as the A. F. L.

affirmation. An assertion or declaration having the same legal validity and penalties as an oath, permitted by the state in lieu of an oath to those persons whose consciences will not permit their taking a regular oath.

agency. 1. Loosely used to mean any governmental administrative office except those of the chief executive and the cabinet members. 2. Specifically used for the office of any person entitled "agent," as for example the Indian agents on the reservations in the United States.

agenda. The pieces of business listed for the consideration of any administrative or policy-making body.

agent provocateur (ah-ZHAHNG prawvah-kah-TYOOR). Literally, a provocative agent. One who incites an underground group to open resistance in order that the authorities may locate and seize those who participate, or one who provokes acts which may be taken as a cause of war.

aggrandizement. Increase, enlargement, or expansion of the size or territorial holdings of a state. Connotation is aggressive expansion.

aggression. The resort to the use of armed force by a state in violation of its international obligations. It has been variously and less satisfactorily defined in the past as a declaration of war, invasion, bombardment, blockade or mobilization, or the refusal to settle disputes peacefully or to cease fire when ordered to do so by an international body such as the League of Nations. Attempts have been made to prevent aggression by the Covenant of the League of Nations, the Draft Treaty of Mutual Assistance, the Geneva Protocol, the Pact of Paris which "outlawed" war, and the United Nations Charter. The war crimes tribunal at Nuremberg took the position that Germany had clearly planned and carried out a policy of aggression and decided that certain of the Nazi leaders had participated in the planning and execution of that policy and hence were personally responsible and punishable therefor.

aggressor. A state which commits an act of aggression. See AGGRESSION.

agitator. A person who stirs up the populace or part of it against the status quo, particularly existing political international relations or local labor relations.

agrarianism. A movement of farmers to improve their position in relation to that of city dwellers or to prevent the exploitation of rural interests by urban interests. It usually is characterized by efforts to prevent excessive charges by money lenders or other unfair credit practices, by attempts to prevent an unduly heavy share of taxes, often tariffs, from falling on the farmers, by opposition to too large a share of the income from farm products going to those who distribute them, and to objection to standards of money and prices that are disadvantageous to farmers. Sometimes such a movement co-operates with laborers who feel themselves threatened by the same forces and conditions. See NONPARTISAN LEAGUE.

agréation. The process by which a

state, before appointing a diplomatic representative to a foreign country, receives assurance that the representative will be acceptable, or persona grata. Seé AGRÉMENT; PERSONA GRATA; PERSONA NON GRATA.

agrément. The approval which a receiving state gives to another state's choice of a diplomatic representative to the former. See AGRÉATION; PERSONA GRATA.

Agricultural Adjustment Act. Law passed May 12, 1933, for the purpose of bettering the economic condition of the farmer by restoring the prices of farm products to a pre-1914 level. The farmers received bonuses for a reduction in specified products and were expected to gain also from the increased prices resulting from reduced production. The money for the bonuses was to come from processing taxes on farm products. This taxing provision was declared unconstitutional in 1936. See PROCESSING TAX.

Agricultural Adjustment Administration. The agency in the Department of Agriculture established to administer the Agricultural Adjustment Act.

Agricultural Adjustment Agency. The agency which in 1942 succeeded the Agricultural Adjustment Administration in administering the Agricultural Adjustment Act.

Agriculture, Department of. The United States Cabinet office for agriculture established as such in 1889. Its basic functions are research and education in such agricultural problems as soils, plants, animal and dairy production, insects, conservation, engineering, and economics.

air jurisdiction. Jurisdiction in the air above a state's territory or territorial waters. It is usually assumed that this jurisdiction extends upward indefinitely, and that airplanes are within the jurisdiction of the state over which they are flying. See INNOCENT PASSAGE, AEROPOLITICS.

air-mail service. Transportation of postal matter via airplane. Begun by the United States Government in 1918 and turned over to private transportation companies in 1927. Since the rates for this service are kept very low it is necessary for governments to subsidize the service in one way or another. In the United States the government contracts with private carriers on a basis fair to them even though this figure may exceed the income from air mail stamps. The government helps indirectly also in airport construction and navigation aids.

Alabama claims. United States claims against Great Britain for British unneutral service in permitting the Alabama and other war vessels, built in Great Britain for the Confederate states to leave port and prey on United States shipping. The claims were settled by arbitration at Geneva, Switzerland, and the award of the tribunal granted damages of $15,500,000 to the United States.

alarmist. One who continually exaggerates the dangers of public policy or proposed policy.

Alcan Highway. See ALL-AMERICAN HIGHWAY.

Alcatraz. A thirty-five-acre island in San Francisco Bay. Used as a military prison from 1886 until 1934, when it was taken over by the Department of Justice for a federal penitentiary.

alderman. Term used for a member of the city council in some United States cities. In some cities the council or one of two legislative bodies of the city is called the board of aldermen. In England part of the county and borough councils are called aldermen, the other members being called councillors.

Alexandretta. City and sanjak, or district, at the northeastern corner of the

Mediterranean, formerly part of the mandated Syria, given by France, the mandatory, to Turkey in 1938 and 1939. Because the area has a large Turkish population, the Turks asked and were given the right of jointly policing the 1938 elections. The autonomous government was then reorganized and made into the Republic of Hatay, which the Turks annexed in 1939.

Algeciras Conference. In 1904 French influence in Morocco was increased by agreement with England and Spain. Germany, omitted in the negotiations, demanded a conference among those who had signed the Morocco agreement of 1880, among them the United States. Germany wished an extension of the open door policy to Morocco, so President Theodore Roosevelt persuaded England and France to attend a conference at Algeciras, Spain in 1906. As the German demands were unreasonable, Roosevelt supported France, which won a privileged position in Morocco. The United States Senate ratified the treaty on the ground that it was to protect American interests in Morocco but did not mean that it was changing its nonintervention policy toward European affairs.

Alianza Democratica (ahl-ee-AHN-sah dem-oh-KRAH-tee-kah). Democratic Alliance. The alliance of a group of political parties in Chile.

alien. Person, usually a resident within a state, who is not a national or citizen of that state.

Alien and Sedition Acts. Four laws passed in 1798 increasing the time necessary for naturalization and providing for the deportation and imprisonment of dangerous aliens and punishment for sedition or hindering the operations of, or defaming, the government. There were several convictions, apparently political, under the last law (Sedition Act) and although the laws were to run only a short time there was a very general reaction against such legislation. It was not until 1917 that such laws were again enacted.

Alien Property Custodian. An official empowered by the Trading with the Enemy Act of October 6, 1917 to hold enemy property and, by later laws, to sell such property as a means of reducing the economic strength of the enemy.

All-American Highway. A series of highways reaching from Fairbanks, Alaska, to Buenos Aires, Argentina. The main route covers 15,494 miles. From Fairbanks to Dawson Creek, Canada, the highway is known as the Alcan and was constructed during World War II. South of the United States, the highway is known as the Pan American; however, the section between Nuevo Laredo (on the Mexican-Texas border) and Panama City is known as the Inter-American Highway.

All-India Moslem League. Mohammedan organization in India which claims to speak for the approximately ninety million Moslems there. Usually in disagreement with the All-India Nationalist Congress party, the League through its leader demands an independent Moslem Indian state of Pakistan.

All-India Nationalist Congress. The chief political party in India. It is largely Hindu in membership but claims to speak for the whole country. The party has been the main vehicle for the independence movement in the country.

All-Russian Congress of Soviets. The title of the representative body in the government of Russia proper prior to the Soviet constitution of 1936. The other constituent republics of the Soviet Union had similar congresses. See UNION CONGRESS OF SOVIETS.

allegiance. The basic obligation of support and loyalty to the state. It is implied as binding on all nationals, but an oath of allegiance is usually required of new citizens, public officials, and new members of the armed forces.

alliance. 1. An agreement between two or more states to support each other in case of war and the subsequent treaty of peace. Often the terms add that the agreement comes into operation only if one of the parties is attacked, that is, the agreement is a "defensive alliance." 2. The group of states that are parties to such an agreement.

Allied Control Council. The supreme authority in Germany after the military government was set up after the defeat of Germany in 1945. It was composed of the four Allied commanders-in-chief of the four zones of Allied occupation.

Allied Council for Japan. An advisory council set up to consult with the Supreme Allied Commander in Japan in the administration of post-World War II allied policy there. The Council was established by the Moscow Conference of Foreign Ministers in December, 1945, and was composed of representatives of the United States (Supreme Commander, Chairman), China, Russia and one member representing Australia, Great Britain, India and New Zealand.

Allied Powers *or* **Allies.** Term used for the United Nations of World War II and for the twenty-one Allied and Associated Powers which were victorious in World War I.

The Allied and Associated Powers of World War I as listed in the Treaty of Versailles were:

Belgium	British Empire
Bolivia	China
Brazil	Cuba
Czechoslovakia	Nicaragua
Ecuador	Panama
France	Peru
Greece	Poland
Guatemala	Portugal
Haiti	Romania
The Hedjaz	Serb-Croat-
Honduras	Slovene State
Italy	Siam
Japan	United States
Liberia	Uruguay

See UNITED NATIONS.

ally. One of the parties of an alliance. A state which has promised to help another state if the latter is attacked.

A.L.P. See AMERICAN LABOR PARTY.

alphabetical agency. A term which came into use during the first administration of Franklin D. Roosevelt to denote government agencies known by their initials, as for example, HOLC (Home Owners Loan Corporation), RFC (Reconstruction Finance Corporation), etc.

alternat. In 1815 the Congress of Vienna decided that the long-familiar *alternat* (taking turns) would determine the order in which states signed treaties. This meant that each state signed its own copy of the treaty first, then the order of the other signatures was determined by lot. In actual practice, however, the other signatures follow the alphabetical order of the names of states as spelled in French.

Amarna Tablets (Tel-el-Amarna). Oldest international correspondence, it consists of over three hundred letters written in Babylonian cuneiform on clay tablets from the kings in Western Asia to Amenhotep III and his son, rulers of Egypt. The tablets were buried at Amarna, Egypt for over three thousand years until found by native diggers in 1888.

ambassador. A diplomatic officer of the highest rank. See DIPLOMAT.

amend. To change a document formally.

amendment. 1. A change in a document

made by adding, substituting, or omitting a certain part. 2. An addition to a constitution which changes a foregoing part. Very often some special procedure is required as in the United States where the Constitution provides that amendments shall be proposed by a vote of two-thirds in both houses of Congress or by a convention called by Congress upon the request of two-thirds of the state legislatures; and shall be ratified by the legislatures or by convention in three-fourths of the states. The amendments to the United States Constitution made the following changes: first 10: bill of rights; 11th: individuals cannot sue a state; 12th: provides for specific election of the vice-president; 13th: abolished slavery; 14th: defined citizenship and the rights and representation thereof; 15th: provides for Negro suffrage; 16th: provides for income tax; 17th: provides direct election of senators; 18th: prohibits manufacture or sale of intoxicating liquors; 19th: provides for women's suffrage; 20th: specifies January 3rd as date for senators and representatives to take office, and January 20th for president and vice-president; 21st: repealed 18th. A proposed amendment giving Congress the power to regulate child labor, submitted in 1924, was ratified by only 28 states by 1938.

America First. Name applied by James True to his organization America First, Inc. in 1934.

America First Committee. Organized in the Summer of 1940 to oppose intervention in foreign wars, announced its dissolution on December 11, 1941 at the same time urging "all those who have followed its lead to give their full support to the war effort of the nation until peace is attained"; named in sedition indictment of twenty-eight persons on July 21, 1942 as an organization supported, used, controlled, or organized to further a conspiracy before and after Pearl Harbor to influence the loyalty, morale, and discipline of the United States armed forces and cause disloyalty, mutiny, and refusal of duty in the armed forces through the medium of various publications and organizations; founded by R. Douglas Stuart, Jr. See AMERICA FIRST PARTY.

American First Party. A quasi-fascist party in the United States headed by the Reverend Gerald L. K. Smith, founded in January, 1942. Leaders of the America First Committee disclaimed any connection between the Party and the Committee. The Party nominated Governor Bricker of Ohio as its presidential candidate in 1944, but Bricker refused to accept, whereupon Smith was nominated. Women United was the special women's organization within the Party. Openly anti-Semitic, anti-Negro, anti-United Nations, it opposes violently the administration and the leaders of both the Democratic and the Republican Parties and blames "communism and international bankers" for all evil in the world.

American Civil Liberties Union. An American organization set up in 1920 to promote and protect, as by furnishing legal counsel, the civil liberties of persons who are in danger of having such liberties infringed because of racial or other prejudice.

American Farm Bureau Federation. An organization of farmers in the United States, with branches in most of the states, the object of which is to secure better conditions for the farmer, partly by legislation. It is a powerful force in securing such legislation.

American Federation of Labor. The oldest and largest American labor union association. It was founded in 1881 at Terre Haute, Indiana under the name of "The Federation of Organized Trade and Labor Unions of the United States of America and Canada." The A. F. of L. was opposed to the more radical Knights of Labor and desired to exclude unskilled workers from its unions and to include only craft unions. Its greatest leader was Samuel Gompers who was President of the A. F. of L. from 1886 to 1924 and became an important figure in American politics. He built the A. F. of L. on the craft union (horizontal) principle, meaning that labor unions belonging to the Federation would organize all workers in all industries performing one particular skill rather than all workers in one industry. Its unions controlled the jobs, rigorously upholding the standards of the craft and being responsible for labor discipline. Sometimes disputes arose between two A. F. of L. unions concerning to whose jurisdiction a particular job belonged. The main aim of the A. F. of L. was to improve working conditions; Samuel Gompers denied socialism and detested Marxism, and accepted capitalism and middle class ideas. By 1900 the A. F. of L. had 548,000 members, by 1920 over four million. By that time unskilled workers were admitted and banded together in special unions. Since 1924 William Green, a former miner, has been President of the A. F. of L. During the 1920's the A. F. of L. declined steadily and by 1933 its membership dropped to slightly over two million. At an assembly in Atlantic City (1935) a minority group led by John L. Lewis demanded the adoption of the principle of industrial (vertical) organization in large industries. This was refused and Lewis together with his United Mine Workers and a few other large unions founded the C.I.O. (Committee for Industrial Organization). The A. F. of L. thereupon demanded the dissolution of the C.I.O., and Lewis and his groups broke away from it. The enmity between the two organizations was rather sharp for some time in spite of occasional attempts to bring them together. In the 1940's many A. F. of L. unions extended their jurisdiction to related trades and industries and to unskilled and semi-skilled workers. In general the A. F. of L. is opposed to governmental intervention, though it sponsored the National Labor Relations Act. In politics it works through a non-partisan political campaign committee which endorses candidates friendly to labor no matter whether Democrats or Republicans. The A. F. of L. supported the old International Federation of Trade Unions and was also represented in the International Labor Organization (I.L.O.). It opposes, however, the new World Trade Union Federation in which Russian trade unions participate, as it regards Soviet trade unions government organizations and not free associations. In 1946 John L. Lewis and his powerful United Mine Workers broke with the C.I.O., and rejoined the A. F. of L. See CONGRESS OF INDUSTRIAL ORGANIZATIONS.

American-German Peace Treaty. The treaty of peace between the United States and Germany after World War I, signed August 25, 1921. It was made necessary by the refusal of the United States to ratify the Treaty of Versailles. This treaty was essentially a copy of the Treaty of Versailles, omitting the first twenty-six articles of the latter, which form the League of Nations Covenant, certain detailed boundary provisions, and the chapter on the International Labor Organization.

American Labor Party. A left-wing third party established in New York City in July, 1936, which received much of its backing from labor union members. It was criticized by both Democrats and Socialists as endangering their votes. It polled some 300,000 votes the following November, backing Roosevelt and the New Deal nationally and later La Guardia locally. In May, 1944 a right-wing group seceded, forming the Liberal Party and charging the A.L.P. with being under Communist domination.

American Legion. Originally established as an organization of veterans of World War I but later included veterans of World War II. It has been effective in securing favorable legislation for veterans. Originally somewhat isolationist, in recent years it has taken a firm stand favoring strengthening of international organization.

American Legislators Association. A national organization of the members of the legislatures of the states of the United States, established in 1925.

American Political Science Association. A nation-wide organization of teachers and students of political science, including a considerable number of government officials. It publishes the bi-monthly *American Political Science Review*.

Americanism. The principles of democracy and freedom on which the government of the United States is based.

Americans for Democratic Action. An organization of liberals formed on January 4, 1947. Its leaders are largely ex-New Dealers and they advocate a program of reform similar to that proposed by the late President Franklin D. Roosevelt. The organization is also openly opposed to Communism, and in this it differs from the Progressive Citizens of America, an otherwise similar organization. Its first co-chairmen were Leon Henderson and Wilson W. Wyatt.

A. M. G. Allied Military Government. The joint Anglo-American army civil affairs branch set up in North Africa, then extended to Sicily and Italy and sent into western Europe with the armed forces. See CIVIL AFFAIRS.

Amgot. Allied Military Government in Occupied Territory. After brief use in North Africa, this name was changed to A. M. G. See A. M. G.

amity. Friendship, especially international.

amnesty. The excuse or forgiveness of a group of persons for some infraction of the law for which they may not have all been individually convicted, as, for example, participation in a rebellion. Amnesty may be extended by Congress as well as the President. See PARDON.

Amtorg. The Amtorg Trading Company, a Russian foreign trade agency incorporated in the United States. It represents the Russian government in its trade relations in the United States.

anarchism. The belief that every coercive central political power in society results in tyranny and oppression, and hence that government is neither essential nor desirable. Anarchists would do away completely with the state and all government; they would form co-operative groups to run factories, farms and stores, and they believe that these groups would co-operate among themselves freely and harmoniously without any government or law-enforcing agency. Anarchism is quite old and appeared first among the early Christians, then reappeared among Protestant sects in England and elsewhere. The apostles of modern anarchism were the Frenchman, Proudhon, and the Russian, Bakunin. Anarchists at the end of the 19th and the beginning of the 20th century believed in trying to attain their ends by violent deeds such as assassinating important military and political leaders who represented the kind of power anarchists oppose. Anarchists influenced syndicalists in many ways and often joined forces. Hence the expression: anarchosyndicalism. Anarchism is the complete opposite of totalitarianism and statism. See SYNDICALISM, CRIMINAL SYNDICALISM.

anarchy. 1. Absence of government. 2. Lack of law and order.

angary. An old rule of international law by which, in case of necessity, a belligerent state could seize and use neutral vessels and crews found in its own ports. In more recent times only the vessels have been seized.

angel. In American slang a wealthy person who contributes heavily to an election campaign fund.

Anglo-Egyptian Alliance. A treaty between Great Britain and Egypt, signed August 26, 1936. It established an alliance by which, in case of war, Egypt was not called upon to fight but merely to provide such facilities as ports and communications. In addition the treaty provided for continued joint control of the Sudan and eventual withdrawal of the British troops in Egypt to the Suez Canal Zone.

Anglo-French-Turkish Treaty. A mutual assistance pact concluded October 19, 1939, by which Great Britain and France promised to aid Turkey if she were attacked, while Turkey promised to aid either of the others in case of aggression by a European state leading to a Mediterranean war, or if either were drawn into war as a result of acting to uphold guarantees previously extended to Greece and Romania. Turkey was not to act, however, if such a step would involve conflict with Russia.

Anglo-French union, offer of. A pro-

posal of the British government when France was being overrun by the Germans in 1940 that France and Great Britain should join to form a union. The matter was broached to the French premier Reynaud on June 16, but that evening Reynaud was removed by Pétain.

Anglo-German Naval Treaty. A British-German agreement of June 18, 1935, in which the British permitted Germany to build a total navy of 35 per cent of the total tonnage of the British navy. Germany's submarines might equal 45 to 100 per cent of the number of British submarines.

Anglo-Iraqi Alliance. A twenty-five year alliance between Great Britain and Iraq signed at Baghdad June 30, 1930. It provided for mutual assistance in case of war and specified that Iraq's contribution should be facilities for the use of the British. Two airports were granted by Iraq for British use for the duration of the treaty and British troops were to remain in two other areas for five years. The document was of special importance as heralding the end of the mandate over Iraq and providing for the entrance of Iraq into the League of Nations in 1932, which was in fact accomplished.

Anglo-Irish Treaty. Treaty of December 6, 1921, which granted the Irish Free State dominion status and defined the new relations between Great Britain and Ireland.

Anglo-Japanese Alliance. An alliance between Great Britain and Japan concluded January 30, 1902. It provided that if either were attacked the other would remain neutral, but that if either were attacked by two states, the other party would come to its aid. The agreement was renewed in 1905 and 1911.

Anglo-phobe. One who dislikes England and the English.

Anglo-Russian Alliances. 1. An alliance of July 12, 1941, providing mutual assistance in the war against Germany and agreeing not to conclude a separate peace. 2. An alliance of May 26, 1942, repeating the 1941 alliance; adding provisions for the preservation of peace, resistance to aggression, and the establishment of security and prosperity after the war, and extending the alliance for 20 years.

Annapolis. See UNITED STATES NAVAL ACADEMY.

Annapolis Convention. A meeting of the representatives of New York, New Jersey, Pennsylvania, Virginia, and Delaware in 1786 to draw up uniform commercial regulations for the states. The meeting was an outgrowth of differences between Virginia and Maryland over jurisdiction of the Potomac River and Chesapeake Bay. Since so few states sent representatives another meeting, the Constitutional Convention, was called at Philadelphia for the following spring.

annex. 1. To take a smaller territory into the domain of a state. 2. An additional part of a treaty or other document.

annexation. The formal action of a state whereby it includes a smaller territory in its domain.

annual message. The message of the president of the United States at the opening of each regular session of Congress. See MESSAGE ON THE STATE OF THE UNION.

Anschluss (AHN-shloos). German term for political union. In recent times applied particularly to the union of Austria and Germany. See ZOLLVEREIN.

anti-clericalism. Political opposition to ecclesiastical influence within a state; especially in European politics, opposition to the influence of the Roman Catholic clergy.

Anti-Comintern Pact. German-Japa-

nese agreement of November 25, 1936 providing that the signatories should consult regarding, and cooperate in executing measures to combat communist activity. Italy, Hungary, Manchukuo, and Spain later adhered to the agreement.

anti-lynching bill. In an effort to control lynching by making it a federal crime bills were introduced in the United States Congress in 1920 and 1921, by Representative Dyer of Missouri. In 1938, an anti-lynching bill did not come to a vote in the Senate because of a thirty-day filibuster by southern senators on the grounds that the South had improved the situation, and that the bill would open the way to federal regulation of state police power (there had been seven lynchings in 1938, a total of 5,120 since 1882). In 1940 the Gavagan Anti-Lynching Bill was approved by the House, but was not considered by the Senate because southern senators threatened a filibuster.

Anti-Saloon League of America. An organization which opposes the liquor traffic and was very effective in securing national prohibition in the United States in 1919 by passage of the 18th amendment to the Constitution. The amendment was repealed in 1933.

anti-Semitism. A modern form of anti-Judaism, meaning a social and political movement against the people of Jewish (Hebrew) origin or religion. Its roots are fairly deep but whereas in the Middle Ages Jews were hated for religious reasons and were regarded as heretics who refused to become converted and whose ancestors crucified Jesus Christ, modern anti-Semitism claims that the Jews are racially different and are thus a peril to non-Jewish (gentile, Aryan) racial purity and culture. In the Middle Ages Jews were in many cities separated into ghettoes and many professions were barred to them. Consequently they employed themselves with commerce and money-lending and became in the latter capacity indispensable to many rulers and noblemen who often offered them high dignities as treasurers etc. Moneylenders, however, are often unpopular with debtors unable to pay and thus the Shylock-legend attached itself to them. In countries where Armenians and Greeks were monopolizing the money market, they were similarly accused of usury and heartlessness and were often called "even worse than Jews." The outcome of this religious and economic resentment was periodical outbursts of mass-hatred and the expulsion of the Jews from southwestern Germany to Poland and Russia, and from Spain (where they attained a respected status at one time) to many parts of Europe. England, too, expelled the Jews and granted their readmission only under Oliver Cromwell.

Racial anti-Semitism started in Germany, where in 1879 the term was coined. It spread to France and particularly to Eastern Europe where it resulted in pogroms (massacres) but subsided around the turn of the century. It was revived and developed to a high point of cruelty and persecution by the National Socialists in Germany where, apart from Hitler, Julius Streicher particularly (one of the chief defendants at the Nuremberg war crimes trial) was its apostle. The Nazi creed made the Jews the scapegoats for the lost World War I, for the Versailles treaty, for the economic depression, and for both capitalist excesses and communist agitation. The Nazis spread the myth of Jewish world-conspiracy. The outcome was the murder of millions of European Jews by the Nazis. In America anti-Semitism has been used by Fascist and semi-Fascist groups, such as the dissolved seditious groups (German-American Bund, Silver Shirts, etc.) and recently by Gerald L. K. Smith's America First Party and the Columbians, as a political catchword.

Anti-Semitism lacks all scientific basis and has been opposed by scientists everywhere. Conservatives, Roman Catholics, liberals, leftists, Protestant Church groups, and nonpartisan groups have repeatedly denounced it. In the United States the National Conference of Christians and Jews and other organizations have as an objective the co-operation between members of different religious and racial organizations and the combatting of such movements as anti-Semitism. See RACE, ARYAN, NAZISM, THIRD REICH, ZIONISM.

antitrust law. Law designed to curb the practices of large business corporations which interfere with a free flow of trade. See SHERMAN ANTI-TRUST ACT; RULE OF REASON; CLAYTON ACT; FEDERAL TRADE COMMISSION; NATIONAL INDUSTRIAL RECOVERY ACT.

appeal. The process by which a case is taken from a lower to a higher court for review or retrial.

appeasement. Giving a state which has clearly embarked on a program of aggression what it wants in a futile effort to prevent its undertaking further aggression by war. Such concession may be made even at the expense of a smaller third state, as was the case in which the term derived its recent meaning when used to describe the Munich Accord of September 29, 1938 whereby Chamberlain gave Hitler what the latter wanted in Czechoslovakia. See MUNICH ACCORD.

appellate jurisdiction. Provision of secondary courts within a judicial system to provide for correction of error in a lower court.

appointment. The process by which a person is assigned to a non-elective public office. The appointment is usually thought of as being made by an administrative official or agency. Sometimes, as in the United States, appointments of higher officers must be confirmed by legislative authority.

apportionment. The process by which the representatives to a legislative body or a convention are distributed among the states, districts, or other units to be represented. See RE-APPORTIONMENT.

appraisal. 1. The value set upon property for tax purposes. 2. The process of setting such value.

approbation. Endorsement of the terms of a treaty without becoming bound by them.

appropriations. Money set aside for government expenditures.

Arab Higher Committee. A group of Arabs claiming to represent the Arab population in Palestine, particularly during the disturbances of the 1930's.

Arab League. An organization of Arab states set up with the signature of its constitution in Cairo, March 22, 1945. The original signatories were Egypt, Iraq, Lebanon, Saudi Arabia, Syria, and Transjordan. A main function is to promote cooperation culturally, economically, and in passport and nationality questions. The members promised to consult in case of aggression, to accept arbitral awards between members, and to settle mutual disputes peacefully. Yemen joined the League subsequently.

Arab Pact. A treaty of "brotherhood and alliance" between Saudi Arabia, the Yemen, and Iraq signed April 2, 1936. It provided chiefly for peaceful settlement of disputes, consultation on meeting aggression, precautions against rebellion, and cultural and military collaboration. The agreement became the basis for a general Arab alliance, aim of the Pan-Arab movement. Other Arab states were invited to join.

arbitration. Settlement of disputes between states or parties to a labor dispute by judges of their own choice. The decision, or award, is binding. See PERMANENT COURT OF ARBITRATION.

archives. 1. A collection of public documents and records. 2. A building where public documents and records are kept.

aristocracy. 1. A government in which the control is in the hands of a small ruling class, the position of which may be based on economic or military power, social or ecclesiastical position, or age, or special training. 2. The ruling class itself in such a government.

armaments. Weapons of the military and naval forces.

armistice. An agreement between belligerents to suspend military operations. Usually the agreement is between military commanders, but a general, as opposed to a local or partial, armistice covering all hostilities may be reached by diplomatic representatives as well as by commanders-in-chief.

Armistice Day. The day (November 11) set aside to commemorate the date of the signing of the armistice terminating hostilities with Germany at the end of World War I in 1918.

armory. Large building used for drilling members of the armed forces and for storing their equipment.

Arms Embargo. Prohibition upon the exportation of guns and ammunition. The United States Neutrality Act of 1935 included an arms embargo prohibiting the sale to belligerents of "arms, ammunition and instruments of war."

Army War College. One of the advanced military training schools in the United States primarily for the training of army officers for the general staff. It was located in Washington, D. C. and suspended instruction in 1940 because of war conditions.

arrondissement (ah-rong-DEES-mong). An administrative local government subdivision in France, usually rural and corresponding somewhat in size to a small American county; in Paris, however, it corresponds to a city ward. It does not enjoy the autonomy of an American county, but is an administrative unit of the national government.

arsenal of democracy. Term used by President Franklin D. Roosevelt in a broadcast on December 29, 1940 to refer to the United States, indicating the role of this country in providing arms, ammunition, and supplies for use against the Axis powers.

artel. The usual type of collective farm in Russia in which the individual may not own land or machinery but may own homes, livestock, and some tools.

Article 10. The tenth article of the League Covenant, one of the two most objected to in the United States. It was the so-called guarantee of the League, and provided that the members would respect and preserve from aggression the territory and political independence of all the members. See ARTICLE 16.

Article 16. One of the two articles of the League Covenant most objected to in the United States. Known as the "sanctions article," it provided that if a member resorted to war, the other members would sever trade and financial relations and support each other economically to minimize resulting losses; and that the League Council should recommend to the members what armed forces they should contribute to uphold the League. See SANCTIONS.

Article 48. The article of the German Weimar Constitution which permitted the president in emergencies to rule temporarily by decree subject to repeal by the Reichstag. In fact such decrees were promulgated by the cabinet; they were not temporary, and the Reichstag never repealed them. From 1930 Germany was ruled largely by such decrees. Article 48 provided that even certain of the fundamental personal rights of the Constitution could thus be set aside by decree.

Article 231. The war-guilt article of the Treaty of Versailles. In it Germany accepted responsibility for causing the losses and damage suffered by the Allies as a result of the war "imposed on them by the aggression of Germany and her allies." This was the basis for levying reparations. See REPARATIONS.

Articles of Confederation. The first constitution for the united American colonies; the predecessor of the United States Constitution. On July 12, 1776 a set of articles was presented to Congress; on November 15, 1777 Congress approved a draft and sent it to the states for ratification; on March 1, 1781 the articles became law. The sole agency of the new central government was a one-house Congress whose powers were limited practically to foreign relations and defense. Otherwise the states retained almost all their original powers, as for example their control of general law-making and criminal jurisdiction.

Articles of Convenience and Necessity. See CERTIFICATE OF CONVENIENCE AND NECESSITY.

Articles of War. Military law enacted by Congress for the "government and regulation" of its army, as the Constitution provides. Included are provisions for punishment and procedure in case of breaches of the regulations. See MILITARY LAW.

aryans. Originally the name of the Sanskrit-speaking people of Ariana or Iran (Persia) who descended from Indo-European stock. During the 19th century, relationships between Sanskrit, Greek, Latin, Celtic, Slavonic and Germanic languages were discovered and students of languages began to refer to the Indo-Germanic or Aryan family of languages as distinguished, for instance, from the Turko-Tartarian and other language families. A few ethnologists and social scientists asserted at the end of the 19th century that there was a close racial kinship between all peoples speaking Aryan languages. Others went further and maintained that the so-called Aryan race was superior to all other races, white, yellow or black. These theories were refuted by the overwhelming majority of anthropologists who pointed out the striking racial mixture peculiar to most Europeans and the doubtful connections between linguistic and racial kinship. Nevertheless the myth of "Aryan supremacy" was embraced by racist political groups, particularly by the German Nazis who ended up by designating the Japanese "honorary Aryans." This unfounded belief, which maintains that "Aryans" are physically, mentally and morally superior to all other races is called "Aryanism." See RACE, ANTI-SEMITISM, NORDIC, NAZISM.

Asia Minor. Roughly the peninsular part of western Asiatic Turkey bounded on the north by the Black Sea; on the west by the Bosphorus, the Sea of Marmora, the Dardanelles, and the Aegan Sea; and on the south by the Mediterranean Sea. The Armenian plateau lies on the east. The term is not in local or official use now. The rise and fall of civilizations in

this area in ancient times is thought by some students to be due to changes in climate, especially changes in rainfall.

aski-marks. Credit in Nazi Germany for goods sent to Germany in excess of goods imported therefrom. The Germans paid this credit only in German goods. The term is a contraction of *Ausländersonderkonten für Inlandbezahlungen* (OWS-lahnd-er-ZAWN-der-kawn-t'n fyoor EEN-lahnd-buh-TSAHL-oong-en).

assassination. Murder of public officials.

assembled examination. See STANDARDIZED EXAMINATION.

assembly. 1. A large general representative international body, as the assembly of the League of Nations, in which all member states were represented. 2. Title of the lower house of the New York state legislature. 3. Occasionally used as the title of the legislature of various states, though in most such cases the official name is "General Assembly."

assemblyman. Most frequently used in the United States as the term for a member of the lower house of the New York state legislature.

assessment. 1. The listing and evaluation of property for tax purposes. 2. Sometimes used for the tax levied against property, as for example a special assessment. See POLITICAL ASSESSMENT.

assistance. Aid in marking ballots permitted by law to persons unable to mark them because of illiteracy or some physical handicap. The aid may be given by an election official or a friend of the voter who is himself qualified to vote.

assizes. 1. British trial courts for more serious crimes. They are held in the counties three or four times a year and are presided over by judges from the High Court of Justice in

London. 2. Intermediate French criminal courts, unusual in that a jury is used.

associate justice. The title given to each judge, other than the chief justice, of the United States Supreme Court.

Asturias, Prince of the. Title held before 1931 by the eldest son of the king of Spain. It was derived from a principality in northwestern Spain created for the purpose in 1388, centering around the city of Oviedo. The name also applies to an ancient Spanish Christian kingdom, the first to achieve its independence from the Moors.

asylum. A government institution for the safekeeping and treatment of the insane.

asylum, right of. The right of a state to extend the hospitality and protection of its legations and ships to non-criminal political refugees. The exercise of this right is very rare.

Atlantic Charter. A joint declaration by President Franklin D. Roosevelt and Prime Minister Winston Churchill, framed on board ship in the North Atlantic shortly before August 14, 1941, the date it was released from the White House. The eight points of the declaration were: (1) no aggrandizement; (2) no territorial changes against the wishes of the people involved; (3) right of peoples to choose their own governments; (4) equal access to raw materials; (5) collaboration for economic and social betterment; (6) peace that would assure all men of freedom from want and fear; (7) free use of the seas; (8) abandonment of the use of force, and reduction of armaments.

Atlantic Wall. The German military defense line in World War II along western continental Europe from the North Sea to the Atlantic Ocean. Following the invasion of Normandy on June 6, 1944 this line was breached by the break-through in the vicinity of Avranches in late July, 1944.

Atomic Energy Act. See ATOMIC ENERGY COMMISSION.

Atomic Energy Commission. 1. A United States board of five members appointed by President Truman under the provisions of the Atomic Energy Act of July 26, 1946. The Act gives the Commission power to control atomic weapons, raw materials, patents, and lands producing uranium or thorium. After a long debate in Congress, the Commission is made up entirely of civilians, without official military representation.
2. A United Nations commission composed of the members of the Security Council plus Canada, the function of which is to study and make recommendations regarding the problems of atomic energy.

atrocities. Acts of unusual and unnecessary cruelty perpetrated usually on large groups of defenseless persons. See WAR CRIMES.

attaché. A military, naval, commercial, or other official of a non-diplomatic government department attached to a diplomatic post.

attainder, bill of. See BILL OF ATTAINDER.

attentat (aht-tawng-TAH). An attempt at crime. Usually used in connection with attempted assassinations that are unsuccessful; but the murder of Archduke Franz Ferdinand of Austria and his wife June 28, 1914 at Sarajevo is often referred to as an *attentat.*

attorney general. 1. In the United States an official found both in the federal and in the state governments who is the chief law officer and the legal adviser to the respective chief executives and department heads. In a state he represents the state in the courts; in the federal system this is done by an assistant, the solicitor-general. The attorney-general of the United States is a cabinet member and heads the Department of Justice. 2. In Great Britain a cabinet member who is the chief law officer and the chief legal adviser of the government and who, with assistants, represents the crown in the courts.

attrition, war of. The type of war in which the enemy is worn down by such means as blockade and destruction of his productive capacities, rather than being defeated by a frontal attack.

auditor. An official found in states and counties whose chief functions are to examine the accounts of collecting and disbursing agents, and, in some cases, to issue authority for expenditures.

Austinian view of law. The idea presented by the jurist, John Austin, in his *Lectures on Jurisprudence* in 1832 that law is a command by a "determinate human superior" receiving "habitual obedience from the bulk of a given society." The view has wide acceptance, particularly as a description of the kind of law handed down by legislatures. It is obviously less adequate as a description of international law.

Australian ballot. The ballot commonly used in the United States, adopted from Australian usage following the Civil War. It is an official ballot provided by the government, it includes the names of all candidates at a given election, and is marked in a private booth. Moreover, the election is regulated by law and administered by special state officials.

Austrian Legion. A proposed armed force of Austrians in exile which was to fight on the side of the United Nations in World War II. Widely criticized in the United States as an instrument for Hapsburg restoration.

Austro-German Customs Union. Germany and Austria announced on March 23, 1931, their intention to join together in a zollverein or customs union. This was opposed by France, her Eastern European allies, and Italy. They asked the World Court if this were legal, as it would be a first step toward political union forbidden by the peace treaties of 1919 and the financial protocol of 1922. The latter was the basis of Austrian loans. Under the political pressure of the opposition Germany and Austria withdrew the plan September 3, and on September 5 the World Court, in an advisory opinion, stated the proposal was illegal under the protocol of 1922.

autarchy. 1. Political self-rule. (Often used incorrectly to mean autarky, as both are pronounced the same in English.)

autarky. Economic self-sufficiency or a relatively high degree thereof.

authoritarian. Pertaining to a governmental system in which the liberty of the individual in theory and in practice is entirely overshadowed by and subordinate to the authority of the state, and in which governmental power is usually centered in a small, autocratic group of leaders. Dictatorships are extreme and arbitrary forms of authoritarian governments.

autocracy. A government in which all or practically all of the power is centered in the hands of the ruler.

autonomy. In a broad, loose sense, self-government. More accurately a share of self-government, usually applied to the right of a state or community to control its own local matters, although not in control of its foreign relations. Before their independence the Balkan states were autonomous portions of the old Turkish Empire; some of the republics of the Soviet Union are now called autonomous republics.

availability. The sum total of the qualifications that make a man a good presidential candidate from the point of view of his party organization. It involves ability as a vote-getter in general and such special factors as his coming from a state which has many electoral votes, particularly if it is a doubtful state, and having no large, well organized groups of voters opposed to him on social, economic, or political grounds.

availability, certificate of. Statement by an employer that an employee was free or "available" for another position. Under the United States War Manpower Commission controls in World War II, a person could not be hired for two months after leaving essential industries without such a statement. These provisions were an effort to minimize migrations from job to job.

Avanguardia. Teen-age Italian Fascist boys' organization.

Aventine Bloc, The. Group of non-Fascist members of the Italian Chamber of Deputies who withdrew in protest at Fascist excesses in 1924. So-called from the practice of the plebeians in ancient Rome in gaining concessions from the patricians by withdrawing to the Aventine Hill and re-

fusing to cooperate in the government. In 1924, however, the result was merely to leave Mussolini in absolute control of the Chamber.

AVNOS. Yugoslav Anti-Fascist Council of Liberation, the supreme governing body of the Yugoslav Partisans. It began first as an executive council, but later took to itself legislative powers. See PARTISANS.

avulsion. A sudden change in the course of a river in which it leaves its old river-bed and cuts a new one. In such cases boundary lines formerly following the river remain in the old river bed and do not change with the change in the river.

award. Term used for the decision of an arbitration tribunal.

Axis. 1. Term used to refer to the Rome-Berlin Axis, or to Germany and Italy and their allies and satellites in World War II. 2. Pertaining to Germany and its allies in World War II.

ayes and noes. A vocal vote in which the presiding officer asks those in favor of the motion to say "aye" (for yes), or "no." He determines the outcome by the volume of sound if it is possible; if he cannot, he asks for a rising vote, or a roll-call may be asked for by the members. See YEAS AND NAYS.

B

B2H2. See BALL-BURTON-HATCH-HILL RESOLUTION.

Bachka, the. A small section of northern Yugoslavia along the Hungarian

border. Its inhabitants include Hungarians, making it a potential source of friction between the two countries.

Back Bench. Seats occupied in the

British parliament, especially in the House of Commons, by rank and file members of the Government or opposition. The leaders occupy the front benches.

"Back to Normalcy." See NORMALCY.

backward territory. An area occupied by peoples whose cultural and economic level, as viewed by the nations of western European culture, is decidedly inferior. It has been usually assumed by the western nations, therefore, that the political and economic shortcomings of "backwardness" should be made up by a greater or lesser degree of imperialistic control.

Baden system. The system of proportional representation in use in Germany under the Weimar republic, whereby each political party received one member in the Reichstag for each 60,000 votes cast by the party. It had the advantage of providing representation closely following the popular vote, though it encouraged the formation of many parties. One disadvantage was that votes were cast only for lists which were arranged by the parties, so a voter had little real choice of representatives. See PROPORTIONAL REPRESENTATION.

Baghdad railway. The project for extending a railway from Constantinople out into central Asia Minor onwards to Baghdad and the Persian Gulf. The contracts, drawn between 1899 and 1903, were given to a group of German bankers by the Turkish government. The railway made possible not merely the economic exploitation of Mesopotamia, but its political domination, should the German government so desire. The project also carried the possibility of German economic and political influence in the Persian Gulf and India. The railway was not entirely finished until forty years later, but the threat occasioned by its planning was one of the major frictions contributing to the outbreak of World War I. Although the railroad was referred to as running from Berlin to Bagdad, in reality it connected the Baltic Sea with the Persian Gulf.

bailiff. In the United States a kind of assistant to the sheriff in the court room. In England most often used in a similar sense as a kind of sheriff's deputy, though also used to cover other officers, especially rent or tax collectors.

balance of payments. The balance of the total international trade transactions of a country, including such items as sales of goods and services, loans, interest, debt payments, tourist expenditures and immigrant remittances. The last two items are good examples of "invisible exports," that is, of items which do not appear in a mere statement of imports and exports of commodities. In a free world economy on the gold standard the balance of trade is "paid for" by a movement of gold.

balance of power. The pattern of international political behavior in which a third state goes to the aid of the weaker of the two parties to a conflict, thus preventing the victory of the stronger state and the annihilation of the weaker, with the consequent upset in the existing relations, or "balance" of power.

balance of trade. A term used loosely to indicate the balance between the value of the imports and the value of the exports of commodities in the international trade of a country. If the value of exports is higher the balance is referred to as favorable, if lower it is referred to as unfavorable. This conception of trade is misleading because it is incomplete, omitting as it does the "invisible" portions of a country's foreign economic relations. See BALANCE OF PAYMENTS. It would be more accurate if the "favorable" balance of trade were referred to as an export balance, and the "unfavorable" as an import balance.

Balfour Declaration. Statement of British policy on Palestine made by A. J. Balfour, the British foreign minister, on November 2, 1917: "His Majesty's Government view with favour the establishment in Palestine of a national home for the Jewish people, and will use their best endeavours to facilitate the achievement of this object, it being clearly understood that nothing shall be done which may prejudice the civil and religious rights of existing non-Jewish communities in Palestine or the rights and political status enjoyed by the Jews in any other country." The statement has often been criticised for its ambiguity.

Balilla. Fascist organization in Italy for boys 8–14 years of age. The name came from the nickname of a national boy hero of the eighteenth century.

Balkan Crisis of 1908. In October, 1908 the existing situation in the Balkans was upset by the Bulgarian declaration of independence from Turkey and the annexation by Austria of Bosnia, the Herzegovina, and the sanjak of Novibazar, which she had occupied since 1878. This annexation cut off Serbia from Dalmatia and Montenegro and prevented the early formation of a united south Slav nation. Serbia was thoroughly aroused, and if she could have secured backing from Russia would perhaps have fought to prevent the annexation. It is commonly said that if Russia had recovered from the Russo-Japanese war she would have backed Serbia, thus precipitating World War I in 1908. It is sometimes stated by historians that after this crisis of 1908, World War I was inevitable.

Balkan Entente. See BALKAN PACT.

Balkan League. The alliance of Bulgaria, Greece, Serbia, and Montenegro in 1912 which fought Turkey in the first Balkan War. See BALKAN WARS.

Balkan Pact. The treaty of February 9, 1934, among Greece, Yugoslavia, Romania, and Turkey, establishing the Balkan Entente. The treaty grew out of a desire to strengthen and make official the more-or-less private Balkan conferences which had been meeting annually since 1930, including the above states and Albania and Bulgaria. These last two refused to sign the pact, Albania because of relations with Italy, and Bulgaria because of boundary claims against the others. The pact provided for a mutual guarantee of frontiers and an obligation to agree on matters of common interest, and set up a permanent council and an advisory economic council which held semi-annual meetings until World War II broke out.

Balkan States. The states south of the Danube in southeastern Europe, Yugoslavia, Bulgaria, Greece, and Albania, plus Romania and Turkey, which, though not entirely within the Balkan area, have been historically connected with it. *Balkan* comes from the Turkish word for mountain.

Balkan Wars (1912–1913). Bulgaria, Greece, Montenegro, and Serbia attacked Turkey in October, 1912 in an attempt to acquire Turkish territory in the Balkans. The venture ended May 30, 1913, but the allies were more successful than they had anticipated and they had no plan for dividing the spoils, which included the important port of Salonika, desired by all but Montenegro. Consequently Bulgaria took up arms against Greece and Serbia on June 29. The latter were joined by Romania in the second Balkan War and before its close Turkey, too, marched against Bulgaria. The war closed in August.

Greece and Serbia received the greatest gains, extending their territories until they met. Bulgaria got a small frontage on the Aegean Sea and Romania received a small section along the Black Sea. Turkey, by her efforts in the second war, pushed the Bulgarian frontier back past Adrianople.

Ball-Burton-Hatch-Hill Resolution. A bi-partisan resolution proposed on March 16, 1943 by four senators: Joseph H. Ball, Republican, Minnesota; Harold H. Burton, Republican, Ohio; Carl A. Hatch, Democrat, New Mexico, and Lister Hill, Democrat, Alabama. It called for the creation of a United Nations Organization to provide relief and rehabilitation, procedures for peaceful settlement of disputes, and a United Nations military force for the immediate suppression of aggression. It was rejected in favor of the weaker Connally Resolution. See CONNALLY RESOLUTION.

ballon d'essai (bah-lohng de-SAY). French for trial ballon. See TRIAL BALLOON.

ballot. 1. Paper on which the names of candidates for public office are printed and on which the voter marks his choice, or writes in a name which isn't printed. Public issues may also appear on a ballot, in which case the voter indicates his approval or disapproval. 2. A vote, as on the candidates at a political convention. 3. The privilege of voting. 4. To vote.

ballot box stuffing. Placing in the box where ballots are deposited more than the legal number of ballots per voter.

ballot stub. Detachable part of a ballot which contains its serial number, used to make sure that the voter, after voting, deposits in the ballot box the same ballot he received from the election clerks, that is, to prevent chain voting. The number is noted by the clerks when the voter is given his ballot, and the stub is detached before the ballot is deposited in the box. See CHAIN VOTING.

baloney dollars. A reference by Al Smith to the dollar after it was devalued in 1934.

Baltic Entente. A loose organization including Esthonia, Latvia, and Lithuania based on a treaty of September 12, 1934. A permanent council for the discussion of common problems was set up. Dropped after August 1940 when these countries became the 14th, 15th, and 16th Soviet Republics.

Baltic States. The countries along the east side of the Baltic Sea, Finland, Esthonia, Latvia, and Lithuania, all formed after World War I. Early in World War II, the last three were occupied by Russia.

banat. Province, from *ban*, Hungarian and south Slav word for governor. The only modern general use is in reference to the Banat of Temesvar, a small territory on the Hungarian-Yugoslav-Romanian boundary, given to Romania in 1919, sometimes referred to as "the Banat" or just "Banat."

Bancor. Proposed name (sponsored in the Keynes Plan, a forerunner of the Bretton Woods Agreements), for an international monetary unit for use in the postwar period. See UNITAS.

bandwagon. Figurative term for the following of a candidate, particularly in a nominating convention, which begins to gather strength and give indications that the candidate will win.

banish. To punish by officially expelling a person from a country.

Bank for International Settlements. An international bank opened at Basel, Switzerland, May 17, 1930 under the terms of the Young Plan for German reparations. The central banks of

Europe were the shareholders and the United States had no official connection, though Americans served as officials. It was founded to aid the movement of international funds and act as trustee for the creditors in regard to German reparations payments. However, the economic crisis of the 1930's greatly limited the bank's effectiveness, and it has served chiefly as an advisory and research body. World War II further curtailed its activities. See YOUNG PLAN.

bank holiday. 1. A British holiday on which banks are closed. The first Monday in August is the only one which does not have some other significance. The others are Good Friday, Easter Monday, Whit Monday, Christmas and Boxing Day (December 26). **2.** The United States bank moratorium of March, 1933. See BANK MORATORIUM.

bank moratorium. The period during which all the banks in the United States were closed beginning March 5, 1933. The closing was necessitated by runs on banks and a number of major bank failures and by state closings of banks in late February and early March. The banks able to do so opened on March 9; others opened later.

bank note. Paper money issued by a bank.

Bank of England. A British bank which is the banker for the British government, privately owned until its nationalization by the Labor government on March 1, 1946. Except for a few minor instances of long historical background, it is the bank which issues notes and is the exclusive deposit, disbursing, and borrowing agency for the government.

Bank of France. A private bank founded by Napoleon which is the bank of issue and performs the other banking functions for the French government.

It came into disrepute because of its control by a very small number of wealthy persons, and was often looked upon as having an excessive interest in its own profits at the expense of the economic welfare of the country. As a result it was brought largely under government control in 1936, and its nationalization was voted by the Constituent Assembly in December, 1945, along with that of four other large banks.

Bankhead Cotton Control Act. A law limiting cotton production in 1934-35 to ten million bales. Each farmer was assigned a quota and was liable for a severe penalty for raising more.

bankruptcy. A process regulated by law by which the assets of an insolvent debtor are distributed proportionately among his creditors.

Banks of the United States. Two banks chartered by Congress for twenty years each in 1791 and 1816. They were banks for the deposit of public funds and loaned money to the national government. They also aided in collecting revenue and issued bank notes. The second was attacked by the state banks and its renewal was a major issue in the 1832 campaign. Jackson opposed renewing the charter and the bank ceased to function in 1836.

bar. 1. Railing before a judge at which the business of the court is carried on. **2.** A system of courts. **3.** Collective term for practicing lawyers or (in England) barristers. **4.** In the Senate the space before the president's desk at which impeached or summoned persons are brought. **5.** The rail at the entrance to the House of Commons beyond which only members may pass.

Barbary pirates. Predatory seafarers who flourished along the North African coast from Morocco to Tripoli, from the 16th century until the French conquest of Algiers in 1830.

The European powers paid them annual tribute to gain immunity for their Mediterranean shipping. Although the United States also made such payments, difficulties arose and Tripoli declared war in 1801. After a conflict largely naval in character, Tripoli sued for peace in 1805. Her annual tribute was abolished, but it was continued to the other Barbary states. During the War of 1812, Algiers seized American ships, but in 1815 Stephen Decatur forced Algiers, Tunis and Tripoli to abandon all payments and an American naval squadron in the Mediterranean assured the future safety of American ships.

Barbary states. The countries along North Africa west of Egypt: Tripoli, Tunis, Algiers and Morocco. The name derives from the Berbers, the principal inhabitants of the area. See BARBARY PIRATES.

baron. European title of nobility, usually of low rank. Most widely used in Britain where it was used after the Norman Conquest to mean roughly any free man, as opposed to serfs, who held land from a feudal lord or the king. Finally applied only to those nobles given the title by the king. Barons have seats in the House of Lords. In France the title was especially prominent after Napoleon I when it was conferred principally as a mark of minor social distinction. See PEERAGE.

baronet. A British title created by James I in 1611, the lowest ranking hereditary title in Great Britain. Baronets do not sit in the House of Lords. They are addressed as "sir," that is, "Sir John Jones, Baronet."

barrister. British attorney who is secured by a solicitor to represent a client in court. See SOLICITOR.

barter. 1. To exchange commodities without the use of money. Used by the Nazis in international commerce to control the foreign trade of smaller countries. 2. The commodities so exchanged.

Base-Destroyer Agreement. An agreement between the United States and Great Britain on September 2, 1940 by which the former was granted 99 year leases to naval and air bases (two were outright gifts) in Newfoundland and scattered places from Bermuda to British Guiana, in return for which Britain received 50 United States over-age destroyers.

Basque. Native of the Basque provinces of Spain or France, lying about the angle of the bay of Biscay.

Bastille. Originally the French name for any fortress, but later limited to the Castle of St. Antoine in Paris, built principally in the 14th century. The Bastille became a symbol of tyranny when used as a state prison by the Bourbons, and it was attacked and destroyed by the revolutionists on July 14, 1789.

Bastille Day. July 14, the French holiday commemorating the fall of the Bastille.

Bataan. A mountainous, jungle-covered peninsula on the Philippine Island of Luzon, west of Manila across Manila Bay. In the opening weeks of World War II the principal units of the United States and Filipino armies withdrew into Bataan in the middle of January, 1942 under the command of Gen. MacArthur. They were forced to surrender to the Japanese, chiefly for lack of supplies, on April 9, 1942 by which time MacArthur had gone to Australia and Gen. Wainright was in command. Wainright held out on Corregidor Island, off the southern tip of Bataan, until May 6. Bataan was liberated by United States troops under MacArthur in February, 1945.

Battle of Britain. Term applied to the German air attacks on Britain in the fall of 1940 following the fall of

France when Britain was threatened with a Nazi invasion. The Nazi air force outnumbered the British by about three to one, but during September the R.A.F. destroyed three times as many Nazi planes as it lost, mostly during daytime raids which the Nazis were forced to abandon. Although British cities suffered heavy damage, the Nazi attack failed to knock Britain out of the war or soften her up for invasion.

Baumes Law. New York law of 1926 making mandatory an existing legal provision that a person convicted of four felonies could be sentenced to life imprisonment. In certain cases it made it mandatory to impose the maximum punishment after two convictions for felony. The mandatory aspects were repealed in 1932.

Bayonne Pawnshop Scandal. See STA- VISKY SCANDAL.

B.B.C. See BRITISH BROADCASTING COR- PORATION.

B coupon. A special gasoline ration coupon in World War II in the United States which permitted car owners to buy extra gasoline for a limited amount of driving beyond that permitted by A coupons.

Beerhall Putsch. The ill-fated attempt of the Nazis to seize power in Munich on November 9, 1923. So-called because the plan was concocted the night before in a beerhall. When the day came, the police and troops remained loyal to the existing Bavarian government and a number of Nazis were shot. Hitler and other leaders were imprisoned for a short time and Nazi control was postponed.

Belfort Gap. A break in the mountains in eastern France permitting easy passage to the Rhine River. Strategically important in many wars, it was used by the United States and French armies in expelling the Germans from France in World War II.

Belgian neutrality declaration. A declaration by Belgium October 14, 1936, that it would enter into no alliances with its neighbors and would maintain a neutral position if they got into a dispute. This policy resulted from the aggressive tactics of Germany and the growing possibility of war. The announcement was a disappointment to France and Great Britain which had hoped Belgium would join them in checking Germany. They released Belgium from its Locarno obligations April 24, 1937.

belligerency. The status in international law which grants to insurrectionary groups within a country the rights and obligations of a state in so far as they are necessary for carrying on civil war. See INSURGENCY.

belligerent. 1. A state at war. 2. A national of such state. 3. Pertaining to such state.

belligerent occupation. See MILITARY OCCUPATION.

belligerent powers. Countries which are parties in a war.

bench. 1. Seat where judges sit. 2. Collective term for the judges themselves.

benefit payment. A subsidy.

benefit theory of taxation. The theory that if a person receives a special, as opposed to a general, benefit from a function of government, he should be taxed for its support in proportion to the benefit received. See ABILITY THEORY.

Berchtesgaden. Hitler's Bavarian mountain retreat in southeastern Germany overlooking Salzburg, Austria. Chamberlain met Hitler there for the first of their meetings leading to the Munich settlement regarding Czechoslovakia in September, 1938. See MUNICH ACCORD.

Berlin to Baghdad Railway. See BAGH- DAD RAILWAY.

Berlin, Treaty of. A major treaty for

the settlement of Balkan and Near-Eastern questions following the Russo-Turkish War of 1877–78. The so-called Congress of Berlin met June 13–July 13, 1878, representing Austria, France, Germany, Great Britain, Italy, Russia, and Turkey. The treaty of July 13, 1878, recognized the independence of Montenegro, Serbia, and Romania and the autonomy of Bulgaria. Austria was allowed to occupy three south Slav territories. Britain was permitted to occupy Cyprus by a separate treaty signed June 4, 1878.

Bertillon system. A method of physical measurements for the identification of criminals established by Dr. Alphonse Bertillon in Paris in 1879. Finger printing has been added since, and is now an essential part of the system.

Beveridge Plan. A system of social security suggested in 1942, in a report by a committee appointed by the British Government and headed by the noted economist, Sir William Beveridge. It has been popularly called "the cradle to the grave insurance plan." The plan proposes the unification of all British social security services by devising a uniform rate of payments and benefits to every British citizen no matter whether rich or poor. It would apply to six classes comprising the whole population: (1) wage earning workers and salaried employees; (2) employers and independently working persons; (3) housewives of working age; (4) persons of working age but not working because of independent income, disabilities etc.; (5) persons below working age; (6) persons above working age. Medical treatment costs, maternity grants, funeral benefits, retirement pensions would be paid to everyone, unemployment benefits and compensation for industrial disabili-

ties to class 1, training benefits to classes 2, 3 and 4.

The British coalition government under Churchill, on the basis of the Beveridge plan, offered a somewhat more restricted social security plan. The Labor Government's Social Security Bill, which is based on the Beveridge Plan, was passed by Parliament in 1946, to become effective in 1948. See SOCIAL SECURITY, SOCIALIZED MEDICINE.

bicameral. With two chambers or houses, as a legislative body.

biennium. A two-year period. Often used in the states of the United States as a fiscal unit.

big business. A general term, usually used in a somewhat derogatory or suspicious sense, to refer collectively to the great industrial organizations of a country or of the world.

Big Five. 1. Term used for the five great powers after World War II—the United States, Great Britain, the Soviet Union, China, and France. 2. The five great banks of England: Barclays and Lloyds, established in the eighteenth century, and the Midland Bank, the National Provincial Bank and the Westminster Bank, all established in the 1830's.

big fix. An American slang term, apparently originating in Chicago in the 1920's, to describe the city-wide graft system designed to control the political activities of the vicinity and to provide immunity from the operation of the law. The system was so extensive it was commonly said that all the angles of danger were "fixed" except agencies of the national government.

Big Four. 1. At the Paris Peace Conference of 1919 the term applied to Clemenceau, Orlando, Lloyd George and Wilson. 2. In World War II, Chiang Kai-shek, Churchill, Roosevelt and Stalin; later, Attlee, Chiang Kai-shek, Stalin and Truman.

big inch. A twenty-four inch pipeline extending like a great inch-worm from Texas to Phoenixville, Pa., constructed in 1942 and 1943 for the transportation of oil. From the latter point two smaller branches went to New York and Philadelphia. A year later the "little big inch," a twenty-inch line, was constructed from Texas to Linden, N. J.

big stick. A policy of forcing through something one desires to achieve. The term is credited to President Theodore Roosevelt who, when asking Congress for a big navy, said that a nation, like a man, should "tread softly but carry a big stick."

Big Three. During and after World War II the term designating Churchill, Roosevelt and Stalin, and later Attlee, Truman and Stalin. Also the countries they represented—Britain, the United States and the Soviet Union.

bilateral. Two-sided, as contracts or treaties between two persons or countries.

bill. A legislative proposal put in the proper form for consideration by a legislative body.

bill of attainder. A legislative enactment providing for the punishment of an individual, usually for a specific alleged crime. Such bills are so opposed to the spirit of a fair trial that they are forbidden by Article I, Section 9 of the Constitution.

bill of rights. In current usage, a list of personal rights and liberties guaranteed the individual citizen by the state. More specifically the term refers to the first 10 amendments to the United States Constitution, and the similar clauses in State constitutions, which were inspired in large part by the English statute of 1689, popularly known as the Bill of Rights. This statute limited the royal power in re-

gard to Parliament and the individual, and is one of the fundamental documents of the English constitution. In France the revolutionists drew up a similar list in 1789, called the Declaration of the Rights of Man and the Citizen, and many European and Latin American constitutions borrowed the idea. In most general usage the rights include freedom of the press, speech and worship; freedom of assembly and petition, trial by jury or by the normal constitutional process, the prohibition of excessive fines or bail, and of cruel and unusual punishments. See CIVIL LIBERTY.

bill-drafting office. An agency established to aid legislators by drafting proposed legislation for them in such a form as best to insure its legal validity. The bill-drafting office of Congress is called the Office of Legislative Counsel.

bi-metallism. A monetary system based on both gold and silver.

bi-partisan. Including representation of two political parties, as for example, a bi-partisan board or commission.

birth certificate. A form issued by a government agency, such as a state or city board of vital statistics, certifying as to the birth, birthday, sex, and parentage of a child; it sometimes includes the race, age, residence, birthplace, and occupation of the parents.

Bituminous Coal Conservation Acts. Two laws of 1935 and 1937 for the regulation of the soft coal industry in the United States. The first, or Guffey Act, was passed after the National Recovery Act was declared unconstitutional, and established what was called a "little N. R. A."—a code authority to determine hours, wages, and prices. Coal was to be taxed 15 per cent, of which 90 per cent was to be returned to coal operators accepting the code. This law was declared unconstitutional in 1936 on the ground that mining was not interstate commerce and thus not under Congressional regulation. The second law, passed in 1937, was an attempt to stabilize the coal market by establishing minimum prices at the mine and setting up marketing regulations under the supervision of the Bituminous Coal Division of the Department of the Interior.

Black and Tan. 1. Term used in the South to refer to Republicans who favor participation of the Negroes in party affairs. See LILY-WHITES. 2. Auxiliary British troops used to quell the Irish revolt in 1920, so called from their khaki uniforms with black bands on their arms and hats.

black bourse. (French, bourse, meaning stock exchange) Illegal banking and, especially, exchange operations. See BLACK MARKET.

Black Dragon. An extremely reactionary Japanese secret society in which the army and navy officers were heavily represented. It was instrumental in promoting recent Japanese aggressive policy. It was officially disbanded when Tokyo was occupied in September, 1945.

Black Hand. The name given to secret societies in Spain, Italy, and Serbia, which used violent means, often assassination, to achieve their more-or-less political aims.

black list. 1. Any list of people, books, organizations, etc. considered undesirable by an individual, organization or state. 2. In international trade, a list of individuals or business firms with which a country forbids its citizens to carry on business, such as the United States black list of firms and individuals in foreign countries, which were claimed during World War II to have had relations with the Axis powers. 3. In labor relations,

an employers' weapon roughly corresponding to labor's use of the boycott; that is, a list of persons whom a firm or a group of firms refuse to employ. Several states have legislation prohibiting certain forms of blacklisting of labor.

black market. A term taken over from the French in World War I to describe a transaction forbidden by law and hence one completed in secrecy or in the dark. Use of the term was widely increased in World War II to describe business carried on in violation of rationing, price, or other regulations.

Black Republican. Term applied in the South after the Civil War to Republicans who helped the Negroes.

Black Shirts. Members of the Italian Fascist political organization, so called because they wore black shirts.

blackout. In World War II, the reduction of light visible out-of-doors to as nearly zero as possible, achieved by extinguishing all exterior lighting, and darkening windows, doors, and other apertures so as to prevent the escape of interior light. The object was to obliterate distinguishing special characteristics of the landscape, such as cities, especially from the air or sea.

Blackstone. Sir William Blackstone (1723–1780), an English law teacher and judge known especially for his famous *Commentaries on the Laws of England.* The *Commentaries* were even more widely used as a legal authority in the United States.

blank check. Figurative term to indicate that a representative has a free hand or authorization to act at his discretion, comparable to the freedom of discretion one has if handed a signed check on which the amount is not filled in.

blanket ballot. A ballot which covers the whole range of government officials; that is, legislative representatives, high executive officers, judges, and all manner of minor administrative officials. Often criticized as putting an unnecessary strain on the voter and obscuring the important phases of an election. See SHORT BALLOT.

blanket code. A set of general rules within which industry as a whole operated under the National Industrial Recovery Act of 1933, unless or until a special set of rules was set up for each separate industry. See CODE OF FAIR COMPETITION.

blanket injunction. An unusually broad injunction forbidding almost all kinds of action against a given party. Usually used to protect the property of an employer against damage by employees.

blitzkrieg. Literally "lightning war" (German). Term used to describe high-speed military tactics of World War II as first used by the Germans, involving especially the co-ordination of tanks and planes. Sometimes shortened to "blitz." When this latter term is used to describe the battle of Britain, it refers only to aerial attack.

bloc. Combination of legislators (not all of the same party), political parties, or states, functioning together to achieve common objectives.

Bloc National (BLAWK nah-syaw-NAHL). A coalition of conservative parties in France, particularly strong after World War I.

block plan. A form of neighborhood organization with the city block as the organizational unit. The plan was used in many American communities during the depression of the 1930's as a means of providing work or relief for the unemployed. During World War II similar organizations were used for the purposes of Civilian Defense and such collections as those of waste paper, tin cans and fats.

blockade. Stoppage of traffic to or from the ports or coast of a belligerent state by the naval forces of the enemy. Recently there has been suggested a similar stoppage of airplane traffic, or air blockade. See PAPER BLOCKADE; PACIFIC BLOCKADE.

blockade runner. A ship engaged in carrying on trade with a blockaded port in contravention of the blockade. Such a ship may be confiscated if caught by the blockading force.

blocked marks. Credits in Germany which the Nazis would pay only in the form of German goods. See ASKI-MARKS.

Blood Purge. The assassination of several hundred Germans, mostly Nazi Storm Troops, by the Hitler government during the week-end of June 30, 1934. They were accused of plotting to overthrow Hitler, but many of the victims were in disfavor with the Nazis for other reasons. Among those killed were Ernst Roehm, leader of the Storm Troops, and the members of that organization found with him in Munich, former chancellor Kurt von Schleicher and his wife, Dr. Erich Klausener, head of the Catholic Action Society, and three secretaries of vice-chancellor Franz von Papen. Von Papen himself was placed under "protective arrest." Following the purge, Hitler's power was greatly strengthened. The Storm Troops were re-organized and reduced in number.

blood-and-soil concept. The Nazi theory that those of "Nordic" blood form a superior race and that they draw their special virtues in part from the soil of the country they inhabit. This idea served as an excuse for the Nazis to commit all sorts of injustices on other peoples, especially Jews and Slavs, in order to preserve and enhance "Nordic" supremacy.

"Blood, toil, tears, and sweat." A phrase used by Winston Churchill in a speech of May 13, 1940, outlining his policy as the new prime minister of Great Britain. He stated that his fundamental principle was to carry on the war, in the prosecution of which "I have nothing to offer but blood, toil, tears, and sweat."

Bloody Saturday. See BLOOD PURGE.

bloody shirt. Symbol of or reference to the Civil War. After the war, when the Republicans laid the responsibility for it on the Democrats, they were said to be "waving the bloody shirt."

bluebacks. Term used to refer to the blue-colored Confederate money to distinguish it from United States paper money, or greenbacks.

Blue Book. One form of commission report to the British parliament, so called because of the blue paper covers. See WHITE PAPER: YELLOW BOOK. Also the United States document exposing the relations between the Nazis and the Argentine Government, issued in February, 1946.

Blue Eagle. Symbol of the N. R. A. See NATIONAL INDUSTRIAL RECOVERY ACT.

blue laws. Laws restricting Sunday amusements.

Blue Legion. Spanish troops used by the Germans against the Russians on the eastern front in World War II.

blue points. See RATION BOOK.

blue ribbon jury. A jury of persons who show special qualities of intelligence and judgment. In New York, for example, such juries are provided for by law if the court so orders because the case is an exceptional one. Such juries are chosen in the prosecution of racketeers or grafters, for example, on the assumption, apparently justified by results, that jurors taken from persons of high standing in the community are less susceptible to pressure and influence than regular jurors.

"blue sky" law. Law for the protection of investors. The term came from the suggestion that some companies were selling shares in the blue sky.

Blut und Boden (BLOOT oont BOH-d'n). See BLOOD AND SOIL CONCEPT.

board. A group of persons elected or appointed to discharge collectively some public function. Usually the group is not very large, very often being of five, seven, or nine members. Its functions may be legislative, as a board of alderman, or more often administrative. In the latter case a board is often considered preferable to a single official, especially if the functions of the office include policy-making in which a variety of interests should be represented.

Board of Economic Warfare. A board whose function it was to promote and co-ordinate the various aspects of United States international economic relations in the field of defense needs. It was first established as the Economic Defense Board July 30, 1941, and changed to Board of Economic Warfare December 17, 1941. On July 15, 1943, the functions were turned over to an Office of Economic Warfare in the Office of Emergency Management. See OFFICE OF EMERGENCY MANAGEMENT.

Board of Estimate. A special organ of city government found in New York and a few other cities which has peculiar functions in regard to the budget and certain other financial matters.

board of review. A board which has the power to uphold or reverse an administrative ruling when appealed to.

Board of Trade. A non-existent British government board theoretically including a number of cabinet members. Its functions are carried out by a president and his office. Formerly the functions primarily involved foreign trade, but now they include patents and copyrights, bankruptcy, temporary control over public utilities, registration of joint-stock companies and control over shipping facilities.

bobby. British nickname for policeman, derived from the name of Sir Robert Peel, who organized the modern London police.

body politic. The people who compose a state, considered collectively.

bolshevik. A member of the Bolsheviki or an adherent of Marxist Communism or Bolshevism. See BOLSHEVISM.

bolshevism. The name of a particular development of Marxism, which was founded by a group of Russian revolutionaries, led by Lenin, the founder of the Russian Communist Party and of the Soviet Union. It is distinguished from Social Democracy and other more moderate schools of Marxism. The Bolshevist theory contends that the proletariat should seize political power through strongly disciplined and centrally controlled local groups as soon as possible, and should not wait until the capitalist system exhausts itself and begins to decay. The clash between moderate Russian Marxists and Lenin's radical group occurred in 1903 at the Congress of the Russian Social Democrat Party, where the radicals gained the majority in the Central Committee, which resulted in their name: Bolsheviki (belonging to the majority) as contrasted with the moderate Mensheviki (belonging to the minority). The Bolsheviki in November 1917 overthrew the moderate Kerenski regime in Russia and established the Soviet Union. They formed themselves into the Communist Party in 1918, the only party of Soviet Russia, which carried out the "dictatorship of the proletariat," rallying behind them at first the workers and then gradually the peasants. Many of the Mensheviki during and after the Bolshevist Revolution joined the majority and merged into the Russian Communist Party. See MARXISM, COMMUNISM, SOCIALISM, CLASS STRUGGLE, PROLETARIAT.

bolt. To leave one's own party and go over to another. Used of party leaders rather than of merely regular voters.

bona fide. Literally, in good faith.

bond. 1. A document or instrument issued by a governmental institution giving evidence of a debt and a promise to repay a specified amount. Such instruments are issued as a part of the process of public borrowing. Usually the obligation extends over a considerable time and the debt is to be paid as a whole, though sometimes provision is made for payment by installments. 2. A money obligation which is forfeited to the city or state if the person for whom it is provided fails to fulfill some duty such as appearing at his own trial, keeping the peace or completing a contract for construction.

Bonneville Power Administration. A federal administrative agency set up August 20, 1937, in the Department of the Interior to market the electric power produced by the Bonneville and Grand Coulee dams on the Columbia River in Washington and Oregon.

bonus. Money granted United States soldiers of World War I after the war in addition to their pay while they were in the service.

Bonus Bill. The bill providing for the soldiers' bonus. See BONUS, ADJUSTED COMPENSATION.

boodle. An American slang term for financial graft.

boodle boys. An American slang term for the men who share in financial graft.

boom. 1. A political campaign which enjoys a marked increase in strength or favor. 2. To cause or try to cause such an increase. See BUSINESS CYCLE.

boondoggling. An American slang term for wasteful or useless expenditure of energy paid for by public funds. The term was applied chiefly during the depression to those projects for which people were employed, usually by the WPA, but the value of which was looked upon by some as very small.

bootleg. Originally, to transport liquor surreptitiously, as in the leg of one's boot. To make, transport, or sell any commodity in contravention of the law.

booty. Spoils taken in war.

bore from within. To undermine the foundations of and to seek to destroy a state or party by working from within its membership.

border states. The slave states which bordered on the non-slaveholding states prior to the Civil War, namely Delaware, Maryland, Virginia, Kentucky, and Missouri. Of these only Virginia seceded.

borough. Town or portion of a large city.

Bosnia. Part of north central Yugoslavia occupied by Austria 30 years before she annexed it in 1908, thus preventing for a time the unification of the south Slavs. It has a very considerable Moslem population, a result of Turkish control for several centuries. In its capital, Sarajevo, occurred the assassination of the Austrian Archduke Francis Ferdinand and his wife on June 28, 1914, which precipitated World War I.

boss. An American slang term for the head of a political machine.

Boston Tea Party. The occasion, on December 16, 1773, on which over 300 chests of tea valued at about $90,000 were thrown overboard in Boston harbor by a group of patriots disguised as Indians, to prevent the landing of the tea and thus the payment of the tax of three pence per pound. The act was one of the most daring in the campaign of the colonists to resist the taxing power of parliament.

boundary. Dividing line between states or political subdivisions.

bounty. 1. Government subsidy to encourage foreign trade. 2. Reward for killing animal pests.

Bourbon. 1. A French dynasty which rules in France, Spain and Naples. Henry IV (1589–1610) was the first Bourbon king of France. Louis XIV 1638–1710) brought the monarchy to the height of its power and influence, but under Louis XV (1710–1774) France slowly decayed. The Bourbons were overthrown when the revolutionists deposed and executed Louis XVI in 1792. After the exile of Napoleon to Elba in 1815, the Bourbon Louis XVIII returned to the throne, only to be driven out during Napoleon's "Hundred Days." When Napoleon was finally defeated and sent to St. Helena, Louis XVIII was again restored. In 1824 he was succeeded by Charles X, who was overthrown by the Revolution of 1830. In Spain, Bourbon rule began in 1700 with the coronation of Philip V, a grandson of Louis XIV. It lasted until 1931, when Alfonso XIII was forced to abdicate. During the Bourbon regime, Spain lost all her American and Pacific colonies. A branch of the family also ruled the kingdom of Naples and Sicily from 1735 until the unification of Italy in 1860, except for a brief period when they were driven out by Napoleon. 2. An unprogressive politician, ruler or business man, often of high economic or social standing, who advocates the old order of things.

bourgeoisie (boor-zhwah-ZEE). French for middle class, hence one who is a property owner or small business-man, as distinguished from the pro-letariat or laboring class.

Boxer Rebellion. Chinese rebellion in 1900 in and about Peking, directed against western control, participated in by the secret society of "Fists of Righteous Harmony." As a result of the damage and loss of life, China indemnified the foreign powers after they occupied Peking. The United States returned about half of its share of the indemnity to China for the purpose of providing funds for the education of Chinese in United States colleges and universities.

boycott. 1. To refrain from doing business with. 2. A general abstention or prevention from doing business with some particular state.

Brahmin. 1. Person belonging to the highest caste of the Hindus. 2. One who is considered a member of the most exclusive social class.

brain trust. 1. Inner group of advisers of President Franklin D. Roosevelt in his early years as president. 2. Any inner advisory group.

branches of government. The great functional divisions of government. In the United States, they are referred to as the legislative, executive, and judicial branches.

breach of the peace. An infraction of the law which is considered as disturbing the tranquillity of the community.

Brenner Pass. Mountain pass between Austria and Italy of great commercial and strategic and, hence, political importance. It lay within Austria prior to World War I but was included in Italy thereafter.

Bretton Woods Conference. An international conference which met at Bretton Woods, New Hampshire, July 1–22, 1944, with a view to improving the world economic situation. The representatives of 44 na-tions brought forth proposals for an International Monetary Fund and an International Bank for Reconstruction and Development with a capital of about $9,000,000,000 each to become effective when 65% of the quotas were subscribed. The purpose of the former is to stabilize currencies and exchange, and of the latter, to provide or guarantee long term loans for economic rehabilitation and development.

bribe. 1. To pay a person such as a voter or public official to act in a way favorable to the one making the offer. 2. The payment for such favorable action, usually thought of in terms of money but often given in political favors.

British Broadcasting Corporation. The nationally owned and controlled British corporation which produces the radio programs in Great Britain. They are not sponsored by private advertisers as in the United States. The corporation was established by parliament whose representative authority is the postmaster general. The administration of the corporation is in the hands of a director-general and board of governors.

British Commonwealth of Nations. 1. The British Empire; political aggregate comprising: (1) the United Kingdom (Great Britain and Northern Ireland); the Channel Islands; the Isle of Man; the British colonies; India; Burma; and (2) the Dominions of Canada, New Zealand, and Newfoundland; the Commonwealth of Australia; the Union of South Africa; Eire. 2. More accurately, the United Kingdom and the Dominions.

British Empire. Accurately, the British colonies. Loosely, the colonies, mandates, protectorates and India. Also used in an inclusive sense to include all territories in any way connected with Great Britain, that is, all the above plus the dominions and Great Britain itself.

British India. The part of India under direct British control as distinguished from the native states which are governed by their own rulers.

British Library of Information. British information and propaganda office in New York City. Its main function is to explain Great Britain to Americans and, during World War II, especially its war effort.

British Museum. British national museum of science, literature, and art, located in London. Known especially for its works of art and its library.

British Union of Fascists. Fascist party in Great Britain.

Brookings Institution. A privately endowed research and training center specializing in studies on public affairs. Located in Washington, D. C.

brown derby. The symbol of Al Smith. The fact that he wore one came into national prominence in the 1928 presidential campaign when he was the Democratic candidate.

Brown House. Headquarters of the Nazi party in Munich.

Brown Shirts. Nazi *Sturmabteilung* or storm troop members, so called from the khaki-colored shirts they wore. See STORM TROOPS.

brownout. The darkening of cities begun February 1, 1945, by the extinguishing of lights on outdoor signs, store show windows, etc., in an effort to save coal by reducing the consumption of electricity. It differed from the blackout in purpose and in the fact that no effort was made to prevent interior lighting from being seen outdoors.

Brussels Conference. A conference held in Brussels in November, 1937, to reach some agreement on methods of stopping the war between China and Japan. The signatories of the Nine-Power treaty of 1922, except Japan, and several other countries were represented. No agreement was reached and the war continued.

Brussels Line. A temporary boundary between Turkey and Iraq drawn in 1924 by the Council of the League of Nations in an effort to keep the peace during a dispute between Turkey and Great Britain. The line received its name from the fact that the special meeting of the Council at which the decision was reached was held in Brussels.

Bryan-Chamorra Treaty. A 1914 treaty between the United States and Nicaragua granting the former the right to build a canal from the Atlantic to the Pacific across Nicaragua, and bases and coaling stations nearby. It was objected to by neighboring countries whose position was upheld by the Central American Court of Justice but ignored by the two signatories.

Bucharest, Treaty of. There have been two recent treaties of Bucharest. The first, dated August 10, 1913, closing the Second Balkan War, divided Macedonia between Greece and Serbia and pulled the Bulgarian frontiers back in the southern Dobrudja. The second, dated May 6, 1918, was a treaty by which Germany forced Romania out of World War I, although Romania re-entered before the war closed. See DOBRUDJA; MACEDONIA.

Buckingham Palace. London home of the British royal family, built in 1703 and bought by George III in 1761. Extensively enlarged and remodelled since then.

budget. A statement of estimated income and expenditure for a governmental unit such as a city or state, over a given period of time taken as a unit for financial purposes, usually one or two years. Such a statement in advance indicates not merely the sources and amounts of income and expenditure but also whether the income and expenditure will balance or which will be larger.

Budget and Accounting Act. United States law of 1921 establishing the General Accounting Office and the Bureau of the Budget.

Budget Bureau. See BUREAU OF THE BUDGET.

budget message. A chief executive's message presenting the budget to a legislative body.

Buenos Aires Conference. A special conference of the countries of the Pan-American Union at Buenos Aires December 1–23, 1936 to consider the maintenance of peace. Three main treaties were signed reaffirming the obligation to settle disputes by pacific means, reaffirming the obligation to refrain from intervention, and providing for mutual consultations in case of threats to the peace.

buffer state. A small, weak state lying between two larger, stronger states. It often continues to exist only by the sufferance of both states, each of which prefers that it continue rather than be absorbed by the other. The buffer serves the purpose of separating the two larger states and thus preventing the friction often induced by the contact of two nations whose common boundary may be the source of trouble. Example: Poland between World Wars I and II.

building code. The law, usually municipal, controlling materials, safety and sanitary features, and other regulations regarding the construction of various kinds of buildings.

building permit. A permit to erect a building. Before issuing such a permit the authorities assure themselves that the building proposed is within the laws prescribed, as, for example, the building code.

Bukovina, the. A province in northern Romania between World War I and

World War II. It was acquired from Austria after the former war, and part of it was lost to the Soviet Union during the latter.

bull. A sealed letter from the Pope, derived from the Latin word for seal, *bulla.*

Bull Moose. Nickname for the National Progressive Party of 1912, formed of progressive Republicans who refused to back Taft for president after his nomination by the Republican convention. The Progressive candidate was Theodore Roosevelt, who received more popular and electoral votes than Taft. Wilson received a large majority of electoral votes, but his popular vote was below that of Taft and Roosevelt combined.

Bund. The German-American Bund, an organization of Germans and Americans of German descent in the United States, with branches in localities where there was any considerable number of such persons. It was strongly pro-Nazi in sentiment and its meetings included Nazi uniforms, swastikas, "Heil Hitlers" and other Nazi trappings. Formally dissolved after the United States was drawn into World War II.

Bundesrat (BOON-tis-raht). German word meaning council of the union. The upper house in the parliament of the German empire, 1871–1918. Its members were appointed by the governments of the German states which were represented more or less according to their populations. It had legislative, judicial and administrative powers. Also the name of the Swiss federal executive council.

bureau. An independent government office or a subdivision of a department.

Bureau of the Budget. An agency in the Executive Office of the President established in 1921 to assist the President in drawing up and controlling the budget. It studies the needs of various governmental agencies and their systems of reporting and keeping of records.

Bureau of the Census. A section of the Department of Commerce devoted to making various enumerations in the United States. The best known is the general census of the population with break-downs regarding age, sex, race, employment, and educational status. Other specialized reports are made on agriculture, industry, business, and foreign trade.

Bureau of Customs. A subdivision of the Treasury Department, established in 1927, charged with collecting customs taxes and enforcing customs regulations such as those regarding smuggling and sanitation. It registers and licenses ships and regulates their entrance into and departure from ports; it also regulates coastal and fishing ships.

Bureau of Engraving. The Bureau of Engraving and Printing is the branch of the Treasury Department which designs and prints or engraves paper money, bonds, and stamps.

Bureau of Foreign and Domestic Commerce. A branch of the Commerce Department set up in 1912 which collects and disseminates information on tariffs and trade regulation, foreign exchange, and other factors affecting foreign commerce, and other information of interest to domestic business concerns.

Bureau of Labor Statistics. A bureau established in 1913 in the Department of Labor which collects and publishes information on working hours, wages, employment, and other factors regarding working conditions.

Bureau of Mines. This bureau, set up in 1910 and long under the Commerce Department but returned to the Department of the Interior, is responsible for the study of our mineral resources and their production, and for collateral functions such as mine inspection, accident prevention, and control of the handling of explosives used in mines.

Bureau of Narcotics. An agency established in the Treasury Department in 1930 for the supervision of regulations regarding narcotics. It licenses cultivation, issues permits for importation, and investigates and tries to prevent violations of the regulations.

Bureau of Standards. A subdivision of the Commerce Department established in 1901, responsible for quantitative and qualitative standards in measuring weights, sizes, temperatures, radiation, metals, chemical products and mechanical appliances. It thus aids also in standardization of industrial products.

bureaucracy. A term applied to government agencies and their officials who are considered to be too much involved with red tape and precedent, tend to increase their power, and lack any direct responsibility to the legislature or the courts.

bureaucrat. Term of derision for an appointed administrative official who is thought of by his critics as thriving on the meticulous administration of the technical details of his office, usually in an arbitrary manner.

Bürgermeister (BYOOR-ger-mise-ter). German word meaning mayor.

burgess. 1. Executive or parliamentary representative of a borough or town. 2. Member of lower house of Virginia legislature before the Revolution.

Burma Hump. The eastern end of the Himalaya range in Burma over which India-China air transport had to pass in World War II. The unusual height for air transport added to the hazards and difficulties of the route. While the Burma Road was closed this air route was the only supply line into China from the southwest.

Burma Road. Road from Burma into southwestern China, closed April, 1942 to January, 1945. Together with the Ledo Road, renamed Stilwell Road in honor of General Joseph J. Stilwell.

bushido (BOO-shee-doh), A Japanese word meaning, literally, "military-knight-way," or "way of the warrior." The ethical code of the Japanese feudal warrier class (samurai). It was developed under Japanese feudalism and is roughly the counterpart of European codes of chivalry, but differs greatly from them in emphasis and character. It stresses above all the complete and absolute devotion of the warrior to his feudal lord, and there were relentless punishments for violation of this part of the bushido. The daily life of the warrior was also minutely controlled so as to place him at every moment at the disposal of the lord if he were needed. The bushido also included an element of sympathy and understanding for the warrior's comrades and also his enemy. When the feudal regime collapsed in Japan around 1860, the bushido was transformed into an equally absolute devotion owed the emperor by his subjects. On the eve of World War II it was revived again by the Japanese militarists, though in practice the element of sympathy for the enemy seems to have been forgotten. See SAMURAI.

business affected with a public interest. A business, such as a public utility, of such a nature that it is felt that the matter of reasonable rates cannot be left, as in most businesses, to the action of free competition. Such businesses have their rates controlled by government.

business cycle. In modern capitalist economies where government control is not complete, there are periods when production and employment are at a high level and also periods when production falls and considerable unemployment exists. At such periods the stockmarket usually collapses also, causing added hardship among investors. Periods of maximum production or full employment are called prosperity or economic boom, while the decline in production and increase in unemployment is called a depression or an economic slump. Business cycles are alternating periods of prosperity and depression. The period between 1922 and 1929 was a period of prosperity in the United States and much of Europe. It was followed in the thirties by one of the most severe depressions that has been known since the beginning of the capitalist system. Alternating periods of prosperity and depression have been known before and can be traced all through the 19th century. Wars usually disrupt the business cycle, causing great increase in production and full employment even to the extent that people usually unemployable or unwilling to accept jobs (very old or very young people, housewives, invalids) are employed. The accumulation of savings through war time results in a postwar period of prosperity after which the regular business cycle is expected to begin operating again.

by-election. A special election between regular elections by which a vacancy is filled. Most often used in connection with special elections for the House of Commons.

C

C. A. A. See CIVIL AERONAUTICS AUTHORITY.

cabal. A more or less secret association of a small number of persons who have common political designs, usually in the sense of plotting against the existing regime. The name comes from the initials of the members of an unpopular ministry under Charles II—Clifford, Ashley, Buckingham, Arlington and Lauderdale.

cabinet. An advisory body to a chief executive or prime minister, composed usually of the heads of the governmental administrative departments. A prime minister is the head of his cabinet, but a president is not considered a member of his.

cabinet of barons. The aristocratic cabinet which served in Germany under the chancellorship of Franz von Papen from May 31, 1932 to November 17, 1932.

cabinet government. A form of government in which the cabinet comprises the working executive and policy-forming body of the state. The members are usually members of the legislative branch and responsible thereto; that is, when they are no longer backed on votes of confidence by a majority of at least one house of the parliament they must resign.

cabinet of monocles. See CABINET OF BARONS.

Cable Act. A law of 1922 regarding United States citizenship for married women. As changed in 1930 and 1934, the rule now is that women gain nationality by naturalization and lose it by renunciation on the same basis as men, except the time for naturalization is somewhat shorter. Marriage of an American to an alien no longer has any automatic effect on a woman's citizenship.

cabotage. The right to engage in coastwise shipping. Usually a state reserves this right along its own shores to its own nationals.

cadastral survey. Land survey used as basis of taxes on land.

Cagoulards (kah-goo-LAHR). Members of a secret French organization of fascist tendencies who in 1937 were discovered planning to overthrow the government. The accomplishment of this was prevented, but such important persons were involved that the whole thing was covered up. See CROIX DE FEU.

Cairo Conference. A conference of President Franklin D. Roosevelt, Prime Minister Winston Churchill, and General Chiang Kai-shek held in Cairo in late November, 1943. In addition to agreements on continuing the war against Japan and renouncing any territorial gains of their own, they declared in favor of taking from Japan all territories acquired since 1914.

calendar. Legislative schedule; schedule of court cases. See HOUSE CALENDARS.

Calendar Wednesday. An infrequently

used rule in the House of Representatives that on Wednesdays it is part of the regular day's business to allow each committee a brief time to bring up bills not placed on one of the other regular calendars.

caliphate. Office of the spiritual head of the Mohammedans. There has been no caliph since 1924.

call. An announcement of the national conventions issued by the political parties during the December or January preceding the convention. It includes the time and place which have been decided upon for the convention, the number of delegates, and sometimes the manner in which they are to be selected.

Calvo Doctrine. The idea that intervention should not be used to enforce against a state foreign private financial claims resulting from contracts or internal violence. The Calvo clause inserted in contracts means that the foreign person or corporation waives the right to resort to diplomatic assistance for the enforcement of his rights, and must be satisfied by remedies provided by the local courts. See DRAGO DOCTRINE.

Camelots du Roi (kah-mi-LOH dyoo RWAH). Small but vigorous royalist faction in France after World War I. Forced to disband by President Lebrun in 1936 after Premier Leon Blum had been beaten by a group of royalists. See ACTION FRANÇAISE.

campaign. 1. The steps taken by a candidate for public office in trying to secure sufficient votes for election. Usually the most prominent of such steps are public appearances, broadcasts, and especially speeches before groups of voters. Also included are such things as advertising and the general management of his presentation to the public. 2. The combined campaigns, in the above meaning, of all candidates running for a single office. 3. The taking of steps as in (1) while running for public office.

campaign fund. Money collected and spent in furthering the election of a person or the party candidates for public office. Limited by corrupt practices acts. See CORRUPT PRACTICES ACTS.

campaign textbook. A handbook published in a presidential election year by each major party. It includes the party platform, information on the candidates, and the stand and record of the party on public issues. It is intended for the active campaigners rather then for the rank and file voters.

Canal Zone. See PANAMA CANAL ZONE.

candidate. A person who may be selected for public office. Usually one who is more or less actively seeking to attain an elective office.

cannon before butter. A statement of German policy attributed to Herman Goering after he became the economic dictator of Germany in October 1936.

canon law. Law governing a church organization.

canton. Political subdivision of a state, especially used in Switzerland and France.

canvass. 1. A count, as of votes. 2. A sampling of opinion. 3. To count votes. 4. To sample opinion.

Cape to Cairo. A project of British imperialism for controlling a continuous series of territories from Egypt south to Capetown. One of the leading exponents was Cecil Rhodes who did so much to bring South Africa under British control. The goal was achieved after World War I when the British received the mandate for Tanganyika, formerly German East Africa. The project also includes a Cape to Cairo railroad.

capital. 1. City which is the seat of government. 2. Relating to a crime punishable by death, or the punishment therefor.

capital gains tax. A tax on the increase in value of property between the time of purchase and the time of sale or exchange.

capital levy. A tax on capital as opposed to one on income.

capital ship. A war vessel of over 10,000 tons displacement carrying guns larger than eight inches.

capital stock tax. A corporation tax levied for the privilege of doing business and based literally on the capital stock.

capitalism. The economic system in which the main tools of production are built by private capital and retained by private ownership.

capitation. A tax per head or per person.

capitol. Building where Congress or a state legislature meets.

Capitol Hill. Small hill in Washington D. C. on which is located the national capitol. Refers also by inference to Congress. In Washington often called "the Hill."

capitulation. Military surrender.

capitulations. Turkish treaties regulating activities and trade of foreigners in Turkey. See EXTRATERRITORIALITY.

capture, right of. The right of a belligerent to seize enemy ships, contraband, or neutral ships running a blockade or performing unneutral service.

career service. Permanent service in a government agency in which appointment and promotion are on an organized merit system. Usually used in reference to the United States foreign service to distinguish the permanent representatives from temporary political appointees. Political appointments have been losing ground in recent years to the career men.

caretaker government. The British cabinet between the dissolution of the Churchill war-time cabinet on May 23, 1945 and the election of July 5, 1945. Churchill continued as prime minister during the interval but there were no Labor Party members in the cabinet.

Carpatho-Ukraine. The eastern tip of Czechoslovakia which Hitler gave to Hungary when he dismembered the former country in 1939. Also called Ruthenia. Transferred by Czechoslovakia to the USSR June 19, 1945, but exchange of populations provided for.

carpet-bagger. One who lived out of a carpet bag, that is a handbag made out of carpeting, hence an outsider. Originally applied to bankers in the western United States who did a temporary rather than a permanent business. Later, a politician from the North who went into the South after the Civil War seeking fortune and political control through manipulation of the Negroes at the expense of the white politicians.

carte blanche (kahrt BLAWNGSH). Literally a white, i. e. blank, card. The term means unlimited authorization. See BLANK CHECK.

cartel. 1. Group of corporations organized with the purpose of controlling the market. 2. French inter-party political grouping. 3. An agreement between belligerents as for an exchange of prisoners.

Cartel des Gauches (kahr-TEL-day GOHSH). Group of parties of the left in France.

Carthaginian peace. A peace settlement in which the defeated side is utterly destroyed, as was Carthage by Rome in 146 B.C.

Carthago delenda est (kahr-THA-goh di-LEN-duh EST). Carthage must be destroyed. The statement with which, it is alleged, Cato closed every speech of his in the Roman Senate after a visit to Carthage in 174 B.C. when he observed that Carthage was a threat to Rome. Often quoted during World War II in regard to Germany, because of the threat which a strong Germany is to neighboring states.

Casablanca Conference. A meeting between President Franklin D. Roosevelt and Prime Minister Winston Churchill and their chief military leaders at Casablanca, Morocco, during the latter part of January, 1943. There plans were drawn up for the succeeding stages of military operations in western Europe, especially the crossing to Italy. From this conference came the demand for unconditional surrender.

"cash and carry." Refers to a provision inserted in the United States neutrality act from May 1937 to April 1939 that belligerents buying goods other than munitions would have to pay for and take title to the goods in the United States and transport them in a vessel not under the United States flag.

caste system. The division of Hindus in India into hereditary social classes.

casting vote. A vote added, usually by a presiding officer, to break a tie vote in a deliberative body.

casus belli (KAH-sus BEL-eye). An occasion or cause for war, such as an attack on territory or representatives of a state.

categorical tonnage. Tonnage by classes or categories of ships for purposes of limiting naval armaments. One view has been that navies should be limited in such a manner, as opposed to a limitation of only the total or global tonnage of a navy.

Catholic Center Party. One of the largest German parties before Hitler came to power. It was supported by peasants, Catholic Trade Unions, middle-class people, small businessmen and particularly by women. It had close relations with the Catholic clergy and institutions, advocated moderate social reforms, friendly relations with the Vatican, international co-operation and in general a middle-of-the-road policy. Its roots go back into the first half of the 19th century when in the legislatures of South German kingdoms and duchies Catholic groups appeared. A Catholic political group was created in Prussia in 1852 which became known as *Zentrumspartei*, or Party of the Center because its representatives sat in the center of the Prussian Chamber. After the formation of the German Empire (1871) the Center Party became a national organization and one of the main parties of the Reichstag. It carried on a fight against Chancellor Bismarck who allied himself with Liberals to fight the Catholic influence in Germany. The Center Party often held the balance between the right and the left. In 1917 it favored peace with the Allies and internal reforms. The Center Party supported the Weimar Republic and together with the Social Democrats and the Democrats participated in most German governments between 1919–1933. Its last leader was Chancellor Heinrich Bruening (1930–32). The party organization in Bavaria was called *Bayerische Volkspartei* (Bavarian People's Party).

caucus. 1. Meeting of leaders of a political group to choose party candidates. 2. Meeting of regular party members in a legislative body to determine the organization of the body and its stand on forthcoming issues.

caudillo. Spanish word meaning chief. Title taken by Francisco Franco in 1939.

Cavite. United States naval base in Manila Harbor.

C.B. See ORDER OF THE BATH.

C.B.E. See ORDER OF THE BRITISH EMPIRE.

C.C.C. See CIVILIAN CONSERVATION CORPS; COMMODITY CREDIT CORPORATION.

C coupon. A special gasoline ration coupon in World War II which permitted a car owner to purchase amounts of gasoline beyond the A coupon limit if extensive use of the car was required in the owner's normal business.

cease and desist order. An administrative order prohibiting a person from continuing a practice which the administrative agency finds contrary to the law and rules.

Cecil-Requin Draft Treaty. See DRAFT TREATY OF MUTUAL ASSISTANCE.

ceiling price. In the United States a price above which a commodity or rent may not legally be raised. Usually fixed by using the price prevailing on a specified previous date. Ceiling prices were part of the government attempt to control inflation during World War II and the period following.

Celestial Empire. A translation of one of the native names for China. Applies to China before 1912, the date when the republic was established.

cell. Smallest unit of a political organization. Used most often in the Communist system.

censorship. Examination of communications, printed material, and moving pictures with a view to preventing transmission, publication, and exhibition of parts which may convey military information or endanger public morals.

censure. 1. A vote of condemnation or disapproval. 2. To vote disapproval.

census. An official count of the population including certain information pertaining thereto such as births, deaths, density, and racial, national and economic groupings.

center. Individuals or parties that follow a middle-of-the-road policy and take a position approximately midway between the reactionary parties of the extreme right and the Communists on the extreme left. Often they are seated literally in the center between the two extremes in parliamentary bodies such as the French Chamber of Deputies. In Germany there was a center party. See CATHOLIC CENTER PARTY.

central administration. National or, less often in the United States, state administrative officers and services as opposed to regional, local, or field offices.

Central American Court of Justice. A court set up to handle cases involving the five Central American republics. It lasted from 1907 to 1917. It was distinguished by permitting not only states but individual persons to appear before it as parties.

Central Executive Committee. See UNION CENTRAL EXECUTIVE COMMITTEE.

centralization. Close connection from top to bottom between different levels of government, for example between national and local, or between field agencies and a central office. See INTEGRATION.

Central Powers. Germany and her allies in World War I: Austria-Hungary, Bulgaria, and Turkey.

Centrists. See CATHOLIC CENTER PARTY.

certificate of convenience and necessity. An administrative order authorizing, as a result of public need and advantage, the establishment or extension of some service, as by a public utility. For example, under the Transportation Act of 1920, the Interstate Commerce Commission was authorized to issue such certificates for extension and new construction of railroads.

certificate of election. Official notification from the proper authorities to a person that he has been elected to office. With the modern rapid reporting of election returns by the newspapers and radio, this is now only a formality.

cessation. Termination. Used very frequently to refer to the end of hostilities.

cession. The legal transference of territory by one state to another. It makes no difference that such transfer may have been the result of war.

C. G. T. See CONFÉDERATION GÉNÉRALE DU TRAVAIL.

Chaco Dispute. See GRAN CHACO.

chain store tax. A state tax levied upon a chain of stores, sharply increasing with the number of stores. Such a tax represents an effort by a state to protect the small individual store-owner from the competition of the big chains.

chain voting. The process by which a voter places in the ballot box a previously marked ballot, the first "voter" in the chain having deposited a facsimile. Unscrupulous party organizations may thus illegally mark the ballots as they desire, away from the voting place, and assure themselves of deposit by not paying the fraudulent voters until they return with a new blank ballot. Called also the Tasmanian dodge.

challenge. To question the right of a voter to vote in an election or, more particularly, to vote a certain party ticket in a primary. If challenged, the voter, in order to vote, must make a statement and in some cases swear that he is eligible to vote as he desires.

chamber. Term synonymous with the word "house" to describe a parliamentary body. In several countries, as for example France, the word may be part of the official name of one of the houses, the Chamber of Deputies, often referred to merely as "the Chamber."

Chamber of Culture. A Nazi German governmental agency under the propaganda ministry which controlled the cultural activities in Germany. Writers, musicians, artists, and radio personnel had to belong to the various divisions or they could not work at their profession.

Chamber of Deputies. Name of the lower house in the national parliaments of a number of countries, the most widely known of which is France.

Chamber of Fasces and Corporations. The lower house of the Italian parliament substituted for the Chamber of Deputies in 1939. Its members came from the Grand Council, the Fascist Party National Council, and the National Council of Corporations.

Chamorro. A native of Guam having the status of an American national.

chancellery. 1. Office of the chancellor. 2. (Plural) Used loosely to mean foreign offices.

chancellor. Prime minister of Germany or Austria. See CHANCELLOR OF THE EXCHEQUER, LORD CHANCELLOR.

Chancellor of the Exchequer. British cabinet member who, as finance minister, is the head fiscal agent of the government. His functions include the collection and disbursing of funds, and government relations with the Bank of England.

chancery. See EQUITY.

chancery courts. See EQUITY.

charge. 1. The instructions a judge gives a jury regarding its responsibilities in reaching a decision. 2. A financial burden of some kind such as interest or rent to be paid.

chargé d'affaires (shahr-zhay da-FAIR). The fourth or lowest class of diplomat. The chargé d'affaires *ad interim* is one who is temporarily in charge of an embassy or legation while the ambassador or minister is absent. The chargé d'affaires *ad hoc* is one permanently in charge of a diplomatic post.

charter. Fundamental law of American cities, including powers and organization, granted by the state legislature. Within each state the different charters may be unique, uniform, or vary by size of city. Charters may also be selected from a few standard forms or the city may be permitted by the state to draw up its own. See GENERAL CHARTER PLAN, OPTIONAL CHARTER PLAN, HOME RULE, and CLASSIFICATION OF CITIES.

Chartist Movement. The first modern effort of the working class to better its political status. It was an English movement prior to 1850, an effort to achieve for the workers the gains received by the middle classes in the Reform Act of 1832.

chauvinism. Blindly excessive and exaggerated patriotism. The term came from the name of Nicolas Chauvin, a most devoted admirer and follower of Napoleon.

cheater. Person paid to vote in one manner who votes in another.

checks and balances. The governmental principle that the three branches of government — legislative, executive, and judicial — should not exercise their powers exclusively but should be somewhat dependent on each other. For example, new laws by the legislative may require the assent of the executive, and then be scrutinized as to constitutionality by the courts, while the executive control of foreign relations may have to have legislative approval.

chef de cabinet (SHEF duh kah-bee-NEH). The chief departmental assistant to a French minister. Each minister in France has a number of advisers who take office with him, a departmental *cabinet*. The *chef* is head of this group.

Cheka. Russian secret police organized by the Communists after their revolution in 1917 to run down and suppress anti-revolutionary activities. In 1922 it was reorganized as the OGPU (Extraordinary Commission to Combat Counter-Revolution.)

Chequers. Country estate placed at the disposal of the British prime minister. It was donated to the government in 1921 by Lord and Lady Lee of Fareham. It received its name apparently from the fact that at an early date it was the home of a clerk to the exchequer under Henry II. The full name is Chequers Court.

Chetnik. Member of Yugoslav regular and irregular forces which continued to attack and harass the German army in Yugoslavia after that country was taken by the Nazis in April, 1941. The forces were led by General Mikhailovich who was minister of war of the Yugoslav government-in-exile, and the political complexion of the organization tended to follow that of preceding governments, that is, favored the continued dominant position of the Serbian part of the country. The Chetniks came into conflict with the leftist Partisans, under Marshal Tito, who received Allied backing after 1942 at the expense of the Chetniks. See PARTISAN.

chief executive. The principal administrative official and head of the executive branch of a government, as the governor of a state of the United States or the president of the United States.

chief justice. Ranking justice of a court, especially the United States Supreme Court. He presides over the court and assigns the work of the court.

chief magistrate. A term sometimes used for the highest executive official, as for example the president or mayor.

child-labor laws. Measures regulating the employment and conditions of employment of children under a certain age. At the beginning of the modern industrial age, toward the end of the 18th century, attention was aroused to the deplorable conditions of children working in factories 12–16 hours a day under unsanitary conditions and deprived of all schooling. Child labor was used particularly in textile mills: in 1832 two-fifths of all persons employed in New England factories were children between 7 and 16 years of age. The legislation to protect the health and morals of working children was passed in England in 1802, the first American Child Labor Laws were passed in Massachusetts in 1836. These laws became gradually more restrictive. Today nearly all civilized nations protect their children from damaging working conditions, prohibiting the employment in mines and factories of children under 14, limiting hours of children between 14 and 18 to eight per day and prohibiting night work altogether.

In the United States most states have their own child labor laws. The first Federal Child Labor Act of 1916 was declared unconstitutional by the Supreme Court in 1918, while similar provisions passed by Congress in 1919 were declared unconstitutional by the Supreme Court in 1922. A Child Labor Amendment to the Constitution was submitted to the states in 1924, by which Congress would be empowered to regulate the labor of children under 18. By 1938 it had been ratified by only 28 states of the 36 necessary to make it an amendment.

In 1936 the Walsh-Healey Act was passed, providing that all government contracts in excess of $10,000 carry stipulations that no boy under 16 or girl under 18 be employed in carrying out the work. (In 1942 the minimum age for girls was lowered to 16).

The Fair Labor Standards Act of 1938, popularly called the Wages and Hours Law, prohibits the shipping in interstate and foreign trade, of goods produced in American establishments where children under 16, or, in case of hazardous occupations, children under 18, are employed. In occupations other than manufacturing and mining, employment of 14- and 15-year-old children is permitted. The act is administered by the Children's Bureau of the Department of Labor.

Children's Bureau. A branch of the United States Department of Labor, set up in 1912, the function of which is the oversight of matters regarding child welfare in general, especially child labor, and maternal health.

Chiltern Hundreds. Three sections of crown lands in Buckinghamshire, England, the stewards of which are appointed by the crown. The offices have been honorary and without real responsibilities for many years, but they have a peculiar significance for the members of the House of Commons. A member of that body, under an old rule, may not resign his seat, but since membership cannot be held by certain officers, appointment to such offices, including the stewardship of the Chiltern Hundreds, is tantamount to resignation.

China Incident. Japanese euphemism for the war in the Far East after 1931.

Chinese Changchun Railway. A merger of the Chinese Eastern Railway and the South Manchurian Railway, both in Manchuria, effected by the Russo-Chinese Treaty of August 26, 1945. The new railway is to be jointly owned and operated by the two countries. See SOUTH MANCHURIAN RAILWAY; CHINESE EASTERN RAILWAY.

Chinese Constitution of 1946. A document approved by the National or Constitutional Assembly of China, December 25, 1946, but without Communist participation. It supplants the Constitution of 1931 and was to go into effect December 25, 1947. The document is a mixture of American,

British and Chinese elements. It provides for a bill of rights, universal suffrage for all over 20, and makes the state responsible for illegal acts by its own officials. Basic power lies with a General Assembly elected for a six-year term; it chooses the President and Vice-President, can amend the Constitution, and has the powers of initiative, referendum, and recall. The President serves for six years and can be elected for only two terms; his powers are similar to those of the President of the United States save that he has wide emergency powers. There are also five Yuans (Councils): Executive Yuan (Cabinet), appointed by the President, with the power of veto; Legislative Yuan, elected every three years, with power to pass normal legislation and over-ride vetoes by a two-thirds vote; Judicial Yuan, a supreme court appointed by the President; Examination Yuan, also appointed by the President, a sort of civil service commission in the ancient Chinese tradition; Control Yuan, to supervise public officials, elected for six-year terms by the Provincial Assemblies. The Communist opposition has declared the Constitution "illegal."

Chinese Eastern Railway. The east-west railway and a southern branch in central Manchuria, an extension of the Trans-Siberian line to Vladivostok. Long a bone of contention between Russia and Japan. See CHINESE CHANGCHUN RAILWAY.

Chinese Exclusion acts. Laws passed in 1882 and 1892 preventing the entrance into the United States of Chinese coolies, and making Chinese ineligible for United States citizenship. They were in contravention of the Burlingame Treaty of 1868, permitting the citizens of each country to enter and reside in the other. The laws were repealed by Congress in 1943, placing Chinese immigration under the quota system.

Chinese-Russian agreements of 1945. A series of agreements between China and the Soviet Union signed August 14 and published August 26, 1945. The first was a thirty-year treaty of friendship providing for military co-operation during and after the current war, no separate peace treaties with Japan, co-operation in peacetime, including respecting each other's sovereignty and territory, and mutual economic assistance. There were five other agreements. The first of these provided for the reorganization of the Chinese Eastern and South Manchurian railways into the jointly owned and operated Chinese Changchun Railway. The second established Port Arthur as a joint Chinese-Russian naval base. The third made Dairen a Chinese-administered free port. The fourth provided for Russian control in the zone of hostilities and control by the Chinese national government in other areas in the three eastern provinces of China into which Soviet troops went while fighting the Japanese. In the fifth Russia agreed to support and assist the Chinese government, to respect Chinese sovereignty, and not to interfere in Chinese internal affairs.

Christian Democratic Party. A post-World War II Italian political party of the moderate left. It is less to the left than socialism, advocating a balance between democratic freedoms and social justice. The leader of the party, De Gasperi, became premier, and in the elections of June, 1946 the party polled 35% of the total vote, almost as many votes as the Communists (18%) and Socialists (20%) together.

Christian Front. One of a number of reactionary, more-or-less pro-fascist and anti-Semitic organizations which sprang up in the 1930's in the United States, composed in part of followers of Father Coughlin.

Christian Mobilizers. An organization of extremists of the Christian Front, set up in 1939.

Christian Social Party. A party of the moderate left which first appeared in the American zone of Germany in October, 1945. It includes many from the former Catholic Center party, which has not reappeared after World War II, and also many from two smaller Protestant parties. Its platform includes the principles of Christian morality, opposition to totalitarianism, maintenance of private property and the co-operation of church and state. In the first four local elections in the zone it received the largest number of votes three times, varying from 30% to 47% of the total votes cast.

Church of England. The episcopal establishment in England, where it is the official church of the state.

C. I. E. See ORDER OF THE INDIAN EMPIRE.

C. I. O. See CONGRESS OF INDUSTRIAL ORGANIZATIONS.

cipher. Code used in diplomatic communications.

circuit court. The name, in certain states, of intermediate state courts between the county courts and the state supreme court. Such courts travel "on circuit," that is, sit in different counties from time to time.

circuit courts of appeals. The ten intermediate courts in the United States federal court system between the district courts and the Supreme Court. They have no original jurisdiction.

citizen. Defined by Amendment XIV of the United States Constitution as a person born or naturalized in the United States and subject to its jurisdiction. See NATIONAL.

citizenship. Full membership in a state. Such membership naturally carries certain rights, but in recent times growing emphasis has been placed on the duties of citizenship.

citizens' ticket. A non-partisan ticket entered by a group of citizens in an election in an effort to clean up local politics.

City, the. Financial center of London.

city charter. The basic law or constitution for the government of a city, outlining its organization and powers. In the United States, as the cities are subdivisions of the states, either the charter or the power to draw up a charter is granted to cities by state law.

city manager plan. Instituted in Staunton, Virginia in 1908. Between 1914 and 1930 the number of cities governed by this plan grew to more than 400. In this plan a properly elected city council appoints the city manager, who is responsible for the administrative office of the city, their personnel and the transaction of the city's business. The elected council and mayor enact ordinances, make appropriations, plan for development of the city, and hire and fire the manager. Thus politics and administration are separate. See INTEGRATION.

city planning. The charting in advance of a city's physical growth and reorganization to care for such needs as easily accessible parks and playgrounds, arterial thoroughfares, and planned business, industrial, and residential areas.

city-state. A city which forms an independent state. Such political units have flourished at various times and places, the situation most often referred to probably being in Greece a few centuries before Christ, when Athens, Sparta, Thebes, etc., were such city-states.

civil. Pertaining to non-military government activity or service; civilian.

Civil Aeronautics Administration. Since 1940 an agency in the United States

Department of Commerce which encourages civilian aviation and supervises routes and facilities and enforces regulations under the direction and supervision of the Secretary of Commerce.

Civil Aeronautics Authority. An independent agency set up in 1938 and given the functions of the United States Department of Commerce in regard to aviation. In 1940 these functions were turned over to the Civil Aeronautics Administration and the Civil Aeronautics Board in the Department of Commerce. See CIVIL AERONAUTICS ADMINISTRATION; CIVIL AERONAUTICS BOARD.

Civil Aeronautics Board. In the United States a board of five members whose functions are to set air rates, establish safety standards and regulations, and investigate aviation accidents. Although a part of the Department of Commerce, the Board exercises these functions independently of the Secretary of Commerce.

civil affairs. Defined by government handbooks as the activities of the government of an area under military occupation and of its inhabitants, except those of an organized military character. Control of such civil affairs is the control of civilian activities in such an area by the armed forces.

civil code. A systematized set of laws applying to the relations of private individuals. See CIVIL LAW; CODE.

civil disobedience. Non-violent resistance by Indians to British rule in India, often led and symbolized by Gandhi. It included such steps as boycotting British goods, picketing liquor stores (an important source of government income), peaceful parades and demonstrations, resignation of Indian officials, and non-payment of salt-taxes and land-taxes.

civil law. The branch of law which

treats of suits between persons or corporations based on wrongs done by one party to the other. See CRIMINAL LAW.

civil liberty. The sum of freedoms which in modern democracies the individual has a right to claim. They consist mainly in freedom of personal action (movement, assembly and association) and freedom of religion and expression of opinion (press and speech). The first ten amendments to the United States Constitution and the state bills of rights guarantee civil liberties for Americans. Democracy alone does not guarantee the rights of the individual, as the majority often suppresses the minority and governments do not always voluntarily exercise restraint unless obliged to do so by constitutional law. Communism and fascism do not believe in civil liberties, though some of them are enacted in their constitutions. British Socialism as represented by the British Labor Party desires to maintain civil liberties in spite of collectivist economic and social legislation. To-day civil liberties are frequently enlarged by such freedoms as "freedom from want" and "freedom from fear," guaranteeing economic and political security, also "freedom to work," recognizing the state's obligation to combat unemployment, and "freedom to be educated," resulting in free educational opportunities. Civil liberties remain the mainstay of liberal thought and one of the cornerstones of free government. See also NATURAL RIGHTS, LIBERALISM, LAISSEZ FAIRE, FREE TRADE, JEFFERSONIAN DEMOCRACY, INDIVIDUALISM, BILL OF RIGHTS.

civil list. Annual appropriation in a monarchy for the upkeep of the royal household.

civil party. A third party to a French criminal trial, namely an injured civilian, if any. While the state prosecutes for the crime the injured private person may in the same trial enter a plea for damages. In the United States this latter action would require a separate civil suit.

civil rights. Rights granted by a state equally to all its citizens or inhabitants. In democracies these rights are considered as protecting a person from the state as well as from other individuals. In the United States the connotation of this term has come to be the equal treatment of all persons regarding the enjoyment of life, liberty, and property, and the protection of the laws. See CIVIL LIBERTY.

civil service. Term applied generally to those employees of a government other than the military. 1. In the United States, agencies of the federal government and some state, county, and municipal governments, are operated by classified and unclassified employees. Characteristics of the classified service are: appointment based on competitive examination (or sometimes on special requirements); tenure; merit promotion; salary standards; and a pension system. Political appointment is typical of the unclassified service. The Pendleton Act, 1883, together with Rules and Orders, 1903, the Classification Act, 1923, an act of 1919 giving war veterans preference, and the Ramspeck Act, 1940, form the basis of the United States Civil Service. The Civil Service Commission report gave the number of employees as 2,908,912 on June 30, 1944. See CIVIL SERVICE COMMISSION. 2. Among highly organized civil services of other countries are those of: (a) China, where the state for centuries conducted public examinations for civil employees. According to the 1928 constitution, the system was revived under the supervision of a special *yuan* (council), and the state became responsible for a national system of education; (b) England, where recruitment on the basis of examination dates from the middle of the 19th century. Before 1854 the term civil service applied to the British administration of India; (c) Prussia (later Germany), where from the early 18th century some civil service employees were recruited by written and oral tests in prescribed subjects.

Civil Service Commission. A commission established by the Pendleton Act, 1883, to administer the United States civil service. Among its functions are recruitment, investigation, examination, promotion, training, and classification of government employees. The President, with the concurrence of the Senate, appoints the three members, only two of whom may be of the same political party.

civil war. A war between the government of a state and a faction or section of the same state, or between two factions or parts of a state neither clearly recognized as the government thereof. Some specifically termed civil wars were: (a) the war between the United States government and the southern states combined in the Confederate States of America from 1861 to 1865. Two chief problems were resolved in the retention of the southern states in the Union and in the abolition of slavery; (b) the war in England from 1642 to 1649 between the followers of King Charles I and the supporters of parliament over the absolute power of the monarch. Charles was beheaded in 1649. See SPANISH CIVIL WAR.

Civil Works Administration. An independent governmental agency set up November 9, 1933, by executive order to provide employment on public works for the unemployed. It ceased to function July 1, 1934.

civilian. A person not a member of the armed forces.

Civilian Conservation Corps

Civilian Conservation Corps. A government agency established by the Emergency Conservation and Reforestation Law of March 31, 1933, for the recruitment of unemployed young men for the preservation of natural resources and building public works. The young men were paid not over a dollar per day and in many cases lived in camps near the site of their work. Their reforestation, beautification of parks and roadways and such projects were one of the least criticized parts of the New Deal. The agency was converted to military purposes, especially for the army engineers between 1940 and 1942, ending its original function in the latter year.

Civilian Production Administration. An agency set up in the office of Emergency Management on October 4, 1945 as a successor to the War Production Board to aid in the transfer of the economy back to a peacetime basis. A primary function was the establishing of priorities and the allocation of scarce materials. On December 12, 1946 its powers were transferred to the office of Temporary Controls for liquidation.

Clark Memorandum. An official interpretation of the Monroe Doctrine drawn up in 1928, made public 1930 by J. Reuben Clark, Undersecretary of State. It receded from the views of Theodore Roosevelt and denied that the Doctrine was an instrument for intervening in the affairs of the Latin-American states. See MONROE DOCTRINE.

classification. 1. The grouping of administrative positions in civil service into classes which require the same qualifications for appointment and performance of the same duties, and which receive the same rate of pay within certain limits. 2. Grouping similar kinds of property for tax purposes. 3. Government projects and materials are sometimes classified for reasons of safety and security, as: secret, confidential, and restricted. There are rules governing the use and handling of such material according to its classification.

classification of cities. The grouping of the cities of a state of the United States into a few classes according to population for purposes of granting charters. In such a plan cities in a given class all receive the same charter, although some states permit slight variations within the classes.

classified service. A term sometimes used for civil service. See CIVIL SERVICE.

class struggle. A social conflict between groups occupying different economic positions in society. The theory of the "class-struggle" has an important part in Marxist teaching. According to Marx, modern capitalist society is split up more and more into two great hostile camps: the capitalist bourgeoisie and the class of wage-earning workers, the proletariat. Between the bourgeoisie, which owns the "means of production" (industries, transportation, banks, etc.) and the proletariat, which they exploit, a struggle ensues which results in the disappearance of the middle classes ground between the two millstones of employers and workers. Marx predicted that this struggle will inevitably end with the victory of the proletariat, which thereupon would establish a new economic system, Socialism, giving rise to a classless society. See MARXISM, COMMUNISM, SOCIALISM, STALINIST, TROTSKYITE, BOLSHEVISM, WORLD-REVOLUTION, PROLETARIAT.

Clayton Anti-Trust Act. A law passed in 1914 redefining restraint of trade and granting greater protection therefrom, but specifically excepting labor unions from being interpreted as combinations in restraint of trade.

Clayton-Bulwer Treaty. An Anglo-American treaty of 1850 by which the two countries agreed that neither should obtain exclusive control over a canal across Central America, nor extend its control there, but that any canal should have their joint protection and should be a free and open waterway.

clean sweep. 1. The house-cleaning of appointive officers which takes place when a different party attains the high executive offices. 2. The winning by one party of all or practically all the elective offices at a single election.

"Clear everything with Sidney." A statement alleged to have been made by President Franklin D. Roosevelt to Robert E. Hannegan, chairman of the Democratic National Committee, at the time of the Democratic National Convention in July, 1944. Held by some to apply only to the nomination for the vice-presidency. "Sidney" refers to Sidney Hillman, chairman of the Political Action Committee. The statement was denied, but was used by anti-Roosevelt forces in the presidential campaign of 1944 to indicate the subservience of Roosevelt to the C.I.O. See POLITICAL ACTION COMMITTEE.

clearing agreement. An agreement between two countries regulating their international trade. Instead of importers paying the persons from whom they buy, they pay through a clearing house in their own country the exporters of their own country. Imports are controlled by each government through import licenses and quotas.

clerk. A county official found in about half of the states who has, as the title indicates, various clerical functions to perform, particularly in keeping records of deeds and acting as the county officer in charge of elections—ballots, returns, etc. In some cases he also keeps the records of the county courts.

clerk of court. A county official who keeps the records of the proceedings and orders of the county court and takes care of the routine matters connected with arranging for and disposing of trials.

Cliveden set. Collective term for the very wealthy, important, and conservative British Tories who represented a British policy of isolationism and appeasement in the late 1930's. So called from the fact that many members of the group often met socially at Cliveden, country estate of Lord and Lady Astor.

closed air doctrine. Each country attempts complete control of its own air and denies access to that air or landing rights on its soil to aircraft of other nations. Sometimes called horse-and-buggy air policy. See AEROPOLITICS.

closed primary. A primary in which only Republicans may vote for Republican candidates and only Democrats may vote for Democratic candidates. See OPEN PRIMARY.

closed seas. Bodies of water not accessible from the open sea, or, if accessible from the open sea, not under the same rules of free use which apply to the high seas.

closed season. The part of the year in which hunting a particular form of game is prohibited.

closed shop. A factory or business in which, by contract between the management and a labor union, only members of the union may be employed.

closure. The process of closing the debate in a legislative body and bringing the matter under discussion to a vote, as in the House of Representatives, by calling for the previous question and voting thereupon. In the Senate, since 1917, the process is started by petition, requires a two-thirds vote and thereafter each senator may still speak up to a total of one hour before the motion is put.

closure by compartments. A device used particularly in the House of Commons to restrict unlimited debate by setting up a timetable stating when debate on the different sections of a bill will be closed and a vote taken.

cloture. See CLOSURE.

C. M. G. See ORDER OF ST. MICHAEL AND ST. GEORGE.

coal and iron police. Police hired by the coal and steel companies to police communities of western Pennsylvania and to protect company property. In the prosecution of their duties, particularly in cases of labor trouble, it has often been considered that these police did not observe the impartiality usually connected with the policing function.

Coal Mines Administration. An agency set up in the Department of the Interior to operate the coal mines taken over by the government by the order of May 1, 1943. The mines were returned to the owners in October, 1943.

coaling station. In former days a port at which naval vessels could refuel with coal. These have tended to disappear with the substitution of oil as fuel for ships.

coalition. A combination of states or political parties.

coalition government. A cabinet or government composed of members of several parties. In a two-party system, such as in Great Britain, this usually takes place only in an emergency such as war, but in a multi-party system a coalition is usually necessary in order to secure majority backing for the government.

Coast Guard. A part of the armed forces of the United States which functions as a maritime police and safety force under the Treasury Department in peace, and as part of the navy in war.

Coast and Geodetic Survey. A branch of the Department of Commerce. Its chief function is to survey the coast and study the tides about the country.

coasting trade. Shipping from port to port along a coast, usually thought of as between the ports of a single state. In such cases this trade is usually reserved to the nationals of the state.

coat of arms. Insignia or symbol of a family or ruling house. Originally the design on the arms, especially the shield, of knights, hence an indication of knighthood.

Cochin Chinese Republic. See INDO-CHINESE FEDERATION.

cockpit of Europe. A term long used for the Balkans as the scene of petty wars.

code. 1. A complete and systematically organized set of laws. In continental Europe and places under its influence the laws of the land are grouped into a series of codes: civil, criminal, criminal procedure, etc. These codes are looked upon as the complete law in their spheres and are not added to by judicial decision as in the Anglo-American system. 2. In the United States legislation is collected and organized in codes but these codes are continually supplemented by judicial decisions. See CODE OF FAIR COMPETITION.

Code Authority. The body established under each of the N. R. A. codes of fair competition to administer the code. They were made up largely of business men in the field covered by the code.

Code Civil. The civil code of France. See NAPOLEONIC CODE.

Code Napoleon. See NAPOLEONIC CODE.

code of fair competition. A set of regulations governing wages, hours, and other working conditions for an industry, set up by the industries and government representatives under the National Industrial Recovery Act. When accepted by both the industry and the government they went into force with the effect of law.

coinage. The process by which a government makes money by stamping pieces of metal. Coins may be of gold, silver, nickel, bronze, copper, aluminum or alloys of these. In the United States the U. S. Mint is charged with supplying the public with the required amount of coin (or change). See MONEY.

collaboration. Joint action of two or more states or political parties.

collaborationist. National of an occupied country in World War II who assisted and co-operated with the Germans or Japanese. Such action was considered traitorous by the patriotic elements of the country. Persons forced to assist the Germans were not considered collaborators.

collection at source. The method of collecting income taxes by having the tax paid by the source of the income before the income reaches the recipient. It is obviously easier to administer in cases in which a person has a single fixed source of income than it is in the case of lawyers fees, for example.

collective bargaining. A method of negotiation between employers and employees by which questions of wages and working conditions are settled between representatives of management and representatives of labor organizations. It is conceded today that the use of collective bargaining and the maintenance of labor unions are inseparable. Bargaining may proceed between a single employer and his employees, a local group of employers with a group of employees, a whole industry with employees of a single craft. The tendency everywhere

seems to be towards industry-wide bargaining. The result of collective bargaining is not a labor contract in the legal sense, but rather a trade agreement imposing no obligation upon employers to offer or to workers to accept work and guaranteeing no jobs. It is rather a statement of the conditions upon which work is offered and accepted. Opponents of collective bargaining argue that it excludes competition between employers for workers and between workers for jobs; defendants of collective bargaining maintain that workers are at a disadvantage in bargaining and that collective bargaining establishes equality of bargaining power. In America the National Labor Relations Act, popularly called the Wagner Act, was passed in 1935 by Congress to insure American workers the right to organize and bargain collectively. The three man National Labor Relations Board was empowered to conduct elections to determine employee representation for collective bargaining purposes and to eliminate those practices among employers which discriminate against employees because of union activities.

Collective bargaining has been generally accepted in the free economies as the best practice of settling labor disputes. Totalitarian countries forbid collective bargaining and settle disputes over wages or working conditions by compulsory government arbitration. The term was first used in London in 1891 by Beatrice Webb, and was popularized in the United States by Samuel Gompers of the American Federation of Labor. See STRIKE.

collective farms. The prevailing system of farming in the Soviet Union. The Russian Revolution in 1917 did not establish socialism in the farming country all at once. During the period of the New Economic Policy (1921–1928) peasants continued to own their land and to sell their products in the free market. In fact a class of well-to-do peasants or "kulaki" had reappeared by 1927. When, however, the first Five Year Plan introduced a system of state controlled and planned economy, Stalin decided to initiate a new system of communist farming. Two types of collective farms were established: the *sovkhazy* (giant state farms mostly in previously cultivated land) and the *kolkhazy* (collective farms formed by making peasants pool their land, livestock and tools and to farm co-operatively). On these farms Soviet experts introduced up-to-date American methods of mechanized agriculture. The number of state farms and collective farms increased rapidly and they are today dominating Russian agriculture, though individual peasant holdings still survive. See COMMUNISM, BOLSHEVISM, NEW ECONOMIC POLICY.

collective security. Immunity from aggression provided by the joint agreement, will, and power of the nations of the world. It is obvious that in such a plan the great powers possess a disproportionate share of both power and responsibility for enforcement.

collectivism. A social system or belief which seeks to run society through co-operative or collective effort. Collectivism is the opposite of individualism. It is also used as a term including collective social and economic systems such as socialism, communism, syndicalism and even fascism. Collectivism sets a special value on doing things in common and merging all individual efforts under a more or less authoritarian leadership. In the economic field collectivism opposes laissez-faire, capitalism and free enterprise. See INDIVID-UALISM, SOCIALISM, SYNDICALISM, COMMUNISM, LIBERALISM, UTILITARIANISM.

collector of internal revenue. The head of one of the taxing districts of the United States, set up for the collection of the internal taxes of the country.

collusive bidding. Bidding for public contracts in which the bidders have agreed before hand on their bids. This obviously circumvents the purpose of competitive bidding and is usually prohibited.

Colonel Blimp. Cartoon character which epitomizes British conservatism, drawn by Low, the famous British cartoonist.

colonial office. A governmental department, the special function of which is the supervision of colonial territories.

colonization. Process of moving a new and usually different population into an area; originally it meant that the area became a colony of the state from which the new population had come.

colony. A territory inhabited largely by people of a more or less backward culture from the point of view of European and western nations, which is controlled by another, and presumably more advanced, state. The territory usually has a number of inhabitants originally from the controlling state.

Colossus of the North. Term for the United States used in the countries of Latin America implying not merely great size but a tendency of the United States to dominate Latin America. Occasions for the use of the term have been more rare since the inauguration of the Good Neighbor Policy.

Columbians, Inc. A secret anti-Negro, anti-Semitic organization founded in Atlanta, Georgia, in 1946 by Homer L. Loomis and Emory C. Burke. It advocated "white supremacy" and was modelled closely on Nazi lines, including uniforms, salutes and terroristic methods. On December 13, 1946 Loomis and Burke were indicted on charges of riot and illegal possession of dynamite.

combatant. One who actively participates in hostilities as a member of the armed forces of a state. Defined by the Hague Conventions as one who is under a responsible commander, who has a distinctive recognizable emblem, who carries arms openly and conducts operations in accordance with the laws and customs of war.

combination in restraint of trade. A group of corporations co-operating in efforts to monopolize an industry or a service.

combine. Term sometimes used for trust or cartel.

Combined Food Board. An Anglo-American board set up June 9, 1942, which Canada joined the following year. Its functions were the production and distribution of food products under war-time conditions.

Combined Production and Resources Board. A joint American-British-Canadian board set up in 1942 for the integration of the war production programs of the three countries.

Combined Raw Materials Board. An Anglo-American board established January 26, 1942 to take care of the raw materials supply problems, particularly in allocation, conservation, and combined purchasing of such essential war materials.

Combined Shipping Adjustment Board. A joint Anglo-American board set up June 26, 1942 to co-ordinate the work of the United States War Shipping Administration and the British Ministry of War Transportation.

Comintern. The Third International. See INTERNATIONAL.

comitadji (kaw-mee-TAH-jee). A member of Balkan armed bands, chiefly Bulgarian and Macedonian, which raid across frontiers and create considerable friction between the countries in the area. Their motives range from private depredations to political independence and their members and methods were often closely related to Bulgarian and Macedonian independence movements. See IMRO.

Comité des Forges (kaw-mee-TAY day FAWRZH). An organization of French iron, steel, and munitions interests, very powerful between the two World Wars. It was not a trust or cartel in the sense of a combination to restrict trade; it was rather a very powerful pressure group established to propagandize for the munitions industry.

comity. The rules of politeness or etiquette in international dealings. They do not have the binding force of law, but are conventional courtesies the exchange of which makes for goodwill; for example, exempting diplomats from general customs duties or extraditing a suspect without treaty stipulations therefor.

command paper. A special report to the House of Commons by some investigating committee or administrative agency. They are called by this name because they are said to be presented to parliament "by command of His Majesty." They are numbered 1 to 10,000 in each series, the first two series having been completed. The first series was labeled C, with a number; the second was labeled Cd. with number; and the third is now in progress labeled Cmd., with number, such as Cmd. 5575. The papers are indexed and can be located by number.

commander-in-chief. The supreme commander of the armed forces. In the United States the president is commander-in-chief of the army and navy.

commerce clause. The clause in Article I, Section 8, of the Constitution which states that Congress shall have power

. . ."To regulate commerce with foreign nations and among the several States, and with the Indian tribes." On the basis of this clause the federal government, through Congress, is empowered to regulate the instrumentalities of transportation, communication, and other forms of commerce if interstate or foreign.

Commerce, Department of. An executive department set up separately in 1903, the function of which is to develop and encourage domestic and foreign commerce including manufacturing, transportation, mining, and fishing. The department collects facts and publishes several censuses, sets up standards of weights and measures, registers patents and copyrights, and develops waterways and aviation.

commercial treaty. An agreement between two or more states defining and regulating their commercial relations.

commissar. Former name for Russian administrative officers, including heads of governmental departments. The latter corresponded to the secretaries of the departments in the United States. Since March, 1946, they have been called ministers.

commissariat. Russian term for government department. Called ministries since March, 1946.

commission. A group of persons delegated to perform some function, usually more or less administrative in nature. This form of administration is particularly useful when policy-forming is necessary or when various interests should be represented in the administration of a particular function.

commission of inquiry. A group of persons, usually selected from the two parties to an international dispute and from outside states as well, whose function it is to determine the facts which bear upon the dispute. This function is of importance because often the two disputing parties begin their disagreement by disagreeing on the facts in the case.

commission system of government. Form of city government in which all powers are in the hands of an elected council. First established in Galveston, Texas as a temporary measure. Between 1908 and 1914 about four hundred cities in the United States and Canada adopted it, but it has since been abandoned in many places. One commissioner is called mayor and acts as chairman. Usually there are five members of the commission who respectively are responsible for five different administrative offices of the city government, but who act jointly on policy making and legislative matters. The system is weak because it lacks administrative unity.

commitment. 1. The process of referring a matter of legislative business to a committee. 2. A pledge by a state that it will act in a certain way or follow a particular line of policy. This may take the form of a unilateral declaration, as well as that of a formal agreement with one or more additional states.

committee. A group of persons, usually rather small, selected to represent a larger group as in the study of a question on which it reports back to the larger group. In the United States the connotation is often in connection with work done for legislative bodies.

Committee of Imperial Defense. A British governmental committee to study problems of the defense of the empire. It includes the cabinet members most closely involved, the heads of the branches of the armed forces, and at times representatives of the dominions.

committee of the whole. A whole legislative body turned into a committee usually for the purpose of taking advantage of less formal procedure, such as no roll-call votes. The House of Representatives has two such, the Committee of the Whole House on the State of the Union, for the consideration of public money bills, and the Committee of the Whole House, for private bills.

Committee of Union and Progress. The group at the center of the Young Turk revolution of 1908 in Turkey.

committee on committees. A committee which designates assignments to other committees. In Congress such committees are party committees.

committee on credentials. A committee in a political convention or deliberative body which judges the admission of delegates or members as the properly authorized representatives of their respective constituents.

Committee on Economic Security. A government agency set up June 29, 1934, to study the problem of social security and to offer legislative suggestions therefor. Its efforts resulted in the Social Security Act. It continues for further study of the problem.

Committee on Fair Employment Practices. An agency set up to eliminate discriminatory practices in employment. It was first placed under the Office of Production Management, June 25, 1941, but transferred to the War Manpower Commission July 30, 1942.

Committee to Defend America by Aiding the Allies. An organization established prior to Pearl Harbor, the purpose of which was to urge that the United States give to Great Britain and later to Russia all aid possible short of actual armed assistance. It was organized on the obvious assumption of its title, that the first defense of America was aid to those fighting the Axis. It was led by the late William Allen White.

Commodity Credit Corporation. A government agency set up in 1933 and transferred to the Department of Agriculture in 1939, the principal purpose of which was to loan money to farmers based on stored crops to help stabilize prices and markets.

Commodity Exchange Administration. An agency set up in 1936 for the purchase and regulation of farm products. It was absorbed in the Agricultural Marketing Administration in 1942.

common carrier. A transportation facility which offers to transport all goods or persons for which the charges are paid, within the limits of the regular service.

common council. Term for the city council or municipal legislative body in certain cities.

common law. The legal system of England, most of the United States and the other English speaking countries. It is based on custom and precedent and on legal commentaries thereon. It is distinguished from statutory or positive law, which is established by legislative bodies (Congress, State Legislatures, Parliament), and also from equity. Common law goes back to the Constitutions of Clarendon (1164) which were the foundation of Anglo-American law and established the supremacy of the King's courts in England. It was brought to America by English colonists. As time went on much of the common law was embodied in legislation, and some of the distinctions between common law and statutory law became therefore somewhat blurred. The legal procedures in English and American law courts such as trial by jury, cross examination of witnesses, etc. were first part of the common law. In most of continental Europe and countries whose cultures spring from the continent, the legal systems are found in one or more codes of law based on Roman law, not on common law. See

---

common-law marriage — page 66

LAW, TRIAL BY JURY, EQUITY, POSITIVE LAW, TRIAL.

common-law marriage. Marital relation based merely on the agreement between the parties and not on any civil or church ceremony recognized by law.

Commons. See HOUSE OF COMMONS.

commonwealth. A term, derived from common weal or common welfare, often applied to states, or officially applied by a state or group of states to itself. For example, in the international sphere there are the Commonwealth of Australia and the British Commonwealth of Nations (which includes the Dominions); among members of the American Union four also use the term, as the Commonwealths of Virginia, Massachusetts, Pennsylvania and Kentucky.

commune. Smallest political subdivisions in France, Italy, and Switzerland.

communique (kuh-MYOO-ni-KAY). Literally, communication (French). An official statement. Used often as the statement of progress of diplomatic conferences or military activities or at the conclusion of a conference.

communism. In a wide sense, the belief in the desirability of social control over economic life and particularly the social or common ownership of the means of production, such as industrial plants, machines, railways, land, banks, etc. Although the term was not known before 1840, the idea of communism is old and can be found in the legends of the "golden age" in which everything belongs to everybody. Early Christian groups practised communism. Today we mean by the term communism usually Marxist communism, the most militant of socialist creeds, which welded Karl Marx's doctrines into a potent political weapon. Its prophets were Marx, Engels, and Lenin, and its greatest hero is Generalissimo Joseph Stalin. Communist parties in more than fifty countries use Marxist ideas in the hope of attaining political power and of establishing a socialist system following the example of Soviet Russia. The Third or Communist International was founded in 1919 and worked for a communist movement on an international scale, distinct from the moderate evolutionist Second International to which the European Social Democrat Parties and the British Labor Party belonged. Its offices were in Moscow and it was dissolved in 1943 because its existence was believed to be an obstacle in the war against Germany in which Russia and the Communists joined hands with countries and groups of all political beliefs pledged to defeat Hitler and Mussolini. Communist parties however continue to receive their inspiration, the so-called "party-line," from Moscow. For tactical purposes Communists following Stalin have dropped their slogan of "world-revolution," and are willing to participate in coalition governments with other parties. Communists believe that they will eventually come to power everywhere and establish dictatorships, and socialist systems according to the Soviet pattern. See MARXISM, SOCIALISM, BOLSHEVISM, STALINIST, TROTSKYITE, CLASS-STRUGGLE, PROLETARIAT, WORLD-REVOLUTION.

Communist Manifesto. A small volume by Karl Marx and Friedrich Engels in 1848. It is the basic statement of socialist doctrine, outlining the inevitability of the class struggle, and the ultimate doom of capitalism.

Communist Party. A political party found in many countries. It follows more or less closely the principles of communism and was more or less closely in touch with the Comintern in Moscow. The United States party was officially dissolved May 20, 1944, but revived in late July, 1945. See COMMUNISM.

Communist Political Association. The Communist organization established in the United States to replace the Communist Party after the latter was officially dissolved May 20, 1944. See COMMUNIST PARTY.

community chest. Fund raised in a city by general private contributions for public welfare purposes, distributed among various welfare agencies. It was evolved in an effort to prevent undesirable competition between agencies and to concentrate the requests and needs of all in a single campaign.

commute. To change a punishment or penalty to a lighter one by an authority with pardoning power.

compact theory. The theory that the state was instituted by a real or implied agreement or compact among its members. About the only real example of such an agreement is the Mayflower Compact. See MAYFLOWER COMPACT; SOCIAL CONTRACT.

compacts, interstate. Agreements between states of the United States regarding common problems such as a common harbor or river. The provision of the Constitution that such agreements cannot be made without the permission of Congress is not enforced too closely in minor matters.

comparative law. The study of several systems of law for the purpose of comparison of their legal principles and institutions.

compensation. The amount awarded by a court to a person in payment for his property taken for public purposes.

competent. 1. Pertaining to the qualified jurisdiction of a court. 2. Pertaining to legal liability of a person, as in respect to age and mental faculties.

competition. See FREE COMPETITION.

Compiègne Forest (kohm-PYEN). Forest some forty miles north of Paris where the armistice of November 11, 1918, was signed. The railroad dining car in which the signing took place remained there until the fall of France in 1940 when it was used again for the signing of the Armistice between France and Hitler's Germany on June 22, and then taken away by the Germans.

compromis (kawm-praw-MEE). An agreement between two disputing parties to submit the dispute to arbitration. It includes the limits placed on the arbitrators and the rules of procedure they must follow.

compromises. Conflicting points of view threatened to prevent acceptance of the United States Constitution, but it is usually considered that the document became acceptable with the insertion of three outstanding compromises: the Connecticut Compromise; the three-fifths compromise; and a third which gave Congress general power over commerce but inserted a prohibition on export duties and on interference with the slave trade before 1808. See CONNECTICUT COMPROMISE; THREE-FIFTHS CLAUSE.

comptroller. An official who supervises expenditures and audits accounts.

Comptroller-General. Head of the General Accounting Office whose function is to approve claims for and against the government of the United States, including general governmental expenditures, and to audit the governmental expenditures.

Comptroller of the Currency. An official in the Treasury Department of the United States whose function is the supervision of all national banks and certain other banks, and the issuance and redemption of Federal Reserve notes and Federal Reserve Bank notes.

compulsory arbitration. Arbitration of certain categories of disputes which states, or parties to a labor dispute, are bound (by previous bilateral or multilateral agreement) to submit to arbitration.

compulsory labor service. A term of physical labor on farms or public works required of the youths of Nazi Germany.

compulsory loans. See FORCED LOANS.

compulsory voting. Voting required of registered voters by law in certain countries of Europe. It has been discussed (but not tried) in the United States as an antidote to non-voting.

Comsomol. See KOMSOMOL.

concentration camp. Prison camps in German-controlled territory for those accused of not being in sympathy with the Nazi regime.

Concert of Europe. The great powers of Europe, whose representatives met from time to time during the 19th century for the purpose of imposing joint peaceful solutions of common problems. Perhaps most successful over a long period in supervising the liquidation of most of European Turkey with only one short war among the powers themselves.

concession. 1. Permission granted by a state more-or-less backward economically to a foreign government or corporation allowing it to exploit certain resources or set up certain services, such as a railway or telegraph, in the territory of the former. Often complete economic and then political control have followed in the wake of such concessions. 2. Small extraterritorial area, as the French concession in Shanghai. See EXTRATERRITORIALITY.

conchy. Abbreviation for conscientious objector.

conciliation. The process of attempting to reach a peaceful settlement of a dispute, either in a labor problem within a country or a dispute involving two or more states, by suggestions of a third party based on a study of the opposing points of view.

The disputing parties are not bound to accept the suggestions. Conciliation differs from mediation chiefly in the assumption that a conciliation commission had been established prior to the dispute.

conciliation commission. A commission which has been established to attempt to settle peaceably either labor or international disputes. The parties to the dispute may be represented, but the essential factor is the presence of those not connected with either party.

Conciliation Service. An office in the United States Department of Labor set up in 1913 to investigate employer-employee disputes. The information secured is turned over to conciliators if such are appointed.

conclave. A closed meeting. Specifically the meetings in Rome of the College of Cardinals to elect a pope.

Concordat. Agreement to which the Pope is one party.

Concordat of 1929. One of the three agreements collectively known as the Lateran Accord. This one provided for the recognition by the Italian government of the Roman Catholic Church as the state church and defined the relations of church and state. See LATERAN ACCORD.

concurrent powers. Powers shared between Congress and the states, as for example the power to tax. See EXCLUSIVE POWERS OF CONGRESS.

concurrent resolution. A resolution passed by both houses of Congress that does not have the force of law but merely indicates the feeling or opinion of Congress on a matter. Since it does not have the force of law, there is no question of its requiring the signature of the president. See JOINT RESOLUTION.

concurring opinion. A judicial opinion in which a member of a court agrees with the conclusion of the majority but by different reasoning.

condemnation. 1. The proceedings by which a court takes property from a private person for public use and by which the amount of compensation is determined. 2. The judicial process by which a prize court turns over to a belligerent state captured enemy vessels and neutral vessels not complying with the rules of contraband and blockade.

condominium. Colonial area in which the sovereignty is shared by two states, as the Anglo-Egyptian Sudan.

confederacy. Confederation. Certain confederations have been known as confederacies, as the Confederate States of America.

confederate. 1. Pertaining to a confederation. 2. Pertaining to the Confederate States of America, the government set up in the South during the Civil War.

confederation. Group of states which, while maintaining their separate independence and entities, combine in the joint exercise of certain governmental functions, often defense and foreign relations. Often a confederation is also a customs union.

Confederation, Articles of. See ARTICLES OF CONFEDERATION.

Confédération Générale du Travail (kohng-fay-day-rahts-YOHNG zhay-nay-RAHL dyoo tra-VAHEE). Literally the General Confederation of Labor. The chief French federation of labor unions, an organization of several million workers prior to the fall of France.

conference of ambassadors. An international conference of several states, whose representatives are their ambassadors accredited to the capital in which the conference meets. After World War I much of the administration of peace treaty provisions was handled by such conferences.

conference committee. Joint committee of the two houses in Congress or the state legislatures whose function is to arrive at and recommend a single version of a bill that has passed the two houses in somewhat different form.

Conférence des Présidents (kohng-fay-RAHNGS day pray-zee-DAHNG). A kind of steering committee in the French Chamber of Deputies, composed of the president, vice-presidents, standing committee chairmen and party leaders, which usually meets weekly to decide what proposed legislation shall be considered.

confirmation. The approval, by a legislative body, required for appointments by the executive.

confiscation. The seizure by a state of property of another state, of nationals of another state, or of its own citizens, without adequate compensation.

congress. 1. International or national representative assembly, most widely known being that of the United States. 2. The two-year term of the United States Congress, based on the regular elections. The Congressmen elected in November, 1946, and the holdovers in the Senate formed the 80th Congress. 3. Less often, a major international conference.

Congress of Berlin. See BERLIN, TREATY OF.

Congress of Industrial Organizations. An organization of labor unions formed in October, 1935 as a protest against the stand of the majority of the American Federation of Labor unions and to "promote organization of workers in mass-production industries and the unorganized workers of the nation." The Committee of Industrial Organization (C.I.O.) was headed by John L. Lewis, chief of the United Mine Workers; Charles P. Howard of the International Typographical Union, Thomas H. Brown of the Mine, Mill and Smelter Workers, Thomas MacMahon of the United Textile Workers, Sidney Hillman of the Amalgamated Clothing Workers and David Dubinsky of the International Ladies' Garment Workers participated in its leadership. In 1936 the A. F. of L. ordered its dissolution as a "dual" movement and the two groups broke. Philip Murray started to organize the iron and steel workers and the C.I.O. grew rapidly under the presidency of John L. Lewis. By 1940 it had a membership of three and one-half million. Antagonism against the more conservative A. F. of L. was sharp, jurisdictional disputes between unions belonging to the two organizations resulting. While the C.I.O. specialized in vertical organization (the organization of whole industries), the A. F. of L. adhered for some time to its principle of organizing certain crafts (horizontal method). The C.I.O. favored government intervention in industry and the New Deal, while the A. F. of L. was often critical of Roosevelt and felt discriminated against by the National Labor Relations Board. Later it came to a break between John L. Lewis and the Roosevelt administration. Lewis took an isolationist stand and in 1942 Philip Murray became President of the C.I.O. Lewis and the United Mine Workers stayed independent and rejoined the A. F. of L. in 1946.

In 1936 the C.I.O. formed Labor's Non-Partisan League as its political arm and in 1944 the Political Action Committee (P.A.C.), which carried out large scale propaganda for the re-election of President Roosevelt. The C.I.O. entered the new World Trade Union Federation.

Congress of Vienna. The international conference held in Vienna after the defeat of Napoleon at Waterloo, between September 1814 and July 1815. It established in particular a new international order in Europe, granting territories which had been seized by the French, to Prussia, Russia, Austria, Holland, and Savoy.

Congress Party. See ALL-INDIA NATIONALIST CONGRESS.

congressional committees. Committees of the members of the houses of Congress in which, in reality, most of the real work on legislation is done. For more or less continuous problems there are standing committees; for temporary problems there are special committees.

The congressional re-organization act of June, 1946, reduced the number of standing committees, permitted joint sessions of committees, and limited the number on which a member may serve. See CONGRESSIONAL REORGANIZATION ACT.

Congressional Directory. A directory of government agencies and officials, not merely congressional but executive and judicial as well. It includes such information as date and place of birth, educational and professional background and other personal items.

Congressional district. In the United States, a geographical division of a state by its legislature in accordance with the conditions laid down by Congress, and on the basis of population after each census. See GERRYMANDER.

Congressional Record. The official report of the proceedings of the two houses of Congress, plus the extensions of remarks. See EXTENSION OF REMARKS.

Congressional Re-organization Act. A measure adopted by the United States Congress on July 26, 1946 designed to increase its efficiency as a law-making body. Its major provisions increase the salaries of Senators and Representatives from $10,000 to $12,500 a year, plus $2,500 a year for expenses (tax free); make Congressmen eligible for federal pensions; give each Congressman an administrative assistant and other clerical help; reduce the number of House committees from 48 to 19, and of Senate committees from 33 to 15; allow joint sessions of committees; call for registration of all lobbyists, including their salaries; set up majority and minority policy committees, and provide for a Joint Legislative Executive Council as a link with the White House.

congressman. A member of the United States Congress, especially a member of the House of Representatives as distinguished from a senator.

congressman-at-large. A congressman elected from a state as a whole because the state has more or less congressmen than congressional districts, due to the failure of a state to redistrict after its number of congressmen has been changed by a reapportionment. If the number is increased the extra ones are elected at large; if the number is decreased below the number of districts, all are elected at large.

Connally Resolution. A Senate resolution passed November 5, 1943, advocating that the United States, through its constitutional processes should join with other sovereign nations in establishing an international authority with power to prevent aggression and preserve peace based on the principle of the sovereign equality of peace-loving states, and providing that the United States should join only by the treaty-making process, that is, with the concurrence of two-thirds of the Senate. See BALL-BURTON-HATCH-HILL RESOLUTION.

Connecticut Compromise. The compromise advanced by the Connecticut delegation in the United States constitutional convention, between the view of the large states that congressional representation of states should be in proportion to population and the view of the small states that there should be equal representation. The compromise was written into the Constitution, Article I, Sec. 2 Par. 1, and Sec. 3, Par. 1: there should be representation in proportion to population in the House of Representatives, and equal representation in the Senate.

conquest. Military subjugation and political annexation of a territory by a state.

conscience money. Money sent to the government to square the sender's conscience for some obligation not fully performed, as, for example, payment of a tax.

conscientious objector. A person who objects to bearing arms or, in some cases, to becoming a member of the armed forces, for reasons of conscience; for example, one belonging to a religious denomination which forbids participation in war.

conscription. Compulsory selection of men for service in the armed forces. See DRAFT.

consent calendar. In the United States House of Representatives, a kind of priority list of bills from the Union or House calendars. This list is regularly taken up in the House the first and third Mondays in each month, and expedites the consideration of bills thereon. The name of this list comes from the fact that consideration of a bill is postponed unless there is unanimous consent when it comes up the first time, and a bill is taken off this calendar if three members object to its consideration after one postponement. See HOUSE CALENDARS.

consent of the governed. The theory that a good society must be based on the consent or consensus of the whole people or a majority thereof. The principle of popular sovereignty is akin to this theory: they form one of the cornerstones of democracy. Among political philosophers who formulated modern democratic ideas the theory of consent was particularly

well expressed by John Locke and
Jean Jacques Rousseau (who formulated the theory of the "general will,"
the will of the people) and John Stuart
Mill (who showed how the people can
govern itself best through democratic
representation). In American political
thinking the idea is particularly
clearly stated in the Constitution of
the United States and in the writings
of Thomas Jefferson. See POPULAR
SOVEREIGNTY, REPUBLIC, SOCIAL CON-
TRACT.

conservation. Preservation or protection of natural resources such as
forests or soil.

conservatism. See CONSERVATIVE.

conservative. One inclined towards conservatism, a political point of view
which desires to "conserve" and
maintain everything essential and
valuable in a nation's past and to accept only such innovations and reforms as are absolutely necessary,
and which do not offend any fundamental traditional ideas. A conservative usually believes in authority
(though not in extreme authoritarian-
ism), in the preservation of the family
and moral values; he will safeguard
the traditional role of aristocracy in a
society and will try to restrain the
direct influence of broad masses in
the direction of the state. Conservatives are also often, but not necessarily, attached to the church and to
monarchy. Conservatives are usually
moderate, occasionally fervent, nationalists. It is often said that while
older people tend to be conservative,
the youth is radical. A rural population as a rule is more conservative
than city-dwellers. The father of
modern British conservatism was Edmund Burke, who violently attacked
the French Revolution and the spirit
of radical change. American historians often compare the more conservative Alexander Hamilton with the

more radical Thomas Jefferson. The
British Conservative Party (Tories) is
a good example of 20th century conservatism. In America the Republican
Party is usually more conservative
than the Democrats, the South more
conservative than the North. Conservative should not be identified with
reactionary, nor should fascists be
likened to conservatives, as fascism
has no real reverence for traditional
values and customs but is a kind of
revolutionary movement. See CON-
SERVATIVE PARTY, REACTIONARY, FAS-
CISM, AUTHORITARIAN.

Conservative. Member of the Conservative Party.

Conservative Party. The name of the
large British party which before 1832
was called the Tory Party. Its official
name today is really "Unionist Party,"
but it is referred to as Conservative or
Tory. It is not opposed to reforms as
such but it prefers moderate, gradual
evolution rather than radical change.
For instance, the Churchill Government, in which the Conservatives
had the majority, favored a social
security plan only somewhat more
restricted than the radical Beveridge
Plan. They were, however, opposed
to radical socialization and favored
continuation of the capitalist system
under government control. The Conservatives uphold many British traditions, emphasize the preservation of
the British Empire, favor the Church
of England and support a strong national defense. The most famous leaders of the Conservative Party after
1832 were Benjamin Disraeli (who
later became Lord Beaconsfield),
Lord Salisbury, Sir Austin and Neville Chamberlain, Lord Balfour,
Stanley Baldwin and Winston Churchill. Britain was ruled by a Conservative Government between 1924 and
1929 and by coalition governments in
which the Conservatives were pre-

dominant between 1931 and 1945. In the National Election of 1945 the Conservative Party was defeated, gaining only 185 against the Labor Party's 395 seats in the House of Commons. See CONSERVATIVE, TORY, REACTIONARY.

consort. Ruler's husband or wife who does not by the marriage receive the title or rank held by the ruler.

consortium. International financial agency set up to aid another state, or to control an industry in two or more countries.

constable. Police officer, in the United States found usually in villages.

constabulary. A police force. Applied in some cases to municipalities in Great Britain; applied in the United States most often to the state police.

Constantinople Agreement. A series of telegrams exchanged in March, 1915 between Russia on one hand and Great Britain and France on the other, in which Russia was conceded much of the territory which is now European Turkey, a strip of the Turkish coast on the east side of the Aegean Sea, and certain Aegean islands, if the allies won the war. This exchange formed one of the so-called secret treaties of World War I. Its provisions were unfulfilled due to the Russian revolution, the Russian peace with Germany, and the Russian renunciation of the secret treaties.

constituency. 1. The people or voters in a representative electoral district. 2. The district itself.

constituent. 1. Pertaining to the power to draw up or amend a constitution. 2. Pertaining to one of several component parts. 3. A person in a constituency. See CONSTITUENCY, 1.

constituent assembly. An assembly whose function is to establish a government or draw up a constitution. A constitutional convention.

constitution. Fundamental or organic law of a state. It is referred to as unwritten if it is not found essentially in a single document, as in England. It may be rigid or flexible, depending on how difficult it is to change or amend.

Constitution Day. September 17, the day commemorating the signing of the Constitution of the United States in 1787.

constitutional. Used to describe a law which is in accord with the constitution, especially in the United States as determined by the Supreme Court.

Constitutional Convention of 1787. The convention which was called to revise the Articles of Confederation but which drew up the United States Constitution. It met in Philadelphia, May 25–September 28, 1787. The Constitution was signed September 17, a date now annually celebrated as Constitution Day. The convention chose George Washington as presiding officer and included among its members an amazingly large proportion of talented men. Some of them were Benjamin Franklin, James Madison, Edmund Randolph, Alexander Hamilton, Gouverneur Morris, all men of wide experience and knowledge of various forms of government.

constitutional law. The law governing the relations between a state and its inhabitants.

consul. Official sent by one state to another to assist and protect its nationals in their commercial relations. Because of their functions consuls are sent to many industrial centers and ports. See CONSULAR SERVICE, CONSUL-GENERAL, VICE-CONSUL, CONSULAR AGENT, DIPLOMAT.

consul general. A consular officer who supervises the consular functions either as an inspector in one office or over a considerable area. See CONSULAR SERVICE.

consular agent. 1. One of the lower

ranks of consular officers. See CON-SULAR SERVICE. 2. Loosely used to refer to any consular officer.

consular privileges and immunities. The privileges and immunities granted to a consular officer. They are less extensive than those granted diplomatic officers. In general they assure sufficient freedom of his person and inviolability of his office to permit him to perform the necessary functions of his office. See DIPLOMATIC PRIVILEGES AND IMMUNITIES.

consular service. The combined consular officers representing a given country. It includes various ranks such as (in the United States) consuls general, consuls, vice-consuls and consular agents. See CONSUL.

consulate. Office of a consul or other consular officer. The office of a consul-general is more correctly called a consulate general.

consumption tax. A tax based on the consumption of, or rather expenditure for, an article. The tax may be collected from the consumer, but more often, as in customs duties, it is collected previous to purchase by the consumer and becomes part of the purchase price.

contested election. An election in which the result is not conceded by the losing candidate. He may demand a recount of the ballots or may, in certain cases, as, for example, in election to the House of Representatives, appeal to the House itself. There the matter is turned over to a committee. If the committee upholds the contention of the candidate, and the House approves, he is given the seat. This power of the House to judge the elections and qualifications of its members is granted by the Constitution. The Senate has the same power.

Continental Congress. The group of representatives of twelve of the American colonies which met in Phila-

delphia from 1774 to 1781. Although it adopted the Declaration of Independence and directed the Revolutionary War, it lacked constitutional basis and was inadequate as a central government. It adopted the Articles of Confederation which were accepted by the states in 1781.

continuing assessment. A system of land assessment in which a constant check is kept on the value of the land by noting sales, changes in use and other indications of value or change thereof. Such an assessment reflects the market value of land more accurately than infrequent periodic assessments.

continuous voyage, doctrine of. The doctrine of international law that a neutral vessel may be captured by a belligerent on the way to a neutral port if thereafter its destination was a port blockaded by the belligerent. In some cases contraband cargo has been treated similarly though bound for an unblockaded port. The theory behind this is that the ultimate destination is enemy territory and that this destination is not changed by an intermediate stop in neutral territory. The Declaration of London attempted to prohibit the application of the doctrine of blockade, but this prohibition was not observed in World War I.

contraband. Goods found by a belligerent on the high sea which are of use in war and are destined for the enemy. Usually the goods are thought of as belonging to neutrals, but occasionally enemy goods are included.

contract labor. Laborers brought to the United States by industries whose representatives bound the workers by contract before giving them passage. The terms of the contract put these people in a condition little better than involuntary servitude and since 1885 persons under such contracts have not been admitted to the United States.

contract theory. The political theory that the basis of the state is one or more contracts or agreements, real or implied, to which the citizen is a party. Often two contracts were assumed, one binding the citizens to each other and a second between the citizens collectively and their government. Underlying the theory is the premise that a governmental obligation to be binding must be accepted by the citizens. See CONSENT OF THE GOVERNED.

convention. 1. Political meeting, as for nominating party candidates for public office. 2. An international agreement, often used with the same meaning as treaty, though more correctly as a less important agreement than a treaty or more restricted in scope. In international politics the first meaning above is not used; an international meeting would be called a conference, not a convention.

conversations. A series of diplomatic discussions, usually of a preliminary nature between the accredited representatives of two, rarely more, states.

conversion. Process of changing over an industry from peace time production to production of war materials. See RECONVERSION.

convict. A person who has been adjudged to have committed a crime, and usually thought of as one who is serving a prison term therefor.

convict labor. Productive work done by prison inmates.

convoy. A group of merchant ships protected in passage by a number of warships.

cooling-off treaty. A treaty in which the parties agree not to carry a dispute to war while it is being investigated by a commission of inquiry, i. e. a period is provided the disputants for "cooling off." The name of William Jennings Bryan is chiefly connected with such agreements, as he negotiated some thirty of them while Secretary of State in 1913–14.

co-operative. A joint business concern established, owned, and operated by a particular group of producers or consumers to save themselves the disadvantages of market control or prices which they meet in dealing with a concern operated for private profit.

Co-ordinator of Inter-American Affairs, Office of. A governmental agency set up July 30, 1941. Its function was to promote inter-American goodwill through educational, cultural, and commercial contacts. It encouraged development in Latin America of agricultural products formerly secured outside the hemisphere and offered assistance in health and sanitary problems. It was taken into the Department of State in 1945.

Copperhead. Person in the North in the Civil War who favored the Southern cause.

copyright. The exclusive right to the publication, production or sale of the right to a literary, musical or artistic work, or the use of a merchandising label, granted to an author, composer, artist or manufacturer. In the United States the period of a copyright is 28 years with optional renewal for 28 more years.

cordon sanitaire (kawr-DOHNG sah-nee-TAYR). A kind of quarantine line to set off one territory from others, especially the line drawn by the western powers along western Russia after World War I in the hope of keeping communistic ideas east of that line.

Corfu incident. In 1923 an Italian, head of an international commission drawing up the Albanian-Greek frontier, was killed in Greek territory. The new fascist regime sent a stiff ultimatum, and when it was only partly accepted by Greece, who had asked the League to settle the question, Italy sent its navy to bombard and occupy the Greek island of Corfu, in the Adriatic. This was one of the first major defeats of the League and the first major fascist victory.

Corfu, Pact of. An agreement among the South Slavs to establish a Serb-Croat-Slovene state. They had been driven from their home lands to the island of Corfu during World War I and the agreement took place there June 20, 1917. The state later changed its name to Yugoslavia.

corn laws. English laws protecting and fostering grain production by limiting imports, paying a bonus for exports, and setting up duties on imported grain. The laws were repealed in 1849 as part of the free trade program.

coroner. An official, in the United States almost always a county official, whose chief responsibility is to investigate the circumstances of deaths apparently not resulting from natural causes.

coronet. A crown, usually less elaborate than that of a king or queen, worn on state occasions by persons of lower rank.

corporation. 1. In the United States a group of persons joined together under the laws of a state and legally forming a new legal entity, i. e. with rights and duties separate from those of the individuals who form the group. The Supreme Court has ruled that corporations are legal persons, and thus are protected as natural persons are by the Constitution. 2. Term also used for city or town, as the corporation limits. 3. In fascist Italy an employer-employee organization in basic groups of industries which were to be the basis for governmental representation. See CORPORATIVE STATE.

corporation tax. See TAX.

corporative state. The economic organization of Italy projected by the Fascists. It was based on a series of "corporations" which included employers and employees which represented their respective organizations (syndicates). The corporations were represented in the National Council of Corporations which began as an economic advisory body but which finally replaced the chamber of deputies.

Corregidor. Fortified island at the entrance to Manila Bay. United States troops there were forced to surrender to the Japanese (on May 6, 1942) after a valiant defense. American parachutists were dropped on the island as the first step in retaking it February 17, 1945.

corrupt practices acts. Laws in the United States which limit the amount of money which may be spent in an election campaign, restrict the sources of contributions to campaigns, and make bribery and other unacceptable methods of influencing the voters illegal.

corruption of blood. The transmission, from the person convicted of the crime, to his children, of the effect of the conviction for a crime, particularly regarding inheritances and titles. The Constitution states that treason "shall not work corruption of blood."

Cortes (KAWR-tez). Spanish national legislative body.

corvée (kawr-VAY). An obligation to a feudal lord, sovereign, or state paid by one's own labor, thus a kind of forced labor. It generally disappeared with the passing of feudalism and substitution of money taxes for labor service.

Cossack. Member of groups of peoples who inhabit the steppe regions of Russia, famous for their horsemanship. Represented by light cavalry forces in the Russian armies.

cost-plus contract. A contract in which the government pays the producer the cost of production plus a fixed percentage, such as six percent, as profit. This scheme is designed to prevent operational loss as well as excessive profit to the producer. Much in use during World War II.

council. A term of somewhat variable meaning used to designate a fairly small governmental body. It may be legislative, as a United States city council or English county council, executive, as the French Council of Ministers, or have some of the attributes of both, as the Council of the League of Nations.

Council of Commissars. See COUNCIL OF PEOPLE'S MINISTERS.

Council on Foreign Relations. Private organization in New York City, engaged in research and dissemination of information on international affairs. Its best-known publication is the quarterly *Foreign Affairs.*

Council of Four. Inner group deciding policies at Paris Peace Conference: Georges Clemenceau (France), David Lloyd George (England), Vittorio Orlando (Italy), Woodrow Wilson (United States). Also referred to as the Big Four.

Council of the League of Nations. The smaller of the two representative bodies in the League organization. It was neither an executive body nor an upper house, but more like a strong executive committee. It included the great powers who were members of the League and usually 9 other elected members. Although its functions were largely shared with the Assembly, it became in time the more important body in the consideration of international disputes, partly because of functions assigned in the Covenant, partly because of its frequent meetings—at least every three months —and partly because it was a smaller and less unwieldy body.

Council of Ministers. French term for the cabinet. It is used to designate the

formal cabinet sessions, usually at the residence of the president of the republic, attended and presided over by the president. The ministers also have a less formal gathering called the cabinet council.

Council of National Defense. In the United States an interdepartmental defense committee set up during World War I made up of the heads of War, Navy, Interior, Agriculture, Commerce, and Labor Departments. Its function was to correlate industrial production and natural resources for national defense. In World War II, its functions were carried on by various agencies.

Council of Nationalities. One of the two chambers in the Supreme Council, or legislative body, of the U. S. S. R. under the 1936 Constitution. The members are elected primarily as representatives of the "nationalities" found in the republics of the Soviet Union or in special regions where nationalities are located.

Council of People's Ministers. The heads of the government administrative departments in Russia, somewhat comparable to a cabinet in western European states. In addition to supervising the work of their individual offices, collectively they plan laws and the budget, and issue administrative orders. Before March, 1946, they were called commissars.

Council of State. French highest administrative court. See ADMINISTRATIVE COURT; COURT OF CASSATION.

Council of State Governments. An association of officials of state governments interested in their mutual problems. It publishes the magazine *State Government* and the biennial *Book of the States.*

Council of Ten. A committee at the Paris Peace Conference composed of the two ranking delegates of the five victorious great powers, France, Great

Britain, Italy, Japan, and the United States. This group, also referred to as the Supreme Council and the Big Ten, made most of the real decisions at the conference. See BIG FOUR.

Council of the Union (U.S.S.R.). One of the two houses of the Supreme Council, or legislative body of the U. S. S. R. Members of this house are elected from electoral districts of 300,000 population.

councilman. In the United States, member of a city council.

counselor. The counselor of an embassy (or legation) is usually the diplomatic officer ranking next to the ambassador or minister. He is the chief adviser to his superior and conducts much of the important business of the post. In the absence of his superior he is likely to serve as the chargé d'affaires.

count. European title of nobility. Descended from the Latin word *comes*, meaning an "associate" of an emperor or king, who in early medieval times was given lands in exchange for feudal service. At the height of the feudal period most counts became actual rulers of these lands, called counties. Now the title seldom has more than an honorary meaning. The British equivalent is earl, whose wife, however, is called countess. The German is *graf*.

countess. Wife of a count or earl, or a woman who holds the title by inheritance, in her own right. See COUNT.

counter-espionage. Efforts to counter-act spying by the enemy.

counterfeit. To make imitations of money to be used for the real article.

counter-revolution. A movement resulting in a forceful attempt to overthrow a successful revolution and to restore an earlier order. See CONSERVATIVE, REACTIONARY, AUTHORITARIAN.

countervailing duty. A tax placed on imports by a state to offset the effects of a subsidy granted on the same products in the country of their origin. It is a tax levied by a state to protect its own producers from advantages of subsidies enjoyed by foreign competitors.

county. Anglo-American political subdivision. In the United States, it is a subdivision of the states, except in Louisiana, where they are called parishes.

county clerk. In the United States an elective official found in most states whose chief function is to keep records of property transfers and to aid in elections by distributing ballots and registering results. In some states he acts also as the clerk of the county court.

county commissioner. One of the members of the legislative or policy-making branch of county government. Usually there is a small number, from 3 to 7, on the board of commissioners. Their functions are chiefly those regarding collection and disbursement of funds and supervising public property and less important highways.

county court. The fundamental judicial unit in the United States system of government. Such a court is found in almost every county, though the judge may serve another county also. Its jurisdiction covers the whole range of civil and criminal cases, barring those that come under the jurisdiction of the federal courts. The court is often given a special name such as court of common pleas, superior court, or district court. They usually have one or more elected judges.

county manager. An administrative officer found in a few counties who functions in the county in a way similar to a city manager in a city. See CITY MANAGER PLAN.

coup d'état (koo-day-TAH). 1. Sudden forcible seizure of government. 2. Sudden stroke of policy.

courier. A messenger carrying official diplomatic correspondence. The general rule is that he is a privileged person and immune to interference in the course of discharging his responsibilities.

court. 1. Place where judges hear and decide cases. 2. Group of judges officiating collectively. 3. Residence and attendants of a ruling sovereign.

Court of Arbitral Justice. International court proposed by the second Hague Peace Conference in 1907. It did not materialize as no agreement could be reached on a method of selecting judges.

Court of Cassation. The highest judicial court in France.

Court of Claims. A court of five judges in Washington D. C. which examines claims against the United States. Its functions include decisions in cases brought by private individuals which may be appealed to the Supreme Court, and a kind of opinion or recommendation to Congress, or a government administrative agency if the claim was referred to the court by it.

Court of Common Pleas. The basic United States county court, also sometimes called the district or superior court. It has both criminal and civil jurisdiction, original jurisdiction in most cases, and often final jurisdiction on the facts.

Court of Conflicts. A French court which decides, when there is a difference of opinion, whether a given case is within the jurisdiction of the Court of Cassation, the highest criminal and civil court, or that of the Council of State as the highest administrative court.

Court of Criminal Appeal. As the name indicates, an English court to which criminal cases may be appealed from the assizes. It is made up of judges assigned from the High Court of Justice. In rare cases appeal may be

taken from this court to the House of Lords.

Court of Customs and Patent Appeals. A federal court of five judges to which appeals are made on rulings regarding customs and patent matters.

court martial. See MILITARY LAW.

court packing proposals. 1. In 1870 President U. S. Grant was accused of packing the Supreme Court when he appointed two justices whose votes reversed the 1869 decision against the Legal Tender Acts. 2. Term applied to part of the proposal in 1937 by President Franklin D. Roosevelt to reform the federal judiciary. This followed in part earlier attempts (1869, 1919) to bring about resignations of federal judges, incapacitated by age or unable to perform their duties, by granting full pay; and allowing appointment of one additional judge for each one, eligible but incapacitated, who did not retire. President Roosevelt proposed substantially the same thing for justices of the Supreme Court but the total number was not to exceed fifteen. The proposal was not enacted.

Since 1789 when the Supreme Court was established with six members its size has been changed six times: four increases and two reductions. President Roosevelt was accused in some quarters of attempting to pack the court in order to avoid having important legislation declared unconstitutional, as had been done with so-called New Deal cases. On the other hand, the Supreme Court was accused of substituting its judgment for that of the people and other branches of the government.

Court of Social Honor. A Nazi German labor relations court made up of employers and employees, which judged cases in which either an employer or employee was charged with infringing on the honor of the group or interfering with the welfare of the state as the Nazis viewed it.

courtesy titles. Subsidiary titles of peers used by their children, either by the older son because his father still bears the ranking title of the family or by a younger son who probably will never inherit the ranking title of the family. A custom followed only if the rank of the father is a high one.

covenant. Term for a kind of international agreement implying greater solemnity and importance than the word treaty.

Covenant of the League of Nations. The first twenty-six articles of the Paris Peace Treaties of 1919, forming the constitution of the League of Nations. See LEAGUE OF NATIONS.

C. P. A. See CIVILIAN PRODUCTION ADMINISTRATION.

craft union. A labor union composed of workers in a single craft or skill such as carpenters or bricklayers. Groups of such unions largely form the American Federation of Labor.

credentials committee. See COMMITTEE ON CREDENTIALS.

crime. An act which is so grave that it is primarily considered an offense against the state rather than against the victim. As such the state prosecutes and, if the person is found guilty, punishes him by fine or imprisonment.

Crimea Conference. A conference of Winston Churchill (England), Franklin D. Roosevelt (United States), and Joseph Stalin (Russia), and their advisers at Yalta, the Crimea, concluded February 11, 1945. The chief decisions were for continued military action against Germany, post-war occupation of Germany by zones under the three powers and France, reparations, Polish and Yugoslav governmental arrangements, and the calling of a United Nations Conference in April at San Francisco to draw up a

charter for an international organization.

Crimean War. War between Russia on the one hand and Great Britain, France, Turkey, and Sardinia on the other between 1854 and 1856, fought largely in the Crimean peninsula on the north side of the Black Sea. It checked Russian influence in Turkey more or less permanently. The war has been famous in literature as the conflict involving the charge of the British Light Brigade.

crime wave. A widespread increase in the commission of crime.

criminal code. A legal code defining crimes and the punishment therefor. See CRIME; CODE.

criminal jurisdiction. The authority of a court to try criminal cases.

criminal law. The law defining crimes and establishing the punishment therefor.

criminal syndicalism. A legal concept which embodies a series of laws known as "criminal syndicalism laws." Their purpose is to prohibit doctrines and activities involving use of violence as a means to social change.

American syndicalism advocated by the International Workers of the World (I.W.W.) for a number of years preceding the first World War was very active particularly among miners, lumbermen and farmhands in western and northwestern states and aroused the fear of employers. When World War I started it was feared that the government's activities would be hampered by the I.W.W. The first criminal-syndicalism laws were enacted in Idaho in 1917, shortly followed by Minnesota and by five more states in 1918. Most criminal syndicalism laws were passed in 1919 and 1920, inspired rather by the Russian revolution than by the I.W.W. strikes. Twenty-one states enacted such laws providing for penalties up to ten years in prison for the advocation of doctrines using crime, sabotage, violence and terrorism for achieving industrial and political reforms. The enforcement of these laws gave rise to lively discussions involving the conflicting problems of freedom of speech and public safety. Prosecution of criminal syndicalism was fairly active in western states between 1919 and 1924. Many sentences however were repealed by higher courts and pardons by state governors were frequent. After 1924 syndicalism and radical left-wing socialism declined in the United States. By 1929 there was no person in a United States prison under the criminal-syndicalism laws. See SYNDICALISM, MARXISM, COMMUNISM, BOLSHEVISM, SOCIALISM, WORLD-REVOLUTION, CLASS STRUGGLE.

critical material. Any raw material absolutely essential in war production for which the supply is inadequate. Term much used during World War II.

Croatia. Northwestern part of Yugoslavia, distinguished from the rest of the country by being Roman Catholic instead of Orthodox and by using the Latin alphabet instead of the Cyrillic.

Croix de Feu (KRWAH duh FUH). Literally: fiery cross. French fascist organization of the 1930's.

Crop Loan Act. Laws of February and May, 1934, providing that the Farm Credit Administration could make loans for crops and livestock in drouth-stricken areas with the first liens on such crops or stock as security.

Cross-of-Gold Speech. A speech by William Jennings Bryan at the Democratic National Convention in 1896 favoring the coinage of silver without relationship to gold, that is "free coinage" of silver. The climax of the speech: "You shall not press down upon the brow of labor this crown of thorns, you shall not crucify mankind upon a cross of gold!" The speech secured for Bryan the presidential nomination.

cross the aisle. To vote with the opposite party on a measure in a legislative body. That is, to vote with the party from which one is divided figuratively, and sometimes literally, by a central aisle.

crown. Office of the king or queen. In Great Britain official actions of the government are usually referred to as being steps taken by the crown.

crown colony. British colonies originally controlled by the English King. Now such colonies are controlled in varying degree by the British Government through the secretary of state for the colonies.

cruel and unusual punishment. A prohibition in the Constitution which has been interpreted as preventing torture, or any punishment or fine greatly out of proportion to the offense.

cruiser. A war vessel of 10,000 tons displacement or less, or carrying guns not larger than eight inches.

Crusades. A series of eight main expeditions by the Christians of western Europe from 1096 to 1291 (supplemented in the intervals by many smaller groups) in which an attempt was made to drive the Mohammedans out of the Holy Land. They were undertaken partly as a result of the request of Alexius Comnenus, emperor of Byzantium, for help against the Seljuk Turks; partly because pilgrims to the Holy Land were interfered with by the Seljuks who had captured Jerusalem in 1071; partly in an effort to find new commercial routes to the East; partly as a means of controlling the feudal barons and their followers; and partly to make Christianity a world-wide religion. Some results were: the Crusaders failed to occupy the East and the Turks became entrenched in Europe; the growth of towns was accelerated; geographical knowledge was widened; feudalism declined further; trade increased; feudal colonies were formed for a time along the eastern Mediterranean; in the end the papacy was weakened, although after a period of greatly increased power; western civilization was brought into contact with another civilization which led to intellectual quickening.

C.S.I. See ORDER OF THE STAR OF INDIA.

cultural attaché. A representative of the Division of Cultural Relations of the Department of State who is attached to an embassy or legation abroad. His function is to make known to the country in which he is stationed the significant cultural contributions of the United States, such as its best books, art, motion pictures, and its scientific and educational opportunities.

cumulative voting. A system of proportional representation in which the voter elects several members of a legislative body. He is given as many votes as there are seats to be filled, and can distribute his votes as he pleases, giving them all to one candidate if he so desires.

currency. See MONEY.

Curzon line. A provisional eastern boundary for Poland suggested by Viscount Curzon to the Allied Supreme Council during the Paris Peace Conference and proposed by the Council. It is generally objectively viewed as approximately the ethnographic boundary between Poles and Russians but since it is considerably west of the 1772 boundary, as well as of the 1920–1939 eastern boundary of Poland, its acceptance by the Poles was, until 1945, sharply resisted.

custody. Imprisonment of a person convicted of crime, or the safe-keeping of one arrested and accused of crime.

customs. A tax on goods imported into a country. Usually the effect of this tax is considered more from the point of view of its protection of home industries than from the point of view of its income-producing aspects.

Customs Tariffs Union. The International Union for the Publication of Customs Tariffs. As the name indicates it is an international organization for the collection and publication of statistics on tariffs and world trade.

customs union. Two or more states that have a common tariff wall around them and none between them. See UNION, ZOLLVEREIN.

C. V. O. See ROYAL VICTORIAN ORDER.

C. W. A. See CIVIL WORKS ADMINISTRATION.

Cyprus Convention. Treaty dated June 4, 1878, between Great Britain and Turkey in which the former agreed to help defend Turkey, if attacked in its Asiatic possessions, in return for which Turkey granted to Great Britain the right to establish a military occupation of the island of Cyprus.

czar or **tsar.** 1. Title for Russian sovereign from 1547 until 1918, the date of the death of the last czar of Russia. Title of the king of Bulgaria from 1908 to 1945. 2. One having absolute authority in some sphere.

Czechoslovak-French Treaty. A 1924 agreement in which France secured a friend on the eastern side of Germany to offset the German threat. The states agreed to settle their mutual disputes peaceably, consult if Germany and Austria threatened to unite, and work together on matters of security.

Czechoslovak-U. S. S. R. Treaty. A mutual assistance treaty signed May 16, 1935, stipulating that each would come to the aid of the other if attacked, provided France also came to the assistance of the victim of aggression.

D

Dail Eireann (dawl ER-uhn). Lower house of the Irish legislative body.

Daily Worker. New York and London newspapers, both organs of the communists.

Danubia. States lying in the Danube valley. Thought by some to form a natural geographical and economic unit which should be formed into some kind of political or economic union. States usually included in such a project are Austria, Hungary, Yugoslavia, Bulgaria, and Romania. Czechoslovakia is also often included; Germany is usually omitted.

Danzig. A free city established by the Treaty of Versailles, the status of which was a result of a compromise between the fact that its population was predominantly German and the fact that it was at the mouth of the Vistula River and the natural seaport for much of Poland. It was under the protection of the League of Nations and its status indicated that it was in neither Germany nor Poland, but it was inside the Polish customs boundaries and Poland carried on Danzig's foreign relations. Hence Germany considered it an irredenta and the Third Reich placed its restoration to Germany high on its list of objectives. Poland received it after World War II.

D. A. R. Daughters of the American Revolution. A women's patriotic organization composed of descendents of those who participated in the American Revolution.

Dardanelles. See STRAITS.

dark horse. A candidate for office who is relatively unknown or not seriously considered as a candidate until the campaign is well under way.

Darlan-Clark Accord. An agreement reached in November, 1942, between Admiral Jean François Darlan and Lieutenant General Mark Clark in preparation for the subsequent landing of American troops in North Africa.

dauphin. An old French title of nobility which was apparently used by only two rulers, the dauphins of Vienne and Auvergne. The dauphinate of Vienne came to be known as the Dauphiné, and when it was acquired by the French king in 1349 a stipulation was added that his eldest son or heir presumptive should bear the title dauphin. The first royal dauphin was Charles V. The title is best known in America as referring to the Lost Dauphin, the son of Louis XVI, who is supposed to have escaped to this country during the Revolution, though there has never been any sound evidence to support the story.

Dawes Plan. The first major revision, made in 1924, of the German reparations for World War I. The plan came as a result of Germany's not paying the reparations as first laid down, with the subsequent occupation of the Ruhr by France. Under the Dawes Plan the Ruhr was to be evacuated, and the reparations were cut down to a series of payments beginning with one billion marks and increasing to two and a half billion annually, to be paid from certain taxes and bonds. There was to be some foreign control of German finances, but Germany was to receive a loan from abroad to help get on her feet. See YOUNG PLAN.

day in court. The opportunity to present one's case before an unbiased tribunal.

daylight saving time. Time one hour ahead of standard time. The plan has been widely utilized to provide an extra hour of daylight late in the day. It is usually used only between April and September.

days of grace. A few days at the beginning of hostilities during which belligerents permit enemy vessels to sail for home.

D-banks. Four banks which formed the backbone of German financial strength, all established prior to the unification of Germany. Some of their funds were invested in certain industries over which they exercised considerable control. They were called the D-banks because their names began with D: Deutsche Bank, Dresdner Bank, Discontogesellschaft, and Darmstadter und Nationalbank.

D. B. E. See ORDER OF THE BRITISH EMPIRE.

D. C. See DISTRICT OF COLUMBIA.

D-day. The day in which a major military operation, such as invasion, begins. D merely stands for day. It is a point of reference for the whole operation; for example, a specific action scheduled for the second day after the operation begins will take place on D plus 2, incorrectly referred to as D-day plus 2. This arrangement makes it possible to plan the time relations of the whole operation accurately without reference to the calendar.

dead-letter office. A division of the United States Post Office with branches all over the country to which letters and packages are sent if they cannot be delivered because of illegibility, wrong address, etc. If possible, after inspection, they are returned to sender. If not, letters are destroyed and parcels are sold at auction.

dean of the diplomatic corps. See DOYEN OF DIPLOMATIC CORPS.

death duties. British term for what are referred to in the United States as inheritance taxes.

debasement. The reduction of value of a unit of money in terms of other units of money or in terms of gold content.

debate. The formal discussion of proposed legislation in a legislative body according to the rules of parliamentary law.

debt limit. The maximum legal limit for a national debt. Presumably it is a legislative check on executive borrowing, but usually when the executive needs to exceed the limit it is raised by the legislative branch.

decentralization. Process of shifting control from a central authority to local ones, as from the national government to states (United States), provinces, counties, or cities. See CENTRALIZATION.

decision. An interpretation of the law in the form of a binding judicial settlement with which a court concludes a case or controversy between two parties who have brought their dispute before the court.

declaration. A unilateral or multilateral announcement or statement of policy which a state or states intend to pursue. It does not as such have the force of law binding other parties, though in time it may come to be generally followed and have such force.

Declaration by the United Nations. An

agreement of January 1, 1942, by 26 United Nations to employ their full resources against those Axis states with which they were at war; to co-operate with the other signatories and not make a separate peace or armis-tice. The preamble stated that the signatories adhered to the purposes and principles of the Atlantic Charter. Other states signed later.

Declaration of Independence. The proc-lamation that the American colonies were free and independent states and no longer subject to England. It was adopted on July 4, 1776, by the Con-tinental Congress. Written principally by Thomas Jefferson.

declaration of intention. Formal state-ment by an alien that he intends to become naturalized. See DECLARENT ALIEN.

Declaration of Lima. A declaration agreed to at the eighth Pan-American Conference on December 24, 1938. The members reaffirmed their soli-darity and their intention to main-tain and defend the principles on which that solidarity is based; they declared of common concern any threat to their peace or security and agreed to consult on the measures to be used in such a case, particularly through meetings of the various min-isters of foreign affairs.

Declaration of London. An unratified agreement on the conduct of naval warfare signed by the leading states of the world in London, February 26, 1909. Its various sections were de-voted to such things as blockade, contraband, unneutral service, prizes and convoys. Although not binding as an accepted treaty, it was com-monly looked upon as a good collec-tion of rules and occasionally cited as authority in subsequent cases.

Declaration of Panama. A statement of policy at the Inter-American Con-ference held at Panama October 1–3,

1939. In an effort to preserve inter-American solidarity it was voted to demand that belligerents should not commit hostile acts within 300–600 miles of the coasts of the Western hemisphere south of Canada, which would have had in part the effect of pushing the 3-mile limit out that far. The conferees also voted to secure compliance from the belligerents, but protests were received instead.

Declaration of Paris. Rules of mari-time international law agreed to by the great powers April 16, 1856, which stated that privateering was abolished; that enemy goods on neutral ships could not be seized nor could neutral goods on an enemy ship be seized; and that blockades to be binding must be effective.

Declaration of Rights. The Declaration of the Rights of Man and of the Citizen voted on August 26, 1789, by the French National Assembly. It was the basic French bill of rights asserting that men are born free and equal in regard to rights of liberty, property, and security, and that the state is established to secure these rights; also that all persons have the right to participate, at least through representatives, in the making of the law. See BILL OF RIGHTS.

declaration of war. See WAR, DECLARA-TION OF.

declaratory judgment. The power exer-cised by the courts in about one-third of the state courts of the United States to interpret the law in answer to a request for such a declaration. See DECISION.

declarent alien. A person who has de-clared his intention to become a citi-zen of the United States or has "taken out his first papers." He may com-plete the process and lose the designa-tion of alien in a minimum of two years and three months if residence requirements are fulfilled.

Decoration Day. See MEMORIAL DAY.

decree. An executive proclamation having the force of law.

decree law. One of a number of laws passed by the French parliament in the 1930's empowering the cabinet in fact to legislate by decree.

dedicate. To devote to public purposes property that was formerly private. Used especially for roads opened to public use.

de facto (dee FAK-toh). Latin for in fact. See RECOGNITION.

defendant. Person who is obliged to defend himself in a legal action taken against him in court.

Defense Homes Corporation. A U. S. government agency set up in 1940 to provide funds for loans for homes in the vicinity of defense plants. Transferred to the Federal Public Housing Authority in 1942.

defense housing. Residence building projects built by either public or private agencies to accommodate workers in war or defense factories.

Defense Plant Corporation. A U. S. government agency set up by the Reconstruction Finance Corporation in 1940 which allocated raw materials, equipment, and manufacturing plants in the production of war equipment.

deficiency bill. A supplementary appropriation bill passed to provide for a financial deficiency. Sometimes this expedient is planned in order to make the original appropriations appear economical.

deficit financing. 1. The practice of meeting a deficit in the public treasury by borrowing on a small scale to cover budgetary miscalculations. 2. Some persons advocate, and the United States government under the New Deal made a policy of, borrowing to meet large anticipated deficits which arise merely because there is no real effort to balance the national budget.

deflation. See INFLATION.

de Gaullist. Follower of General Charles de Gaulle. Also Gaullist. See FIGHTING FRENCH.

de jure (dee JOO-ree). Legal or legally. See RECOGNITION.

delegate. 1. Representative to a political convention or conference. 2. Nonvoting representative from United States territories to the House of Representatives. 3. Member of a House of Delegates. See HOUSE OF DELEGATES. 4. To empower a person to act as a representative.

delegation. 1. Group of delegates or representatives. 2. The authorization by one party that certain of its functions shall be performed by another.

delegation of powers. The turning over of certain governmental powers by a branch of government or an official to another branch of government or person. Under the United States Constitution there is a rather strict limit on this transfer of power by branches of government, though the president may delegate executive functions more freely to subordinate administrative officials.

deliberative body. A law-making body.

delinquency. A minor infraction of the law by an adult, or any infraction of a law by a juvenile. In the latter case an act is not considered an offense of the same seriousness as if it had been committed by an adult, on the theory that a young person is less responsible for his acts.

demagogue. A person who tries to gain political backing by appealing to the prejudices of the masses of the people by such means as fantastic promises or the development of group hatreds.

démarche (day-MAHRSH). French word meaning a step. Used to mean a diplomatic step or some decisive diplomatic action.

demilitarized zone. Area from which

fortifications and troops have been removed.

demobilize. To release large groups from the armed forces.

democracy. Government by the people, usually set up in practice in such a way that control is exercised by the majority of the total number of qualified voters using the privilege of voting on issues or officials at an election, and by the majority of a body of representatives thus elected. Sometimes, in a "pure" or "direct" democracy the qualified voters vote directly on all policy issues, as in a New England town meeting. In addition to this rule of the majority, democracy has implied a second aspect, namely that the minority has certain rights so fundamental that they may not be infringed even by the majority in the regular legislative, executive or judicial processes.

democrat. One who believes in the principles of democracy.

Democrat. Member of the Democratic Party.

democratic. Showing the attributes of equality and acceptance of majority rule and minority rights.

Democratic Party. One of the two major American parties. Its spiritual father was Thomas Jefferson and it appeared under its present name during the presidency of Andrew Jackson (1829–1837). It is usually looked upon as the more liberal and progressive of the two parties, though due to the problem of states rights and the Solid South it was not the party which emancipated the slaves. It was also considered originally as the states-rights party, advocating the limitation of the power of the federal government; also a low-tariff advocate. Under President Franklin D. Roosevelt the New Deal was instituted in 1933. Democratic conservatives now claim the New Deal has set up its own party, ignoring the Democrats as such.

Democratic-Republican Party. A name used to describe both the Republican party which arose as an anti-Federalist party in 1792 and the party which elected Andrew Jackson in 1828. The latter group, however, was only a faction of the former group. Both are the ancestors of the present Democratic Party.

demonetization. The discontinuance of the use of a given metal as a monetary standard, as, for example, silver.

denunciation. Formal notice by a state that it considers a treaty terminated or at least no longer binding upon it.

département (day-pahrt-MAHNG). The largest administrative subdivision in France. It has an executive, the prefect, and a general council with limited powers of legislation. The *département* is a unit of national administration primarily, and its own local powers are much less extensive than those of the states of the United States. There are 92 of these units, three of which are in Algeria.

department. The name given in the United States to the various great administrative divisions of the government at the head of each of which is a cabinet member. In many other countries they are called ministries.

dependency. Any political unit which is not entirely independent but controlled to a greater or less extent by another state.

deport. To send out of a country, usually now applied to undesirable aliens.

depose. To force a ruler from a throne.

depressed classes. A new and less harsh term for the Untouchables in India. See UNTOUCHABLES.

depression. Technically a low point in the business cycle. Specifically the reduction of trade and business activity which, except for military preparations, largely characterized the 1930's. It was signalized in the United States by the collapse of the stock market in October, 1929, and in Europe by the failure in June, 1931, of the big Vienna bank, the Kreditanstalt, and the subsequent departure of Great Britain from the gold standard.

Deputies, Chamber of. Lower house in several national legislatures, the best known of which is that of France.

deputy. 1. Person authorized to represent another person or group of persons. 2. Member of a Chamber of Deputies.

deputy sheriff. An assistant who acts in place of the sheriff.

dereliction. Failure adequately to discharge a duty.

desert. To quit the service of the armed forces without authorization.

despatch. Message sent by a diplomatic officer abroad to the foreign office (in the United States the Department of State) in his home capital. See INSTRUCTIONS.

despot. A ruler who wields absolute and arbitrary power.

despotism. A system of government in which the ruler exercises absolute and arbitrary power.

destroyer deal. See BASE-DESTROYER AGREEMENT.

detention home. A place where juveniles are confined while awaiting trial or sentence, or sometimes while serving a term of punishment. Such a place is provided to keep youths away from adult offenders in a jail.

Deutsches Nachtrichten Buro (DOY-chis NAHKH-rish-ten byoo-ROH). Official Nazi German news agency, usually known as D.N.B.

devaluation. Reduction of the value of money in terms of its former values, other currencies, or gold.

devolution. British term used to indicate a delegation of the work of the House of Commons, as to adminis-

trative agencies or the parliament for Northern Ireland.

d'Hondt system. A method of apportioning seats in a plan of proportional representation in which the vote of each party is divided first by one, then by two, then by three and so on. Seats are given to the parties which after each division have the largest number of votes, until all seats are taken. Often used in connection with a list system.

diarchy. The system of the separation of governmental functions in British India whereby the governments of the Indian provinces and of the central government exercise certain functions while certain others are reserved to the British. In the central government the reserved powers are defense and foreign relations.

dictatorship. Arbitrary rule by one man.

dictatorship of the proletariat. Domination of government by the wage-earners, the goal of a socialist or communist party. See PROLETARIAT.

dictum. Plural, dicta. See OBITER DICTUM.

die-hard. Person who relinquishes his preconceptions most reluctantly. Usually used to refer to conservatives rather than to radicals.

Dies Committee. A special committee of the United States House of Representatives under the chairmanship of Rep. Martin Dies, Democrat, of Texas, set up in 1938 for the investigation of un-American activities. It was widely criticised as being inquisitorial in its methods and as being much less interested in running down activities of a fascist nature than those of a communist nature. Dies retired from the House in 1944, but the committee was put on a permanent basis and called the Committee on Un-American Activities in January, 1945.

dimout. A partial blackout, in use

during World War II. It meant a sufficient reduction in the outside lights in a city so that the normal glow they create would be eliminated. It was particularly used in American coastal cities so that vessels near the shore would not be silhouetted against the sky, thus becoming targets for submarines.

diplomacy. The practice and methods of carrying on relations between sovereign states.

diplomat. A person who is the political representative of his state at the capital of another state. There are four ranks: ambassadors, ministers, ministers resident, and chargés d'affaires.

diplomatic agent. 1. Often used as a synonym for diplomat. See DIPLOMAT. 2. A special diplomatic representative not included in the four regular classes of diplomats.

diplomatic corps. The total body of diplomatic officers at a given capital. See DOYEN.

diplomatic correspondence. The messages sent between a diplomatic agent and his superiors in his home capital. See DESPATCH, INSTRUCTIONS.

diplomatic intervention. Interference in the affairs of a state by a diplomatic agent of another. Distinguished from interference by armed force. See INTERVENTION.

Diplomatic List. A monthly publication of the Department of State giving the names of the members of the various diplomatic staffs in Washington, D. C.

diplomatic mission. 1. The term of service of a diplomatic agent at a foreign capital. 2. The diplomat and his staff at a foreign capital.

diplomatic pouch. Sealed bag in which diplomatic correspondence is transported between the department of state or foreign affairs and the diplomatic representatives abroad. Usually such correspondence is unmolested and kept completely private en route.

diplomatic privileges and immunities. As a representative of a sovereign or state it is assumed that in general a diplomatic officer is not subject to local jurisdiction where he is stationed, and that he must not be hindered in the performance of his duties. As a result, he is not bound by the local laws in his official capacity, and his home, office, family and suite, or official family, are all also more or less free from local jurisdiction. There are a few exceptions, such as quarantine regulations and certain private business transactions, and the diplomatic agent may in special cases voluntarily come under local jurisdiction.

diplomatic protection. The protection extended by a state to its citizens within the territory of another state. Every state possesses the right thus to protect its citizens abroad. This right is exercised through the diplomatic representatives of the state.

diplomatic service. The total group of diplomatic agents of any one state. See FOREIGN SERVICE OF THE UNITED STATES.

diplomatist. Term often used instead of diplomat.

direct action. The use of force and threats of force to achieve one's political ends, as the forceful seizure of offices, election machinery, or factories.

direct election. An election in which the voter casts his ballot directly for a candidate. United States senators were originally elected indirectly by the state legislatures, but now they are chosen by direct election.

direct legislation. Direct participation by the people in the process of legislation. See INITIATIVE, REFERENDUM.

direct primary. An election in which the voters of the various parties nominate their candidates for the final election. A primary.

direct tax. See TAX.

directive. An order or set of instructions.

disarmament. Abolition of armaments, or their reduction or limitation.

Disarmament Conference of 1932. A disarmament conference sponsored by the League of Nations. It failed largely because the demands of Germany could not be accommodated by the other powers. After that Germany, Italy, and Japan rapidly increased their armaments in preparation for World War II.

Disaster Loan Corporation. An agency established in 1937 in the Commerce Department under the general supervision of the Reconstruction Finance Corporation which makes loans to those who have suffered losses from floods.

discharge. 1. To dismiss a special committee after it has reported to the legislative body of which it is a part. 2. To release a person from the armed forces.

discipline, party. Party control over members which impels them to act according to the directions of the party. These directions may be democratically or autocratically determined, but the rank and file must obey. This is what provides party strength and solidarity either at election time or in debate in a legislative body.

discovery. Act of finding territory which was previously unknown.

discretion. Freedom to make choices in the administration of a policy.

discretionary. The kind of power which involves freedom of choice. See MINISTERIAL.

discrimination. The making of laws which treat people unequally, or the administration (or application) of laws or regulations in an unequal manner.

disestablishment. Separation of church and state. See ESTABLISHED CHURCH.

disfranchisement. The denial to a person of the privilege of voting.

dispatch. See DESPATCH.

displaced person. The term applied during and after World War II to the war refugees who had been forced from their homes by the tides of military action, and also to those who had been separated from their homes by policy, as for example, the Poles and others taken by the Nazis to Germany as laborers.

disputed elections. See CONTESTED ELECTIONS.

dissenting opinion. The legal opinion of a judge who disagrees with the decision of the majority of a court.

dissolution. The ending of the term of a parliamentary body, such as the House of Commons, usually as the result of a vote adverse to the government.

district attorney. 1. The attorney for the federal government who presents to the grand jury evidence of violation of federal laws and prosecutes in the district courts cases in which the grand jury returns indictments. 2. Title of an officer with similar functions in a county. See PROSECUTING ATTORNEY.

District of Columbia. The territory on the north side of the Potomac River provided for in the Constitution of the United States as the seat of the federal government. Washington is located therein. The Constitution grants Congress the exclusive power of legislation there. Hence, although it is surrounded by Maryland, it is not part of that state. It has a kind of commission form of government, with the commissioners appointed or assigned by the president. There are no locally elected officials and the inhabitants can vote for government officials only by retaining a legal residence in one of the states.

district courts, federal. The courts comprising the lowest level of the three in the regular federal judiciary system. They are courts of original jurisdiction, which includes almost all cases within the federal jurisdiction. Appeal from them is taken to the circuit courts of appeals, or in a few instances, to the Supreme Court. The courts are about 90 in number, and they are scattered over the country in specially drawn districts, one court per district, so that they serve an approximately equal number of people.

district judge. A judge who presides in a federal district court. He is appointed by the president and serves for life or good behavior.

divide et impera (DI-vi-dee et im-PEER-uh). See DIVIDE AND RULE.

divide and rule. The principle of keeping subjects or enemies at odds among themselves on the theory that it is easier to control divided subjects than those who are unified. Rome is usually cited as having followed the principle; Great Britain is accused of recently doing so, particularly in India.

divine right of kings. The theory that a king's right to rule is founded on the law of God and the law of nature. Kings must succeed by heredity alone to the rights of their ancestors, who in the beginning were divinely appointed to rule. This theory should be distinguished from beliefs in the divinity of the monarch (such as the now defunct Japanese myth that the person of the Emperor is divine). The divine right of kings was particularly widespread after the end of the Middle Ages, supporting the claims of kings to their thrones on the basis of heredity and legitimacy. It was used to support the Stuart restoration in England (Charles II and James II) and by the so-called Jacobites who were unwilling to recognize the rights of the House of Orange to the British crown. Romanticists supporting monarchies in the 18th and 19th century continued to hold this belief and there are still small groups today in Europe who cling to it.

division. 1. A recorded vote in a legislative body. 2. A subdivision of a government department.

Division of Central Administrative Services. A central general administrative office of various war-time emergency agencies such as the Office of Price Administration, Office of Civilian Defense, Office of Defense Transportation, etc. It handled their budgeting, accounting, purchasing, and other administrative needs.

division of powers. Distribution of governmental functions between the federal government and the states. Federal powers are listed in Art. I., sec. 8, of the Constitution of the United States; other powers are exercised by the states. See SEPARATION OF POWERS.

D. N. B. See DEUTSCHES NACHRICHTEN BÜRO.

Dobruja (DAW-broo-jah). The area between the Black Sea and the lower reaches of the Danube, south of the river's mouth. It has long been a bone of contention between Bulgaria and Romania and was divided between the two by the peace treaties following World War II.

docket. List of cases to be tried by a court or a list of items of business for a deliberative body.

doctrinaire. 1. Pertaining to excessive adherence to theoretical considerations. 2. One who adheres excessively to theoretical considerations or considerations of political doctrine.

documentary evidence. Proof in the form of official papers.

Dogger Bank episode. An incident in

1904 during the Russo-Japanese War which was the first of its kind turned over to a commission of inquiry. Russian ships off the Dogger Bank in the North Sea had fired on British vessels thinking they were Japanese. The commission found the facts to indicate the Russians were at fault and Russia paid damages to Great Britain.

dole. Cash grants or relief given to persons who are unemployed. A system used particularly in Great Britain. See WORK RELIEF.

dollar. Monetary unit divided into 100 cents used in the United States, Canada, and a few other countries. The term is said to come from thaler, or Joachimsthaler, a silver coin once made at Joachimsthal, Bohemia. The United States coinage act of 1792 made the United States dollar the equivalent of the Spanish dollar of that time. The intrinsic value of the United States dollar has varied in the vicinity of 410–15 grams of silver or about 24 grams of gold, but coinage in gold ceased in 1934.

dollar-a-year-man. A person who gives his time and services to the government, particularly in time of national emergency. In order that such a person may become a fully responsible government official he is given a nominal salary, often one dollar per year.

dollar diplomacy. The execution of a foreign policy which has the primary aim to enlarge and protect the investments of private capital from a given state in another state, usually less advanced economically.

domain. Territory over which a state has jurisdiction.

Domei (DOH-MAY). Official Japanese news agency. Abolished under the allied occupation.

domestic. Pertaining to matters of national internal interest and control, as opposed to international matters.

domestic dependent nations. Term used to describe the status of the American Indian tribes. The status of the native states of India is somewhat similar. In both cases the Indian group has no foreign relations, but often its relation to the protecting state is defined by a treaty which the latter considers binding.

domestic violence. Serious disorder occurring within a state.

domicile. A place of residence looked upon as the permanent residence of a person, one to which he will ultimately return if he leaves even for a considerable time. The word residence is often used in this sense as, for example, for those who have lived a long time in Washington, D. C. but retain what is called a residence, really a domicile, in their home states for voting purposes.

dominion. The term for the status of the self-governing portions of the British Commonwealth of Nations, namely Canada, Australia, New Zealand, the Union of South Africa and Newfoundland.

Dominions Office. British cabinet office charged with conducting relations with the British dominions.

Donets Basin. Basin of the Donets River in southwestern Russia, seat of a very considerable part of pre-World War II Russian industry. During and just before the war, much of this industrial equipment was moved east to the Ural Mountains, thus enabling Russia to save this equipment from the Germans and keep it operating during the war. Also called the Donbas.

donkey. Symbol of the Democratic Party, originated by the cartoonist Thomas Nast.

Dooley, Mr. Mythological newspaper character of the turn of the century, created by Finley Peter Dunne, given to pungent comment in a strong

Irish brogue on the American political scene and other general observations.

Dopolavoro (doh-poh-lah-VOH-roh). A fascist organization in Italy for leisure time activities. It had several million members and provided sports events, libraries, lectures, excursions, and entertainment.

D.O.R.A. British Defense of the Realm Act, war-time law for the protection of the national security.

double citizenship. See DOUBLE NATIONALITY.

double jeopardy. Liability of a person for a second trial after being acquitted of the charge at a previous trial. Prohibited by the Constitution.

double nationality. The condition of a person who is a citizen or national of two states, due to his acquiring one nationality and not automatically at the same time losing his former nationality. This formerly happened frequently in cases of naturalization, with the state of original allegiance claiming military service of the person if he returned to that country. Most such difficulties have been cleared up by treaties.

double taxation. Two taxes collected from the same tax base. Injustice is usually implied in the use of the term, but chiefly because the double taxing does not apply to all cases of the same base. It is obvious that double taxation is unjust if certain cases are exempt from one of the taxes or the other.

doubtful states. States that do not go consistently either Republican or Democratic in an election but change from one to another, usually due to a switch in the independent voters who are sufficiently numerous to determine the outcome. Such states are of special importance in the presidential elections if they have a large number of electoral votes, such as New York, Pennsylvania, Ohio or Illinois.

dowager. A word added to a woman's title to indicate that her husband, from whom she received the original title by marriage, is dead. Examples: the Dowager Empress of China, the Dowager Queen Mary of Great Britain.

Downing Street. Street near the Parliament buildings in London on which is located the residence of the prime minister. Hence, the office of the British prime minister.

doyen of the diplomatic corps. The dean or ranking diplomat of all the diplomatic representatives at a given capital. Usually he has served there longer than any other representative. He is the spokesman for the entire group.

D. P. See DISPLACED PERSON.

draft. 1. To draw or select by lot physically qualified men for military or labor service. The first military draft in the United States was that of 1863 during the Civil War, which also provided that draftees could send a substitute or could avoid service by paying $300. During World War I the Selective Service Act of 1917 provided for a draft without the possibility of substitution or payment. In World War II it was used again under the terms of the Selective Training and Service Act of 1940. A labor draft was widely used in Europe during World War II, notably by the Nazis, and while advocated by President Franklin D. Roosevelt in this country, it was never enacted. See SELECTIVE TRAINING AND SERVICE ACT. 2. To draw up a preliminary sketch of a law or treaty, or the sketch itself.

draft board. In the United States, a group of citizens set up in each community and in various sections of metropolitan areas to administer the provisions and exemptions of the

Selective Training and Service Act of 1940.

draft dodger. A person who avoids or tries to avoid his responsibility for serving in the armed forces under the draft regulations.

draft registration. The registration of men of certain ages in preparation for providing those needed for a draft for the armed forces.

Draft Treaty of Mutual Assistance. A proposal made in 1923 to strengthen the League of Nations by having its members agree to give real assistance to a victim of aggression. The attempt failed because the nations were not willing to consent to such general commitments. See GENEVA PROTOCOL.

Drago doctrine. Doctrine of international law forbidding the use of force in the collection of international public debts. See CALVO DOCTRINE.

drainage district. Special administrative districts established for the purpose of draining land lying in different townships, counties, or states.

Drang nach Osten. (DRAHNG nahkh OSE-tun). German phrase meaning drive to the east, a historic trend in German history. It began with Charlemagne's conquest of the Saxons and Czechs, was continued by the Teutonic Knights in the Baltic states and by the partitions of Poland in the 18th century. It was revived by the Second Reich before 1914 with the emphasis toward the southeast— the Balkans, Turkey and the Persian Gulf. Hitler's Polish and Russian campaigns revived the older form, and those in the Balkans and North Africa united it with the newer, Middle Eastern version.

drawback. A refund on a tariff on imported raw materials, granted to a manufacturer if the raw materials are made into finished products which in turn are exported.

Dred Scott decision. A Supreme Court decision in 1857 which was one of the important incidents in the slavery controversy. Dred Scott, a slave, had been taken by his master to Ft. Snelling, near St. Paul, Minn., which was in that part of the Louisiana Purchase made free territory by the Missouri Compromise. Scott later, in Missouri, sued to obtain his freedom on the ground of residence in free territory. He lost in the state courts and was refused by the United States Supreme Court on the ground he was not a citizen. Moreover the court declared the Missouri Compromise unconstitutional since the limitation on slavery in a United States territory infringed the right of property stated in the Constitution. The matter of Congressional regulation of slavery in the territories was an issue until the Civil War.

Dreyfus affair. The case of the French army captain, Alfred Dreyfus, who was arrested on a charge of treason in 1894, was sentenced to lifelong imprisonment on Devil's Island, later retried and acquitted, and finally rehabilitated in 1906. Dreyfus was of Jewish origin and was convicted on flimsy and partly forged evidence. The long and complicated struggle of a group of French liberals, among whom Georges Clemenceau and the writer Emile Zola were prominent, to prove the innocence of Dreyfus and to break down the nationalist, anti-Semitic and militarist attitude of the French army, violently rocked French political and social life. It brought to the surface many latent conflicts in French society, such as the position of the army in a liberal republic, the position of the Catholic Church, anti-Semitic movements, etc. See ANTI-SEMITISM, MILITARISM.

Druze revolt. The revolt of a peculiar religious sect, chiefly concentrated in southern Syria some 50 miles east of the Mediterranean sea, against French rule under the Syrian mandate, in 1925.

dry. A person who favors prohibition of the sale of intoxicating liquor.

dual access. The principle in the Japanese government by which both the prime minister and the minister of war could speak directly to the emperor on matters of policy. This made it possible for the minister of war to circumvent the prime minister and act independently of the civil control of the government. Abolished in 1945 under the allied occupation and by the constitution of 1946.

dual alliance. In general a term used to describe any two-party alliance. Often used to refer to the German-Austrian alliance of 1879 which became the Triple Alliance when Italy joined in 1882, and also to the Franco-Russian alliance completed in 1894 which Great Britain later joined to form the Triple Entente.

dual citizenship. The citizenship in the United States and also in a state of the union which is possessed by resident citizens within the United States. Almost all American citizens have both a national and a state citizenship, but there may be exceptions, as, for example, when a person, having a national citizenship, has a permanent residence abroad, and is not technically a citizen of any of the states of the union. See also DOUBLE NATIONALITY.

Dual Monarchy. Austria-Hungary as organized between 1867 and 1918. Austria and Hungary each had a separate parliament, but they had a monarch in common who was Emperor of Austria and King of Hungary. See REAL UNION.

dual nationality. See DOUBLE NATIONALITY.

duce (DOO-chay). Italian word for leader. Title taken by Mussolini.

duchess. Feminine for duke. See DUKE.

due diligence. The reasonable degree of care expected of a state, as in preventing unneutral activities by its citizens when it is a neutral or in the protection of aliens within its territory.

due process of law. A protection granted an individual which provides that the laws by which he is governed fall within the law-making power of the appropriate legislative body, and that his administrative and judicial treatment under the law shall not be arbitrary and unreasonable but fair and just.

duke. A European title derived from the Latin word *dux*, or leader, at first applied to leaders of the Roman imperial armies and later to the ruler of a large territory within the empire. The title was carried over into the middle ages and many dukes were independent monarchs, as the dukes of Burgundy. Most of them were later made subject to a king or emperor and the title now is merely a badge of high nobility. In Britain where dukes form the highest class of the peerage, the royal princes are given the title but most of the dukes are not of the royal family. See PEERAGE.

Duma. Name for the Russian parliament set up in 1905 and ended by the Bolshevik revolution of 1917.

Dumbarton Oaks Conference. A double conference held at the Dumbarton Oaks estate in Washington, D. C., ending October 7, 1944. In the first part the United States and Great Britain met with Russia, which was replaced by China in the second part. The result was a proposal for a charter of an international organization whose details were to be decided upon at a later date. In general structure the proposal was in many respects somewhat similar to the League of Nations, but it provided for a much stronger council with power to act, and for armed forces for the suppression of aggression. See SAN FRANCISCO CONFERENCE.

dumdum bullet. Bullet with a soft point or core which expands in flight or when it strikes an object. Because of its unusual frightfulness its use was prohibited by the Hague Conventions of 1899 and 1907.

dumping. Process of selling goods in international trade without regard to the cost, usually to dispose of a surplus.

Dunkirk. Battle at Dunkirk, Belgium, in the closing days of May, 1940, which ended British military strength on continental Europe for 4 years, although the British by ingenuity and persistence salvaged some 300,000 men, but little equipment, from the defeat. The word has since been used, not quite correctly, as a losing last stand from which there is no escape.

duress. Illegal compulsion or restraint used to force a person or state to do something. A contract signed under duress, for example, may be voided by the person forced to agree to it. In international relations a state may practically be forced to sign a treaty, under threat of a continuation of war, for example, but a state may void a treaty which its agents or diplomatic representatives have been forced to sign.

dust bowl. The western great plains region of the United States, where in the dry seasons in the middle 1930's thousands of farms were seriously affected by wind erosion.

duty. 1. A legal obligation. 2. A tax on imports or formerly exports. See TARIFF.

dynamic policy. A polite term for an aggressive, expansionist policy. The fascist countries liked to call what they did "dynamic."

E

eagle. 1. Symbol of the United States of America. 2. A gold coin of the United States worth $10, weighing 258 grains.

E.A.M. In Greek, *Ethnikón Apeleutherotikon Metopon* (eth-nee-KAWN ah-pel-ew-THER-oh-tee-kawn MET-oh-pawn) National Liberation Front. A Greek leftist political organization which tried to gain control of Greece in late 1944 and early 1945. It was opposed chiefly by the E.D.E.S. See E.D.E.S.

earl. British title of nobility equivalent to that of count in other European countries. An earl's wife is a countess. The title ranks between those of marquess and viscount in the British peerage. Originally an earl was the king's representative in a county, but now the title is merely a hereditary badge of nobility. See COUNT; PEERAGE.

earmarked. Pertaining to a tax or fund set aside for a particular purpose and not to be used for general expenditures. A gasoline tax might thus be set aside for building or maintaining roads.

earned income. A distinction in income made for income tax purposes to indicate that part derived from salaries, wages and fees for professional and other personal services, as distinguished from income derived from investments, which are classed as "unearned."

eastern front. In World War I and World War II the military fronts in the Balkans and more particularly the places where the Germans fought the Russians.

Eastern Locarno. A settlement for the eastern boundaries of Germany, similar to the Locarno treaties on the western boundaries of Germany. Such a settlement on the east was never concluded. See LOCARNO TREATIES.

Eastern Question. The problem of the formation of the different states and colonies which might result from the breakup of the Turkish Empire. During the 19th century this was one of the major problems confronting both the great powers of Europe and the subject peoples within the empire.

E Award. An award presented jointly to manufacturing establishments in the United States by the War and Navy Departments for excellence in production during World War II. It was symbolized by an "E" pennant presented to the company or organization and by "E" lapel pins given each employee. It originated in the award for excellence given ships in the Navy.

Economic and Social Council. One of the constituent parts of the United Nations organization, a body of eighteen members whose function is to promote the economic and social welfare throughout the world, particularly by studies and reports, recommendations and draft conventions.

economic barrier. Any hindrance to the free flow of goods in international trade, such as a tariff or quota.

Economic Conference of 1933. A conference held in London in June and July, 1933, under the auspices of the League of Nations, in an effort to reverse the effects of the depression: widespread reduction in employment, prices, international trade and national incomes, and the departure of about half the countries of the world from the gold standard. The United States was willing to discuss tariff reductions, but certain European countries, particularly France, Belgium, Holland, and Switzerland, still adhering to the gold standard, felt it was useless to realign tariffs until the currencies were stabilized. The United States had not yet revalued the dollar and in the middle of the conference President Franklin D. Roosevelt decided this country could get out of the depression faster by itself than by world co-operation and so refused to discuss stabilization. The conference failed to solve the main problems, though there were minor agreements regarding sales of silver, tariffs, and international banking facilities.

economic depression. See BUSINESS CYCLE.

economic determinism. The theory that the policies of states and events of history result from economic forces and causes.

economic imperialism. The establishment by one country of economic domination over other countries due to such factors as geographical proximity, the fact that the dominant state provides the best markets or sources of supply for the special needs of the others, or political pressure.

economic nationalism. The principle and policy that a nation in its dealings with other nations should advance the economic welfare of itself and its citizens to the exclusion of the welfare of others. The nation is thus considered as an economic, as well as a political unit. The principle is dominant, for example, in a nation's efforts to control markets and sources of raw materials.

economic penetration. The process by which a state gains economic dominance in another state or a colonial area, as by the more or less exclusive exploitation of raw materials or by providing essential needs in the latter's markets.

economic warfare. An extreme degree of economic competition between two or more states. Such a degree of competition usually is marked by a resort to means not usually in use in international economic relations, such as the boycott and discriminatory tariffs.

economy. The total system of production, distribution, and consumption of goods and services within a state.

Economy Act. A law of March 20, 1933, granting to the president of the United States the power to cut government salaries and veterans' payments for disabilities not received in connection with their military service. In the long run it affected only minor economies.

economy of scarcity. The theory or policy that the economic welfare of a country is advanced by a limitation of production and hence by the increase of the price of goods per unit.

E.D.E.S. *Ellinikós Dimokratikos Ethnikos Stratós* (hel-ee-nee-KAWS dee-maw-krah-tee-KAWS eth-nee-KAWS strah-TAWS). National Democratic Army, the Greek right-wing political organization competing with the E. A. M. for control of the government in late 1944 and early 1945.

edict. Public proclamation or decree.

Education, Office of. See OFFICE OF EDUCATION.

educational qualification. A qualification for voting in certain states based on the citizen's education, for example, proof that he has completed the fifth grade at school.

effective. In operation in fact, as, for example, the occupation of a territory or the actuality of a blockade. "Effective" money, when asked for at a European frontier, means currency and coins but not travelers checks.

efficiency rating. A record of the quality of work done by an employee in the civil service. It is usually taken into consideration in regard to the promotion of the employee.

egalitarian. Pertaining to equality, derived from the French word *égalité* and the revolutionary slogan, *Liberté, Egalité, Fraternité*, Liberty, Equality, Fraternity. One of the key-words in the liberal movement of the 19th century in Europe.

Egyptian-British Alliance. See ANGLO-EGYPTIAN ALLIANCE.

eighteenth amendment. Amendment to the United States Constitution prohibiting the manufacture, sale, transportation, importation, or exportation of intoxicating liquors. It was proclaimed January 29, 1919, and repealed by the twenty-first amendment in 1933.

Einheitspartei. See SOCIALIST UNITY PARTY.

E.L.A.S. *Ellinikós Laïkós Apeleutheratikos Stratos* (hel-ee-nee-KAWS lah-ee-KAWS ah-pel-ew-THER-ohtee-kawn strah-TAWS). Hellenic Peoples Army of Liberation, the fighting branch of the E. A. M., Greek leftist political organization. See E. A. M.

elastic clause. The statement in Article I, Section 8, of the Constitution that Congress shall have the power to "make all laws which shall be necessary and proper for carrying into execution" the preceding list of specific powers. This is the legal basis for the implied powers of Congress. See IMPLIED POWERS.

elder statesman. Any one of the former group of older advisers to the emperor of Japan chosen because of experience and prestige, but no longer holding public office. Known as the *genro.* Hence any elderly statesman of outstanding experience and prestige.

election. The formal process of selection of officials, and sometimes the determination of issues, by the marking and deposit of ballots by the voters.

elector. 1. A voter. 2. In the United States, a member of the electoral college.

electoral college. The body of representatives or "electors," equal to the number of a state's representation in Congress, chosen by the voters of the states. They cast the formal vote for president and vice-president of the United States. Originally this voting was a matter of free choice but in time the vote became merely a reflection of the popular vote by states, as all the electoral votes in a state go for a single candidate.

electoral commission. The commission of five senators, five representatives, and five members of the Supreme Court which passed upon the disputed electoral votes from southern states in 1876. The commission included eight Republicans and seven Democrats; all disputed electoral votes were given to Hayes, the Republican candidate, who then won, 185 to 184.

electoral count. The count of the votes of the electoral college for president and vice-president. Legal provisions for this count include determination of correctness or for the throwing out of conflicting returns.

electoral vote. 1. The number of members of the electoral college from a given state. 2. The number voting for a given candidate. 3. The members of the electoral college as a whole (531).

electorate. Total number of persons qualified to vote.

electric voting. The process of voting used in some state legislatures whereby the legislator pushes one of two electric buttons on his desk to indicate his yea or nay vote. In most cases, the votes are added automatically as recorded, thus saving a great deal of time in counting the vote.

elephant. Symbol of the Republican Party, originated by the cartoonist Thomas Nast.

eligible list. List of applicants for a civil service position who have passed the examination with a sufficiently high grade (usually about 70 per cent) to be eligible for appointment. Appointments are usually filled from the three on the eligible list with the highest grades in the examination.

eligibility of officers. Qualification for public office regarding legal requirements such as age and citizenship.

elite. A group considered as the upper class. Fascism claims government should be by the elite.

Elite Guard. See SCHUTZSTAFFEL.

Elk Hills. United States oil lands in California reserved for naval use which were leased to the Pan-American Petroleum Company by Secretary of the Interior Albert B. Fall in 1922. A Senate investigation disclosed that Fall borrowed $100,000 without security or interest from E. L. Doheny, president of the company. In 1927 the Supreme Court sustained decisions of lower courts that the lease was corruptly obtained and that the property should be returned to the Government. Doheny was acquitted but Fall was convicted of bribery. Both men were acquitted of criminal conspiracy. These lands were again in the news when Congress learned in June, 1943 that the Navy had contracted with the Standard Oil Company of California to extract oil there. The company agreed to drop the contract when the Department of Justice claimed it was illegal. See TEAPOT DOME.

Élysée Palace. The Paris residence of the president of France, located on the Champs Élysée.

emancipation. The process of liberating, particularly applied to the slaves after the American Civil War, or the serfs in Russia in 1860.

Emancipation Proclamation. A proclamation by President Lincoln dated January 1, 1863, and issued under the war powers, proclaiming the freedom of the slaves in the part of the South still in active rebellion.

embargo. A governmental prohibition on the departure of ships for, or export of goods to, a foreign country. An ordinary or pacific embargo applies to ships of the state applying the embargo and is not illegal. A hostile embargo applies to the vessels of the state against which the embargo is declared and is a violation of its rights.

embassy. The office of an ambassador, often including his residence.

Emergency Banking Act. Law passed by Congress March 9, 1933, giving the president power to regulate or prohibit foreign exchange transactions, gold exports, or the hoarding of money, and giving the secretary of the treasury the power to call in all gold.

emergency measures. Legislation intended to deal quickly with a sudden and unforeseen situation. Usually governments have special provisions that such legislation need not go through all the technical steps required of ordinary laws before coming into effect.

emergency powers. A loose term used to refer to certain implied powers of Congress that flow chiefly from the power to declare war, such as the power to draft men for the army and to punish espionage.

emigration. Departure of a person from the country of which he is a national with the intention of residing in and becoming a citizen of another state.

émigré government. See GOVERNMENT-IN-EXILE.

eminent domain. The right of a state to take private property for public use upon the payment of just compensation.

emoluments. Salary and other profits of public office. See PERQUISITES.

emperor. Title of the ruler of an empire.

empire. Monarchy including diverse peoples or scattered territorial holdings which are constitutionally inferior to the central unit of the whole.

"Empire," the. 1. The first French Empire under Napoleon, from 1804 to 1815. 2. Holy Roman Empire.

enabling act. An act of Congress permitting the people of a territory to draw up a constitution for a state of their own.

Enabling Act in Third Reich. The law of March 23, 1933, granting Hitler dictatorial powers for four years (later extended). It was passed by a vote of 441 to 94. All opposing votes were cast by Social Democrats; 26 of their number and all the 81 Communist members were forced to stay away. The majority thus not only included the 288 Nazis and their 52 Nationalist party allies, but all the center parties as well.

enact. To pass a law.

enacting clause. The clause at the first of an act which begins: "Be it enacted that," followed by the provisions of the law.

enactment. 1. An act as passed by a legislative body. 2. The process of passing acts by a legislative body. Loosely used to cover all forms of laws.

encirclement. Process of drawing the neighbors of a state together politically with the result that the state finds itself more or less completely surrounded by a hostile coalition.

en bloc (ahng BLAWK). Literally, in a bloc; as a unit.

enclave. A territory, such as the Republic of San Marino in Italy, completely enclosed by the territory of a foreign power. In common usage, an enclave may be a territory almost but not entirely enclosed in this way, as was formerly the case with the Lado Enclave in Equatorial Africa. An enclave may also be a territory with a seacoast, surrounded only on the landward side by the territory of a foreign power, i. e. Gibraltar. The term is also used to describe a group of people of one nationality surrounded by a larger group of a different nationality, as for example, a German enclave, in Romania.

encyclical. Letter from the Pope to the bishops of the Roman Catholic Church. Papal pronouncements on world affairs often take this form.

enemy. 1. An opposing state in a war. 2. A national of an opposing state in war. 3. Pertaining to an opposing state in a war or nationals of such a state.

enemy alien. A person within a state who is a national of a second state with which the first state is at war.

enfranchise. To extend the privilege of voting.

English-speaking Union. Cultural organization of English-speaking peoples, emphasizing the common interests of Great Britain, the Dominions, and the United States.

engrossed bill. A printed bill in the final form in which it is passed in one house of a legislative body.

enlistment. Process of voluntarily entering the armed forces.

enrolled bill. A copy of a bill as printed in the form passed by both houses of Congress, signed by the presiding officers of both houses and presented to the president for his signature.

entangling alliance. An alliance which would either limit the United States in its future freedom of action or involve it in the politics of Europe—in fact, any alliance.

entente. 1. An international agreement of friendship or alliance. 2. The group of states bound together by such an agreement. See TRIPLE ENTENTE, LITTLE ENTENTE, ENTENTE CORDIALE.

Entente Cordiale (ahn-TAHNT kawr-DYAL). An Anglo-French agreement of 1904 settling mutual outstanding differences regarding Africa, providing particularly that France would not interfere with the British in Egypt and that Britain would permit France a free hand in Morocco.

entrepot (ahngtr'-POH). 1. Port where goods are transshipped. 2. Bonded warehouse (French).

enumerated powers. The powers of Congress which are specifically listed in the Constitution, as, for example, the power to declare war, coin money, tax and regulate interstate commerce.

enumerator. A person who takes the census or some special count, such as the school census or "enumeration."

envoy. In a general sense a diplomatic agent of any rank. Specifically part of the title of a diplomatic agent of the second rank. See MINISTER.

E Pluribus Unum (EE PLOOR-i-bus YOO-num). One out of many, the motto of the United States.

equal protection clause. A provision of the 14th Amendment of the Constitution that "No state shall . . . deny to any person within its jurisdiction the equal protection of the laws." This has been interpreted to mean that states shall not unjustly discriminate against any class of inhabitants in the making or administering of the state laws.

equality. Character of being the same in some respect or other. In a democracy persons have equality in terms of rights before the law and protection by the law. Voters have an equal voice in law-making. In international law states also have equal rights before the law. Protection, however, is just now being considered on a basis of equality and certain practical exceptions are made to the equality of states in making new rules in international law.

equity. A legal system originating in the power of the English king and later the chancellor, to dispense substantial justice in cases not provided for in the law. In time the cases became so numerous that a court system was set up to care for them, the courts of the chancellor or chancery courts. These courts developed special rules and procedures of their own. They were merged in 1875, with the law courts in a unified system which handled cases in equity as well as law, and the Chancery Division was made a division of the High Court of Justice. In the United States by Article III, Section 2 of the Constitution the jurisdiction of the federal courts extends to all cases "in law and equity" and that system has been followed in most of the states, although in a few the original English system of separate courts for law and equity were established and still remain. See INJUNCTION, LAW, COMMON LAW.

"Era of Good Feeling." The period from 1817 to 1824 in United States political party history, so-called because there was no clear-cut cleavage between two parties. The general following of the Jefferson tradition was, however, divided into several personal factions.

ersatz. German term for synthetic substitute, taken over rather generally into English.

escalator clause. The provision in certain naval disarmament treaties that upper limits on tonnage limitations could be raised under certain conditions.

escape clause. See ESCALATOR CLAUSE.

espionage. Spying, or the organization of spying.

Espionage Act. A United States law of 1917 defining spying and establishing the punishment therefor.

Established Church. A state church, as, for example, the Church of England.

Estate of Trade and Industry. The branch of Nazi German governmental economic control devoted to industry, commerce, banking, insurance, and electric and water power. It was a union of trade associations in these fields, controlled at the top by the Minister of Economics, who regulated production, distribution, costs, and standards.

estimates. The calculations of necessary funds turned in by the various branches and departments of government to the budgeting agency. These are revised and combined to form the expenditure side of the budget.

Estrada Doctrine. A doctrine advanced in 1930 by the Mexican foreign minister, that a government should be recognized automatically when it comes to power regardless of the methods employed, thus making recognition a matter of fact rather than implying a judgment.

etatisme (ay-tah-TEEZM). See STATISM.

ethnic. Pertaining to races or racial groups.

ever-normal granary. An objective of Henry A. Wallace when Secretary of Agriculture (1933–1940). He hoped to avoid wide fluctuation of agricultural products on the market by storing all the surplus above "normal" in the good years and throwing it on the market in years of poor crops.

Evian Conference. A conference held at Evian, France, in July 1938, to assist the refugees of Europe to escape from the persecuting states. A committee was set up to handle the problem, but before anything substantial was accomplished its work was interrupted by World War II.

ex officio. Latin term meaning because of one's office. For example, if a governor of a state is an *ex-officio* member of an appointive state commission he is a member because he fills the office of governor, not as one of the regularly appointed members.

ex post facto law. A law passed after an act is performed, making that act a crime, or a more serious crime than it had been when committed, increasing the punishment for the act or making conviction thereof easier. Such laws are prohibited by the Constitution of the United States.

exarchate. A chief see or province of the Eastern Orthodox Church, the bishop of which was called an exarch. One exarchate which has survived territorially is that of Bulgaria, which has become the Bulgarian Orthodox Church. It was also a political unit under the Byzantine Empire, administered by an exarch, such as the Exarchate of Ravenna.

excess profits tax. A tax on corporate incomes which are in excess of a certain return on invested capital or an average normal income. In the United States it was used primarily as a war measure to prevent excessive war profits. In World War II the years 1936–39 served as the base for the average income, and most of the time the tax (after an exemption of $10,-000) amounted to 95% with a possible 10% refund. It was abolished in 1945, beginning January 1, 1946.

exchange of populations. The mutual transfer by two states of the citizens of each who, because of nationality, ancestry, race, culture or some other reason, would appear to fit better into the population of the other state.

exchange of prisoners. The mutual trade by two belligerents of prisoners of war.

exchange rate. See RATE OF EXCHANGE.

exchange stabilization fund. A fund which may be drawn upon to prevent excessive fluctuations in a rate of exchange.

Exchequer. Ancient English office of royal revenues which has lent its name to the title of the head of the British Treasury. See CHANCELLOR OF THE EXCHEQUER.

excise tax. See TAX.

exclusion. The prohibition of entrance. See CHINESE EXCLUSION ACT.

exclusive powers of Congress. Governmental powers which are vested wholly in Congress by the Constitution and are not shared with the states, such as the coining of money and naturalization.

execute. 1. To carry out, as a law or a death sentence. 2. To complete or make valid, as a deed.

executive. The branch of government charged with the enforcement and administration of laws.

executive agreement. A form of international agreement less formal than a treaty and not requiring ratification.

executive departments. The divisions of the administrative branch of the United States government presided over by the cabinet members.

Executive Office of the President. An office established under the Reorganization Act of 1939 in which were grouped, under the close supervision of the president, the following agencies: White House Office, Bureau of the Budget, Liaison Office for Personnel Management, Office for Emergency Management, Committee for

Congested Production Areas, and the War Refugee Board.

executive order. A rule or regulation issued by the chief executive to amplify the general terms of legislation.

executive session. A closed session of the Senate, from which visitors and reporters are barred, usually for the consideration of treaties, and formerly of appointments, in which it is felt open discussion is not in the general interest.

executor. Person appointed by one making a will to see that it is carried out.

exequatur. Formal permission granted by a state to a consular officer of another state to perform the functions of his office. See LETTER OF CREDENCE.

exile. 1. Compulsory or voluntary departure of a person from his home state because of incompatibility between himself and his government. 2. A person who has so departed.

expanding bullet. See DUM-DUM BULLET.

ex parte (eks PAHR-tee). From one part or party, or on behalf of only one side of an argument.

expatriation. Process of losing one's nationality, as by continued absence from a country or by naturalization in another state.

expediency. A policy of pursuing immediate possible advantage at the expense of principles.

expediter. A person who presumably accelerates the speed of government business by transporting and explaining memoranda, requests for materials and research, etc. In the worst cases the function can degenerate into that of an expensive messenger-boy. In the higher salary brackets such a person is called a liaison officer.

expeditionary force. A military force sent abroad for a special purpose. See A. E. F.

Export-Import Bank. A United States government agency established in 1934 to provide financial aid in the stimulation and facilitation of foreign trade.

express powers of Congress. Powers specifically granted to Congress by the Constitution. See IMPLIED POWERS.

expropriation. Process of taking of private property by the state, without adequate compensation.

expulsion, right of. The right of a state to rid itself of undesirable aliens.

expunge. To remove or erase from a public record, as a certain part of a debate.

extension of remarks. Speeches, documents and other material inserted by members of Congress into the Congressional Record which were not presented during debate on the floor of the House or Senate. They may be anybody's speeches, not just those of members.

Extension Service. A service of the Department of Agriculture for the dissemination of information and providing demonstrations of improved methods in agriculture.

exterritoriality. Shortened form of extraterritoriality.

extra-legal. Beyond, but not contrary to, the provisions of the law.

extra session. An extraordinary or special session of a legislative body, held at a different time and in addition to the regular sessions.

extradition. The delivery on demand of a person accused of or convicted for a crime, to the officers of the state in which the crime was committed, by the officials of the state to which the accused had fled. The accused may be tried only for the crime for which he is extradited.

extrality. Much contracted form of extraterritoriality, chiefly used by those who have lived under the system in the Far East.

extraterritoriality. The right of a state to extend its jurisdiction over its nationals into the territory of another state. Several nations thus exercised their own jurisdiction within China and pre-World War I Turkey. In a somewhat similar fashion warships, embassies, and legations are under the jurisdiction of the home state and outside the jurisdiction of the foreign state in which they are located.

F

Fabian Society. An organization of British socialist intellectuals established in 1884. They tried to sell socialism to the middle class and advocated its adoption on a gradual basis.

faction. Portion of a political party. Used by George Washington in the sense we now use the word party; parties as we know them were undeveloped in the United States at that time.

Fair Labor Standards Act. A law passed in 1938 establishing minimum wages and maximum weekly hours for persons engaged in interstate commerce or in producing goods for interstate commerce. It also forbade child labor in these occupations (under 16 years, or 18 years if the occupation is hazardous).

fait accompli (fe-tah-kohng-PLEE). An accomplished fact or deed.

Falange Española (fah-LAHN-hay es-pah-NYOH-lah), or Falangists. A Spanish fascist organization created in October, 1933 by the eldest son of General Primo de Rivera, Dictator of Spain (1923–30). It was suppressed by the republican government in 1936 but almost immediately became the backbone of General Franco's forces. United in April, 1937 with the Traditionalists and other small pro-Franco parties into the *Falange Española Traditionalista* (FET), they were led by a so-called *Junta Politica* of fifty, and headed by the *Caudillo* (leader), Generalissimo Francisco Franco, who asserts responsibility only "to God and history." After the Civil War the original Falangists completely dominated the moderates in the party and established a totalitarian state on the model of Nazi Germany and Fascist Italy, save that it was closely tied to the Roman Catholic Church. Violent reprisals against former loyalists and all possible opposition, abolition of popular suffrage and regional autonomies, a regimented press and radio, were essential parts of their program. They also returned confiscated property to the great landlords and industrialists, created Falangist-controlled trade unions (*sindicatos*) and carried out a social program. The *Falange* has a Youth Movement, its own police, and branches in many Latin-American countries, one of their aims being an eventual union of all Spanish-speaking people. Their foreign policy was friendly to Germany and Italy and hostile to Soviet Russia. After 1943 Franco endeavored to restrain the *Falange* by including moderates in his government and curtailing the Falangists' powers. In order to win the favor of the Allies, Franco dissolved the Falangist secret police and gave some freedom to the press. See TOTALITARIANISM, FASCISM, NAZISM.

false colors. False flag used on a ship in time of war to deceive the enemy, as, for example, to elude capture. Before opening fire a ship must run up its own flag.

family of nations. Term used for the community of states of the world.

F. A. O. See FOOD AND AGRICULTURE ORGANIZATION.

Far East. That part of Asia east of India, including Burma, the Malay archipelago, Thailand, Indo-China, China, Japan and eastern Siberia.

Far Eastern Commission. A commission composed of representatives of Australia, Canada, China, France, Great Britain, India, the Netherlands, New Zealand, the Philippines, Russia and the United States, set up to formulate and review the Allied policy for Japan. It was established by the Moscow meeting of foreign ministers in December 1945, and succeeded an earlier Far Eastern Advisory Commission.

farm bloc. Congressional (or state) representatives who have large agricultural constituencies and who vote and act together to secure advantages for the farmer. Usually thought of as being largely representative of the Middle West.

Farm Bureau. See AMERICAN FARM BUREAU FEDERATION.

Farm Credit Administration. An agency set up in the Department of Agriculture in 1933 to consolidate all the preceding farm credit agencies such as the Federal Land Banks, Intermediate Credit Banks, Banks for Cooperatives, etc.

Farmer-Labor Party. A radical United States political party of the 1920's and 1930's supported chiefly by farmers and laborers. It never achieved national strength but dominated Minnesota politics for over a decade.

Farm Mortgage Moratorium Act. A law (the Frazier-Lemke Act) passed in 1934, and in amended form in 1935, providing for a moratorium on foreclosures of farm mortgages. The first was declared unconstitutional, so amendments provided certain changes and the amended act was upheld by the courts in 1937.

Farm Security Administration. An agency of the United States Department of Agriculture the chief function of which is to encourage settlement on farms by providing loans and technical assistance. Established in 1935 as the Resettlement Administration, an independent agency, and renamed and transferred to the Agriculture Department in 1937.

fascism. An extremist, totalitarian, revolutionary system of government first developed in Italy and later, under other names, in Germany and Spain. Some or all of the elements of fascism have been adopted by political parties in many other European countries and by various groups and leaders in the Americas, notably by President Peron of Argentina. The term comes from the Italian word "fascismo," the name for the ancient Roman symbol of authority, a bundle of rods and an axe, which was borrowed by Benito Mussolini and his Black Shirts. Wherever it has appeared, fascism has exploited the social disintegration caused by World War I, economic depression, the struggle between capitalists and the labor movements, and the decline of the hold of religion and traditional morality on the masses. Its doctrines are not as clear-cut and logical as those of Marxism, which it violently opposes, and derive from many sources. Fascism appeals first of all to the lower middle classes, but also to those businessmen and bankers who are frightened by socialist or leftist trends and seek safeguards against them. It has been able in most cases to rally behind it those peasants and farmers who resent the labor movement, and even large groups of workers disappointed by unsuccessful strikes and the fights between rival leftist and liberal parties. Army leaders are attracted by the extreme fascist nationalism, which creates a myth asserting that the nation has a special mission to rule humanity, or at least its neighbors, and that for the purposes of aggression and war the individual has to be completely subordinated to the state. It believes in the "leader principle" and exalts the Leader of the Party (*Il Duce* in Italy, *Der Fuehrer* in Germany, *El Caudillo* in Spain) as a sort of demi-God and as the only man who can save the nation from ruin and lead it to the fulfillment of its "historic mission." A large, fanatical party led by dynamic leaders versed in the arts of modern propaganda keeps the people in a perpetual frenzy, both before and after the party comes to power, if it does. The party youth from the earliest age are regimented into uniformed marching groups and indoctrinated with fascist ideas. Once the party is in power, all other parties are abolished, along with such democratic institutions as a free press, free assembly, free speech, and free trade unions. Elections become plebiscites in which fascist candidates or policies are forced through under such pressure that the opposition does not dare to raise its head. Fascism comes to power either through forceful methods, as in Italy and Spain, or by undermining the foundations of the democratic state and then gaining a majority in its legislature or electing its leader to office, as in Germany and Argentina. Once in power, fascism usually favors imperialism and militarism, a self-sufficient economic system, territorial expansion and an aggressive foreign policy towards all non-fascist countries. All criticism is ruthlessly suppressed by uniformed party-armies and secret police. Totalitarian methods are applied in every field, and economic, social, cultural and even religious institutions are brought under the domination of the fascist party and state. Extreme nationalism may or may not be developed into racism coupled with anti-Semitism; Italian Fascism was at first friendly to the Jews, but after 1938 it yielded to pressure from Germany—where anti-Semitism was a cardinal principle of German fascism, or Nazism—and Mussolini enacted anti-Semitic legislation. In the United States fascist groups such as the Silver Shirts and Columbians have all been violently anti-Negro as well as anti-Semitic. See NAZISM, FALANGE ESPAÑOLA, FASCIST PARTY, TOTALITARIAN, THIRD REICH, REACTIONARY, COUNTER-REVOLUTION, IMPERIALISM, MILITARISM, NATIONALISM.

Fascist Grand Council. A group of about 25 which formed the inner circle of the Italian Fascist Party. In later years as the party and the government became merged, it was given state functions, including consultation on the most important legislation and the status of an advisory body in case successors to the king or Mussolini were to be chosen. See FASCISM.

Fascist Party. The party, led by Benito Mussolini, which came to power after the March on Rome of October, 1922, instituted the subsequent dictatorship, and continued to control Italy until World War II. It developed after World War I and had only 35 members in the Chamber of Deputies prior to gaining power, but the violence committed by its Black Shirt gangs gave it a political strength greater than its membership would indicate. See FASCISM.

Fascist Triplice. Germany, Italy, and Japan as allied prior to 1943.

Fascist Youth Organization. An organization of young Italians which served as a training ground for fascist party members and leaders and a place of indoctrination. It was divided into four age-group sections for boys and four for girls. The boys groups were called *Figli della Lupa, Balilla, Avanguardia,* and *Giovani Fascisti.* See FASCISM

Fashoda. An island in the Nile in the Sudan where the French found their desire to control central Africa blocked by the British in 1898. The French conceded the British control, thus helping pave the way for the alliance existing between the two by 1914.

fat cat. American slang term for a person whom a party organization makes a candidate for some office because he will contribute enough money to pay for a large share of the expenses of the party's entire campaign.

favorite son. Candidate for the presidential nomination at a party convention who has the enthusiastic support of the delegation from his own state.

F. B. I. See FEDERAL BUREAU OF INVESTIGATION.

F. D. I. C. See FEDERAL DEPOSIT INSURANCE CORPORATION.

federal. 1. Pertaining to a federation. 2. Pertaining to the North in the Civil War. 3. Term used in the United States relating to the national government as opposed to the governments of the states.

federal aid. Financial assistance granted

by the national government in the United States to the states.

Federal Bureau of Investigation. An office in the Department of Justice which investigates and collects evidence regarding violations of national laws except in such cases as postal and internal revenue violations, where the departments concerned have their own investigation staffs. The F. B. I., as it is usually called, has gained high prestige from its record of carrying its cases through to convictions in the courts.

Federal Communications Commission. A commission set up in 1934 to regulate domestic and foreign wire and wireless communications. In World War II, it was given special functions such as reporting foreign broadcasts.

Federal Council. The seven-man executive of Switzerland. It enjoys the regular executive functions, and is the outstanding example of a national plural executive.

Federal Crop Insurance Corporation. A government agency in the Department of Commerce set up in 1938 to insure cotton and wheat crops. After 1943 its only function was to liquidate prior obligations.

Federal Deposit Insurance Corporation. An independent agency which began to operate in 1934, the main function of which, from the viewpoint of the average person, is to insure bank deposits. In addition it is empowered to take certain steps to try to prevent bank failures and to re-establish national banks which have failed.

Federal Emergency Relief Administration. An independent agency which functioned between 1933 and 1938 to help the unemployed and drouth-stricken farmers by a program of work relief. Merged with the Civil Works Administration in 1938.

Federal Farm Board. An agency established in the Department of Agriculture in 1929 to increase the sale of agricultural products and to achieve for the farmer an equality with industry. Liquidated in 1933.

Federal Farm Mortgage Corporation. A government agency set up in 1934, the function of which was to assist in financing farmers through the Federal Land Bank. It was transferred to the Department of Agriculture in 1939.

Federal Home Loan Bank Administration. The top administrative agency supervising the work of the Federal Home Loan Bank System, Federal Savings and Loan Associations, Federal Savings and Loan Insurance Corporation, and the Home Owners Loan Corporation.

Federal Housing Administration. A government agency set up in 1934, the functions of which were to back banks on loans for repairs on homes and to encourage a long-term home construction program. Later it insured mortgages on homes for war workers.

Federal Land Banks. A chain of banks set up throughout the country by the government in 1916 in an effort to provide a banking system for farmers somewhat like the federal reserve system for banking interests. The land banks did not loan to individuals but to national farm loan associations which ultimately acquired almost all the capital stock.

Federal National Mortgage Association. An agency established in 1938 within the Department of Commerce to finance and aid in construction of small homes and rental housing projects, and to establish a market for first mortgages on such houses.

Federal Power Commission. A government agency established in 1930 which sets up reservations for power purposes, issues licenses for power projects and regulates the details of the sale of electricity. It also has jurisdic-

tion over the export and import of natural gas.

Federal Public Housing Authority. An emergency government agency established in 1942 by executive order for the purpose of facilitating war housing and aiding in slum clearance and low-rent housing.

Federal Radio Commission. A government agency set up in 1927 for regulation of radio. It was replaced by the Federal Communications Commission in 1934.

Federal Register. A government publication of United States administrative documents including presidential proclamations, executive orders, and the orders, rules and regulations of government administrative agencies.

federal relief. Relief funds granted by the national government.

Federal Reserve Board. Changed to Board of Governors of Federal Reserve System in 1935.

Federal Reserve System. A series of 12 banks set up by Congress in 1913, located in 12 federal reserve districts scattered throughout the United States. These banks are not for individuals but for "members," i. e., the national banks in the district and the state banks who wish to join. According to the act establishing them, their function is "to furnish an elastic currency to afford a means of rediscounting commercial paper, to establish a more effective supervision of banking in the United States."

Federal Savings and Loan Insurance Corporation. A government agency set up in 1934 to insure the accounts of various kinds of savings and loan or building and loan associations and certain co-operative banks.

Federal Trade Commission. A government commission established in 1914 for the purpose of prosecuting antitrust suits and cases of unfair competition. As part of its program it investigates deceptive advertising and labeling, and discriminatory prices.

Federal Works Agency. A government agency established in 1939 which combined the Works Progress Administration, Public Works Administration and the United States Housing Authority. In 1942, its housing functions were assigned to the National Housing Administration.

federalism. The principle of dividing the exercise of the powers of a state between the central government and certain subdivisions of the state. See FEDERATION.

Federalist, The. A series of essays written in the first half of 1788 by Alexander Hamilton, James Madison, and John Jay explaining and advocating the adoption of the Constitution, particularly by the New York state convention. New York did ratify in July. The series has never been equaled as a commentary on the Constitution and gives us perhaps our best view of the intentions of the authors.

Federalist Party. One of the first United States political parties, recruited from the wealthier classes and favoring particularly a strong national or federal government. It was strongest during the administration of President John Adams and ceased to be of major importance after the War of 1812, which many of its members opposed.

federation *or* **federal state.** A state composed of political subdivisions that have certain governmental powers of their own, or in which certain powers are shared between the central or national government and the subdivisions. From the international point of view, however, the whole is considered a single independent state, and the foreign relations for the whole are generally carried on by the central government.

At present almost half of the world is governed by federal states of one kind or another: United States, USSR, Brazil, Canada, India, Australia, Union of South Africa, Switzerland, Austria, Yugoslavia, etc. The British Commonwealth of Nations as such is not a federation, as the independence of the Dominions from the mother country is incomparably greater than it could be in a federal state; it is, however, somewhat more than a personal union under King George VI, as bonds of sentiment, similar political, cultural institutions, and economic policy hold the dominions together. The Union of Soviet Socialist Republics (U.S.S.R) differs in its principles of federalism from the United States. The centralized Communist Party, issuing directions to all its organizations, dominates every executive and legislature of every republic; and the succession of centrally constructed Five Year economic plans have united the country more tightly than many non-federal, constitutionally unified countries. See CONFEDERATION.

fellow-traveler. A person who sympathizes and agrees with the communist point of view but is not a member of the Communist Party.

felony. One of the more serious crimes such as murder or robbery.

F. E. P. C. See COMMITTEE ON FAIR EMPLOYMENT PRACTICES.

Festung Europa. (FES-toong oi-ROE-pah). Fortress Europe, the German term for that part of continental Europe dominated by German troops in the latter part of World War II, that is, that portion of the continent west of Russia and Turkey, excepting Sweden and Spain, and entirely surrounding Switzerland. The Nazis gave the impression that this whole area was as impregnable as a single great fortress.

feudalism. A social, economic and political organization found in much of

Europe and the Far East prior to the formation of modern national states. Its major characteristics were a system of land-holding whereby tenants were granted land by nobles and ultimately by the king, and a series of mutual duties, for example military service by the vassal and protection by the lord. It has been influential on later political organization, as for example on the ideas of allegiance and territorial jurisdiction. If used to refer to a state at present the meaning is usually that of a country in which there is a landed nobility with the land worked by a peasantry which does not exercise or enjoy many political rights.

"Few die and none resign." A paraphrase of a mournful observation of Thomas Jefferson in a letter of July 12, 1801, to Elias Shipman regarding the Federalists still holding office in the national government, and apparently lending some encouragement to what later became known as the spoils system: "If a due participation in office is a matter of right, how are vacancies to be obtained? Those by death are few; by resignation none."

F. F. I. See FRENCH FORCES OF THE INTERIOR.

F. H. A. See FEDERAL HOUSING ADMINISTRATION.

fiat. An order or decree. It usually carries the connotation of being an executive decree of a more or less arbitrary nature which has the force of law, and not a statute enacted by the constitutional authorities for lawmaking.

fiat money. Paper money which receives its value entirely from government action or fiat, and not because it is backed by or redeemable in gold or silver.

fifth column. Group undermining a cause from within. When General Mola approached Madrid in the Spanish Civil War in the autumn of 1936, he stated he had four attacking columns but that they would be aided by a fifth column inside the city.

fifth freedom. See FIVE FREEDOMS.

"Fifty-four forty or fight." An expansionist slogan of the Democratic party in 1844, demanding the whole of Oregon Territory (up to the parallel 54° 40′) which had been occupied jointly with Great Britain since 1818. The Democrats won the election, but because of the war with Mexico were unwilling to press the demand. Congress instructed President Polk to end the agreement for joint occupation, and the dispute was settled by a treaty of June 15, 1846 dividing the territory along the present boundary line, the 49th parallel, giving almost half the territory to Great Britain.

Fighting French. Organization of active followers and sympathizers of General Charles de Gaulle after the fall of France in June, 1940. Originally called the Free French movement. From this group were set up the provisional French government and assembly in Algiers early in 1944. These were moved to Paris after its liberation in August of that year.

Figli della Lupa (FEEL-yee del-lah LOO-pah). Sons of the wolf, Fascist youth organization of boys 6–8 years of age. See FASCIST YOUTH ORGANIZATION.

filibuster. 1. The practice of holding the floor in a legislative body by talking endlessly in order to block the measure under consideration or to force acceptance of the speaker's view in some other respect. It is particularly effective in a body like the United States Senate in which there is no general limit on debate, especially near adjournment time when pressing business must be considered. 2. To hold the floor by speaking endlessly in the above fashion.

filibustering expedition. A private adventurous military expedition.

finance department. Administrative department in state or city government the responsibility of which is the collection and disbursement of public funds.

fireside chat. A kind of informal radio address to the nation made popular by President Franklin D. Roosevelt. The effect striven for, as the name indicates, was a kind of personal chat with the American people grouped about their own firesides.

First Bank of the United States. See BANKS OF THE UNITED STATES.

First Empire. French rule under Napoleon as Emperor from 1804 to 1815.

"First in war, first in peace, and first in the hearts of his countrymen." A characterization of George Washington made by General Henry Lee in his funeral oration for Washington, delivered in Philadelphia at the request of Congress on December 26, 1799, about two weeks after Washington's death. General Lee, known as "Light-Horse Harry" Lee, was the father of Robert E. Lee.

First International. See INTERNATIONAL.

first papers. The declaration of intention which an alien files with a court in the United States as the first step in naturalization.

First Reich. The Germanic empire which existed in Europe from the establishment of the Holy Roman Empire under Otto I in 996, to 1806 when the Hapsburg emperor of Austria ceased to be Holy Roman emperor. See HOLY ROMAN EMPIRE.

First Republic. The first republican government of France. It arose under the Convention in 1792 and during the period 1792–5. It continued under the Directory (1795–99) and declined during the Consulate (1799–1804) ending with the establishment of the First Empire in 1804.

fiscal year. The twelve-month period used as the unit in the collection and appropriation of funds. For many governments it does not correspond to the calendar year. For example, the fiscal year of the United States government begins July 1 and ends the following June 30.

Fish and Wildlife Service. A branch of the Department of the Interior formed in 1940 by the union of the Bureau of Biological Survey and the Bureau of Fisheries. Its function is to preserve fish and wild life by study and research, establishment of refuges, administration of conservation laws, propagation of fish and supervision of fishing industries.

fishing expedition. American slang for an investigation that does not stick to the purpose for which it was organized but goes wandering off unearthing all sorts of information of a more or less irrelevant nature.

Fiume incident. The seizure of the city of Fiume at the northeast corner of the Adriatic Sea by a group of Italians led by Gabriele D'Annunzio in September, 1919. The city was not granted to Italy by the secret treaty of London of 1915 and was occupied by Yugoslavs or an international force after the war. A large number of Italians lived there and D'Annunzio seized it on these grounds, but his control lasted only about four months. The Italian government tried to reach agreement with Yugoslavia over details of the problem until Mussolini came to power and later annexed the city.

five-five-three ratio. The ratio of capital ships established by the Washington Disarmament Conference in 1922. Japan was to have three-fifths the tonnage in capital ships allowed to the United States and Great Britain. France and Italy were assigned one-third the tonnage of the United States and Britain.

five to four decision. A decision of the Supreme Court established by the agreement of five judges although the other four dissent. Such decisions have been relatively rare, but many of them have concerned important social and constitutional issues thereby creating an unfavorable impression with the public, because the opinion of the court was so nearly evenly divided.

five freedoms. Various privileges accorded civil aviation accepted by varying numbers of states at the International Civil Aviation Conference of 1944. They were the privilege to fly over foreign territory, to land without change of passengers or cargo, to discharge passengers and cargo from the plane's state, to take on passengers and cargo for the plane's state, and to discharge and take on passengers and cargo to or from any state. The last was referred to as the fifth freedom, and was accepted by a smaller number of members than the other four.

five minute rule. A rule of the United States House of Representatives which can be invoked when it is meeting in Committee of the Whole and general debate on a measure has been closed. Under the rule two members are permitted to speak five minutes each for and against each amendment to the bill under consideration. This is to prevent the prohibition of all debate on amendments after the House has closed general debate.

five year plans. Programs for the industrialization and socialization of the Soviet Union, drawn up as over-all "plans," each to cover a five-year period. The first three were announced in 1928, 1933 and 1938, but the third was interrupted by the outbreak of World War II. A fourth plan

was announced in the winter of 1945–46.

fix. An American slang expression meaning to provide immunity from the operation of a law by paying such officers as policemen, prosecutors, mayors or judges not to carry out their normal functions impartially in respect to the person making the payment, or of someone in whose interest the payment was made. Payment need not be limited to cash.

Flag Day. A national holiday in the United States in honor of the flag, observed on June 14.

flag of truce. A white flag used by armed forces as a request that the bearer should not be attacked by the enemy. It is used to indicate a desire to surrender or that the bearer carries a message to an enemy commander.

flapper vote. Slang term for the women's vote, especially in the 1920's when women first voted in a United States national election and younger women first voted in Great Britain.

flexible constitution. A constitution which may be changed sufficiently easily so that it may be kept fairly well abreast of current political and economic problems.

flexible tariff. A tariff in which the law provides that rates may be altered by the action of the president upon recommendation of the Tariff Commission.

floater. A person who votes illegally in different election districts in the same or subsequent elections.

floating debt. A public debt for whose liquidation an accumulation of funds has not been provided.

floor leader. The leader of a party in a legislative body. He keeps the members in line, indicates who is to get the floor to speak on certain measures and facilitates the course of business in accordance with the rules of the body.

floor wage. Minimum wage.

Fonopostal. An Argentine postal service for the transmission of domestic messages by means of recordings.

Food Distribution Administration. An agency of the Department of Agriculture set up in 1942 to take over the work of the Agricultural Marketing Administration and various food units of the Office of Price Administration. It procured and allotted food to the army and occupied territories.

Food and Agriculture Organization. The first of the new international organizations set up after World War II. Its function is to collect and distribute information, and to recommend and assist in national and international action in regard to research and education, conservation, processing, and financing and marketing of agricultural, fisheries and forest products to prevent starvation and to better nutrition among the peoples of the world. Its deliberative body is called the Conference. It meets annually and each member state has one vote therein. There is an Executive Committee which directs the work of the organization between sessions of the Conference.

Food and Drug Administration. A government agency for the inspection and analysis of food, drugs, and cosmetics, and for enforcing the laws regarding purity, standards, and labeling of such products. Following the passage of the first Food and Drugs Act of 1906, these functions were exercised by the Agriculture Department until 1940, when the reorganized functions were turned over to the Federal Security Agency.

food stamp plan. The method of administering the rationing of food in World War II by requiring the surrender of so many stamps or "points" for each purchase of rationed food. These stamps were periodically issued to each person by local rationing boards. Rationing was made variable by increasing or decreasing the number of stamps or points required, as for a pound of butter. A few other commodities were covered by the same system, notably shoes.

forced labor. Work by laborers conscripted by a government for purposes and upon terms designated by the government.

forced loans. Money borrowed by a government from persons regardless of their desire to loan.

Foreign Bondholders' Protective Council. An American non-profit, semipublic agency set up in 1933 to help protect the interests of persons owning foreign government bonds. It does not act as an agent of bondholders, but intervenes on their behalf in cases of default.

foreign commerce. Trade to and from a state across its national boundaries.

Foreign Economic Administration. A United States government agency set up in 1943 to aid the State Department in the formation of economic foreign policy and in the collection of information. It also secured supplies abroad.

Foreign Funds Control. A war agency in the United States Treasury Department in World War II which regulated or disposed of neutral and enemy funds located in the United States.

Foreign Legion. A part of the French army, recruited chiefly from foreigners, used principally in protecting the various parts of the empire, especially North Africa.

foreign minister. The administrative head of the government department dealing with foreign relations. He shares with the head of the state the right to speak officially for the state on foreign affairs.

foreign office. The government department charged with carrying on the foreign relations of a state. At its head is the foreign minister, or minister of foreign affairs.

foreign policy. A series of objectives pursued by a state in its dealings with other states. In so far as specific methods for achieving these objectives are also planned, the use of these methods is also part of the foreign policy.

Foreign Policy Association. A New York organization, with branches in many other cities, for educating the public on international affairs. The various groups have periodic meetings with qualified speakers. The Association publishes biweekly *Reports*, a weekly *Bulletin*, and periodic Headline Books.

foreign service. The diplomatic and consular services of a state.

Foreign Service List. A quarterly publication of the Department of State giving the names and locations of the United States diplomats and members of the Foreign Service.

Foreign Service of the United States. The combined diplomatic and consular services as joined together by the Rogers Act in 1924. A person may now move from one to the other of the formerly separate services.

forest preserve district. A special governmental district overlapping regular township, county, or state lines, established for the preservation of forests therein.

Forest Service. A branch of the Department of Agriculture set up in 1905 to administer the national forests and help the states and private individuals in forest protection.

fortification. 1. A position of military defense provided with cannon and troops and strengthened by construction, for example, of walls, to aid in resisting attack. 2. The process of establishing such a position.

Founding Fathers. Those who contributed particularly to the establishment of the government of the United

States, especially the leading signers of the Declaration of Independence and the Constitution.

Four Freedoms. In his message at the opening of Congress, January 6, 1941 President Franklin D. Roosevelt stated as the objectives of United States foreign policy the smashing of militarism, the liberation of the subjugated nations, and the "establishing and securing freedom of speech, freedom of religion, freedom from want, and freedom from fear everywhere in the world."

4-H Clubs. Educational clubs of rural youth sponsored by the Department of Agriculture and the county agricultural agents. The purpose is the stimulation of appreciation and skills of rural life and the making of better citizens. The symbol is a four-leaf clover on each leaf of which is an H, indicating the goal of betterment of health, head, hand and heart.

Four-Power Pact. A project of Mussolini's for setting up a consultative arrangement among Great Britain, France, Germany, and Italy, for the discussion of common problems, thus excluding Russia. It was signed at Rome July 15, 1933 but not ratified.

Four-Power Treaty. A treaty drawn up at the Washington Disarmament Conference and signed December 13, 1921 by the United States, Great Britain, France, and Japan. The treaty provided for the mutual respect of the rights of the signatories in their insular possessions in the Pacific Ocean. Disputes among these powers were to be settled by conference, and threats from other states were to be the subject of discussion by the signatories.

Four-Year Plan. A German program of economic self-sufficiency begun in 1936, in preparation for war.

Fourteen Points. American war aims as expressed by Woodrow Wilson in an address to Congress on January 8, 1918. They included open diplomacy, freedom of the seas, reduction of economic barriers and armaments, adjustment of colonial claims in the interest of the peoples affected, evacuation of Russia and Belgium, restoration of Alsace Lorraine, Romania, Serbia, Montenegro and Poland, new boundaries for Italy along lines of nationality, autonomy for the peoples of Austria-Hungary and the Arab parts of the Turkish Empire, and the establishment of a league of nations.

fourth estate. The press. At the close of the feudal system three great social divisions or estates were recognized namely, the nobles, the clergy, and the commons. The term "fourth estate" was applied variously to other groups, such as the Army and has been applied to the press since about the middle of the 19th Century.

Fourth of July. A United States national holiday commemorating the signing of the Declaration of Independence in 1776.

Fourth Republic. The post-World War II government of France. After several elections and interim governments a constitution was agreed upon and the new government thereunder went into office in January, 1947.

franchise. 1. Right granted to a person by a governmental unit to carry on a certain business, such as the operation of a street-car line. 2. The right to vote.

franchise tax. 1. A tax levied on the franchises of privately-owned utilities. In certain states these taxes have almost superseded the general property tax. 2. A tax on the formation of a corporation or the right to operate as a corporation.

Franco-German Armistice. The armistice between France and Germany concluded June 22, 1940, which took France out of World War II. Signed in Compiègne Forest, where the armistice was signed ending World World War I.

Franco-Soviet Treaty of Mutual Assistance. A treaty signed by France and Russia May 2, 1935, in which the signatories promised to consult if aggression threatened and agreed to come to the aid of the victim of aggression if either were attacked.

Frankfort, Treaty of. The treaty concluding the Franco-Prussian War, signed May 10, 1871. One of the chief provisions was for the German annexation of the formerly French areas of Alsace and Lorraine.

franking privilege. The privilege of having mail delivered without the usual charge. Government agencies are granted this privilege for official business. Members of Congress are also given the privilege and often criticised for abusing it by mailing personal campaign literature free of charge.

fratricidal. Pertaining to the killing of brothers, that is, to a civil war.

fraud. Illegally inducing a person to do something by misrepresenting the facts. A vote fraud is the securing of a large number of votes by such illegal means as false registration.

Frazier-Lemke Act. See FARM MORTGAGE MORATORIUM ACT.

free competition. An economic system in which prices are regulated by supply and demand and in which the supply is offered by vendors competing freely with each other for the customer's trade without any advantages for any one of them established by private monopoly or governmental action.

free economy. An economic system in which supply and demand are permitted to operate freely with no specially politically-derived advantages for any, and with only minor regulation on behalf of the public welfare and to secure freedom from the growth of monopoly.

Free French. See FIGHTING FRENCH.

free port. See FREE ZONE.

free ships, free goods. The rule of international law (of the conventions of armed neutrality of 1780 and the Declaration of Paris of 1856) that a belligerent could not confiscate enemy goods found in a neutral ship on the high seas.

free trade. The free exchange of goods between countries, unhampered by regulations or duties designed to keep out foreign goods. The main argument for free trade is that if every nation concentrates on producing what it is best fitted to produce, and exchanges goods freely with other nations, everybody would benefit. The mutually beneficial nature of foreign trade was not understood for a long time; the mercantilists, for instance, believed in regulated trade and high tariffs on the importation of foreign goods in order to attain a favorable balance of trade and to accumulate gold and money. Adam Smith, the father of classical economic theory and of laissez-faire, the principle of non-interference by the state with the economy, also believed in free trade. Free trade gained ground only gradually between the end of the 18th and the middle of the 19th century. So-called prohibitive duties which made the importation of goods virtually impossible were abolished. The struggle in Britain against the Corn Laws, which made the importation of French grain to Britain impossible and resulted in corresponding French tariffs against British manufactured goods, ended victoriously and opened the road for free trade. It was led chiefly by the so-called Manchester liberals, a group headed by Richard Cobden and John Bright. The commercial treaty between France and England in 1861 established free trade between these two countries. The most-favored-nation-clause giving signatories of trade treaties the advantage of any lower duties subsequently granted to any other country came into general use. Cobden and his friends believed that free trade would usher in a period of international peace and prosperity. But a general system of free trade was never established. Industrially backward countries imposed protective tariffs on foreign goods to build up their own industries by keeping out foreign competition; Germany and America were following this policy in the last century. In Britain the policy of "imperial preference" advocated by Joseph Chamberlain tended to draw the Colonies and Dominions closer together and to raise tariff barriers against the rest of the world. These trends sharpened after World War I, enhanced by nationalism and economic depressions. Free trade and the most-favored-nation-clause gave way to strictly bilateral treaties and the so-called quota system which prescribes the quantity of goods to be exchanged between two countries. The United States never embraced free trade to any extent. The tariff of 1913 showed signs of abandoning the policy of protecting the by then well-developed American industry from foreign competition, but in 1921 America returned to high protective tariffs. Cordell Hull's policy of attempting to lower tariff barriers through bilateral treaties particularly with Latin American countries was much opposed in Congress and was only partly effective. Since the close of World War II the necessity for larger American exports has been realized, as the home market will prove too small for the increased productivity of American industry. This however, will only be possible in the long run if America permits the importation of foreign goods. The competition of foreign goods is feared by many domestic industries, as American wages are higher and rate of exchange of the dollar such as to make foreign goods seem even cheaper than they really are. See LAISSEZ-FAIRE, LIBERALISM, MERCANTILISM, TARIFF.

free zone. A port or part of a port through which goods to or from one or more foreign states may pass without being liable for import duties, inspections, etc., by the state in which the port is located.

freedman. A slave who was granted his freedom as a result of the American Civil War or by the 13th Amendment to the Constitution.

freedom. The absence of various kinds of restraints preventing or hampering the development and self-realization of a person or a group. The history of human freedom is as old as mankind. The great variety of human beings, the constant change in the size, number and nature of human groups, the different ends and methods people pursue in expressing themselves make freedom a term which means different things to different people. In modern history the struggle for freedom for a group and freedom for the individual have gone hand in hand. An excellent example of a time when people desired to achieve both national and individual freedom was the American Revolution. Yet today there are nations which are completely free from any outside restraint but do not grant freedoms (civil liberties) to their citizens. Freedom of the group led in the 19th century to the nation-state and to the principle of national self-determination. Freedom of the individual was the aim of liberalism and was realized in the bills of rights and constitutions of democratic nations. Re-

ligious freedom was achieved by the tolerance of all religions. Political freedom was founded in free opinion and in political equality, in every man's and woman's right to vote and to run for election. Economic freedom was at first based on the freedom to hold private property and to use it freely, which led to the systems of free trade and laissez-faire. Today it has been found that the individual's economic freedom needs to be protected not only from an all-powerful state, but from too-powerful groups, such as monopolies, trusts etc., which prevent free competition. The ideas of economic equality and economic freedom often conflict, though a compromise between the two may be possible. Freedom from want and freedom from fear are not traditional freedoms, but were included in the Atlantic Charter. In addition the modern state seems to recognize other freedoms: freedom to work, by trying to combat unemployment and also freedom to be educated by providing free education. Collectivist states are mainly interested in freedom for the group, and leftist collectivists believe in economic equality; individual freedom is likely to suffer thereby. To strike the right balance between freedom of the group and freedom of the individual, between liberty and equality is the great problem which confronts free governments. See LIBERALISM, RADICALISM, INDIVIDUALISM, NATURAL RIGHTS, RIGHTS OF MAN, CIVIL LIBERTIES, FREEDOM OF RELIGION, LAISSEZ-FAIRE, FREE TRADE.

freedom of religion. The right to worship freely according to the dictates of one's conscience. Freedom from interference of the government in the exercise of religion (or freedom of conscience) is guaranteed in the First Amendment of the American Constitution: "Congress shall make no law respecting an establishment of religion, or prohibiting the free exercise thereof." Freedom of worship is also one of the Four Freedoms enunciated in the Atlantic Charter.

The idea of toleration of all religions is not old in the Western World; only in the 17th century the term "freedom of conscience" was coined by the English "Independent" (Congregational Church) and even they did not include Roman Catholics or Quakers among the tolerated religions. The Roman Catholic Church still regards every Christian who does not follow its doctrine as a "heretic," and until the 18th century heretics were persecuted everywhere with the help of state authorities. Early protestant churches were even less tolerant. Anglicans persecuted Presbyterians in England, Presbyterians persecuted Lutherans or Independents in England, Scotland, Geneva and Puritan Massachusetts. Tolerance spread only gradually and the idea that two or more denominations could peacefully live in the same community was not understood for a long time. Religious tolerance triumphed only when religious fanaticism was at an ebb and the principle of the separation of church and state was generally accepted. By the beginning of the 20th century freedom of religion was well established in Europe and America, but the anti-Christian and violently anti-Jewish Nazi and Fascist creeds revived religious persecution, as did Communist atheism. The Russian Government, however, later showed itself much friendlier toward religion, lost its interest in militant atheism and guaranteed a certain amount of religious freedom to most churches. See NATURAL RIGHTS, CIVIL LIBERTIES, FREEDOM.

freedom of speech. The right to say or publish anything one wishes subject to the operation of the laws of slander and libel. A right granted in most bills of rights, including that of the United States Constitution. (First Amendment.)

freedom of the press. The right freely to publish newspapers, magazines, books and pamphlets without such government restrictions as licensing or censorship, or the registration of the writers and publishers, but subject to the laws of libel.

freedom of the seas. The rule of international law that in times of peace the high seas are open to use by all and cannot be placed under the jurisdiction of any state. In times of war this freedom is limited by belligerent rights regarding enemy property, blockade and contraband.

French Committee of National Liberation. A committee formed as the first step toward a provisional government of France during World War II. See FIGHTING FRENCH.

French Forces of the Interior. Organized French guerrilla troops which arose within France to aid the cause of the allied invasion in the summer of 1944.

French Line. The compromise Italian-Yugoslav boundary suggested by France during the negotiation of the Italian peace treaty after World War II. It was largely followed in the treaty. It lay to the east of the frontier advocated by Russia and to the west of the boundaries put forward by the United States and Great Britain.

French Union. Term used following World War II by the French Government to designate the French colonial empire and France itself. The precise terms under which the various colonies would belong to the Union were to be developed later.

Front Bench. The first of the five rows of benches in the House of Commons to the right of the Speaker. It is occupied by the members of the cabinet who are members of the House of Commons.

front porch campaign. Presidential campaign in which the candidate does not do a lot of traveling but stays home and occasionally makes political speeches literally from his front porch to visiting delegations of the party. Particularly used by McKinley in 1896 and Harding in 1920.

Front Opposition Bench. The front row of benches to the left of the speaker in the House of Commons, occupied by the leaders of the opposition party.

frontier. 1. National boundary of a state. 2. In U. S. history that part of the nation involved at a given period in expansion and settlement.

fry the fat. American slang expression meaning to secure political contributions from wealthy individuals or corporations in return for economically advantageous political favors.

Fuehrer (FYOOR-er). German word for leader. Title used by Hitler as the supreme leader of the Nazi organization and state.

Fuehrerprinzip(FYOOR-er-prin-tseep). Literally, the leader-principle. The Nazi doctrine that the leader is the physical embodiment of the people and as such fully represents them and can act in their stead and make decisions for them.

full faith and credit clause. Article IV, Section 1 of the Constitution states, "Full faith and credit shall be given in each state to the public acts, records, and judicial proceedings of every other state." This means that, in general, each of the United States recognizes the civil laws, decisions, and decrees of the other states.

full powers. Complete authorization from a state to represent it in the negotiation of an international agreement, as given to a diplomatic agent at an international conference.

functional representation. Representation in a parliamentary body on some other basis than territorial, usually by one of the voter's own economic or professional group. Attempted after a fashion in fascist Italy, though the representatives were appointed rather than chosen in a free election.

fundamental law. The law which serves as the underlying foundation for the structure and functions of the government of a state; a constitution.

fusion. The union of two parties or factions of two parties for the backing of a candidate. It is found most often in city politics when the support of a candidate cuts across party lines, for example, the Fusion party of New York City which supported Mayor Fiorello H. La Guardia.

G

Gadsden Purchase. A strip of United States territory along southern New Mexico and Arizona bought from Mexico in 1853. It is named for James Gadsden, ambassador to Mexico from 1853–56, who negotiated the treaty which included the terms of the purchase. The cost was $10,000,000 and also included the settlement of various claims by Mexico against the United States.

gag law. A law placing serious limitations on the freedom of speech or freedom of the press.

gag rule. A rule which can be proposed by the rules committee in the House of Representatives. If its use is approved by the House, a minority is prevented from taking charge of procedure or getting before the House a bill the majority does not want to consider.

Gallipoli Peninsula. The peninsula which forms the west shore of the Dardanelles. The British suffered a major reverse there at the hands of the Turks in 1915.

game preserve. An area in which game hunting is prohibited for the sake of the preservation of wild life.

game warden. An official whose function is to enforce the fishing and game laws.

gangster. A member of a group or gang of persons who makes a profit promoting or protecting by force some illegal activity such as bootlegging or gambling.

gangway. A transverse aisle across the House of Commons, cutting through the benches beyond the center of the room from the speaker. Third parties and less influential members of the other parties are seated "below the gangway," furthest from the speaker.

gasoline tax. Federal and state taxes of several cents per gallon on gasoline. In many cases the income of this tax is earmarked for road construction and repair.

gas warfare. The use in war of poisonous gas as a weapon. In spite of efforts to make its use illegal, it was often used in World War I, though scarcely at all in World War II, probably because both sides were fairly well supplied and prepared to meet it, thus reducing the element of surprise, by which it is most effective.

Gau (GOW). (Plural, **Gaue**). German word for district. Used as an administrative unit in the Nazi party.

Gauleiter (GOW-lie-ter). District leader of the Nazi party. See GAU.

G. B. E. See ORDER OF THE BRITISH EMPIRE.

G. C. B. See ORDER OF THE BATH.

G. C. I. E. See ORDER OF THE INDIAN EMPIRE.

G. C. M. G. See ORDER OF ST. MICHAEL AND ST. GEORGE.

G. C. S. I. See ORDER OF THE STAR OF INDIA.

G. C. V. O. See ROYAL VICTORIAN ORDER.

General Accounting Office. An independent agency of the U. S. Federal government set up in 1921, the functions of which are the general auditing and accounting for the government departments and agencies and the settling of all claims in which the national government is either debtor or creditor. The office is headed by the comptroller-general.

General Act. The General Act for the Pacific Settlement of International Disputes was a combination of treaties providing for adjudication, arbitration, and conciliation proposed by the League of Nations in 1928. Something over a dozen nations acceded to it.

General Assembly. 1. The deliberative body of the United Nations, in which each member state is represented and receives one vote. It may consider any matter within the competence of the organization except disputes before the Security Council. It shall promote international cooperation, particularly in law, economic and social relations and education and health. It receives the reports of related agencies, approves the budget and votes on new members of the General Assembly, Security Council and other United Nations Agencies. It meets regularly in annual sessions, but may convene in special sessions. See UNITED NATIONS. 2. The name for the legislature in a number of states of the United States.

general charter plan. The plan for providing all the cities in a state with the same charter established by state law. This plan is usually not considered flexible enough for the needs of cities of differing size.

general delivery. The delivery of mail at the post office to those who, for some reason such as lack of permanent residence, cannot be reached by a mail carrier. In communities too small to have a mail carrier a large proportion of the mail may be handled this way.

General Council. The legislative body found in the French *départements*. Its functions are naturally local in character, including chiefly the regulation of relief, public property, and traffic, and the voting of the budget.

general fund. The sum of the general income of a governmental taxing unit, from which general expenditures may be made. It does not include special income from which special expenditures are made.

General Land Office. A branch of the U. S. Department of the Interior which disposes of public lands and develops the minerals therein. It also issues land patents, carries on conservation measures, and sets up grazing districts.

general property tax. A tax on all real and personal property assessed according to the value of the property. It has long been and generally still is a basic tax for state and local purposes, but has become increasingly unsatisfactory in proportion to the growing amount of intangible personal property, the taxation of which is difficult.

general strike. A strike of all workers at the same time. A wide-spread strike in England in 1926 is thus referred to. Such a strike would, of course, have a paralyzing effect on the entire economy of a country. In certain labor circles it is held as the goal of the movement, which will, when carried out, provide labor with the control of production.

general welfare. The well-being of the community or state as a whole. It is one of the goals of democracy, and its promotion was one of the reasons for establishing the Constitution, as stated in the preamble.

general welfare clause. The first sentence of Article I, Section 8 of the United States Constitution states that "the Congress shall have power to lay and collect taxes, duties, imposts and excises, to pay the debts and provide for the common defense and *general welfare* of the United States." This has been interpreted to mean that Congress can tax and spend for the general welfare but cannot otherwise legislate concerning such matters.

Geneva Arbitration. See ALABAMA CLAIMS.

Geneva Award. See ALABAMA CLAIMS.

Geneva Conference. See GENEVA NAVAL CONFERENCE; DISARMAMENT CONFERENCE OF 1932.

Geneva Convention of 1864. See RED CROSS.

Geneva Convention of 1929. A treaty concerning the treatment of prisoners of war, signed at Geneva July 27, 1929 by 47 nations. The treaty provides for the humane treatment of prisoners, the administration of prison camps, work by the prisoners, their discipline and repatriation.

Geneva Naval Conference. A conference of the United States, Great Britain, and Japan held at Geneva in the summer of 1927. The object was cruiser limitation, but the conference reached no agreement on the subject. See WASHINGTON CONFERENCE, LONDON NAVAL CONFERENCE OF 1930.

Geneva Protocol. A project of the League of Nations in 1924 by which war and aggression were to be renounced, disputes settled peacefully, and aggression defined as resorting to war after refusing to submit to, or accept, a peaceful settlement. Rejected by the British in 1925, and never put into effect.

Genoa Conference. An unsuccessful effort in 1922 toward an agreement between Russia and the other European powers to settle their conflicting claims over cancelled debts and damages for intervention.

genocide. Strictly, murder of a race, or, more often, murder of large groups of people. A term which came into use as a result of the Nazi policy of killing off masses of non-German peoples. Declared an international law crime by the Legal Committee of the United Nations Assembly.

genro. See ELDER STATESMAN.

gentlemen's agreement. An understanding between statesmen who, considering each other to be dependable gentlemen, do not demand that the agreement be put in formal treaty form. Such an agreement was that of 1907–8 between the United States and the Japanese providing that the United States would continue to permit Japanese to come to the United States, and that the Japanese government would discourage Japanese laborers from taking advantage of this permission. The understanding was ended by the immigration act of 1924 excluding Japanese and certain others.

Geological Survey. A branch of the U. S. Department of the Interior, the function of which is the study of the mineral and water resources of the United States, the making of topographic surveys and the classifying of public lands. It also is in charge of the leasing of public and Indian lands for the extraction of gas, petroleum, and minerals.

geopolitics. A science which studies the relationship between geography and the life of great powers and empires. The term was coined by the Swedish scholar Kjellén after World War I, but the influence of geographical conditions on international politics and warfare has been studied since antiquity. One of its most remarkable experts was the American Admiral Mahan who wrote on seapower. Another was Sir Halford Mackinder, who based his theories on land power, that is, world control from the Eurasian "heartland." German geographers, military and political scientists developed geopolitics into a "science" of aggressive expansion serving the ideas of a self-sufficient, militarily strong German world empire. General Karl Haushofer, a professor at the University of Munich who founded the first Institute of Geopolitics, was its main apostle. Hitler's deputy, Rudolf Hess (one of the chief defendants at the Nuremberg War Crimes Trial), was a student of Haushofer's and introduced the general to Hitler. Geopolitical ideas play an important role in Hitler's *Mein Kampf*, the Nazi Bible. National Socialism gradually adopted geopolitics as its tool, merged it with totalitarian and racial ideas and made it one of the compulsory subjects to be studied by budding party officials. The Nazis also developed a so-called geostrategy, a science dealing with the methods of conquering the world through a thorough knowledge of geographical conditions affecting world-strategy. See IMPERIALISM, NAZISM, THIRD REICH.

German-Italian Alliance. Two treaties between Germany and Italy signed May 7 and 22, 1939 providing for consultation on common problems, economic collaboration, military assistance and no separate armistice or peace treaty in case of war. The alliance was to run for ten years.

German-Polish Declaration. A joint declaration of the two states agreed upon January 26, 1934 providing that for a period of ten years the two states would base their relations on the Pact of Paris (Kellogg-Briand Pact, 1928) and specifically that they would discuss mutual problems, settle disputes peacefully and would "agree under no circumstances to use force to settle such disputes." This agreement was in force when Germany attacked Poland in 1939.

German-Russian Non-Aggression Pact. A treaty signed August 23, 1939, in which the two countries agreed to refrain from aggression against each other. Each also agreed not to aid a third power at war with the other signatory. They agreed also to consult on problems of mutual interest and to settle mutual differences by peaceful means. In practical effect, the treaty provided each signatory with the breathing space needed before the two came to grips with each other. Russia was given time to prepare a defense against Germany and Germany was given time in which to wipe out France in preparation for attacking Russia, as Hitler had proposed in *Mein Kampf*.

gerrymander. The establishment of electoral districts in such a way that the party dominating the redistricting is favored by the scattering of its voters through as many districts as possible, while the votes for the opposite party are placed in the smallest possible number of districts. This naturally results in districts of peculiar shape, although contiguous and compact areas are now required by law. The name is derived from Governor Elbridge Gerry of Massachusetts who signed a state law which was guilty of this practice in redistricting the legislature. An especially unusually shaped district was said by one person to resemble a salamander, but another man commented that it looked more like a gerrymander.

Gestapo. Abbreviation for *Geheime Staatspolizei* (guh-HIE-muh SHTAHTS-poh-lee-tsei). Literally the home state police, the secret state police of Germany. Long directed by Heinrich Himmler, it was the leading instrument of Nazi repression and one of the most effective means for the maintenance of Nazi control.

get-out-the-vote movement. A movement in the interests of better government aimed at getting the largest possible number of people to the polls on election day. There are always large numbers of Americans who do not vote in any given election. This movement is based on the theory that most of the non-voters are among the more intelligent citizens, so that increasing the number of voters will increase even more the number of intelligent voters. Sometimes such movements are based on the idea that stirring a person up to vote will force him to educate and interest himself in public issues and affairs.

ghazi. Title conferred by the Turkish Grand National Assembly on Mustapha Kemal, later Kemal Ataturk, first president of the Turkish Republic. The title means "conqueror," and was granted because Ataturk had repulsed the threat of Greek conquest of Turkey in 1921.

Ghent, Treaty of. The treaty between the United States and Great Britain concluding the War of 1812, signed at Ghent December 24, 1814. In addition to the cessation of hostilities between themselves and with the Indians, the agreement provided for settling by commissioners from each nation the ownership of certain islands off the eastern boundary, and disputed points in the boundary along eastern Maine, in the St. Lawrence River and through the Great Lakes to the Lake of the Woods. The two powers also promised to try to abolish the slave trade.

G. I. Bill of Rights. The Servicemen's Readjustment Act of June 22, 1944 providing servicemen and women, after their honorable discharge from the armed forces, with unemployment compensation of $20 per week for a period depending on the time in service, a governmental guarantee of 50 percent on loans up to $4000 for the purchase of a business, farm or home, and the financing of educational expenses for a period equal to the time spent in the service. See PUBLIC LAW 16.

gift tax. A tax on a gift by one person to another. Often the rate is the same as the inheritance tax rate, on the theory that the gifts are made to avoid the inheritance tax, that is, are made in anticipation of death.

G. I. O. General International Organization—the title of the world organization suggested in the Dumbarton Oaks proposals. Changed at the San Francisco Conference to United Nations.

Giovani Fascisti (joe-VAHnee fah-SHEES-tee). The eldest of the fascist youth organizations for boys, those 18 years old and above. The name means "Young Fascisti." See FASCIST YOUTH ORGANIZATION.

"Give me liberty or give me death." The closing lines of the appeal of Patrick Henry to the members of the Virginia Convention, on March 23, 1775, to take up arms against England in defense of their liberty.

Glass-Steagall Act. A Federal law passed in 1933 after the bank moratorium to strengthen the position of banks, individually, by stricter regulation of the use of funds and by insuring deposits, and collectively by pulling the banking system of the country closer together under the Federal Reserve system. The law also established the Federal Deposit Insurance Corporation.

global. 1. Pertaining to the whole world, as a global war, one going on all over the world. 2. Pertaining to the entirety of a thing. See GLOBAL TONNAGE.

global tonnage. Tonnage of an entire navy. This has occasionally been sug-

global war 126

gested as a basis for naval limitation, as opposed to the plan of limiting ships by categories or classes.

global war. Term applied to a war of worldwide extent involving most of the people of the world.

globaloney. An American slang term of derision directed at the consideration of global problems. Coined by former Representative Clare Boothe Luce of Connecticut.

gobbledygook. The wordy, stilted and technical-sounding verbiage of many governmental orders and communications, presumably the natural language of the bureaucrat. Invented by Maury Maverick of Texas.

Godesberg Memorandum. An ultimatum given by Hitler to Prime Minister Neville Chamberlain during a night meeting at Bad Godesberg on the Rhine, September 22–23, 1938 for transmission to the Czechs. It demanded that the Czechs evacuate part of the Sudeten area by October 1, permit Sudeten Germans in the Czech army to go home, liberate German political prisoners, and establish a new boundary by plebiscite before November 25. See MUNICH ACCORD.

gold certificate. Paper money specifically redeemable in gold.

gold clause. Statement in a contract that the principal or interest must be paid in gold if so demanded. When the United States went off the gold standard in 1934, the Supreme Court held that the action nullified gold clauses.

gold reserve. 1. Gold held by a government as a reserve for redeeming paper money if demanded. 2. Gold certificates held by the Federal Reserve system as a reserve for Federal Reserve notes.

Gold Reserve Act. The law passed in January, 1934 permitting the president to reduce the value of the dollar to at least 60 cents (the new value was

set at 59.06 cents). The new dollar was redefined in terms of gold but paper money was not redeemable in gold.

gold standard. See MONEY.

Gondra Treaty. A Pan-American treaty signed May 3, 1923 at the Santiago Conference providing that disputes not settled by diplomacy or arbitration should be submitted to a commission of inquiry for investigation and report.

good-neighbor policy. The United States foreign policy in regard to Latin America since Franklin Roosevelt became President. In his inaugural of March 4, 1933, however, Roosevelt used the term in relation to the total United States foreign policy. See MONROE DOCTRINE.

good offices. See TENDER OF GOOD OFFICES.

G. O. P. The Grand Old Party—the Republican Party.

Gosplan. The Russian State Planning Commission, the top planning agency of the Soviet Union.

governance. The process or act of government. Rarely used, but intended to be more explicit than the word government.

government. 1. The combined organs and mechanisms by and through which the state functions. 2. The total processes or acts of the organs of the state for the control or regulation of the people thereof. 3. Used in Europe, especially Great Britain, to mean the cabinet or administration.

government bill. A bill sponsored by the administration in office.

government enterprise. The carrying on of business functions by a governmental agency as opposed to having them carried on by private individuals. Also referred to as public enterprise.

government-in-exile. A government

which has been forced to leave its homeland, but secures permission to continue its existence and to function, within the possible limits, within another state. During World War II London was the seat of several such governments of states occupied by Germany.

Government of India Act. Two fundamental laws for India passed by the British parliament in 1919 and 1935 and both given the same name. Each provided an increasing degree of self-government for India. The former established the principle of diarchy. The latter provided for a federation of the 11 provinces and the native states, with a two-house legislative body. As in the earlier plan, certain important powers are reserved for British control. See DIARCHY.

"government of laws and not of men." Article 30 of Part I (Declaration of Rights) of the Massachusetts Constitution of 1780, written by John Adams, specifically states that the legislative, executive, and judicial departments of the state government shall not exercise each other's powers "to the end that it may be a government of laws and not of men."

government ownership. The ownership of some business undertaking by a local or national government, such as a street railway or electric system.

Government Printing Office. A government agency set up by Congress in 1860 which prints and distributes the publications of Congress and the different executive departments and administrative agencies. See also BUREAU OF ENGRAVING.

governor. 1. The highest administrative official of a major governmental subdivision. He may be an appointed head of a province in a centralized state or the elected chief executive of one of the United States. 2. The executive of a Federal Reserve Bank.

Governor-General. Title of the chief representative of the Crown in the British Dominions and most important colonies.

G. P. U. See O. G. P. U.

graft. The diversion of public funds or property or the use of political power for personal or party gain.

Gran Chaco. An area part of which was long in dispute between Bolivia and Paraguay. The dispute broke into war in 1928, and, in spite of half-hearted attempts by other American states to settle it, again in 1932. After unsuccessful efforts on the part of the League of Nations to solve the difficulty, several major American states again took a hand and in 1935 the disputants reached a preliminary solution. The final treaty and boundary were settled in 1938 with most of the disputed area going to Paraguay.

Grand Council of Fascism. See FASCIST GRAND COUNCIL.

grand jury. A group of persons selected to aid in the administration of justice by determining whether evidence discovered by themselves, or more usually presented by the prosecuting attorney, warrants the criminal trial of an accused person. If they find a trial is warranted they return an indictment against the accused person. See INDICTMENT.

Grand Mufti. Title appropriated by Haj Amin el Husseini, the mufti or Moslem religious leader of Jerusalem who, in the 1930's, assumed the leadership of the Palestinian Arabs. He spent the later years of World War II in Axis countries and after the war he was banned from Palestine.

Grand Old Party. Republican Party. Usually abbreviated to G. O. P.

grandfather clause. A clause inserted in the constitutions of several southern states waiving certain voting requirements if a person's grandfather had the right to vote at the time of the

Civil War. Such provisions were an obvious attempt to disfranchise the Negroes. They were declared unconstitutional by the Supreme Court in 1915.

Grange. The name for the local unit of the Patrons of Husbandry, a farmers' organization along the lines of a secret fraternal society, set up in 1867. See GRANGER LEGISLATION.

Granger. Member of a Grange.

Granger legislation. State laws promoted by farmers providing for fair freight rates and preventing discrimination. These laws were later declared unconstitutional, but the movement continued and aided in the establishment of the Interstate Commerce Commission.

grant-in-aid. A contribution by the Federal government to the states for various purposes, among the first of which were agriculture and roads. Now the grant is matched by state funds. In return for the grant the national government insists on minimum standards or varying degrees of regulation.

grass roots. 1. The earthy, individual, and usually rural foundations of United States political opinion. 2. Pertaining to these foundations.

Grazing Service. A branch of the Department of the Interior set up in 1934 which controls the grazing on federal grazing lands and the conservation thereof.

Great Britain. The official title of the political unity of England, Wales and Scotland. It was adopted formally in 1707 with the union of the crowns of England and Scotland, but it had been used informally by many writers for many years. See UNITED KINGDOM.

great powers. The nations which, because of history, political and economic strength and military might are generally acknowledged to be the most influential nations in the world.

Between the World Wars they included France, Germany, Great Britain, Italy, Japan, the United States, and the U. S. S. R. Prior to World War I Austria-Hungary was also included.

great seal. The seal of the United States which is affixed by the Department of State to laws and other public documents. This seal and its reverse (unused as a seal) are found on the back of the one dollar silver certificate.

Great Wall. An artificial defense barrier built of stone, finished in 214 B. C., to protect ancient China from the northern barbarians. It averages about 20 feet in height and has a road on the top. It extends from the west shore of the Gulf of Liaotung to the middle of Kansu Province, and covers about 1500 miles.

Great White Father. The ceremonial name the Indians give the President of the United States.

Greater East Asia Co-Prosperity Sphere. Euphemistic title given by the Japanese to the empire they won during World War II and planned to hold on a permanent basis. It included Japan itself, Korea, Manchuria, Indo-China, the Philippines, the Dutch and British East Indies, Malaya and occupied China. They hoped to add the rest of China and exploit all of it for the benefit of Japan.

Greco-Turkish exchange of populations. By an agreement of 1923, Greece and Turkey undertook, with minor exceptions, to return the Greeks in Turkey to Greece and the Turks in Greece to Turkey. It was a major social operation but it apparently ended the friction of centuries' duration arising from these minorities.

Greco-Turkish War. The war between Greece and Turkey following World War I. It grew out of the Greek occupation of Smyrna and its hinterland, permitted by the Allies; it came to a practical conclusion when the Greeks, after having penetrated almost to Ankara, were driven out of Smyrna in September, 1922.

greenback. 1. Originally paper money not backed by gold, issued during the Civil War. So-called because one side was printed in green. 2. Later, and more loosely, any United States paper money.

Greenback Party. A United States minor party active in the elections of 1876 and 1880. Its main object was the unsuccessful effort to prevent the redemption and retirement of the greenbacks. See GREENBACK.

Greenbelt communities. Government-built, more-or-less co-operative communities for persons of low income modeled on the pattern of the one established a short distance from Washington at Greenbelt, Maryland.

gross income. The total income of a person or corporation. Certain deductions from this for expenses and exemptions are allowed before the taxable income is reached.

Grossraumwirtschaft (GROHS-rowm-virt-shahft). The German and especially Nazi doctrine that the Reich needed more room or territory in which to achieve its historic mission. It was of no consequence to the Nazis that the part of this territory outside the boundaries of Germany was already inhabited by other peoples.

Guadalupe-Hidalgo, Treaty of. Treaty of peace between the United States and Mexico ending the Mexican War, signed February 2, 1848, ratified on May 30. It confirmed the Rio Grande as the boundary and also gave the United States the present states of California, Arizona, Nevada, Utah, and parts of Colorado and Oklahoma, as well as recognizing the annexation of Texas. The United States paid $15,000,000 and assumed certain claims of United States citizens against Mexico.

guerilla. 1. Originally a member of an armed band carrying on hostilities without the authorization of a state. 2. Later broadened to mean authorized resistance by relatively small groups, often detached from the main body of the army, as for example behind enemy lines. 3. Pertaining to such mobile, hit-and-run hostilities by small armed groups.

Guffey Coal Act. See BITUMINOUS COAL CONSERVATION ACTS.

guild socialism. A kind of socialism under which most of man's relations would be taken care of by the functional or professional group or guild to which he belonged. A certain political control, weaker than that of the present states of the world, would be retained as a referee between the functional groups.

guillotine. 1. Beheading device, named after its inventor (J. I. Guillotin), used at the time of the French Revolution. 2. A variety of closure found in the House of Commons by which the House votes to end all debate on a bill at a specified hour on some given future date, or, more recently, thus to end debate at fixed times on parts of a bill.

H

H. R. House Bill.

habeas corpus. A writ or order of a court bringing an accused person before it to inquire whether he is being lawfully detained.

Hagana. A Jewish resistance movement in Palestine, originally organized during the 1920 and 1921 troubles with the Arabs as the National Defense Organization. In recent years its strength has been directed toward the Zionist objectives of an independent Jewish Palestine state. It numbers several tens of thousands, with subdivisions according to degrees of armed activity.

Hague Conventions. A series of treaties concluded at the Hague Conferences of 1899 and 1907, regarding the laws of land warfare, a number of problems in naval warfare, neutrality and the use of force in the collection of contract debts. They are usually referred to by number and date, as the fourth Hague Convention of 1907.

Hague Peace Conferences. Two international conferences which met at The Hague, the Netherlands, in 1899 and 1907. At the first was established the Permanent Court of Arbitration; at both were signed a number of agreements regarding warfare known as the Hague Conventions.

Hague Tribunal. See PERMANENT COURT OF ARBITRATION; PERMANENT COURT OF INTERNATIONAL JUSTICE.

Half-breed. The liberal wing of the Republican party during the administrations of Hayes, Garfield, and Arthur (1877–85). See STALWART.

Hall of Mirrors. The great mirror-lined hall in the palace of Versailles where the German empire was established after the Franco-Prussian War in 1871 and where the Treaty of Versailles was signed June 28, 1919.

hammer and sickle. The insignia of the Communist Party, and on the flag of Union of Soviet Socialist Republics.

hands-off policy. A policy of non-interference in a particular matter.

Hansard. Nickname of the *Parliamentary Debates*, the record of the debates in the British parliament. The name is that of the original publisher of the *Debates*, Luke Hansard (1752–1828).

Hapsburg, house of (also Habsburg). A ruling dynasty of Europe. Their power centered first in Austria, until Rudolph I was elected German king in 1273, founding the family's greatness. From 1483 until the empire's dissolution in 1806, the Hapsburgs were also Holy Roman emperors. Maximilian I (1459–1519) added Burgundy and The Netherlands, and Philip I (1478–1506) became king of Spain. Philip's son, Charles V (1519–1558) united the Hapsburg lands into one of the greatest empires in history, including most of Central Europe and Italy, and Spain and her colonies. In 1556 his dominions were divided, the Austrian branch becoming Holy Roman emperors and adding Bohemia and Hungary. Philip II (1556–1598) ruled Spain, The Netherlands and a large part of Italy. He also conquered Portugal and its empire, but his designs against England ended with the defeat of the Armada in 1588. The Spanish Hapsburgs lost Portugal in 1640 and The Netherlands in 1648, after bloody revolutions, and the family died out in Spain in 1700. The Austrian Hapsburgs continued as Holy Roman emperors until 1806, but lost their Italian possessions during the unification of Italy, ending in 1860. In 1867 they re-organized their remaining lands as the Austro-Hungarian dual monarchy, and ruled this state until World War I, when Charles I abdicated in 1918. His son, Archduke Otto still maintains the Hapsburg claim to the thrones of Austria and Hungary. During the American Civil War, the French emperor Napoleon III sent troops to Mexico to found a French empire under the Austrian Hapsburg Maximilian. With the end of the Civil War, the French troops were withdrawn after American protests, and Maximilian was overthrown and executed in 1867. See HOLY ROMAN EMPIRE.

hara-kiri. A Japanese form of suicide by slashing the abdomen. Committed particularly as a result of failure in responsibility to the emperor.

hard money. See MONEY.

Hare plan. A system of proportional representation in which the voter lists his first, second, third, etc. choices for office. To be elected a candidate needs a number of votes equal to the total votes cast divided by the number of candidates plus one. When a candidate receives the required quota, his excess ballots are given to the candidates receiving second choice thereon, and so on. When the number of excess votes fails to elect another candidate, the candidate with the smallest number is thrown out and his ballots distributed among the second choices and so on until the required number of candidates is elected.

Hartford Convention. A meeting of New England Federalists, opposed to the War of 1812, convened in December 1814 at Hartford, Connecticut. They agreed to the right of secession if necessary, but the successful conclusion of the war precluded the determination of the issue at that time.

Hatch Acts. Two laws which Congress passed in August 1939 and July 1940 to strengthen corrupt practices legislation. The former extended to all federal administrative officials, except the highest policy-making officers like the president and department heads, the regular provisions of the civil service prohibiting soliciting funds and direct participation in election activities. The latter extended these provisions to state and local officials whose income is derived at least in part from federal funds. It also limits individual campaign contributions to $5000 and total campaign expenditures of each political organization to $3,000,000.

hat in the ring. An American slang expression used to indicate that the person who owns the hat is a candidate for office.

Havana Conference. The sixth Pan-American Conference held in 1928. It made the chairmanship of the governing board of the Pan-American Union an elective office instead of having the United States Secretary of State serve automatically in that capacity, accepted compulsory arbitration in principle, and also accepted a codification of private international law.

Hawes-Cutting Act. Law for Philippine independence passed by Congress in

January, 1933. It provided for a ten-year transition period after which the Islands would become independent if the plan was approved by the Filipinos. They did not approve, so the law was replaced by the Philippine Independence Act of the following year. See PHILIPPINE INDEPENDENCE ACT.

Hawley-Smoot Tariff. The United States tariff act passed in June, 1930. It was very extensive, including some 20,000 items, and is a leading contender for the dubious distinction of being the world's all-time highest tariff. It is commonly looked upon also as in part responsible for the world depression of the 1930's.

Hay-Pauncefote Treaty. A United States-British treaty of 1901, superseding the Clayton-Bulwer Treaty, and by which Great Britain conceded to the United States the sole control and protection of a canal across Panama if it were to be open to the warships and merchant vessels of all nations equally.

H. Con. Res. House Concurrent Resolution.

"He kept us out of war." Democratic campaign slogan in the election campaign of 1916, referring to Woodrow Wilson.

head tax. See POLL TAX.

headlands theory. A theory of international law, unaccepted in general and especially by the United States, that a maritime boundary, instead of following the shore line closely, should be a series of straight lines from headland to headland, as, for example from Cape Lookout to Cape Fear.

hearing. 1. A session of a legislative committee in which the views of non-members are heard. 2. The opportunity to defend one's self against the rulings of an administrative body before that body or a court. 3. Preliminary criminal proceedings. 4. Trial in equity.

hearth tax. A tax on fire-places in vogue some 250 years ago, levied on the theory that the number of fire-places in a home was an indication of ability to pay. See ABILITY THEORY.

heartland. The great central northern plain of the Eurasian land mass. In German geopolitics the base from which world control was possible.

heckle. To interrupt a speaker by questions or comments with the intention of upsetting his composure.

heeler. See WARD HEELER.

hegemony. The preponderant position of a state within a group of states.

heimatlos (HIME-aht-lohs). German word for homeless, used in international law to indicate a person who has no nationality because he has lost one without gaining another. Such is often the case when boundaries change and some persons in the locality do not conform to regulations for gaining the nationality of the new jurisdiction.

Heimwehr (HIME-vayr). Literally home guard, the German regular army.

heir apparent. An heir to a throne who is first in the line of normal succession, usually from father to son or daughter.

heir presumptive. An heir to a throne who is not first in the line of normal succession; such as, the younger brother of a king who will succeed to the throne only if no heir is born to the king before his death. See HEIR APPARENT.

hemispheric defense. A suggested defensive policy for the United States, prior to 1941, based on meeting with armed force an attack directed against any point in the western hemisphere.

hemispheric solidarity. The goal of a western hemisphere united in efforts to repel fascist aggression or penetration. The Pan American Conferences have taken important steps toward realizing this goal.

H-hour. The hour at which a particular military movement begins. See D-DAY.

high. Principal or important, as in high policy or the high contracting parties.

high commissioner. Chief commissioner. A title often used for an appointive administrative office; for example, the British administer Palestine through a high commissioner.

High Court of Justice. The three trial divisions of the British Supreme Court of Judicature. See SUPREME COURT OF JUDICATURE.

high seas. The oceans with their connecting bodies of water and bordering bays which are not within the territorial jurisdiction of any state.

Hindu. A follower of Hinduism, the religious and social creed of over 250 million inhabitants of India. The beliefs are polytheistic and include the re-incarnation of a person or animal in the form of another person or animal after death. In India religion tends for many to demand a loyalty superior to that given the state, with a result that the people often are Hindus first and Indians second.

hinterland. The land lying inland from the coast.

hinterland doctrine. The international law doctrine advocated by certain imperialistic states in the late nineteenth century that an effective occupation of a sea-coast in a colonial area carried with it a title to the unoccupied territory lying to the interior.

Hitler-Jugend. See HITLER YOUTH.

Hitler Youth. Uniformed youth organizations set up for the purpose of physical training and indoctrination in Nazi ideology.

H.J.Res. House Joint Resolution.

Hoare-Laval Agreement. An agreement between Sir Samuel Hoare, British foreign minister, and Pierre Laval, French premier, reached on December 8, 1935 which gave Italy a large fraction of Ethiopia and put that country under mostly Italian advisers, provided that Mussolini would halt his Ethiopian war. The offer was not accepted by Mussolini and the war went on.

Hohenzollern, house of. Former German ruling family. It originated in South Germany, but in the 15th century moved to Brandenburg, around Berlin. The family lands were expanded by marriage and conquest, and in 1701 Frederick I became king of Prussia. Frederick the Great (1740–1786) made Prussia a major military power, chiefly by wars with Austria. In the 19th century Hohenzollern Prussia won control of Germany from the Austrian Hapsburgs, and William I was crowned emperor of Germany (Second Reich) in 1871. Their power came to an end after World War I with the abdication of William II in 1918. Other members of the family have been princes and kings of Romania since 1866. See SECOND REICH.

HOLC. See HOME OWNERS LOAN CORPORATION.

hold-the-line-order. An executive order of April 8, 1943 limiting increases in prices and wages (the latter by the Little Steel formula) the object of which was to "hold the line" against inflation.

holding company. A company which is set up, not as a producing or operating company, but solely for the purpose of owning all or part of one or more other companies and thus achieving a greater or less degree of control over them.

hold-over. An elective official who has been re-elected, or "held over," from the previous term.

Holy Alliance. An agreement signed by Russia, Austria and Prussia in 1815, and later by all European states except the Papacy, Great Britain and Turkey. The instigator was Czar Alexander I of Russia. It stated merely that the signers would conduct themselves according to Christian principles. The term came into disrepute between 1815 and the revolutions of 1848 because the same powers contributed to the repression of European liberalism, especially in Italy and Spain, where armed intervention was used. The Monroe Doctrine was in part a result of the fear that the Alliance might extend its influence into the new republics of North and South America.

Holy Place. A place of special religious significance to some particular religion. Mecca, Medina, and Jerusalem hold such holy places for Mohammedans; Jerusalem also holds such holy places for Christians and Jews.

Holy Roman Empire. The European empire founded by Otto I in 962 and dissolved by the Hapsburg emperor Francis I in 1806. Throughout its history there was a wide gap between its real political power and its theoretical position in Europe. At its height (roughly, 962–1250) it was a loose German-Italian confederation and the emperor's power was usually limited to his own family possessions and such nobles as he could overawe with superior force. But in medieval political theory it was the descendent of imperial Rome and the empire of Charlemagne. Medieval theory demanded unity in both church and state, with the papacy providing one and the empire the other. However, their powers and claims overlapped, causing frequent conflict. At one time or another the empire laid claim to almost every European state, but its real power was always limited to Germany, parts of eastern France, and (before 1250) to Italy. All the emperors were at least theoretically elected, after 1356 by a body composed of seven German princes or electors. There was also an administrative body, the imperial Diet, but its powers were vague. Among the greatest emperors were: Otto I of Saxony (962–973); Henry III of Franconia (1039–1056), perhaps the most powerful of the medieval emperors; Henry IV of Franconia (1056–1105) whose struggle with pope Gregory VII marked a turning point in the relations between the two powers; Frederick Barbarossa of Hohenstauffen (1152–1190) and the brilliant Frederick II of Hohenstauffen (1212–1250), under whom the conflict with the church continued, ending in the downfall of the Hohenstauffens and the virtual destruction of the medieval empire. It was revived by the Hapsburgs as an essentially Germanic confederation around which revolved the other Hapsburg titles and possessions. All the emperors after 1483 were Hapsburgs. The empire lasted on into the 19th century, when it lost all political significance and was dissolved during the Napoleonic wars.

Home Loan Banks. A series of banks set up in 1932 to lend money on mortgages to banks and building and loan associations. The function was later enlarged in the Home Owners Loan Corporation and the Federal Housing Authority.

Home Office. British Department of Home Affairs, the duties of which cover miscellaneous domestic matters, particularly the oversight of the police throughout Great Britain, elections, and naturalization.

Home Owners Loan Corporation. An independent U. S. government agency set up in 1933 to stabilize the real estate market and prevent excessive foreclosures on mortgaged homes by providing loans with which to finance first mortgages. It has been liquidating its loans and not loaning since 1936.

home rule. 1. The plan of government

which permits a city (or in some cases a county) to draw up its own charter and establish a form of government of its own choosing, within the general framework of state laws. See CITY CHARTER. 2. Term applied to the political goal of the Irish (and some Scottish) who desired independence from England.

homestead. 1. A farm which was formerly public land, worked and lived upon by the person who owns it or is in the process of becoming the owner. Often it is more or less exempt from the normal seizure of property for debt. 2. To settle on and work a farm which was formerly public land with the intention of qualifying as the owner.

homestead policy. A government policy of giving public land in the West to settlers for a very low price. Under the Homestead Act of 1862, a person could get 160 acres for a $10 registration fee and a promise to cultivate the land for five years. In some cases title could be obtained in less than five years at a nominal price, such as $1.25 per acre.

honest broker. Term applied to Bismarck, German Imperial Chancellor, as a result of the Berlin Conference, at which all the great powers except Germany received some territorial additions. On the surface it appeared that Bismarck had been honest and disinterested in supervising gains for others without claiming any for his own state, though he had in fact thereby preserved a strong diplomatic position for Germany, and the continued diplomatic isolation of France which he desired. See BERLIN, TREATY OF.

honest graft. A distinction made by the New York politician George Washington Plunkett, meaning that a political figure can legitimately use his inside information for financial gain,

such as the unearned increment on land which will result from forthcoming public improvements. The profit will go to someone anyway, he said, so he considered it quite honest for a politician, knowing of the pending improvements, to buy the land and pocket the increase in value.

Honor Court. See COURT OF SOCIAL HONOR.

Hoover moratorium. The suspension of payments of principal and interest on war debts and reparations from July 1, 1931, to June 30, 1932. The plan was suggested by President Hoover in the hope of mitigating the world financial crisis.

Hoovercrat. Southern Democrat who voted for Herbert Hoover in 1928 when Hoover broke the Solid South.

Horst Wessel Lied (HAWRST VES-uhl LEET). Nazi song written by Horst Wessel, young storm troop leader shot in 1930. He was living at the time with a prostitute.

hostage. 1. Person seized by enemy armed forces to induce his fellow countrymen to act or refrain from acting in a certain way. If they refuse, his life is forfeited. 2. Any person held as a forfeit for the conduct of others.

hostilities. Overt acts of war such as the capture of ships or attacks by armies. At the beginning, during (as by a truce or armistice), and at the end of a war, hostilities need not coincide precisely with the legal state of war. See WAR.

hot oil. American slang term for oil produced or taken from storage in amounts over a permitted state quota. The power of the president to enforce these quotas by forbidding the transportation of such oil in interstate commerce was thrown out by the Supreme Court in the "Hot Oil" cases of 1935. Congress then explicitly forbade shipment of such oil.

hot potato. American slang for a hot political issue.

hot pursuit, doctrine of. The rule of international law that pursuit of a vessel which has committed an offense within the territorial waters of a state may be continued out upon the high seas if begun within territorial waters.

House, the. Term for the House of Representatives.

house arrest. A form of official detention requiring a person to remain in his home.

House Calendars. The schedules of bills reported to the House of Representatives. Appropriation bills, which must originate in the House, are placed on the Calendar of the Whole House on the State of the Union, usually referred to as the Union Calendar. Nonappropriation public bills are placed on the House Calendar. Private bills are placed on the Private Calendar, the full title of which is the Calendar of the Committee of the Whole House. This separation makes it possible to consider together various bills in the same category.

House of Assembly. Title of the lower house of parliament in the Union of South Africa and formerly in India.

House of Commons. The elective or lower house of the British parliament. It is much more important than the House of Lords. Dissolution of the Cabinet results from an adverse vote in the House of Commons and this house may, under special circumstances, pass legislation not requiring passage in the House of Lords.

House of Councilors. Upper house in the Japanese Parliament, established by the Constitution of 1946 to replace the House of Peers. Its members are elected.

House of Delegates. The name of the lower house of the state legislature in Maryland, Virginia and West Virginia.

House of Lords. The upper house of the British parliament. It is composed largely of the members of the hereditary English peerage, but includes also 26 "lords spiritual" (2 archbishops and 24 bishops of the Church of England), about 35 representatives of the Scottish and Irish peers, 7 "law lords" and the royal princes.

House of Peers. Former upper house of the Japanese parliament, replaced by the House of Councilors in the Constitution of 1946. Its members were part hereditary peers, part elected, and part appointed by the emperor for life.

House of Representatives. The lower and larger house in the United States Congress, many state legislatures and the Japanese parliament. In Congress the House of Representatives has the special function of originating money bills. In most cases its members are apportioned according to population.

housing. The problem of providing satisfactory residences. In many countries it has come under government direction in order to provide better accommodations for low economic groups or to provide residences quickly in the vicinity of factories turning out supplies needed for war.

H. R. House Bill.

H. Res. House resolution.

H. R. 1776. In the United States Congress, House Resolution 1776, the Lend-Lease Act of January 29, 1941. See LEND-LEASE ACT.

Hull trade agreements. See RECIPROCAL TRADE AGREEMENTS.

Hundred Days. The term used for the time between the return of Napoleon to Paris from Elba, March 20, 1815, and the date of the restoration of the Bourbon monarch, Louis XVIII, on June 28. Hence, any brief return to power.

Hungarian optants. Persons of Hungarian nationality prior to 1918 residing in territories taken from Hungary by the Treaty of Trianon who chose to remain Hungarian and who moved to Hungary after the territories came under the control of other states, especially Romania. Those who did not thus "opt" for Hungarian citizenship, but remained in the territories, took on the nationality of the new jurisdiction, as for example Romanian.

Hussein-McMahon Agreement. A series of letters exchanged between King Hussein of the Hedjaz and Sir Henry McMahon of Great Britain between July 1915 and January 1916. The former claimed the right to rule practically all the Arabian peninsula in return for revolting against Turkey, while the latter made exceptions of Turks, Christian Arabs, semi-independent Arab chiefs, British interests in Mesopotamia and British obligations to France. There was no common understanding as a result of these letters, and the term "agreement" is misleading.

hustings. British counterpart of the term stump as used in the United States. Literally any place from which a candidate speaks during a parliamentary election campaign.

hyphenate *or* **hyphenated American.** A person whose nationality is described by some other word in addition to American, as German-American or Irish-American. Such distinctions were particularly deplored by Theodore Roosevelt, who coined the term and who wanted Americans to have a loyalty only to the United States.

I

ICC. See INTERSTATE COMMERCE COMMISSION.

"I'd rather be right than be president." Statement used by Henry Clay on more than one occasion to his friends, and in a letter in 1839, and again in a speech in the Senate in 1850.

idealist. One who believes that politics should function according to ideals or lofty principles. The term is usually applied to a person advocating such ideals without any knowledge of, or willingness to compromise with, the practical difficulties involved.

identic. Identical, for example, as applied to diplomatic notes dispatched by two or more states to another state.

ideology. The sum of the political ideas or doctrines of a distinguishable class or group of people, such as the communist, fascist or middle class ideology.

"I do not choose to run." Equivocal response of President Calvin Coolidge in answer to a question as to whether he would be a presidential candidate in 1928. Having served parts of two terms it was not clear whether his candidacy would violate the then tradition of a president's serving only two terms. He meant he was willing to be drafted, but nobody drafted him.

I. G. F. I. G. Farbenindustrie—German chemical trust which reached into much of German industry, and whose plants were to be destroyed under the provisions of the Potsdam Declaration in 1945.

I.L.O. See INTERNATIONAL LABOR ORGANIZATION.

immigration. The movement into a country of persons who are not citizens thereof. Such "immigrants" are usually thought of as seeking a more or less permanent residence and are not merely tourists or itinerant business men or students. See IMMIGRATION LAWS.

immigration laws, of United States. Laws governing the entrance of aliens into the United States. In general paupers and criminals are barred. Up to 154,000 Europeans may enter each year on a basis of quotas for different countries based on the proportion of each nationality in the United States population in 1920. Many of the larger quotas have not been filled for many years. Latin Americans have no special restrictions. Asiatics, except Chinese, are excluded because they are not eligible to become citizens. There are exceptions to these general geographical rules for transients and students.

immunity. The exemption from the application of a rule or jurisdiction. See, for example, DIPLOMATIC PRIVILEGES AND IMMUNITIES.

impartiality. One of the basic responsibilities of a neutral toward a belligerent in wartime. See NEUTRALITY.

impeachment. Charges of crimes and misdemeanors against civil officials produced as grounds for removal of the officials from office. In Congress impeachment is a function of the House of Representatives, where the charges are drawn up after committee investigation. The trial on the charges is held in the Senate. The impeach-

ment is often inaccurately confused with the trial itself.

imperial. Pertaining to an empire or an emperor.

Imperial Conference. A meeting of representatives of the British Commonwealth for the discussion of common problems. It usually meets every four years with occasional special meetings. There is a permanent secretariat located in London.

Imperial House Law. The law regulating the succession to the throne in Japan.

imperial preference. Economic policy within the British Commonwealth by which members grant preferential treatment to imports from other parts of the Commonwealth over imports from the rest of the world.

Imperial Service Order. A British honor bestowed upon distinguished civil servants. It is not one of the orders of knighthood. See ORDERS OF KNIGHTHOOD.

imperialism. A policy which aims at creating and maintaining an empire, a state of vast size comprising many nations and tribes, all of which are subject to one central government. The first Empire in western civilization was created by Alexander the Great of Macedonia who ruled much of Europe and Asia. The Roman Empire contained even vaster regions in Europe, Asia and Africa. The Holy Roman Empire of the Middle Ages, the Turkish or Ottoman Empire, the colonial Empire of Spain, the huge Empire of the Russian Czars, the British Empire branching over six continents, the Austrian Empire containing many nations in Central Europe, Napoleon's French Empire and finally Hitler's short-lived German Reich or Empire, are all examples of various kinds of imperialism. In the Far East, Japan and China founded vast empires.

Some empires serve military conquest, others economic or religious expansion. Some arise through gradual or sudden forceful annexations, others, less often, by voluntary associations. Successful imperialism usually carries some spiritual message: the appeal of a deified emperor, the message of a universal faith, the knowledge of a common past, the desire for a common future or the blessings of civilization. In the modern age empires were created by the ideal of economic self-sufficiency, mercantilism and isolation from the rest of the world. Modern imperialism was greatly stimulated by the discovery of America and Australia and the unknown parts of Asia and Africa that lent themselves to economic exploitation.

The term can also be used to connote any development of foreign trade, which makes use of political means to attain its ends. Financial control enables a large power to run backward nations without directly assuming political responsibility. At the beginning of the 20th century the United States foreign policy was called imperialistic, when conducting a so-called dollar-diplomacy in Latin America.

President Wilson's idea of self-determination of nations was directly opposed to imperialism. In another way the British tendency of developing the Empire into a free association of independent dominions, the British Commonwealth of Nations, works toward the liquidation of imperialism. The principle of international trusteeship over colonies advanced by the UN charter also aims at combatting imperialism. See ISOLATIONISM, MERCANTILISM, NAZISM, SELF-DETERMINATION, DOLLAR-DIPLOMACY, WILSONIAN DEMOCRACY, UNITED NATIONS CHARTER (APPENDIX).

imperium in imperio (im-PEE-ree-um in im-PEE-ree-oh). Literally a rule, dominion or jurisdiction within another, meaning that a segment within a jurisdiction is not under its control but a rule unto itself. For example, a small aristocratic or militaristic group within a state which is above the rule of the state and acts as it sees fit.

implied powers. Powers that are not expressly granted by the Constitution of the United States to Congress, but which may be implied as residing in Congress because of other powers which are expressly conferred. The first important question of this kind arose over the establishment of a bank by Congress. Power to do this was not stated in the Constitution, but was implied from the powers specifically granted Congress to tax, borrow money, regulate commerce, and support the army and navy.

import duty. A tax on goods imported into a country.

impost. A tax or duty, particularly on imports.

impressment. Seizure of individuals and forcing them to serve in the armed forces.

I. M. R. O. *or* **Imro.** Internal Macedonian Revolutionary Organization. A revolutionary group organized about 1895 working for the independence of Macedonia, the hinterland of Salonika, Greece. When the group was organized both Bulgaria and Macedonia were still under Turkish control and the Imro worked also for Bulgarian independence. Its chief weapons were assassination, terrorism, and crisis-producing raids by comitadjis or armed bands into neighboring countries. See MACEDONIA, COMITADJI.

in absentia (in ab-SEN-shuh). Latin phrase meaning in one's absence.

inauguration. The formal installation

into office of an elected president or governor.

incentive payment. A kind of bonus to induce a person to perform his tasks in a certain way. Such payments have been made by the Federal government to farmers under the Agricultural Adjustment Administration for changing the production of certain crops, and to industrial concerns to their employees for superior production records.

incident. An event which attains political significance because it creates friction, particularly between two or more states.

income tax. Tax on a person's income, as opposed to a tax on his capital or property.

incorporated territories. United States territories in which practically all the provisions of the Constitution are extended to the inhabitants because they are considered to be a part of the United States in a way that the other possessions are not. Arizona, New Mexico, and Oklahoma were such territories before becoming states; Alaska and Hawaii are now. See UNINCORPORATED TERRITORIES.

indemnity. 1. Charges assessed against a person or state for compensation for a wrongful act. 2. Charges assessed against a vanquished state by a victor in war. Recently the term reparations has been used instead.

indenture. A long-term contract binding a person to work for another, usually as a servant. Such contracts were numerous in the 17th and 18th centuries in the American colonies as a way of supplying needed labor. Some indentured persons came of their own will, others were kidnapped and some were convicts. Terms of service varied from three to seven years. The indentured person was commonly given a small tract of land which was his after the indenture ex-

pired. They were mostly English, Scotch and Germans.

independence. Control by a state of its own foreign relations as well as of its own internal affairs.

independent agency *or* **establishment.** A United States administrative agency or organization not a part of one of the ten departments presided over by cabinet members. Among the first were the Civil Service Commission and the Interstate Commerce Commission. Many of the alphabetical agencies established as part of the New Deal or for the administration of the war effort have been such agencies.

Independent Labor Party. A small British labor party favoring immediate and broad socialization of the means of production and industrial unionism as opposed to craft unionism. Founded by Keir Hardie in 1893. Philip Snowden was one of its prominent leaders. Although always small, it served to propagandize socialism, and the Labor Party has adopted part of its program. It elected 3 members in the parliamentary elections of 1945.

independent voter. A person who does not feel himself a party "regular," but votes for whoever he believes is the better candidate for office, regardless of party.

indeterminate sentence. A sentence which does not have a definite time limit.

Indian National Congress. See ALL-INDIA NATIONALIST CONGRESS.

Indian Office. The office of Indian affairs in the U. S. Interior Department. This office oversees the health, and general welfare of the American Indians, and provides for their education.

Indian reservations. Part of the public land of the United States set aside for the use and habitation of the Indians. See INDIAN OFFICE.

Indiana ballot. A ballot in which the candidates for office at a given election are placed in columns according to their party affiliation, all the Democrats in one column, all the Republicans in another. Often called a party-column ballot, as opposed to the office-group, or Massachusetts ballot. See MASSACHUSETTS BALLOT. Usually there is a circle or square at the top of each party column in which the voter may indicate by a single cross his desire to vote for all the candidates of a single party.

Indians, status of. American born Indians who were not citizens were granted citizenship by law in 1924. Over 200,000 still live on reservations and thus have the government as a kind of guardian.

indictment. The formal charge that a person has committed a specified crime and that a trial is warranted. Usually drawn up by a prosecuting attorney and given by him to a grand jury. If the grand jury agrees that the person should stand trial, it labels the indictment "a true bill," and the person, if apprehended, is brought to trial.

indirect election. A method of selecting elective officials whereby the voters choose representatives who do the actual voting for them. The United States Constitution provides for the indirect election of the President and Vice-President by an Electoral College, but in practice its members no longer exercise their own discretion but vote as directed by the majority or plurality of voters in each state. Before 1913 United States Senators were indirectly elected by the state legislatures, but this was abolished in favor of direct election by the 17th Amendment to the Constitution.

indirect tax. A tax which is not paid directly but indirectly, as, for example, as part of the price of goods bought in a retail store.

indispensable man. A term applied to President Franklin D. Roosevelt, particularly when running for re-election in 1940, seriously by his friends and ironically by his opponents.

individualism. The conviction that people should be allowed to think and act for themselves and to regard themselves the best judges of their own interests. Individualism is often used as the opposite of totalitarianism. Modern individualism arose partly through a belief in the supreme worth of the individual and partly through the emergence of an economic system based on private property and free exchange. The Reformation strongly emphasized the individualistic elements of Christianity and such principles as freedom of conscience became one of the pillars of individualism. The prophets of modern individualism lived in the 18th and 19th century, mainly in France, England and America. They were John Locke, Adam Smith, Jeremy Bentham, John Stuart Mill, Benjamin Franklin, Thomas Jefferson, Thomas Paine. They believed that the state and the government should not enforce uniform behavior on its subjects but should rather protect their individual rights and liberties. The American Bill of Rights is an eminently individualistic document. In the economic sphere individualism believes that the absence of government regulations, free trade, a spontaneous division of labor and a free exchange of goods and services increases the welfare of everybody. Extreme individualism results in chaos and anarchy, while the neglect of individual rights and of the dignity of man results in tyranny or totalitarianism. See LIBERALISM, UTILITARIANISM, FREE TRADE,

Indo-Chinese Federation

142

LAISSEZ FAIRE, FREEDOM, LIBERTY, CIVIL LIBERTY.

Indo-Chinese Federation. The name given by the French Government after World War II to their former colony of Indo-China, in response to promises of greater self-government made by General deGaulle during the war. On March 7, 1946 the French High Commissioner at Saigon recognized the Viet Nam Republic (formerly Annam) as a "free state within the Indo-Chinese Federation and French Union." On June 1 a similar announcement was issued concerning a new Cochin Chinese Republic, and on September 15, 1946 an agreement was signed in Paris between the French Government and President Ho Chi-minh of Viet Nam. However, there was basic disagreement as to the degree of independence to be given the two states, and revolt flared, especially in Viet Nam. General Leclerc was sent to Indo-China with re-inforcements for the French in December, 1946.

indoctrination. Process of establishing in the minds of others the acceptance of certain principles which have been set up as bases for the achievement of certain political ends.

Indonesia, United States of. A plan for granting independence to the peoples of the Dutch East Indies while maintaining their allegiance to the Dutch Crown. It was adopted by the Netherlands Parliament on December 20, 1946. The plan was agreed upon by the Dutch and Indonesians with the aid of a British mediator, and it includes: (1) Dutch recognition of the Indonesian Republic (the islands of Java, Sumatra and Madura); (2) formation on January 1, 1949 of a United States of Indonesia to consist of the Indonesian Republic plus the autonomous states of Borneo and East Indonesia (Bali, Celebes and the islands to the east except New Guinea); (3) a Netherlands-Indonesia Union under the Dutch Crown, each member to have equal status. The plan was the result of a bitter conflict between Javanese nationalists and the Dutch (aided by British troops) which broke out after World War II. The movement in Java was lead by President Achmed Soekarno and Premier Sutan Sjahrir of the Indonesian Republic, who helped formulate the new plan. The Provisional State of East Indonesia was proclaimed by Queen Wilhelmina on December 25, 1946.

inductee. Person conscripted or "inducted" into the armed forces.

industrial revolution. The economic and technological developments which during the 18th century in England (and later in the rest of the civilized world) established the modern industrial system. Based on new sources of power, the main features of this revolution were: (1) invention of new machines, such as Watt's steam engine, spinning machines, coke-smelted iron, Wedgwood's new process of making pottery, etc., revolutionizing the manufacturing of certain basic goods; (2) the rise of a class of big industrialists owning large plants and factories and the gradual decline of the small independent masters and artisans; (3) the corresponding rise of a larger wage-earning class and the disappearance of close personal relations between employers and employees; (4) expansion of domestic, foreign and colonial trade, improvement of roads and sea transportation; (5) growth of large industrial cities and depopulation of the countryside in consequence of the new factory system; (6) expansion of banking and financial facilities, and of joint stock companies, which attracted capital and savings of private individuals and laid the basis of the modern capitalist system.

Industrial Workers of the World. A revolutionary industrial union founded in the United States in 1905 in opposition to the craft unionism of the American Federation of Labor. It opposed collective bargaining and political activity in favor of strikes and sabotage. It reached its height in 1912 with about 100,000 members, but has since lost ground to the Communist party and the Congress of Industrial Organizations. Popularly known as the "Wobblies."

industrial union. A union which enrolls or tries to enroll all the employees of a given industry, even though they have widely varying functions. Most units of the C.I.O. are industrial unions. See CRAFT UNION, CONGRESS OF INDUSTRIAL ORGANIZATION.

infant industry. A term used during the controversies over a high protective tariff to mean those industries in the United States which were new and needed protection from foreign competition. There was a tendency, however, to maintain their tariff protection long after they had become well-established.

infiltrate. To penetrate and permeate. Used in connection with the dissemination of new or foreign political doctrines, or of troops or guerillas within enemy lines.

inflation. The process which occurs in an uncontrolled or partly controlled economy, where prices may rise and fall, when the amount of money which is used for spending becomes relatively larger than the amount of goods and services available in the market. As a result more money is available for less goods and services, and the general price level goes up as consumers begin to compete for the goods in which there is a relative shortage. If the supply of money for spending continues to expand, prices will go up correspondingly and a spiral ensues sending prices higher and higher. As a result a dollar will buy less and less. If this inflation is not stopped by reducing in some way the amount of money available for spending, or by fixing prices, or producing more goods, it might develop into a so-called "runaway inflation" in which money loses its value almost completely. When this occurs people lose faith in the currency and money changes hands faster and faster, starting an additional spiral which accelerates the increase in prices, and so on.

Deflation is the opposite of inflation. It occurs in a free-market economy when the amount of goods and services available for consumption is not, or cannot be, bought with the amount of money available in the public's pocket for spending. This results in a downward spiral of lowered wages and prices, in decreased production, and in unemployment. In a deflation the value of money rises, in so far as the same amount of money will buy more and more goods as prices continue to fall.

The effect of inflation and deflation is different for different groups of people. In an inflation those people who receive their income in fixed amounts of money (salaries, wages, fixed interest-bearing investments, pensions, etc.) will suffer most. Even if their incomes are raised, they will hardly keep pace with the rise of prices and will, in fact, always lag behind them. Wages will usually be raised somewhat faster than salaries or pensions because wage earners are organized in unions in most cases and can win a rise in wages in case the cost of living rises. People living on business profits, no matter whether owners of large industries or of a small store, fare far better in an inflation as their incomes tend to increase proportionately with the rise in prices. At the end of the inflation this group will be relatively better off than those whose income is fixed in terms of money. In a runaway inflation people try to get rid of any money in their possession, and rush to buy real estate, precious stones, and other tangible things of continuing value. After wars and revolutions this often happens, as goods are scarce and inflationary trends are accelerated by the people's lack of confidence in the government and in the currency. Such a runaway inflation occurred in Germany in the early 1920's, resulting in an impoverishment of the salary-earning middle classes. A similar situation took place after the second World War in Greece, Hungary, Romania and several other countries, etc. See BUSINESS CYCLE.

information. An official statement by a prosecuting attorney that the facts regarding some act warrant a criminal trial. It is a substitute for an indictment by a grand jury and is used in many states to facilitate the administration of justice. It is not used in the federal courts as the Constitution requires an indictment or presentment by a grand jury.

inheritance tax. A tax levied on property or a share of property which is inherited. It is a graduated tax with a low rate on small amounts and a high rate on large estates.

initial. To give a preliminary assent, as in the negotiation of a treaty, to the general principles laid down. It is not as formal and binding as a signature, and arises from the suggestion of changes, for example, or some other factor the agreement to which the negotiator must secure from his government.

initiative. The process by which legislation or constitutional amendments are proposed by the people in the form of petitions. It is in use in many states and cities in the United States. Indirect initiative permits the people to propose legislation for consideration by a state legislature or city council, and in some cases there is a provision that the voters may vote directly for the issue if it fails to pass the legislative body. Direct initiative provides for the popular vote on the issue without reference to a legislative body. The petitions must be signed by a given number or percentage of the qualified voters before the issue is placed on the ballot. Initiative is usually linked with referendum and recall. See REFERENDUM, RECALL.

injunction. A court order directing a certain person or certain persons to do, or more usually, to refrain from doing a particular act. It is the most important of the remedies of equity. See EQUITY.

Inland Waterways Corporation. A United States government agency set up June 3, 1924 under the War Department and later transferred to the Commerce Department. Its function is to develop inland water and rail transportation and water terminals.

innocent passage. The right of merchant ships to pass freely through the territorial waters of a state without, except technically, being considered as coming into the jurisdiction of that state. It is not settled whether warships enjoy this right except along international highways. The degree to which this right should be extended to airplanes is coming in for increased consideration. See AEROPOLITICS, AIR JURISDICTION.

inquest. An official inquiry. Usually refers to the one held by a coroner regarding the facts of death from unusual causes.

Inquisition. The office founded by the medieval Roman Catholic Church for inquiry into heresy. As organized in the 12th and 13th centuries to combat heresy in South France, Germany and Italy, it was usually in the hands of the Dominicans or Franciscans, but the secular authorities were normally involved in the proceedings, and the death penalty by burning was carried out by the State rather than the Church. Torture was sanctioned as a means of extracting confessions, but repentance was the chief aim of the Inquisition at least as long as it remained under the control of the Church. It gained its greatest notoriety in Spain and the New World when it was used by the Spanish monarchy for essentially political purposes.

in-service training. Training to make a person more efficient in his job, taken after the person has been employed and is in service.

inspection laws. Laws providing for control of certain commodities, or standards thereof, by official inspection, as for example food products.

instructions. 1. Directions to delegates to the national party nominating conventions to vote for a certain candidate. Delegates who are free to vote in any way they please are "uninstructed." 2. Directions to diplomatic and consular agents of a country from their superiors in their home capitals. See DESPATCH.

Insular Affairs, Bureau of. A branch of the War Department which had control of certain United States island possessions. This function was turned over to the Division of Territories and Island Possessions of the Interior Department July 1, 1939.

insular possessions. The island possessions of the United States, such as the Hawaiian Islands, Virgin Islands and Puerto Rico. See also INCORPORATED and UNINCORPORATED TERRITORIES.

insurgency. The status in international law granted to a group of revolutionists who do not possess sufficient organization to warrant the granting of the status of belligerency. They are granted certain belligerent rights and their actions at sea, for example, are not considered as piracy. See BELLIGERENCY.

insurgent. 1. In international law, a supporter of an armed revolution which has been granted a recognition of insurgency. See INSURGENCY. 2. In U. S. history, a general term applied to a party member who revolts against the party leadership. More specifically, one of the Republicans who rebelled against the conservative party leadership in 1909 and 1910. Most of them joined the Progressive Party in the election of 1912.

insurrection. An armed uprising against the internal authority of a state.

intangible property. Property which does not have physical substance but represents a legal right with property value, such as a bond, a share of stock, or a patent.

intangible property taxation. Taxation of intangible property. It is not a very satisfactory form of taxation as this kind of property lends itself so readily to concealment.

Integralista. Member of a subversive pro-Nazi organization which existed in Brazil until its unsuccessful attempt to seize power in 1938.

integration. Close co-ordination between administrative offices on any given level of government such as a city or state. The city manager plan of city government is one of the best examples of an integrated administration. See CENTRALIZATION.

intention, declaration of. Statement filed by an alien affirming his purpose to become a United States citizen. This statement is commonly referred to as taking out one's "first papers."

inter-Allied debts. Debts of the various Allies of World War I owed to one another, chiefly to the United States. Commonly referred to as war debts, as distinguished from reparations, or debts owed by the losers.

Inter-American Affairs, Office of Coordinator. See CO-ORDINATOR OF INTER-AMERICAN AFFAIRS

Inter-American Defense Board. A board of military experts which met regularly in Washington to discuss and recommend measures of hemisphere defense. It was set up in January 1942 at a meeting of the foreign ministers of the American republics at Rio de Janeiro.

Inter-American Highway. See ALL-AMERICAN HIGHWAY.

Inter-Governmental Committee on Political Refugees. An international committee set up after the Evian conference on refugee problems in 1938 for the purpose of resettling the refugees from Germany. See EVIAN CONFERENCE.

Interior, Department of the. One of the major United States executive departments, established March 3, 1849. Its chief function is the promotion or control of various internal matters such as mining, parks, conservation and wild life, the geological survey, Indian service, and national territories.

intern. To detain and prevent from departure or moving about freely, usually for the duration of a war, of enemy aliens, prisoners of war or, in the case of neutrals, of members of the armed forces or war vessels of a belligerent.

internal improvements. In general, any project built within the borders of a country, such as canals, roads, or improvements in river and rail transportation. In United States history the

term is applied more specifically to the movement in the first half of the 19th century which urged the use of state and national funds for such projects. In national affairs Henry Clay was a leading advocate, and was opposed by those who believed the Constitution did not grant the federal government such powers. The Erie Canal was an example of state-financed improvements, and the Cumberland or National Road, from Cumberland, Maryland, to Illinois, was an example of national projects. Many of the early railroads were also aided by state or national grants of money or land. Such improvements have since become standard practice, notably highways, river improvements and airports, and the term has almost dropped out of use.

Internal Revenue, Bureau of. The complete title of this bureau is the Office of the Commissioner of Internal Revenue, and it was established in the Treasury Department in 1862. It is primarily charged with the collection of the internal revenues or domestic federal taxes such as the income tax, profits taxes, and taxes on alcoholic beverages and cigarettes.

internal revenue. Taxes collected from sources within a country as opposed to those collected on imports. In the United States the chief sources of this revenue are taxes on incomes, profits, amusements, and production of articles like tobacco, liquor, and playing cards.

international. Pertaining to more than one state.

International. A name applied to three international workingmen's organizations known as the First, Second and Third Internationals. The *First International* was founded in London in 1864 by Karl Marx and Friedrich Engels. Its full title was the International Working Men's Association, and it was also known as "The International." It was a loose organization of trade unions and it became increasingly socialist in policy. The collapse of the Paris Commune in 1871, which the French members of the First International joined but did not instigate, and the split between the Marxist Socialists and the Bakunin Anarchists in 1872 lead to its decline. Its last meeting was in Philadelphia in 1876. The *Second* (*Socialist*) *International* was founded in 1889 as an organization of the various socialist parties. Its early congresses were devoted to discussions of party tactics and the like, but it made a serious though unsuccessful effort to organize the working classes against the outbreak of World War I. During the war it fell apart, but was rebuilt, chiefly at Hamburg in 1923, when the Communists (who had already formed the Third International) were excluded. The *Third* (*Communist*) *International* was founded in Moscow in 1919 under the leadership of Lenin and Trotsky as the international organ of the various Communist parties. It was known as the Comitern and revived much of the revolutionary policy of the First International. Russian influence was always strongest, though it was active all over the world. It was dissolved in May, 1943 during World War II.

international boundary commission. A commission established for the purpose of delimiting an international boundary.

International Brigade. One of the military units fighting on the side of the Loyalists in the Spanish Civil War. It received its name from the fact that it was largely composed of non-Spaniards—Americans, French, Russians, British, and others.

international concession. A right granted by one state, usually technologically backward, to another or to a foreign corporation for the construction and operation of some service like a railway, port, or telegraph line.

International Court of Justice. An international court, the statute, or constitution, of which was drawn up at the United Nations conference in San Francisco in 1945. It is a court for the United Nations, but it differs little in composition or powers from its predecessor, the Permanent Court of International Justice. The judges, again nominated by the national groups of the Permanent Court of Arbitration, are elected by the General Assembly and the Security Council of the United Nations, and obligations under the Optional Clause of the previous court are continued under the new court. See PERMANENT COURT OF INTERNATIONAL JUSTICE, OPTIONAL CLAUSE.

international crimes. A popular expression meaning any flagrant violation by individuals or states of rules established by international law, such as piracy, slave-trading, opium smuggling, war crimes, etc. Leaders of countries preparing for aggressive wars or persecuting religious, racial or political minorities may also be counted among international criminals. See WAR CRIMES, WAR CRIMES TRIALS, INTERNATIONAL LAW, SANCTIONS.

international deliquency. A failure on the part of a state to conform to its international duties.

international ethics. The moral principles which should guide nations in their relations with each other. Such principles have been of influence in the establishment of some of the rules of international law, as for example those which attempt to mitigate the horrors of war.

international highway. Road or waterway open to the free use of more than one nation. See INTERNATIONAL WATERWAYS.

International Labor Office. The secretariat of the International Labor Organization. See INTERNATIONAL LABOR ORGANIZATION.

International Labor Organization. An international institution set up in 1919 under the provisions of the Versailles Treaty. Its aim is the improvement of labor conditions throughout the world. It draws up draft conventions to be submitted to the member nations and carries on extensive research. Members of the League of Nations were automatically members of the I.L.O., but the organization has worked independently of the League. Other nations may join, as did the United States in 1934. The I.L.O. has a General Conference which meets at least once a year and is composed of four representatives from each member, two nominated by the government of the country, one by labor and one by management. The representatives, however, vote as individuals rather than as a national unit. The International Labor Office, in Geneva, is the permanent secretariat of the I.L.O.

international law. The body of rules commonly observed and considered as binding in the relations of states. Such rules grow from international agreement and custom, and may be found also in the decisions of international tribunals and in the commentaries of authoritative writers. Agreements among states appeared in the interstate relations of antiquity, but the present concept is modern, Hugo Grotius (1583–1645) of the Netherlands being known as the father of international law. The rules included such things as the classification of states, their rights (such as territorial jurisdiction) and duties, the matter of nationality and naturaliza-

tion, and the regulation of relations in time of war, both between belligerents and with neutrals. In addition to gradual growth, they have been expanded from time to time in such great international conferences as the congresses of Vienna and Berlin, the Hague Peace Conferences and the conferences of Paris in 1856 and 1919 and of San Francisco in 1945. International law lacks certain of the advantages of municipal law, as there is no international legislature to formulate new universally binding rules, there is, as yet, no international policing agency, and the persons in international law are sovereign states which cannot be bound without their own consent. See SANCTIONS, AGGRESSOR, NEUTRALITY.

international legislation. There is, of course, no real international lawmaking in the sense of a national legislature passing by majority vote a new law which will be binding on all persons within the jurisdiction of the state. The term international legislation is used to describe great multilateral treaties which formulate new broad general rules of international law. Usually such treaties establish some form of international administrative organization set up to perform some needed function within the community of nations. See INTERNATIONAL LAW, INTERNATIONAL ORGANIZATION,

international organization. Organizations the members of which are states represented by properly accredited delegates. In a sense any large alliance of states is an international organization. The most important and ambitious international organizations attempt to promote the peace, welfare and security of the whole world (League of Nations, UN); others deal only with certain regions (Pan American Union); others again only with certain fields of international co-operation (International Labor Organization, International Postal Union etc.). See INTERNATIONAL LEGISLATION, INTERNATIONAL LAW, LEAGUE OF NATIONS, UNITED NATIONS.

international police. A body composed of representatives from, and set up and administered by or on behalf of, a group of states. Such a force has been used in a few instances of limited scope. Currently the question is raised as to the advisability of establishing such a force on a worldwide basis.

international relations. 1. Any dealings between states. Usually used to describe official political relations. 2. The study of international relations in the sense of 1.

International Settlement. Prior to World War II a separate municipality, forming a part of Shanghai, which enjoyed extraterritorial rights. It was jointly administered by the leading foreign powers, except France, which had a separate concession nearby. Its Council included American, British, Chinese, and Japanese citizens.

International Telecommunications Union. The oldest public international union which began in 1865 with the control of telegraph and was later extended to radio. Periodic conferences are held and the permanent office or bureau is at Berne, Switzerland. It publishes a monthly journal and such special items as an international listing of radio ship and shore stations.

international waterways. Rivers, canals or straits which are open to the commerce of all nations, often by international agreement or treaty. The Suez, Panama and Kiel canals are such waterways, and are also open to the warships of all nations, at least in peacetime. Among international rivers are the Rhine, Elbe, Congo, Amazon, Danube and St. Lawrence.

Internationale, The. Anthem of the revolutionary working class movement, especially of the Third International. First sung in 1871, the music by Adolphe Degeyter and the original French words by Eugene Pottier. See THIRD INTERNATIONAL.

internationalism. A belief that widest possible co-operation between nations would considerably advance the welfare of mankind and would assure lasting peace. Some internationalists envisage a world-state as controlling all nations without, however, destroying their identity or independent functions. Various forms of world government were suggested by William Penn, the Abbé de St. Pierre, and the German philosopher Immanuel Kant. A particular kind of internationalism is the orthodox Marxist idea of the world rule of the international proletariat. The establishment of the League of Nations after World War I, although failing its purpose of ensuring peace, greatly stimulated the development of internationalism. The United Nations Charter is considered widely among internationalists as a step in the right direction. Internationalists today maintain that the gradual shrinking of the world through the ever increasing speed of air transportation demands a closer drawing together of all nations. The main obstacles in the way of a final success of internationalism are: nationalistic political, economic and military interests; unequal development of the various nations ranging from primitive South Sea Island tribes to highly industrialized countries; existence of different and often hostile political theories in various nations, i. e., fascist Spain, democratic United States and Britain, communist Soviet Russia. See ISOLATIONISM, LEAGUE OF NATIONS, UNITED NATIONS.

internationalize. To place under the control of two or more states concurrently, as a waterway.

internment camp. Place of detention of persons who have been interned. See INTERN.

internuncio. A diplomatic representative of the pope of a class below that of nuncio, hence of the same rank as minister. See NUNCIO, MINISTER.

Interparliamentary Union. An organization made up of members of the legislative bodies of the various countries of the world. They do not officially represent their governments in the meetings, and the organization has thus been an informal and useful means of discussing international problems. It was instrumental in the establishment of the Hague Court of Arbitration.

interpellation. A formal written question on a matter of policy by a member of the French Chamber of Deputies directed to a cabinet minister. It opens the matter for general debate and a vote adverse to the ministry usually forces it from office. The process is found with certain variations in some other parliamentary bodies.

interstate citizenship. Term applied to the right of a citizen of one state of the United States to be eligible, usually after a lapse of time, to be treated on an equal footing with the local citizens in another state. This right is granted in Article IV, Section 2 of the Constitution, that "citizens of each state shall be entitled to all privileges and immunities of citizens in the several states."

interstate commerce. Business relations across state lines involving, for example, the transportation of passengers and commodities by any of the common carriers, or the transmission of fluids through pipelines or messages by wire or radio.

Interstate Commerce Commission. A commission set up February 4, 1887, for the regulation of matters pertaining to commerce in the United States which crosses state lines. Transmission of information and messages as well as goods is included. Rate-fixing is a most important function, but safety appliances, wages and other things are also regulated.

interstate compact. An agreement between two or more of the United States regarding some common problem such as the distribution of the waters of a river for irrigation purposes.

intervention. Illegal interference by one state in the affairs of another.

interventionist. Term used to indicate a person in the United States who, prior to Pearl Harbor, advocated active participation in World War II or at least whole-hearted support of Britain and Russia.

intransigent. Unwilling to retreat from a diplomatic position, usually a rather extreme one.

intrastate commerce. Business relations in which the movement of goods, persons, or ideas does not extend across the boundaries of a state.

invasion. Movement of an armed force across a boundary line and into a foreign country with the intention of making war.

investigations, Congressional. Inquiries by committees of either house of Congress or by joint committees of both houses. They have been used, especially in the Senate, as a means of overseeing and criticising the activities of the Executive Branch, which is otherwise difficult for Congress to accomplish under the American system of, the separation of powers. While certain investigating committees have been attacked as being inspired chiefly by a desire for publicity, most have served a useful purpose.

inviolability. The principle that a state and certain of its representatives shall not be violated, intruded upon, interfered with, or harmed by agents of another state. It applies to territory, sovereigns, and diplomatic agents, and to such property as legations and consular files.

Invisible Empire. Term used for the Ku Klux Klan. See KU KLUX KLAN.

invisible exports. Items which do not appear on the balance of trade in goods, such as tourist expenditures. See BALANCE OF TRADE.

invisible government. Control of one or more of the various branches of government by a political boss.

"I propose to fight it out on this line if it takes all summer." Word sent by General U. S. Grant from near Spotsylvania Court House, Virginia, to General Henry W. Halleck in Washington on May 11, 1864.

Irgun Zvai Leumi. The National Military Organization, a Zionist extremist resistance group in Palestine, organized in 1935 among members of Hagana who wished to use more forceful means than the Hagana then used. During recent years it has spearheaded the attack in the resistance to British administration in Palestine.

Irish representative peers. Twenty-eight Irish peers elected to membership in the House of Lords for life. They are elected by the whole number of Irish peers.

Iron Curtain. Churchill's term for the barrier preventing the free exchange of persons, ideas and information which the Russians have erected along the western side of the territories under their control or occupation after World War II.

Iron Guard. Romanian fascist organization.

iron ring. Military encirclement, particularly as seen on the part of her neighbors by Germany. See ENCIRCLEMENT.

irreconcilables. Those who cannot be won over to another point of view. Occasionally used to refer to a group of senatorial hold-outs.

irredentism. The principle of nationalism which asserts that a group of people outside the borders of a state that has the same cultural characteristics (or "nationality") as those within the state should be joined to the state. It involves the annexation of the territory the group inhabits. The word is derived from *Italia irredenta*, unredeemed Italy, the term used by the Italians to refer to the Trentino area with its 400,000 Italians which was held by Austria prior to World War I. Occasionally the term was also applied to Corsica and Nice, held by France, Malta, held by Great Britain, and the Italian-speaking sections of Switzerland.

I.S.O. See IMPERIAL SERVICE ORDER.

isolationism. A belief and policy favoring the deliberate abstention of a nation from political and economic co-operation with other nations. Isolationism is often coupled with imperialism, because a large and militarily strong and economically self-sufficient nation may easily believe that it can isolate itself from the rest of the world. This was the idea behind the "splendid isolation" which for a long time dominated British foreign policy. The most remarkable example of isolation from international politics was the American foreign policy in the 19th and early 20th centuries. American isolationism was greatly enhanced by a feeling of security created by the two oceans separating America from the rest of the world. Recent immigrants often turned isolationist from an urge to forget Europe. America's non-participation in the League of Nations and in the World Court; opposition to the repeal of the Neutrality Laws, to Lend-Lease, to the UN and the 1946 loan to Britain were all related to isolationist beliefs. The closer economic and political contacts of the world and the occurrence of two global wars have rendered isolationism a weak basis for national policy. See IMPERIALISM, INTERNATIONALISM, LEAGUE OF NATIONS, WORLD COURT, UNITED NATIONS, NEUTRALITY, NON-INTERVENTION.

isolationist. An advocate or believer in isolationism. See ISOLATIONISM.

issue. A question of public policy in which there are two or more alternatives upon which members of a legislative body may vote, or upon which

the public may express its choice, either directly, as in a referendum, or indirectly, by electing representative officials pledged to carry out a certain alternative.

item veto. The power of an executive official to veto parts or items of bills without vetoing the whole bill. This power is provided the governors of several states, but it has not been given the president of the United States.

ius sanguinis. See JUS SANGUINIS.

ius soli. See JUS SOLI.

I.W.W. See INDUSTRIAL WORKERS OF THE WORLD.

Izvestia. Official newspaper of the government of the USSR, published in Moscow.

J

jackpot. American slang expression for a fund collected during the early years of the century in Illinois from parties interested in the passage or defeat of certain legislation and at the end of the session distributed among the members of the legislature who "went along" and voted on these measures as directed.

Jacksonian democracy. Democratic principles as advocated by President Andrew Jackson (1767–1845). Jackson opposed the aristocratic principle of government and came out vigorously for popular sovereignty. He believed that the common people should govern themselves, to the greatest extent possible, as by holding

public office, even though this might result in an inefficient administration. He expanded manhood suffrage and abolished the congressional caucus system which in the absence of national conventions carried out the nomination of candidates. Jacksonian democracy favored the simple people, the "backwoodsmen," the West against the eastern city population. It opposed bankers and capitalists in a rather emotional way. It tried to unite mechanics and frontiersmen into one strong party. Its opponents often pointed out that Jacksonian democracy led to a somewhat emotional and not always reasoned system of government, could be easily exploited by political demagogy and could give rise to half-dictatorial presidents identifying their actions with the will of the people. It cannot be denied, however, that Jacksonian democracy did much to make the name of democracy popular. The Democratic Party regards Jackson as its founder and commemorates him with annual dinners. See JEFFERSONIAN DEMOCRACY, WILSONIAN DEMOCRACY, POPULAR SOVEREIGNTY, REPUBLIC.

Jameson raid. An unsuccessful attempt by Dr. Leander S. Jameson, friend of Cecil Rhodes and administrator of Rhodesia, to lead a group in seizing the Transvaal from its Boer government in late December, 1895. The incident temporarily halted British expansion in South Africa and intensified the imperialistic friction between Germany and Great Britain.

Japanese Constitution of 1946. A document adopted on August 24, 1946 after approval by General MacArthur, the Allied Supreme Commander. It replaced the Constitution of 1890 and was radically anti-militaristic—renouncing war "forever" as a national policy and prohibiting the maintenance of an army, navy or air force. It abolished the House of Peers, substituting an elective House of Councilors. The powers of the emperor were strictly limited and the special privileges of the Minister of War abolished. It includes a bill of rights and provision for a strong and independent Supreme Court.

Jay Treaty. A United States-British treaty signed for the United States by John Jay on November 19, 1794. It provided for extradition, British withdrawal from certain frontier posts, settlement of various claims for failure to observe the rules of neutrality, commercial and navigation agreements, and the proposal to settle outstanding boundary disputes by a series of commissions.

Jeffersonian Democracy. Democratic principles held by President Thomas Jefferson (1743–1826). They can be found in the American Declaration of Independence of which he was the author. As the chief representative of 18th century enlightenment in America, Jefferson believed strongly in the inalienable rights of the individual to "life, liberty and the pursuit of happiness." He violently opposed despotism, in fact any government which would not respect the Rights of Man and would rule without the consent of the governed. He had a strong belief in reason and in humanity, in the necessity to educate people and in humanitarian principles. He opposed industrialization and the rise of great, densely populated cities. He believed that rural life was far more natural and less artificial than city life. His ideal was an independent, economically self-sufficient community of free farmers governing themselves under the leadership of a benevolent gentry through democratic-republican ideas and institutions. He believed in a weak national authority, in the preservation of state and local government, and in a decentralization of powers as the best safeguard against the rise of despotism. In a sense Jeffersonian democracy relies on enlightened, free, educated and responsible individuals, while Jacksonian democracy emphasizes the will of the broad masses and is frankly sceptical about the disinterestedness of aristocratic leaders. See JACKSONIAN DEMOCRACY, WILSONIAN DEMOCRACY, POPULAR SOVEREIGNTY, LIBERALISM, NATURAL RIGHTS.

Jewish Agency. Organization of Zionist and non-Zionist Jews set up in 1929 as the representative in Palestine of the Jews of the world.

Jewish National Home. Term referring to Palestine, taken from the Balfour Declaration. The Zionists infer that Palestine should become a Jewish-controlled state but the Declaration is ambiguous and there is no unanimity of opinion as to its meaning. See BALFOUR DECLARATION.

Jihad (ji-HAHD). A holy war waged by Mohammedans against unbelievers. In the early days of Mohammedanism the Jihad was considered an essential element of the faith, and under its inspiration Moslem conquests were rapidly expanded. With the decline of Mohammedan power, especially that of Turkey, its use also declined. In 1914 the Turkish Sultan, acting as Caliph, called for a Jihad against the Allies, but he was obeyed chiefly in Turkey itself.

"Jim Crow" Laws. Laws passed by the legislatures of Southern States and in Southern cities following the end of the Reconstruction period, designed to separate whites and Negroes in social life and discourage the Negroes' desire for social equality. Originally these laws concerned travel in trains and other conveyances, but the term now covers legislation forbidding intermarriage and for compulsory separation in schools, restaurants, theaters, factories, hotels and similar places. A Negro is usually defined as anyone possessing one-eighth Negro blood, or more. In 1917 the United States Supreme Court declared unconstitutional city ordinances requiring residential segregation, but the decision has not checked the maintenance of actual segregation through legal subterfuge or unwritten local custom.

jingoism. Aggressive, war-like and militaristic national policy. Derived from the song popular in the British music halls when Disraeli threatened to intervene in the Russo-Turkish war of 1877–78:

> We don't want to fight
> But by jingo if we do,
> We've got the ships, we've got the men
> And we've got the money too.

John Bull. Cartoon and symbolic character typifying Great Britain. The name was first popularized in Dr. John Arbuthnot's *History of John Bull* (1727).

John Doe Warrant. Warrant made out with a fictitious name such as John Doe, made necessary by the fact that the real name of the person wanted is unknown.

Johnson Act. Law of April 13, 1934, prohibiting borrowing in the United States by countries which had defaulted on previous loans.

joint. Participated in by two or more parties.

Joint Board. The joint board of the War and Navy departments set up July 17, 1903, for the study of any matter calling for the common consideration of the two departments. Other joint Army-Navy boards whose titles indicate their functions have been set up since: the Aeronautical Board, the Joint Economy Board, the Joint Munitions Board, and the Joint Committee on Welfare and Recreation.

joint committee. Committee representing two houses of a legislative body. In some states regular committee consideration of legislation takes place in such committees.

Joint Economic Committees. Committees composed of American and Canadians set up June 17, 1941, for coordination of defense resources and the minimizing of postwar reconversion dislocations.

joint resolution. Resolution passed by the Senate and House of Representatives of the U. S. It has the effect of law and may be vetoed.

155

joint session. A legislative session attended by two houses, as, for example the Senate and the House of Representatives of the United States, to hear a message from the President or other chief executive.

Joint War Production Committee. A United States-Canadian agency set up November 5, 1941, for the purpose of achieving maximum war production by the most efficient use of combined raw materials and specialized production.

Jones-Connally Act. A Federal law of 1934 adding cattle, barley, rye, flax and peanuts to the list of goods receiving benefit payments under the original Agricultural Adjustment Act, namely corn, wheat, cotton, rice, tobacco, hogs, and milk products. The Jones-Costigan Act added sugar cane and sugar beets.

journal. Official minutes of the actions taken by a legislative body. It does not, however, include debates.

judge. One who dispenses justice in a court along lines of established law when presented with a controversy between two parties.

judge-made law. Law as formulated in judicial opinions rather than by statute.

judgment. 1. Decision in a legal case. 2. An obligation, as to pay damages, included in a legal decision.

Judicial Committee of the Privy Council. A British court of appeal from decisions of the courts in the dominions, India and the colonies, and the courts of the British church. It is composed of the president and a few members of the privy council, the law lords of the House of Lords and jurists from the dominions and India. Technically it does not render decisions but advises the Crown from which the decision then comes.

judicial review. The power of a court to say whether a law is or is not in accord with the constitution, or is "constitutional." With the United States Supreme Court this is an important power as it provides for the scrutiny of both federal and state laws.

judiciary. 1. The branch of government whose function is to interpret the law. 2. The whole system of courts set up to perform this function. 3. The judges who compose these courts.

Junker (YOON-ker). Originally a member of the landed aristocracy of Eastern Prussia. Under the Second Reich, and later, the word was applied to the members of this class who formed the military aristocracy of Germany. Their power centered in the General Staff and lasted practically undiminished through the Weimar Republic. They made an alliance with Hitler, and though various members of the group opposed him, Junkers dominated the Wehrmacht in World War II. The destruction of the Junkers' General Staff was one of the Allied objectives announced at the Crimea Conference in 1945 and was carried into effect after the surrender of the German armies.

junket. A trip, at public expense, ostensibly with a public purpose such as that of a Congressional investigating committee, which in reality the members are taking principally for the ride.

junta. 1. A Spanish term for legislative or administrative council. 2. Italian provincial administrative council which both reviews the work of local officials and acts as the lowest administrative court. 3. Used also in the sense of junto. See JUNTO.

junto. A small group of persons banded together for some political scheme such as the maintenance or seizure of the political control of the state. Often more or less secrecy is implied in either the persons or plot involved.

jure sanguinis. See JUS SANGUINIS.

jure soli. See JUS SOLI.

juridical. Term pertaining to law, a legal system, or to the administration of justice. Also used instead of "legal."

jurisdiction. The power and right of a political or legal authority to function over a certain territory or people or in a certain field. The jurisdiction of a court of law means that a particular court has the constitutional or statutory power to try a certain type of case in a certain territory, i. e., the United States Customs Court in New York City can handle only cases involving goods imported into the United States. The jurisdiction of a government department means that that department has been empowered by Act of Congress or presidential ruling to administer certain matters. In international law, the jurisdiction of a state means the right of a state to extend its control in general over the persons and things within its territorial limits. So-called "jurisdictional disputes" between two courts, two government agencies or even two offices within the same government department, or between two labor unions, are not infrequent as there are usually many border-line cases concerning which laws, rules or orders do not clearly apply; in addition the jurisdiction of courts of law or of government departments often apparently overlap. See SOVEREIGNTY, INTERNATIONAL LAW, SUBSOIL JURISDICTION, MARITIME LAW. For exceptions see EXTRATERRITORIALITY, DIPLOMATIC PRIVILEGES AND IMMUNITIES.

jurisdictional dispute. See JURISDICTION.

jurisprudence. In the widest sense the science of law. It is concerned first with the philosophy of law, namely with the task of ordering human relations through the use of law and, second, with the means of performing this task, namely with legal institutions and with law itself. In a more narrow sense it is the science of comparing and analyzing the laws and legal systems of civilized societies.

jurist. A close student of the law, particularly a judge.

juristic. 1. Pertaining to a jurist. 2. In accordance with law or jurisprudence.

jury. A body of impartial men and women (usually 12 or 6) without legal training, selected from the neighborhood and obliged under oath to listen to evidence and return verdicts. The judge presides in the court, determines the procedure and asks questions from witnesses and from the jury, also advises the jury on the law. The jury determines the facts in a given case and concludes whether or not the accused is guilty as charged. Trial by jury is deeply rooted in Anglo-American common law and dates back to the Middle Ages. It is often called one of the ways in which a free, democratic society protects its citizens from oppression and arbitrary practices. As such it has been embodied in the United States Constitution which clearly says that "the trial of all crimes except in case of impeachment shall be by jury." Article VII of the Bill of Rights also emphasizes that "the right of trial by jury shall be preserved." Trial by jury has been adopted by most democratic countries (many of them using Roman Law and not Common Law as their legal system). In America today there is also the "grand jury" which is called upon to determine whether there is ground for a criminal accusation, and a "coroner's jury" or "jury of inquest" to inquire into the causes of death. See TRIAL, COMMON LAW, MILITARY LAW.

jury trial. A trial, usually of a more important nature, in which questions of fact are decided by a group of disinterested people, usually twelve in number, called a jury. See JURY, TRIAL.

jus belli (JUS BELL-eye). See LAW OF WAR.

jus sanguinis (JUS san-GWINE-us). Literally the law of the blood. The rule that a child receives its nationality by blood or parentage.

jus soli (JUS SOH-lie). Literally the law of the soil. The rule that a child receives its nationality from the soil or place of birth.

just compensation. Fair payment for property taken from a person for public use. This payment shall not vary materially from the value which may, by courts and experts, be placed upon the property. In fact it is usually determined by such methods and usually is higher than the price would be if the property were sold to another private person.

justice. 1. Fairness or right, particularly as determined by judicial process. 2. A judge, as, for example, a judge of the United States Supreme Court.

Justice, Department of. One of the executive departments of the United States Government the functions of which are the enforcement of federal law, the furnishing of legal counsel in cases involving the federal government, and the interpretation of the federal laws when requested by other federal agencies. The Attorney General heads the Department. It was established in 1870, and prior to that time the Attorney General had been a cabinet member (since 1789) but not the head of a Department.

justice of the peace. The lowest judge in the American and British local court systems. His jurisdiction is limited to minor local matters, criminal and civil in the United States but only criminal in Great Britain. Similar officials are often found elsewhere with somewhat the same title, as in France.

justiciable. Legal as opposed to political. A dispute in which the parties are agreed as to the validity of the existing law, but do not agree on its interpretation. Often they are willing to accept settlement by an impartial body such as an established court.

juvenile court. A special local court which handles cases involving young people and particularly their crimes and misdemeanors.

K

kamikaze. 1. Suicide dive bomber pilot used by Japan late in World War II, mostly against American naval ships and transports in the waters of the Philippines and Okinawa. From the Japanese, meaning divine wind. 2.

Relating to the tactics of suicide-bombing.

kangaroo closure. A type of closure used in the British House of Commons after 1909. It gives the chairman authority to select sections of the bill which he considers important for discussion. This means jumping from section to section—hence "kangaroo." In 1919 the standing orders of the House incorporated kangaroo as part of the regular procedure.

kangaroo court. A court which hands down decisions without proper, and sometimes without any, legal or official authorization to do so.

Kapp Putsch. A reactionary attempt to seize power from the Weimar Republic in Germany in March, 1920. Some 8000 soldiers under Dr. Wolfgang Kapp drove the government and government forces from Berlin and were in control for about a week. The movement was broken chiefly by a general strike of labor. Kapp fled the country but later returned and died in prison while his trial was pending.

Karageorgevich. The Serbian dynasty named after George Petrovich, known as Kara George or Black George from his dark complexion. He led the Serbs in their revolt against the Turks (1804–13). The last three kings of Serbia and Yugoslavia, King Peter II, his father Alexander, and his grandfather Peter I, were of this dynasty.

Karlsbad demands. A series of demands on the Czech government by Konrad Henlein and the Sudeten Germans dated April 24, 1938. It included the recognition of autonomy under German officials in recognized Sudeten districts, protection of Sudetens outside these districts, removal of and reparation for "injustices" since 1918, and the right of the Sudetens to become part of the Nazi Pan-German movement.

K. B. See KNIGHT.

K. B. E. See ORDER OF THE BRITISH EMPIRE.

K. C. B. See ORDER OF THE BATH.

K. C. I. E. See ORDER OF THE INDIAN EMPIRE.

K. C. M. G. See ORDER OF ST. MICHAEL AND ST. GEORGE.

K. C. S. I. See ORDER OF THE STAR OF INDIA.

K. C. V. O. See ROYAL VICTORIAN ORDER.

Kellogg-Briand Pact. See PARIS, PACT OF.

Kemalism. The principles of government laid down by Turkey's first president, Kemal Ataturk. They included nationalism, republicanism, secularism, a partial governmental participation in an otherwise fairly free economy, adherence to the principles of the Kemalist revolution and the development of social, economic, legal, and political equality.

keynote speech. One of the first speeches made at a political convention, the one outlining the general policies supported by the party.

K. G. See ORDER OF THE GARTER.

Khyber Pass. Mountain pass between northwest India and Afghanistan, area of occasional raids, minor wars, and local resistance against British rule.

Kiaochow. Port in north China on the south side of the Shantung peninsula for which a 99 year lease was secured through force by Germany in 1897. Japan seized the area in 1914, but it was turned over to China at the Washington Conference of 1922.

kid-glove diplomacy. American slang for international dealings carried on with finesse rather than with bluster.

kid-glove politics. American politicians' slang term for political movements backed by the wealthier classes and advocating principles, candidates, and methods favored by those classes.

Kimpai. The imperial Japanese secret military police, a counterpart of the German Gestapo. Abolished under allied control.

king. Male ruler of a state, or kingdom.

The title is usually hereditary. Most kings in modern times have been sovereign rulers, like the king of Great Britain, but some have been subject to an emperor, as the king of Bavaria to the emperor of Germany.

king can do no wrong. A natural corollary of absolute monarchy and the divine right of kings. In one extreme sense it was taken to mean that the king could do anything he wanted to do, responsible to no man but only to God. In another sense it was used to indicate that since the king was the source of law, all his acts were legal. See PREROGATIVE.

King-Crane Commission. An American commission which visited the Arab countries of the Near East and Turkey after World War I in an effort to ascertain the desires of the inhabitants regarding their political future. Its report was not officially published, but it recommended preferably American mandates for Armenia, Constantinople, and Asia Minor. It conceded that the first desire of the inhabitants was for independence.

kitchen cabinet. An informal group of advisers which a president may assemble and on which he depends more than on the regular cabinet. First referred to in connection with Andrew Jackson.

K.K.K. See KU KLUX KLAN.

Kleinburgertum (KLINE - byoor - gertoom). German for lower middle class.

knight. A British title originally involving military service due the king in return for land, but now given as a recognition of outstanding service of any kind to the nation. A knight may belong to any one of a number of Orders of Knighthood, such as the Order of the Garter, of the British Empire, of St. Patrick, etc, or be one of the Knights Bachelor (K. B.) The title is not hereditary, nor does it give the holder a seat in the House of Lords.

Knights of Labor. An early American labor organization, secret at first, which flourished between 1870 and 1890. It aimed to include practically all labor and advocated the eight-hour day and a broad program of arbitration, prohibition of child labor, equal pay for equal work, and health and safety legislation.

Know-nothing party. A small United States political party in evidence chiefly in 1856. Its program was primarily anti-foreign and anti-Catholic. It began as a secret organization and its name came from the early disinclination of its members to admit any knowledge of it.

Kokuikai. The State Strength Society, a Japanese organization set up in 1932 composed of members of parliament, high civil officials, and less radical army officers. It was a kind of unofficial planning commission for Japanese economic policy. Abolished after World War II.

Kommandatura. The inter-Allied governing authority of Berlin, planned in the Allied statement of June 5, 1945 regarding the control of Germany under military occupation. It is composed of four commandants appointed by the commander-in-chief of the four Allied occupying forces in Germany. Also spelled less often Komendatura.

Komsomol. Communist youth organization in the USSR for those 16 years old and up. It is a place of party indoctrination from which it is expected that future party leaders will be recruited.

Koran. Holy book of the Mohammedans, written by Mohammed between 610 and 632 A.D.

K.P. See ORDER OF ST. PATRICK.

Kraft durch Freude (KRAHFT doorsh

FROY-duh). See STRENGTH THROUGH JOY.

Kredit-Anstalt (KRAY-deet AHN-shtahlt). Great Vienna banking institution the collapse of which, in June, 1931 heralded the world depression in continental Europe.

Kreis (KRISE). German county, literally the German word for circle.

Kremlin. The citadel of Moscow within which are the highest government offices and the meeting places of the USSR. Hence a term used as a synonym for the Soviet government.

kriegie. American slang for a person taken as a prisoner of war in World War II. The term is derived from *Kriegsgefangene*, the German word for prisoner of war.

Kronstadt mutiny. A mutiny of the Russian sailors at the Kronstadt naval base in March, 1921 which arose from opposition to the policies of the new Bolshevik government in socializing the country, and particularly to the food requisition policy with its resulting hardships especially for the peasants.

Krupp. Family name of the founders and managers of the great German steel corporation bearing their name, used synonymously with German munitions. The head of the family, Gustav Krupp von Bohlen und Hal-bach, was one of the original defendants in the Nuremburg war guilt trials in 1945–46, but his trial was postponed because of senility. The family was accused of giving financial support to Nazi plans for world conquest.

K.T. See ORDER OF THE THISTLE.

Ku Klux Klan. 1. Secret organization in the South set up after the Civil War for the maintenance of white supremacy. 2. Secret anti-Negro, anti-Jewish, anti-Catholic organization established during World War I and of greatest importance in the 1920's when it achieved some political influence in a number of southern and middle-western states. Revived on a smaller scale after World War II, especially in Georgia.

kulak. Wealthiest of the Russian peasants. They were an object of special repression by the Communists as particularly interfering with the policy of collectivization of the farms.

Kultur (kool-TOOR). German for culture or civilization, particularly the German brand which, in addition to the English meaning of the term, carried with it a strong emphasis on militarism.

Kuomintang (KWO - min - TAHNG). Chinese National Peoples Party, in recent times the party in power and the dominant Chinese party.

L

Labor, Department of. One of the United States government executive departments. It was set up in 1913 for the purpose of promoting employment and improving working conditions and the general welfare of wage-earners. From 1903–1913 it was part of the Department of Commerce and Labor.

Labor Front. The sole Nazi German economic organization of workers and employers. It was set up, after the Nazis attained power, as a substitute for former labor unions, but the employers were included. In 1935 it became an auxiliary of the Nazi party.

labor legislation. Laws regarding hours, wages, or working conditions of wage-earners.

Labor-management Relations Act, 1947. An act amending the National Labor Relations (Wagner) Act, passed after President Truman had first vetoed it on January 20, 1947. Its effect was to reduce the strength of the position of labor established by the Wagner Act. It ruled out the closed shop, permitted employers to present their views on labor relations to their employees, made strikes subject to injunction, especially where national health or safety are involved, and made labor organizations liable for suits over contracts.

Labor Party. The large British Socialist Party. In the 1945 National Elections it gained 395 of 622 seats in the House of Commons and its leader,

Clement Attlee, was asked by the King to form a Government. The Labor Party was founded in 1900 by trade unions and socialist groups in order to establish a distinct Labor group in Parliament promoting legislation in the interest of Labor. Until then labor representatives were included among Liberal candidates and were called Lib-Labs. The Labor Party is based upon the British trade unions, co-operative societies and a few other associations which give it a strong financial basis. It developed gradually since the beginning of this century, became in 1922 the second strongest party in the House of Commons and formed a government in 1924, but stayed in power only for nine months. The failure of the general strike of 1926 meant a further setback. In 1929 the Labor Party became the strongest party in Parliament, but did not have an absolute majority. Its leader Ramsay MacDonald became Prime Minister. In the general elections of 1931 the party suffered a crushing defeat and split into two; Ramsay MacDonald heading the smaller group, the so-called National Labor Party, which joined with the Conservatives and National Liberals to form the new Government-coalition that was in power until the fall of Neville Chamberlain in 1940. The Labor Party entered Winston Churchill's National Government in 1940 and left it only in the summer of 1945, demanding a general election, which ended with Labor's victory. The party's program contained the nationalization of the Bank of England, gradual socialization of certain key industries, mining, railways and shipping, the carrying out of the Beveridge Plan, extensive housing and other social legislation. It is, however, opposed to full socialism and its roots are not in revolutionary Marxism, but in English socialist movements such as the Fabianists. It does not believe in the class struggle and in the dictatorship of the proletariat and has several times rejected Communist requests to join forces. It upholds parliamentary democracy and civil liberties. See SOCIALISM, MARXISM, INDEPENDENT LABOR PARTY.

Labor Service. A German compulsory six months term of work for the state in labor camps instituted by the Nazis. The camps were run on a military basis and provided an opportunity for further Nazi indoctrination.

labor union. An organization of workers established for the purpose of securing higher wages and better working conditions from their employers by means of joint demands and joint action.

lack of confidence. A vote in the House of Commons, or other legislative body under a parliamentary form of government, against the policy of the cabinet. That is, a vote indicating that the cabinet no longer enjoys the backing or the "confidence" of a majority of the members of the body. After such a vote the cabinet resigns, and in the British system a new election is held. In other countries, France for example, a new cabinet may be formed instead.

laissez faire (le-say FAIR). Originally in French *laissez faire, lassez passer*—

let one do (as he will), let things move (as they may). It is used as a name for the classical economic theory and expresses its main principle, namely that economic affairs will take care of themselves best if neither the state nor any other compulsory authority interferes with them. This principle is based on the theory that a harmonious order is possible in which individual action, unhampered by state regulations, will determine the economic process to the benefit of all. In other words *laissez faire* assumes that rationally conceived self-interest will in the long run be identical with the interest of all. This theory had its beginning in the 17th century but was popularized and developed by a group of French economists, the so-called physiocrats, led by Turgot. The theory was adopted by Adam Smith, the father of classical economics, in his book "The Wealth of Nations" (1776). See LIBERALISM, UTILITARIANISM, FREE TRADE.

lame duck. A member of a legislative body whose term continues and who remains as a full voting member of the body after an election in which he failed to be re-elected. The term was particularly applied to members of Congress prior to 1934, who failed of re-election in November but whose terms ran until the following March 4, and who participated in the intervening short session. This problem of having a whole regular session in which there were always many members recently repudiated at the polls was solved by the Lame Duck or 20th Amendment to the Constitution.

Lame Duck Amendment. The 20th amendment to the Constitution proclaimed October 15, 1933. It provides for unusual instances of filling the presidency, and particularly that the president and vice-president shall take office January 20 and Congressmen on January 3, instead of March 4 as formerly, thus eliminating the former short session "lame ducks." See LAME DUCK.

Land (plural, **Länder**) (LAHNT, LAYNder). German word for land, meaning the states which were the subdivisions of Germany.

land bank. See FEDERAL LAND BANKS.

land-grant college. An agricultural and mechanical college or state university of which such a college forms a part, which by the Morrill Act of 1862, received early assistance from grants of United States land given to the states for the promotion of agriculture and the mechanical arts. Most of the states in the Middle West have such schools. See MORRILL ACT.

landslide. An overwhelming majority of votes cast for one candidate or party in an election.

Lansing-Ishii Agreement. An American-Japanese agreement of November 2, 1917, in which Japan conceded the principle of the open door and the territorial integrity of China, but the United States admitted that Japan, because of its location, had special interests in China.

Lateran Accord. An agreement of February 11, 1929 between the Italian government and the Pope consisting of three parts. The first was a treaty in which Italy recognized the temporal sovereignty of the Pope over Vatican City and his jurisdiction over certain churches and the Pope's summer home outside Vatican City, the Pope renouncing other outside jurisdiction. The second indemnified the Pope for the loss of territory held previous to 1870. The third, the Concordat, established the position of the Catholic Church in Italy and its relation to the state. Roman Catholicism was made the official religion, tax free and public-supported, in charge of religious education in the public schools.

Lausanne, Conference. See LAUSANNE, TREATIES OF.

Lausanne Reparation Agreements. A series of agreements concluded July 8, 1932, at Lausanne providing for the scaling down of the German reparations bill to $714,000,000, the continuation of the Hoover moratorium until the first agreement went into effect, settlement of reparations of other countries, and a study of international trade and the calling of an economic conference. A "gentlemen's agreement" was added that the reparations would be reduced only if the United States would similarly scale down the war debts. The United States refused and the agreement regarding German reparations never went into effect. See HOOVER MORATORIUM; REPARATIONS; WAR DEBTS.

Lausanne, Treaties of. (1) October 18, 1912, following the war in Tripoli over Turkey's attempt to check Italy's influence there. Turkey had exercised more or less control over the territory since the early sixteenth century. However, the treaty forced Turkey to withdraw from Tripoli with the exception that the sultan retained religious authority, through his representative, as caliph. (2) July 24, 1923, following World War I in which Turkey was an ally of Germany. Some provisions were: Turkey lost its former Arab lands, and territory in Europe beyond Adrianople and the Maritsa River; Turkey promised judicial reforms, accepted treaties to protect minorities, and paid no reparations; the Straits were demilitarized and open to ships of all nations in peace, and in war if Turkey remained neutral, but if not, enemy ships only might be excluded. On April 11, 1936 Turkey asked the signatories for permission to refortify the Straits. The request was approved a few months later in the Montreux convention.

Laval-Mussolini Accord. A French-Italian agreement of January 7, 1935, by which France ceded territory adjoining Libya and Eritrea, and gave Italy a share of the Djibouti railway to Addis Ababa, special privileges for Italians in Tunis, and a free hand in Ethiopia. There was also provision for consultation if Germany threatened to seize Austria.

law. A rule for human actions prescribed by authority. There are different kinds of laws according to their origin and their purpose. There are laws of God, the so-called "natural law," written laws made by the sovereign (King, Parliament, Congress, etc.), common law based on tradition and precedent, equity, etc. International law is concerned with the relations of states (nations) with each other, federal or national law is valid for a whole country, state law (in America) and municipal law are valid for the subdivisions of a country, although the term municipal law is also used to mean all forms of national and local law within a country, as opposed to international law. Today constitutional government is government by law, while dictatorships, absolute monarchies and totalitarian states place their leader above law and maintain that their leaders represent the will of the people and whatever they do is therefore right and legal. The science of law is called jurisprudence. See JURISPRUDENCE, SOVEREIGNTY, COMMON LAW, POSITIVE LAW, MILITARY LAW, TRIAL, TRIAL BY JURY, EQUITY.

law lords. The Lords of Appeal in Ordinary and certain other jurists in the House of Lords. They are the members who exercise the function of the House of Lords as a court of last appeal from the British lower courts.

law of nations. Term often used for international law.

laws of war. A branch of international law dealing with rules generally observed by nations at war. Many of these rules were formulated by the Hague Conventions of 1899 and 1907 and by the Geneva Convention (regarding war prisoners) of 1929. They deal with matters such as the definition of belligerency, declaration of war, safeguarding of diplomats and emissaries of the enemy, duties towards neutrals, treatment of prisoners of war, military occupation including conduct toward enemy civilians and their property, actions against spies and civilian snipers, facilitation and safeguarding of the work of relief societies such as the Red Cross, naval blockades, hostages and reprisals, the prohibition of certain weapons, negotiations for truce and armistice, etc. In the last war many of these rules were broken at one time or another but it would go too far to say that the laws of war were uniformly ignored by either side, though the Axis powers violated them more frequently than the Allies. The violation of the laws of war are generally called war crimes for which the death penalty is applicable. Moreover the War Crime Court at Nuremberg attempted to establish the new principle according to which aggression and preparation for war itself should rate as a war crime and the leaders of the nation can be held responsible for aggression. See INTERNATIONAL LAW, WAR CRIMES, WAR CRIMES TRIALS, WAR GUILT, NEUTRALITY, AGGRESSOR SANCTIONS.

lay on the table. In parliamentary practice a motion to table, or lay on the table, postpones indefinitely action on a pending motion.

League of Free Nations Association. One of the United States organizations established during World War I to advocate the formation of a league or association of nations.

League of Nations. Organization of the Allied nations, exclusive of the United States, after World War I, to establish permanent peace. The League of Nations came to life mainly through the efforts of President Wilson, who insisted at the Paris Peace Conference in 1919 that the Covenant of the League of Nations be incorporated into the Treaty of Versailles.

The main points of the Covenant were: (1) the maintenance of peace; (2) the peaceful solution of international disputes by law, public debate, impartial investigation and conciliation; and (3) international cooperation in general. The League of Nations came into existence on January 10, 1920 and was virtually dead at the outbreak of World War II. The United Nations Assembly supplanted it in January, 1946. At Geneva, Switzerland, immense buildings were erected to house the extensive Secretariat and other permanent offices of the League.

The fact that the United States did not enter the League was the first blow it suffered. It consisted originally of forty-two member states. By 1928 the number was fifty-four including Germany. After that date six more states entered, among them the U.S.S.R., Turkey and Mexico, while Japan withdrew from the League after refusing to agree to any settlement suggested regarding its conflict with China over Manchuria. Germany withdrew soon after Hitler came to power. Sanctions imposed by the League when Italy invaded Ethiopia (Abyssinia) proved ineffective, as the powers would apply neither oil sanctions, nor the threat of armed intervention. After the war Italy also withdrew. Smaller disputes were set-

tled amicably. Disarmament conferences promoted and arranged by the League were a failure. Russia was expelled from the League because of her war against Finland in the winter of 1939-40. The League was more successful in the field of humanitarian activities such as international control of drugs, white slave traffic, support of stateless persons and refugees, and general health work.

The failure of the League of Nations was due primarily to: (1) unwillingness of some great powers to enter it and withdrawal of others once the League decided against them; (2) hesitation to apply effective sanctions against aggressors and offending member states; (3) great power politics continued outside the League; (4) general strain caused by the economic depression; (5) appeasement policy of western powers toward Germany and Japan; (6) failure to implement the League with armed forces.

Some of the League's features have been incorporated into the Charter of the United Nations. See SANCTIONS, AGGRESSOR, INTERNATIONAL ORGANIZATION, INTERNATIONAL LEGISLATION, UNITED NATIONS, COVENANT OF THE LEAGUE OF NATIONS.

League of Nations Society. The name of British and French organizations set up during World War I to back the League of Nations.

League of Women Voters. See NATIONAL LEAGUE OF WOMEN VOTERS.

League to Enforce Peace. An American organization set up in 1915 advocating a rather advanced form of league of nations, with power to enforce the peace, as the name indicates. One of its most enthusiastic backers was Senator Henry Cabot Lodge, Senior, who later opposed entry of the United States into the League of Nations.

leasehold, *or* **leased territory.** A portion of a state leased to another state, such as Port Arthur to Russia prior to 1904 and the Panama Canal Zone to the United States.

leave to print. Permission granted Congressmen to insert in the *Congressional Record* speeches they have not delivered in their respective houses, and speeches and articles by others.

Lebensraum (LAY-buns-rowm). Literally living room or living space. The doctrine adhered to particularly in Nazi Germany that a great people has a right to expand and extend its boundaries at the expense of weaker neighbors.

Ledo Road. A road built during World War II from northeastern India joining the Burma Road in northern Burma to furnish a supply line to western China. This road was made necessary by the Japanese seizure of the western terminus of the Burma Road. The Ledo and Burma roads have been renamed Stilwell Road in honor of General Joseph J. Stilwell.

left. A term including liberal, radical, socialist, anarchist and communist parties. Their ideas are often described as "leftist." The origin of this expression is found in European parliamentary practices, according to which the parties sit in a semi-circle, the conservatives occupying the right side, the middle-of-the-road groups the center and the liberal, radical and socialist groups the left side as seen from the position of the presiding officer. Communists would sit on the extreme left, Fascists or arch-conservatives on the extreme right. Nowadays it is often doubted whether a liberal belongs to the left, and liberals believing in capitalism and free trade are often counted as belonging to the center or even to the right. See LIBERAL, RADICAL, SOCIALISM, COMMU-NISM, MARXISM, ANARCHISM, SYNDICALISM.

legal. Pertaining to, or in accordance with, the law.

legal tender. See MONEY.

legality. Quality of conforming to the law.

legate. A papal diplomat who is also a cardinal. Otherwise the same as a nuncio.

legation. The office or official residence of a diplomatic agent below the rank of ambassador.

legation, right of. The right to exchange diplomatic representatives with other states.

Legion of Honor. French military and civil order established by Napoleon. Granted to many American soldiers in World War I.

legislation. 1. The process of law-making. 2. The laws after enactment.

legislative. Pertaining to law-making or legislatures.

legislative committee. A group of members of a legislative body whose function it is to go thoroughly into the advisability of passing certain bills and to present recommendations as to this advisability to the body as a whole. In a body where hundreds of bills are proposed it is clearly impossible to consider each before the whole body. Thus the real work of such a body tends to be done in a series of committees.

legislative council. In the United States a council set up in several states composed of members of each house of the legislature, the function of which is to plan the legislative program for the next session of the legislature. It is a joint committee for legislative planning and has been set up to preclude the criticism that legislative bodies fail to provide adequate leadership.

legislative courts. A collective term for the various courts such as the Commerce Court, the Court of Claims, the District of Columbia courts, etc., which are based on Congressional legislation as opposed to the regular federal court system which is provided for in the Constitution.

legislative day. Sometimes it is impossible for a legislative body to complete on the designated day some of the business which may have to be done on that day. In such a case the business is carried over to the next day, but completed as of the legislative day preceding. Many legislatures run past midnight of the day on which they are required by law to close, but the work completed thereafter is completed as of the last legislative day of the session. Sometimes clocks are stopped or covered to make the legislators feel that they are observing the technicalities.

legislative drafting bureau. See BILL-DRAFTING OFFICE.

Legislative Reference Service. In the United States a reference service for legislators in connection with their work, providing material necessary for bill drafting and sometimes also technical help in setting up proposed bills in suitable form. Part of the Library of Congress.

legislature. The part of the government which makes the laws. It is usually the most numerous branch and is thought of as representing the people more closely than an executive, since each member is responsible to a smaller number of voters.

legitimacy. 1. Attribute of a monarch who attained office by the established law of succession. 2. State of being legitimate.

legitimate. 1. Pertaining to a government which came to power by legal means. 2. Pertaining to a person born of legally wedded parents.

legitimation. The process of placing an illegitimate person on the same footing before the law as a legitimate person.

Leipsic trials. The unsuccessful efforts of the Allies after World War I to try German war criminals. The Kaiser was not turned over by the Netherlands and only a few minor officers were finally brought to trial in Leipsic. The trial was conducted by German judges and the accused received nothing more than light sentences.

Lend-Lease Act. Law of March 11, 1941, authorizing the president to sell, exchange, lease, lend, or otherwise dispose of whatever articles of defense he saw fit to any state whose defense he considered vital to the United States. Under this law about forty-three billions of dollars worth of American munitions, machinery, raw materials, and other articles were transferred to other countries for the common defense. See REVERSE LEND-LEASE.

Lend-Lease Master Agreement. The identical agreement used by the United States and other countries as the basis for extending lend-lease aid. The first was one with Great Britain of February 23, 1942; the one with China was dated June 2, 1942; the one with Russia was completed June 11, 1942. Many more were agreed to.

Leticia dispute. A disagreement between Peru and Colombia over the port of Leticia, on the upper Amazon, and surrounding Colombian territory where the two countries join. The area was seized by Peruvians September 1, 1932, and there was armed conflict during the early months of 1933. The dispute was finally resolved in May 1934 and Peru withdrew due to direct negotiations and the friendly offices of a League of Nations committee.

"Let's take a look at the record." A favorite expression of Al Smith in his campaign for the presidency in 1928.

letter of credence. Letter carried by a diplomatic agent from his home government to the government to which he is accredited indicating who he is, his rank, and functions. He begins his duties only after this is presented to the head of the state or, if he is only a chargé d'affaires, to the foreign minister.

letters of marque and reprisal. Commissions by a government to its citizens permitting them to seize the property of a citizen of another state in satisfaction for damage done to them by the second state or one of its citizens. Such activity was abolished by the Declaration of Paris of 1856.

lettre de récréance. See RECREDENTIAL.

Levant. Collective term for the countries at the east end of the Mediterranean Sea.

Levant Federation. One of the forms of union advocated for the countries at the eastern end of the Mediterranean. Included in this project are Syria, the Lebanon, Palestine, and Transjordan. The degree of union varies among different advocates, confederation rather than federation appearing more likely at first, with a customs union and other elementary economic and political co-operation. See ARAB LEAGUE.

levée. 1. A morning reception held by a sovereign or personage of high rank. 2. In Great Britain, a court assembly held in the early afternoon and attended only by men. 3. In the United States a reception held by the President or other high official.

levée en masse. The spontaneous armed rising by the population of territory for the purpose of resisting an approaching invader. According to the Hague Conventions such persons should be treated as belligerents if they carry arms openly and respect the laws of war. Sometimes spelled *levy*. See BELLIGERENT.

levy. 1. To collect money (as taxes) or men (as troops) for public purposes. 2. To assess, as a fine. 3. (plural) troops.

Liaison Office of Personnel Management. A branch of the Executive Office of the President set up in 1939. As the name implies it assists the president in the management of personnel and is his point of contact with the personnel policies of the various government agencies.

liaison officer. A person who maintains relations of one government agency with one or more other agencies. He is something more than merely a very high-class messenger boy because he ranks so high that he is in a position to explain and discuss the information which he transmits.

Liaotung Peninsula. A peninsula in northern China under lease to Russia which lease Japan acquired as a result of the Russo-Japanese War. In it are located Dairen and Port Arthur, the latter of which was made a joint naval base by the Chinese-Russian treaty of August 26, 1945.

libel. 1. Malicious publication by writing, or some other permanent form, of matter injurious to the character or reputation of a person. Such publication gives the injured person cause to sue for damages or enables criminal prosecution of the offender. 2. A process in admiralty law instituting action in regard to a claim against a vessel arising either from seizure in war or for some act for which damages may be collected.

liberal. In a wide sense a person, political party, or philosophy which believes that man has a free will and should be permitted to develop himself as freely as possible. Political liberalism in the beginning of its development worked for limiting the interference of the state, of privileged traditional aristocracies or of domineering churches with individual liberties and for promoting the development of human personality. This was an individualistic creed. Thomas Paine and Thomas Jefferson were eminent early liberals. Freedom of the press and of opinion in general was one of their main principles and religious, racial or social intolerance was strongly opposed by them. They favored free trade, free enterprise, civil liberties, equal rights for women, self determination of minority rights and opposed the influence of royalty, the church, aristocracy and army leaders in political and social affairs. The 19th century was the age of liberalism, supported chiefly by the middleclasses. Representative, parliamentary democracy and the creation of the nation-state were liberal achievements. When more radical, collectivist movements sprang up, liberals became relatively more conservative and less reformist: they tried to preserve what they had achieved. In the 20th century European liberal parties were fighting a losing fight, ground between the two millstones of conservatives and socialists, and often between fascists and Marxists. The British Liberal or Whig Party had to yield its place as one of the main British parties to the Labor Party. The French and Belgian liberals suffered a crushing defeat in the elections of 1945 and 1946. In America liberal often still means a person desiring radical reform. See RADICAL, LEFT, UTILITARIANISM, LAISSEZ FAIRE, FREE TRADE, REPUBLIC.

Liberal National Party. A British party formed in 1933 from part of the Liberal party. It supported the national government when the Liberals joined the opposition.

Liberal Party. A British political party known as the Whig Party before the reforms of 1832. In the 19th century it was the party of the middle class and also of the great industralists, opposed to the Conservative Party of the upper classes and the land owners. Under the leadership of William E. Gladstone, from 1865 to 1895, the party was anti-imperialist, and passed important social reforms, save in the field of factory legislation. Gladstone's Home Rule policy for Ireland split the party in 1886, an important group joining the Conservative or Unionist Party. The Liberals came back to power in 1906, and in the ministries of Campbell-Bannerman and Asquith passed far-reaching social and factory legislation. It came into open conflict with the House of Lords over a tax on land values, and the Parliament Act of 1911 finally limited the power of the upper house and established the dominance of the House of Commons. After World War I the party suffered from the trend toward the extremes of Conservatism and Socialism (Labor Party), and in the early 1930's it split into three small factions, one group, the Liberal National Party supporting the coalition or national government in 1933. In the elections of July, 1945 the Liberals won only 11 seats, the Liberal Nationalists, 14, though they polled over two million votes.

liberalism. See LIBERAL.

liberation. Freeing or emancipation.

Liberté, Egalité, Fraternité (lee-ber-TAY, ay-gahl-ee-TAY, frah-ter-nee-TAY). Liberty, equality, fraternity— the slogan of the French Revolution.

liberty. The right to be free from unnecessary external restraint or autocratic control. The right or power to choose a course of action.

"Liberty and Union, Now and Forever, One and Inseparable." Closing statement of Daniel Webster in his speech in the United States Senate, January

26, 1830, in reply to Hayne on the Foote Resolution. The resolution was on the question of the sale of public lands, but the debate turned upon the powers of the federal government, Hayne claiming that, as a confederation, it had no real power of its own. Webster's reply advocated real power for the federal union.

Liberty Loans. Four United States Government bond issues to finance World War I; brought out between May 14, 1917 and April 21, 1919. The fifth issue was known as the Victory Loan. Sales were made direct to the people and pleas were made by volunteer speakers in all sorts of places such as hotels, churches, and theaters. A vast organization of Liberty Loan Committees canvassed almost the entire population. The issues remaining after those that have matured, have been refunded at a saving of interest and called Treasury bonds.

library district. A special governmental district established to provide library facilities for the people within the district.

Library of Congress. Originally set up in 1800 as a library for Congress, it has grown into a national library. As the repository of books deposited for copyright, it has copies of practically everything published in the United States.

license. In the United States a certificate of permission to perform a certain act such as sell cigarettes or drive an automobile. The requirement to secure such permission is made on the theory that control of such acts is socially necessary, but the fees paid for such licenses sometimes form a considerable part of a state's revenue.

Lidice. Czech community annihilated by the Germans in World War II in retaliation for the murder of Acting Reich Protector Reinhard Heydrich, known as The Hangman. The word has been sometimes used as a term for ruthless and punitive obliteration of a community.

Lieber's Code. General Orders No. 100 of the War Department, "Instructions for the Government of the Armies of the United States in the Field" prepared by Francis Lieber and dated April 24, 1863. The United States Army rules for the conduct of hostilities. Subsequently brought up to date.

lieutenant-governor. An official in most of the states of the United States corresponding in general in functions to the vice-president of the United States, i. e., he succeeds to the governorship if the governor does not finish his term, and he presides over the state Senate.

lily whites. White Republicans in the South who oppose Negro participation in the party organization.

Lima Conference. The 8th International Conference of American States (Pan American Union) held at Lima, Peru, December 9–27, 1938. Its major actions were the Declaration of Lima, a declaration of American principles, further study of pending problems of codifying international law, and a series of resolutions and recommendations regarding cultural, educational, and commercial relations. See PAN AMERICAN UNION.

Lima, Declaration of. A declaration of the members of the Pan American Union at Lima December 24, 1938, reaffirming their continental solidarity and the principles on which it is based, their decision to maintain these principles and their own sovereignty against all foreign intervention, and their intention to consider as of common concern, and to consult regarding, any threat to the peace, security, or territorial integrity of any one of them.

limitation of armaments. The process of reducing the armaments of a country by setting maximum limits. Prior to World War II there were certain temporary successes in limiting naval armaments, but general limitation of land armaments defied solution. See WASHINGTON CONFERENCE, DISARMAMENT CONFERENCE OF 1932.

Lincoln's Birthday. The anniversary of birthday of Abraham Lincoln, February 12, observed as a legal holiday in some of the United States.

Lincoln Brigade. American volunteer troops on the Loyalist side in the Spanish Civil War 1936–9.

line of succession. 1. The order in which a throne or other hereditary office is occupied by candidates eligible for the office. 2. The persons who have attained a throne or other hereditary office.

lion. Symbol of Great Britain. Derived from the lions on the coat-of-arms of the English kings.

liquidate. 1. To wind up business affairs. 2. To remove, get rid of or do away with: sometimes by execution, as in the case of a person or persons considered inimical to the state.

liquor traffic. The manufacture, transportation, and sale of alcoholic beverages.

list system. A plan of proportional representation in which the voter votes merely for a certain party's list of candidates. The number elected depends on the votes cast for the list, and the persons elected depend on their ranking on the list, the voter thus having nothing to do with picking particular candidates. In Germany under the Weimar constitution each party received one representative in the Reichstag for each 60,000 votes cast for the party list.

literacy test. About half of the states in the United States require some proof of literacy as a qualification for voting. Such proof may be a certificate of completion of a certain amount of schooling or the voter may be asked to write or read or even interpret something, as for example a statement from the Constitution.

Little Englander. An Englishman who was opposed to British imperialistic ventures, as for example, Gladstone.

Little Entente. Czechoslovakia, Romania, and Yugoslavia, as bound together in special treaty relations during much of the 1920's and 1930's.

little group of wilful men. A small group of senators so characterized by President Wilson for preventing, by a filibuster just prior to March 4, 1917, Congressional authorization for arming United States merchant vessels against submarines. Wilson gave the authorization by presidential order on March 12.

Little N. R. A. See BITUMINOUS COAL CONSERVATION ACTS.

Little Steel Formula. In the United States, a governmental policy stated first in a directive of the National War Labor Board in a case involving the so-called "Little Steel" companies— Bethlehem, Republic, Inland, and the Youngstown Sheet and Tube Co. It was repeated in the president's executive order of October 3, 1942, and in the Board's statement of policy of November 6, 1942. It provided for a pay increase ceiling of 15 per cent over January 1, 1941, on the basis of the estimated 15 per cent cost of living increase since that date as determined by the Bureau of Labor Statistics. Those who had received increases of 15 per cent or more as of September 15, 1942, could receive no more except in unusual cases; those receiving less than a 15 per cent increase since January 1, 1941, could request and presumably receive, an increase up to 15 per cent.

LNC. *Levizje Nacional Clirimtare.* Albanian resistance movement in World War II.

loan flotation. Borrowing by the successful offering of public securities.

lobby. 1. One or more lobbyists for a particular interest who are bringing pressure to bear upon a particular legislative body; or all such lobbies dealing with a legislature. See LOBBYIST. **2.** To try to secure special favors as above.

lobbyist. A person who works for a particular interest. Usually thought of as a paid, professional promoter or representative of certain interests before legislative bodies.

local government. Government of small local units such as the village, city, or county.

local legislation. Laws passed by Congress or a state legislature that are purely local in application or effect, as for example certain building, road or harbor projects, or personal claims. Such laws detract from the time to be used for general legislative matters, but voters demand a certain amount of them as evidence that the representative is doing a good job of representing his district.

local option. The right of a village, city, township, or county to set up certain restrictions within such local areas. The term is usually used to refer to the right of such local units to prohibit the liquor traffic therein.

Locarno Treaties. A series of treaties negotiated at Locarno but signed at London, December 1, 1925. They were ratified September 14, 1926 after Germany had joined the League of Nations. The most widely heralded treaty was the Rhine Security Pact by which Germany, France, and Belgium promised to respect each other's frontiers, not to invade each other, and to settle all mutual disputes peacefully. Great Britain and Italy undertook to guarantee these provisions. There was

also a series of treaties between Germany and Belgium, Czechoslovakia, France, and Poland providing for submission of disputes to arbitration or conciliation. France also signed treaties of mutual guarantee with Czechoslovakia and Poland.

Log Cabin and Hard Cider Campaign. In the United States the presidential campaign of William Henry Harrison, the Whig candidate, in 1840. Both the cabin and the cider were used as symbols of the homely virtues of the candidate and the cause.

logrolling. The process by which one legislator helps other members get their pet bills passed by a legislative body and they do the same for him. The term came from the days of building log cabins, when the neighbors would come in and roll logs for a man building a new cabin, thus making possible a building impossible for a single builder. The new owner would return or pass on the favor in time.

London County Council. The governing body of the administrative county of London. It has both legislative and executive power, the latter exercised through committees and appointed officials. Its functions include the normal functions of a great municipality such as fire protection, sewers, health, housing, transportation lines, and education, but not policing which is handled by the metropolitan police district.

London, Declaration of. A declaration agreed upon at London by the sea powers in 1909 formulating rules regarding neutral rights and the treatment of neutral trade in time of war. It was not generally ratified but is considered an enlightened statement on the subject.

London Economic Conference. See ECONOMIC CONFERENCE OF 1933.

London Naval Conference of 1930. A

conference of the five naval powers, held January 21—April 22, 1930 in London. Great Britain, the United States, and Japan agreed to limit their cruiser and destroyer tonnages to a ratio of about 10:10:7, and they agreed on a common maximum submarine tonnage. France and Italy did not enter these provisions because of the question of their mutual tonnage relation. The capital ship "holiday" set up in 1922, that is, no building until 1936, was reaffirmed, and there was added an escalator clause permitting upward revision in case a state felt threatened.

London Naval Treaty of 1936. A treaty signed as a result of a naval conference held in London December 9, 1935—March 25, 1936. Japan refused to sign because it was not granted equality with Great Britain and the United States, and Italy refused because of the League of Nations sanctions then in force against her. The treaty did not limit naval armaments except the tonnage of certain smaller classes. It extended the holiday on small capital ship building till 1943 and provided exceptions to the rules if the states were threatened. After 1936 naval limitations were off in reality.

London Roundtable Conferences. 1. A series of three conferences between representatives of Britain and India held in London 1930–32. The first two achieved little but the third concluded recommendations later embodied in the 1935 constitution or Government of India Act. **2.** Two parallel conferences between the British and the Arabs and the Jews held in February and March 1939 to discuss a settlement for Palestine. No constructive conclusions were reached.

London, Secret Treaty of. The secret treaty Italy signed April 26, 1915 with Great Britain, France, and Russia on the basis of which she joined them in World War I. They agreed she should receive Austrian territory north and east of the Adriatic, the Dodecanese Islands near Turkey, an undefined control over southern Turkey and more territory in Africa if France and Great Britain did.

long session. The first regular session of the United States Congress prior to the passage of the Lame Duck Amendment. It met in December and ran until late the next spring. See SHORT SESSION.

loose or **broad construction.** The interpretation of the Constitution that the powers of the federal government include all those which may be reasonably inferred as flowing from the powers specifically granted. See STRICT CONSTRUCTION, IMPLIED POWERS.

Lord Chancellor. In England the presiding officer of the House of Lords, and the cabinet member who heads the British judicial system. He presides also when the law lords sit as a judicial body, recommends the higher judges, and appoints judges to the inferior courts.

Lord Mayor of London. Title of an honorary and ceremonial, rather than functioning, official. The Lord Mayor presides over the three councils or "courts" of the city of London, but is not an executive official.

Lord Privy Seal. A British cabinet position which carries with it no administrative functions, a kind of ministry without portfolio. It was formerly the office of the keeper of one of the royal seals.

Lords of Appeal in Ordinary. Seven members of the House of Lords appointed for life because of their legal qualifications. They are the only paid members. Their function, and that of the other "law lords" is to represent the House of Lords as the highest court of appeals. See LAW LORDS.

Lords Spiritual. The twenty-six members of the House of Lords representing the Church of England. They include the two archbishops of Canterbury and York and twenty-four bishops.

Lords Temporal. The members of the House of Lords other than the Lords Spiritual. See LORDS SPIRITUAL.

Louisiana Purchase. 1. The purchase of the territory of Louisiana by the United States from France in 1803 for $15,000,000. It included a great expanse of territory north and northwest of the present state of Louisiana, greatly increasing the extent of United States territory and assuring free access to the Gulf of Mexico via the Mississippi River. **2.** The territory included in the purchase.

Louvre. Greatest of the palaces of Paris. It houses a museum containing a magnificent collection of pictures and other works |of art. The scholars in charge of it founded the famous *École* (school) *du Louvre* in 1882.

Low Countries. Belgium and the Netherlands; the latter means low countries.

lower house. One part or house of a legislative body, as the House of Representatives of the United States, which for various traditional reasons such as the popular election of its members, is, or was originally, thought of as being somewhat inferior to the other chamber. See UPPER HOUSE.

loyalist. 1. One loyal or faithful to the legitimate government during a revolution, particularly those faithful to the Republican regime in Spain during the Civil War of 1936–39, or to the British Government during the American Revolution, 1776–1781.

Lublin government. A post-war Polish government established in Lublin, Poland by pro-Russian Poles after the Nazis had been driven out of the city by the Russian troops in World War II. Until after the end of the war this government was at odds with a Polish government-in-exile in London. The government recognized by the United Nations is a merger of the Lublin government and individual members of the London group.

Lufthansa. German pre-1939 civil air service.

Luftwaffe. German army air force.

lynch. To inflict death upon an accused person, as when a mob hangs a suspect, or even, in some cases, one who has been tried.

Lytton Commission. A commission appointed by the League of Nations December 10, 1931 to investigate the dispute between China and Japan. The chairman was Lord Lytton of Great Britain. France, Germany, Italy, and the United States were also represented. It traveled to the Far East and its report, made public October 2, 1932, recommended autonomy for Manchuria, direct Sino-Japanese negotiation of new treaties redefining the political and commercial relations of China and Japan, and a promise by both parties not to exert influence in Manchuria and to settle disputes peacefully. This report came too late to have any effect.

M

mace. A heavy, ornamented staff used by various officials as a symbol of authority. The two best known are: the wooden mace covered with gold leaf and topped by a gold crown which symbolizes the authority of the British king and rests on the Treasury bench in the House of Commons during each session; the simpler mace, topped by an eagle, which stands beside the desk of the speaker of the American House of Representatives.

Macedonia. An area lying about the port of Salonica, Greece, at the northwest corner of the Aegean Sea. Its boundaries have changed throughout history, but many of its inhabitants have been striving for independence which the area has not had in modern times. For centuries it was part of the Turkish empire, but after World War I it was divided between Greece and Yugoslavia, with a small part going to Bulgaria.

Machiavellian diplomacy. Diplomacy using unscrupulous means to attain its ends. Named for Niccolo Machiavelli (1469–1537) whose book, *The Prince*, cites many examples of the successful use of such methods.

machine. A term applied to a well-disciplined, usually unscrupulous political organization or part of such an organization. Usually machines are found only in large cities or in states, rarely on a national basis.

Machtstaat (MAHKHT-shtaht). Literally a power-state. A German conception of the state as an organization of power, ready to use its power freely, especially military, to achieve its aggressive ends.

Mackinac Declaration. Statement on foreign policy adopted by the Republican Post-War Advisory Council at Mackinac Island, September 7, 1943. It included: "1. Prosecution of the war by a united nation to conclusive victory over all our enemies . . . 2. Responsible participation by the United States in post-war co-operative organization among sovereign nations to prevent military aggression and to attain permanent peace with organized justice in a free world."

maffia. Italian, or more specifically Sicilian, secret organization which rules its members without regard to local law, especially in regard to the meting out punishments or revenge.

Maginot line (mazh-i-NOH). Series of fortifications built by France along the German frontier. Its extension along the Belgian frontier was not completed before World War II. It was named in honor of André Maginot, several times minister of war and a staunch defense advocate. It proved inadequate as a defense against mechanized warfare.

magistrate. Judge of a minor court, such as a police court. See CHIEF MAGISTRATE.

Magna Carta. The Great Charter, the most influential document in English history. It was an agreement between King John and his rebellious barons issued in the form of a charter or grant in 1215, after a meeting at Runnymede, and it guaranteed to the barons certain feudal rights and privileges involving inheritance, law courts, feudal dues and the like which John had violated. The serfs and townsmen were only briefly mentioned. John was forced to issue the charter against his will and later repudiated it, but it was re-issued in 1216 and 1217 by Henry III. From the 17th to 19th centuries the document was interpreted in a sense very different from its actual feudal character. It was declared to be a symbol of the supremacy of the constitution over the king, a guarantee of trial by jury and a bulwark against taxation without representation. Although these claims were only partly founded in fact, they gave the Magna Carta an immense influence in the development of British and American institutions.

Magyar (MAHDJ-yahr). Hungarian.

Maharajah. Literally, great rajah, one of the highest titles of the princes of the native states of India.

mahatma. In India a kind of prophet or saint. The word means "great soul."

Mahdi. The last of the Mohammedan prophets who is still expected to appear on earth. The title has been assumed by several Moslem leaders, notably the one the British met in the Sudan in the 1880's.

Mahratta Confederacy. A confederation of native princes in west and central India, destroyed by the British in 1818.

majority. 1. The major or greater part, that is, more than half, or the group that controls a vote of that size. 2. The excess of the largest number of votes for a candidate over the next highest number for another. 3. 21 years of age.

majority floor leader. Floor leader of majority party. See FLOOR LEADER.

majority rule. See RULE OF THE MAJORITY.

Make the world safe for democracy. "The world must be made safe for democracy." Statement of President Wilson in his address to Congress April 2, 1917, asking for a declaration of war against Germany, later adopted as a popular slogan.

malfeasance. Performance of a wrongful act, particularly by a public official.

managed currency. A currency not based on gold but changed in amount, availability and value from time to time for the purpose of securing stability of prices and thus of business as a whole.

Manchu dynasty. Rulers of part or all of China intermittently between the 12th century and 1912, whose original home was in Manchuria.

Manchuria Industrial Development Corporation. A Japanese holding company established in 1937 for controling the coal, iron and steel, magnesium, gold, oil, and soya bean development in Manchuria. Its establishment indicated a marked step in the growing co-operation of capitalists and militarists in Japan.

mandamus. An order of a court commanding an administrative official to perform one of his functions in a specific case.

mandate. 1. The authorization under the League of Nations granting to a state a kind of trusteeship over an area which is not sufficiently developed to be recognized as independent. Territories taken from Germany and Turkey after World War I were so organized, in three categories: the A mandates were those in which the inhabitants were almost ready for independence; the B mandates involved those less ready; and the C mandates practically perpetuated a colonial status. One A mandate, that over Iraq, was in fact resolved according to plan and Iraq joined the League in 1932. 2. The document embodying the authorization. 3. A territory under mandate, more accurately referred to as a mandated territory.

mandatory. A state which has been granted a mandate over a backward territory.

manhood suffrage. A voting system in which all men, with minor exceptions as in the case of those mentally incapacitated, are granted the privilege of voting.

manifest destiny. A kind of imperialistic predestination, the feeling of many Americans that it was our obvious destiny to expand imperialistically across the continent, into the Caribbean, and out into the Pacific. A term in use prior to 1850; used by McKinley to refer to the United States annexation of the Hawaiian Islands.

manpower. The number of men and women available for productive employment in industry, agriculture, transportation, and other essential services.

manslaughter. Unlawful killing of a person without malice, that is, with some justification but not sufficient to prevent the act from being illegal.

maquis (mah-KEE). French underground organization and a member thereof. The term is the French word for scrub, bushy vegetation in Corsica or land covered therewith. Hence the organization of patriots who "took to the bush."

March. See MARK, 2.

March on Rome. The descent upon Rome in late October, 1922, by about 50,000 blackshirted Fascists. This display of power was instrumental in making the King of Italy offer the premiership to Benito Mussolini on October 29. He took office the next day and brought the Fascists to power.

Marco Polo Bridge incident. An armed clash, on July 7, 1937 between Chinese and Japanese troops during night maneuvers and patrol duty at the Marco Polo Bridge near Peiping. This shooting opened the second phase of the Sino-Japanese War begun in 1931; it continued into World War II.

mare nostrum (MAY-ree NOS-truhm). Latin term meaning "our sea," that is, the Mediterranean. Taken over by the Italian Fascists to indicate their imperialistic ambitions regarding the sea and the nations bordering it.

marginal sea. The sea along the coastline out to the three-mile limit. This area is under the jurisdiction of the state whose shore the sea washes.

Marianne. Feminine figure with revolutionary cap, symbolic of France.

maritime law. A collection of rules dealing chiefly with rights and duties in the handling of ships. Maritime law dates back to ancient civilizations and has been built up almost entirely on customs which are often identical or similar in most sea-faring countries. It includes provisions as to registry, license, mortgage, inspection, navigation, equipment, seizure and forfeiture of ships. It also deals with all kinds of maritime contracts which include the hiring of ships, carriage of passengers and goods, marine insurance, wharfage and towage, purchasing of supplies, wages of seamen, pilotage and salvage. Several international conferences have done much to unify the maritime rules in various sea-faring countries.

Maritime Provinces. The eastern coast of Canada: the provinces of Nova

Scotia, Prince Edward Island and New Brunswick. Also used under the Czar to refer to the eastern provinces of Siberia.

mark. A medieval Germanic word for a border region. One of the most important was the mark of Brandenburg. The Nazis revived the word and applied it to Austria after the annexation of 1938, calling it the Ostmark, or East Mark. In Britain the same word was spelled march, especially applied to the Welsh and Scottish Marches. From the words are derived the titles margrave, marquess and marquis, originally applied to their rulers. 2. German unit of money, formerly valued at 40 cents. Officially, Reichsmark.

Marne, Battles of. Two battles in which the Germans in World War I were stopped at the Marne River just short of Paris. The first battle occurred in the second week of September, 1914 and the second during the last half of July and the first week of August, 1918.

marquis, marquess. European title of nobility. Marquis is the French form, marquess British. Originally a ruler of a border region called a mark or march, but the term has lost this meaning and is now merely a symbol of nobility. In Britain a marquess ranks between a duke and an earl in the peerage. The German equivalent is margraf, often called margrave in English. The feminine forms are marquise (French), marchioness (English) margraefin or margravine (German). See MARK.

marquise, marchioness. In French and English respectively, the noble title held by the wife of a marquis or marquess. The German form is margraefin or margravine. See MARQUIS, MARQUESS.

Marseilles assassinations. The murder on October 9, 1934 of King Alexander I of Yugoslavia and French Foreign Minister Louis Barthou, in Marseilles, during the former's state visit to France to consider a French-Yugoslav agreement. The assassin was Vlatko Georgieff, a Macedonian terrorist, and the crime stemmed from Macedonian and Croatian discontent under Yugoslav rule. See IMRO.

marshal. 1. A high military title, usually outranking that of general. In Britain and Germany the full title is Field Marshal, but Britain also has Air Marshals. In the United States Army the corresponding rank is that of General of the Armies. The name is descended from the early medieval title given the royal official in charge of the king's stables, who later was put in charge of military affairs. 2. An officer exercising certain police functions for the United States Federal courts, such as arresting and detaining accused persons, serving papers and carrying out judgments. 3. Village police officers in many of the United States. 4. In American cities, the head of the police or fire department.

martial law. The temporary government of the civil population of a state by the military forces of the state because of military or other necessity.

Marxism. The principles of socialism as advocated by the German philosopher Karl Marx (1818–1883). Marxists believe in an economic interpretation of history, according to which history can be best understood by observing the means of economic production, the distribution of property, and the resulting conflict of interests. Political and social institutions and beliefs are all dependent on the underlying economic system. With technological progress economic systems change, property is redistributed and new economic classes arise. In every society there is a ruling economic class, which creates a hostile class and the "class-struggle" ensues. Thus according to Marxism the rule of the capitalists, which began in the 18th century created an evergrowing hostile class of wage-earning workers, the proletariat. The overthrow of the economic and political rule of the bourgeoisie, the class of capitalists, who own the "means of production" and exploit the workers by taking away part of their just reward (the so-called "surplus-value") is the aim of the enlightened or "class-conscious" proletariat. The worker has a "right" to his own "product" and therefore the struggle against capitalists is just. The state (the government) is run by the capitalists, in order to keep down the workers and once the workers come to power they will have to remake the whole social and political order and establish a more equitable economic system: socialism. The socialist society according to Marx will be classless and therefore a political government will become eventually superfluous.

The theory of capitalist exploitation was expounded by Marx in "Das Kapital" (Capital) and the appeal to the workers of the world to rise, in the revolutionary pamphlet, the "Communist Manifesto." Marx's theory was the driving force behind many, though not all, Socialist parties and was adopted by the Russian, Lenin, the founder of modern Communism. The Soviet Union is the only country where Marxism has completely triumphed, but according to Soviet theorists, the USSR is only on its way to the final stage of socialism, in which according to Lenin, the state political government will "wither away." See CLASS-STRUGGLE, COMMUNISM, SOCIALISM, STALINITE, TROTSKYITE, BOLSHEVISM, WORLD-REVOLUTION, PROLETARIAT.

Mason-Dixon Line. The line separating free states from slave states. Part of it, the boundary between Pennsylvania and Maryland, was almost completely surveyed between 1763 and 1767 by two surveyors named Mason and Dixon, to settle a dispute between the two colonies.

Massachusetts ballot. A ballot with all the candidates for a given office grouped together in one column. A straight party ticket cannot thus be voted by marking a single cross for all the candidates of a given party. See INDIANA BALLOT.

master race doctrine. The Nazi theory that the German Nordics were a superior race and as such were justified in pushing aside, mistreating, or even exterminating their inferior neighbors. See RACE, TOTALITARIAN.

Material Co-ordinating Committee. A joint American-Canadian emergency war agency set up May 14, 1941, to facilitate the exchange of information regarding raw materials of defense value.

matriarchate. State in which the rule is held by women.

May Crisis. The international crisis of May 1938 precipitated by the interference of Hitler in the Czechoslovak municipal elections. It was his first move against Czechoslovakia and was stopped by the Czech mobilization and by assurances for Czech backing from London, Paris, and Moscow.

May First. An international labor day celebrated by socialists and communists and made one of the most important national holidays in Russia.

Mayflower Compact. The agreement drawn up by the Pilgrims on the Mayflower en route to America in 1620 as a basis for their colony. It stated that they would draw up and obey such laws as the majority of the community decided upon. It is often referred to as an example of an explicit social contract. See SOCIAL CONTRACT.

mayor. Title of chief executive official in many cities in the United States and the British Commonwealth.

M. B. E. See ORDER OF THE BRITISH EMPIRE.

M. C. Member of Congress.

McDuffie-Tydings Bill. See PHILIPPINE INDEPENDENCE ACT.

M-day. Mobilization day. In countries that have compulsory military service it signifies the day of return of the national manpower to the armed forces and the shift of transportation and industry to a military basis.

measure. Term used for projected or enacted legislation.

Mecca. City in Saudi Arabia, birthplace of Mohammed, and one of the Mohammedan holy cities. It is a place of pilgrimmage and the place toward which Mohammedans turn when they pray.

mediation. An attempt by a third party to reach a settlement in a labor or international dispute by making suggestions based on a compromise between the views of the disputing parties. Submission of a dispute to mediation does not imply that the disputing parties are bound to accept the suggestions of the mediator. See CONCILIATION; TENDER OF GOOD OFFICES.

Mein Kampf. Two-volume work by Adolph Hitler, the first part of which was written while he was in Landsberg prison serving a short sentence for starting an armed revolt against the German republic, November 9, 1923. It is a confused combination of autobiography and plans for a great new Germany. The latter part was chiefly a repetition of earlier pan-German doctrines plus a chapter on propaganda. The title means "my struggle."

Memel Territory. The port of Memel, Lithuania. The city, almost entirely German in population, was taken from Germany by the Allies at Versailles. It was occupied by Lithuanians in 1923. The end result was a large degree of autonomy in local government, an international committee to control the port, a free zone for Polish shipping, and continuous friction between the German inhabitants and the government of Lithuania. It was occupied both by Germans and later Russians in World War II. Now part of the USSR.

Memorial Day. A United States national holiday to commemorate the members of the armed forces who gave their lives in the Civil War. In recent years it has been extended to include those who fell in the Spanish American War, World Wars I and II. It is celebrated in the North on May 30, and is a legal holiday in most states. In the Southern States a similar day is celebrated as Confederate Memorial Day on April 26 in Alabama, Florida, Georgia and Mississippi; May 10 in Kentucky and North Carolina; May 30 in Virginia; June 3 in Louisiana and Tennessee.

mending fences. The occupation of an elected legislator in cultivating the voters of his district, looking forward to getting their support at the next election.

Mensheviki. The minority and less radical element of the Russian socialists. See BOLSHEVIKI.

mercantilism. An economic theory and policy asserting that a nation is economically strengthened by exporting more goods than it imports, thereby achieving a so-called favorable balance of trade. Mercantilism favored state support and protection of industry, facilitation of exports and imposition of tariffs against the importation of foreign goods. This was partly based on an express intention to protect domestic industry from damaging foreign competition and partly on a belief that gold and money are identical with wealth and that an excess of exports over imports resulting in a net import of gold and money would also mean an increase of wealth. Mercantilism prevailed particularly in the 16th and 17th centuries as a reaction against medieval economic systems in which money played a subordinate role and where international trade was based on barter. Mercantilism was succeeded in turn by a policy of free trade. Mercantilism re-appeared at the end of the 19th and in the 20th centuries mainly as a result of attempts to protect domestic industries from better or cheaper foreign products. This so-called neo-mercantilism resulted in protective tariffs throughout the whole world. See FREE TRADE, TARIFFS, TARIFF WAR, PROTECTIVE TARIFF, INTERNATIONAL TRADE.

mercenaries. Hired troops not of the nationality of the army in which they are incorporated. Rarely found in recent times. Example: the Swiss troops hired by many European powers and the Papacy.

merchant marine. Strictly speaking, the merchant vessels owned and operated by a state. In some states in peace, and in most states in war, this tends to include all the merchant ships flying a state's flag. The term is often used loosely in this latter sense.

merchantman. Merchant ship, usually thought of as a freighter rather than as primarily a passenger ship.

merit system. A system of recruiting and promoting public employees on the basis of merit or worth, as opposed to a spoils basis. Often used synonymously with civil service. See CIVIL SERVICE.

Mesopotamia. A Greek word meaning between the rivers, applied to the region between the Tigris and Euphrates rivers in the Middle East, roughly equivalent to the modern state of Iraq. It is one of the cradles of ancient civilization, dating back at least to 3000 B.C. It has formed a part of the Babylonian, Assyrian and Egyptian empires, the empire of Alexander the Great, of Persia, Parthia and, more recently, Turkey. In biblical times it was known as Aram or Padan Aram. It was the site of such famous cities as Babylon, Ur of the Chaldees, Nineveh, and Bagdad, the present capital of Iraq.

message on the state of the Union. Any message which the president may send to Congress under the provision of Article II, Section 3 of the Constitution of the United States which provides that, "He shall from time to time give to the Congress information of the state of the Union, and recommend to their consideration such measures as he shall judge necessary and expedient." Usually thought of as the annual message which the president sends to Congress at the opening of each regular session.

Metals Reserve Company. An agency of the United States Commerce Department set up by the Reconstruction Finance Corporation on June 28, 1940 to stockpile and distribute under the priorities established by the War Production Board the minerals and metals needed in the war production program.

metropolitan region. The area surrounding a large city and its dependent municipalities, townships and counties. A few beginnings have been made toward centralizing control of certain matters of common interest throughout such regions such as water supply, sewage disposal, parks and port facilities.

middle class. Those persons, and their

Middle East

families, whose essential economic status is neither that of the large employer of labor nor that of a person working for wages as one of a large group hired by such employer. The group tends to include doctors, lawyers, teachers, and the other professions, and those whose businesses depend to a large extent on their own efforts. The group is distinguished as a "middle" class also in that its economic income is in general higher than that of the common laborer and below that of the large employer.

Middle East. Strictly speaking, Iraq, Iran, and Afghanistan, that is, the countries between the Near East, or states bordering on the eastern Mediterranean, and India. The British often include Egypt, Palestine, Transjordan, Syria, and the Lebanon, in the Middle East. Hence in World War II the Middle Eastern armies and supply centers were centered in Egypt. See NEAR EAST.

Middle Eastern Pact. A treaty signed July 8, 1937, by Afghanistan, Iran, Iraq, and Turkey at Saad-Abad Palace near Teheran, Iran. It contained agreements for non-aggression, no raiding, and peaceful settlement of disputes among the parties, and for consultation in case of any international conflict of common interest.

Middle West. A term used to designate roughly the states between Ohio and Nebraska inclusive, north of the Ohio River and the southern boundary of Missouri and Kansas.

midnight judges. Judges commissioned as late as midnight on March 3, 1801, by President John Adams. The new judgeships had recently been provided by Congress, but the appointments were rushed through in an effort to prevent Jefferson, who took office March 4, from filling the positions from members of his own party.

migration. 1. Movement, usually of a considerable number, of people changing their places of residence. 2. The people participating in this movement.

militarism. A belief that war and the preparation for war are the most important functions of a nation and the highest form of public service. The militarists exalt military service, personal courage, loyalty to superiors, physical endurance and rigid discipline. They would like to introduce certain military ideas and customs into civilian fields and have in general only disdain for the "weak civilians." They favour the profuse use of flags, decorations, orders; the establishment of exclusive military associations, the holding of ceremonies and parades. In militaristic countries the officers' corps generally forms an exclusive and special class, admired by the rest of the people and highly influential in political, social and spiritual life of the nation. War usually furthers the growth of militarism. The Kingdom of Prussia which, with the other German countries, formed the German Reich in 1871, is the best example in modern history of triumphant militarism. German militarism prepared the ground for Hitler's Nazism. Pre-war Japan was dominated by militarism and was driven into aggression by the highly influential army circles. An anti-militaristic feeling was brought to America by English colonists and is still maintained by the overwhelming majority of the British and American people. See TOTALITARIANISM, FASCISM, NAZISM.

militaristic. See MILITARISM.

military government. The government set up and maintained by the armed forces of a state over territory of the enemy which they have occupied and its inhabitants, and over domestic territory taken from enemies or rebels recognized as belligerents.

military law. The body of rules which governs the administration, organization, and discipline of an army and which also provides for the punishment of violators. Its essence is that members of the armed forces are governed by separate rules and that those who break the rules should be punished by special military courts. In America military law is called the "Articles of War" which are valid for both war and peace time. They grew up upon English foundations. A military court is called court-martial and to court-martial a person means to try him under military law. Courts martial usually operate with a jury drawn from both officers and enlisted men. Courts martial do not belong under the judicial branch of the United States Government but are part of the armed forces and are as such a part of the executive branch.

Martial law deals with civilians, not with members of the armed forces. See LAW, POSITIVE LAW, TRIAL BY JURY.

military necessity. The doctrine, subject to humanitarian considerations, that a belligerent may use any amount and kind of force in compelling the submission of the enemy with the greatest economy of lives, money, and time.

military occupation. Control by a state's armed forces of the territory of an enemy or recent enemy. This control, though complete, is temporary and does not in itself make the occupant sovereign. See OCCUPATION.

military service. Service in the armed forces of a state.

Military Service Act. See SELECTIVE TRAINING AND SERVICE ACT.

military training. Instruction in military science and organization. Usually discussed in terms of such instruction in time of peace and the degree to which it should then be required, if at all.

militia. An armed force consisting of non-professional or citizen soldiers. The institution of civilians called up for national defense in war time or for training in peace time is very old. The true militia system is based upon the obligation of every citizen to serve his country. Therefore it should be distinguished from the draft (which exists only in war time or in emergency situations) and also from the National Guard in the United States, which is a voluntary force. In Washington's army 41% were militia and the rest volunteers. To-day Switzerland has one of the few militia systems which dispenses completely with any professional army except a small group of officers, the so-called "army instructors." The merit of a militia system is that it safeguards democracy from the danger of aggressive militarism, which may arise within a large professional army. The Swiss regard their military service as a kind of civic education. The system's weaknesses are that it cannot be adjusted easily to modern warfare which relies on highly trained specialists. See MILITARISM.

"Millions for defense but not a cent for tribute." Toast offered by Rep. Robert G. Harper of S. Carolina at a dinner given by Congress June 18, 1798 in honor of John Marshall, who had just returned from France. It was a challenge to build a navy to protect United States ships from the depredations of the French. Also ascribed to Charles Pinckney, United States ambassador to France, who was asked indirectly for $250,000 on October 26, 1797 in return for stopping the attacks.

minimum wage law. A law setting a minimum rate for wages.

minister. 1. Diplomatic agent of the second class. The full title is Envoy Extraordinary and Minister Plenipotentiary. 2. Cabinet member, as a minister of foreign affairs or foreign minister.

ministerial. Pertaining to administrative functions, the institution and operation of which are so closely prescribed that practically no choice is available to the administrator. Used as opposed to discretionary.

ministerial responsibility. The accountability of a cabinet minister to a legislative body in a cabinet form of government. If a minister's policies are not backed by his parliament on a vote of confidence, he resigns.

minister resident. Diplomat of the third class sent to very small countries. See DIPLOMAT.

ministry. 1. Collective term for cabinet, particularly in Great Britain. 2. Office of a cabinet minister, as the ministry of war.

Minnesota Mortgage Moratorium. A Minnesota state law postponing payments and preventing foreclosure on mortgages. In 1934 the Supreme Court held such laws passed by a state to be valid in view of the economic emergency.

minor. Individual under legal age.

minority. 1. Group of people in a state forming less than half and often a small fraction of the total population, who differ in race, cultural background or for some other reason from the majority of the people of the state. 2. A vote comprising less than half the vote cast.

minority party. A party whose representation in a legislative body is a small proportion of the total.

minority report. A report from a minority, as of a committee, disagreeing with the committee report or majority report.

minority representation. See PROPORTIONAL REPRESENTATION.

Minseito Party. One of the two major political parties in Japan prior to World War II, the other being the Seiyukai Party. Under other names it dates back to 1882, and it became the Minseito Party in 1927. It was the more liberal and internationalist of the two, drawing its main support from the cities. It sponsored the manhood suffrage act of 1925 and supported the London Naval Treaty. But like the Seiyukai it was an alliance of politicians, industrialists and land owners, and its close connections with the Mitsubishi interests gave it the popular name of the Mitsubishi Party. In 1940 it was abolished when the fascist Imperial Rule Assistance Association was made the only party in Japan. See SEIYUKAI PARTY; MITSUBISHI.

mint. 1. Place where metal money is made. 2. To coin or make metal money.

minuteman. A kind of militia formed by the patriots just before the American Revolutionary War who were prepared to mobilize on a minute's warning.

minutes. Record of the actions taken in a meeting such as that of a legislative body or committee.

misdemeanor. Minor infraction of the law. See CRIME.

misfeasance. Wrongful performance, particularly by a public official, of an act which ordinarily is legal.

mi-souverain (mee-soo-VRANG). See SEMI-SOVEREIGN.

mission. 1. Some special function to be performed such as the negotiation of a special international agreement. 2. The persons sent to carry out such a function, such as a military or diplomatic mission. 3. In the sense of 2, the staff of an embassy or legation.

Missouri Compromise. A group of

measures passed by the United States Congress in 1820 temporarily solving the question of slavery in new states. Missouri had applied for admission to the Union in 1818, but the Senate and House of Representatives disagreed on whether slavery should be permitted there. The solution was to admit both Missouri and Maine, the former a slave state and the latter not, and to prohibit slavery in the rest of the Louisiana Purchase north and west of the southern boundary of Missouri.

Mitsubishi. Great Japanese financial house, second in importance only to Mitsui. Its holding companies were dissolved by Gen. MacArthur in January, 1946. See MITSUI.

Mitsui. Great Japanese financial concern, Mitsui and Company. Prior to 1945 its control reached into the major interests of the country in banking, industry, and trade. Like Mitsubishi's, its holding companies were dissolved by Gen. MacArthur in January, 1946.

Mitteleuropa (MIT-uhl-oi-ROH-pah). Literally middle Europe. A German concept of a fairly well integrated central Europe, naturally to be dominated by Germany.

mixed commission. An international commission composed of representatives of the two or more states in a dispute.

mixed courts. A series of civil and commercial courts set up in Egypt in 1876 including both Egyptian and foreign judges, the latter in a majority and representing the states having capitulatory agreements with Turkey. See CAPITULATIONS.

mobilization. The process of calling up the members of the armed forces, including those normally in civilian life, and organizing their units in preparation for war. Whether the process includes marching against an enemy, is a matter of national interpretation.

modus vivendi (MOH-duhs vi-VEN-die). Literally a method of living (together). An arrangement by which two states can compose their differences at least well enough to get along together until further, more permanent agreement can be reached.

Mohammedan. Follower of Mohammed; adherent of Mohammedanism. See MOHAMMEDANISM.

Mohammedanism. Religion based on the teachings of Mohammed and on the belief in God and Mohammed as a prophet of God. A religion dominant in North Africa, the Near and Middle East, Northwest India, and parts of the East Indies and Central Asia.

Molly McGuires. Members of lawless secret organizations in Ireland and, just following the Civil War, in the hard coal region of Pennsylvania.

monarchy. Rule of a state by a single person. Referred to as "absolute" if the rule was actually controlled by the monarch alone, and "limited" if the ruler were aided in the exercise of his functions, especially by a parliamentary body for law-making.

monetary. Pertaining to money; financial.

money. Money in modern society serves two purposes: it acts as a medium of exchange and serves as a common denominator of value. As a medium of exchange money must be generally acceptable and easily transferable. It may take the shape of gold, silver, or metal coins (also called hard money); or printed or engraved paper (paper money, banknotes); or (in primitive society) shells or colored stones; or (in advanced society) promises of payment, such as checks etc. The expression "currency" refers to money which is current or which circulates subject to public regulation. In modern society all money is currency, though in times of inflation or economic chaos old and out-of-date gold coins suddenly appear and are used as money instead of currency. Currency is also called legal tender. Modern money carries on it an inscription bearing the name of the unit of account or a multiple or a fraction thereof. Hence money serves as the common denominator of value even in cases where actual physical money is not used, as in business transactions which appear in accounting without money changing hands, simple barter, etc.

When the currency system is founded upon a precious metal (gold, silver), the unit of account corresponds to the legally defined value of the precious metal; paper money in such a system could be exchanged for (converted into) the precious metal. Nowadays, however, most countries have established a so-called convertible currency system, in which the unit of account is a fiction corresponding to something in the past. Currencies (or monetary systems) may follow various standards: gold standard; silver standard; gold and silver standard (bimetallism); exchange standard (or related to the value of another currency); managed through the limitation of issue (index standard). They may be convertible, partly convertible or inconvertible into the precious metal they are bound up with, or they may have no external standard whatsoever and be entirely dependent on public faith.

The most important standard in recent history has been the gold standard which had a certain international validity in the 19th century. It collapsed over a large part of the world during the 1930's and has been maintained in other parts only formally. It was based upon the principle of the free mintage of gold with silver, bronze or nickel coins and banknotes mainly as a subsidiary kind of money, all convertible into gold. This made international monetary transactions simpler and rendered currency more stable. Money if convertible into gold is less apt to depreciate suddenly, but if it is not convertible, the possession of huge gold reserves will have little effect. (This is the case in the United States, where in Fort Knox, Kentucky, much of the world's gold is stored). The value of the money is only partly dependent on restrictions of the quantity issued, but much more on the relationship between cash money owned by the public and intended for consumption, and the available supply of goods. The value of money is also greatly dependent upon public faith, the lack of which may cause depreciations as in the case of revolutions when the public may refuse to accept the money printed by the new regime. In the past money based on the gold standard was called "sound money" and was contrasted with "managed" currency which had no intrinsic value in itself. Later the term "sound money" was applied to those currencies in which the public had faith and accepted without hesitation.

money bill. A bill appropriating funds for governmental use. Under the United States Constitution such bills must originate in the House of Representatives. Occasionally the Senate so amends such a bill, as a tariff bill, that few of the provisions really originating in the House are left.

monopoly. Control of any sale, service, or source of supply, more or less exclusively in the hands of one person or firm. Much early legislation in the

United States promoting a free economy took the form of prohibiting such control. Certain services are exempted.

Monroe Doctrine. A United States policy regarding Latin America. President Monroe's message to Congress of December 2, 1823 stated that "the American continents by the free and independent condition which they have assumed and maintain, are henceforth not to be considered as subjects for future colonization by any European powers" and that the United States would consider as an unfriendly act any attempt at interposition or intervention in Latin America and any extension there of European political systems. This statement was intended to back up the new South American republics still fearing reconquest by European colonial powers and was at the same time a warning to Russian plans of expansion on the northwestern coast of America. The doctrine was revived in the 1840's when Britain and France tried to prevent the annexation of Texas by the United States, and when conflicts over Oregon with Britain arose. It was unsuccessfully invoked in the 1860's when Spain took over the Dominican Republic and France intervened in Mexico. After the Civil War France withdrew from Mexico. The doctrine was also used in an effort to prevent Europeans from constructing a canal across the Isthmus of Panama, and to end a blockade imposed by Britain, Germany, and Italy against Venezuela.

President Theodore Roosevelt gave the Monroe doctrine a new interpretation as a justification for United States' intervention in the area. In 1904 he stated that continued misconduct in a Latin American state might compel the United States to intervene in order to keep Europe out. This is called the Roose-velt corollary. President Wilson in 1913, repudiated Roosevelt's "big stick" policy. Yielding to Congressional pressure Wilson succeeded in having the principle of regional understandings, such as the Monroe Doctrine, included in the Covenant of the League of Nations. The Monroe Doctrine lost much popularity during the first two decades of this century as many Latin American countries were afraid of United States domination. In 1930 the Clark Memorandum denied that the Monroe Doctrine was an instrument for intervening in Latin-American affairs. The Good Neighbor policy since 1933 has done much to lessen their fears. In Europe, however, the Monroe Doctrine is still often understood as establishing Latin America as a "sphere of interest" of the United States. The Charter of the United Nations, like the League, permits regional arrangements between States. See GOOD NEIGHBOR POLICY.

Montagu-Chelmsford Report. A report on the India problem, drawn up by the British Secretary for India and the Viceroy, published in July, 1918, and used as the basis for the Government of India Act of 1919, increasing the electorate and setting up a Council of State and Legislative Assembly.

Montevideo Conference. The Seventh Pan American Conference which met December 3, 1933, notable particularly as the first occasion on which the United States agreed to the principle of non-intervention in Inter-American affairs.

Montreux Convention. A treaty signed July 20, 1936, redefining the regulations of the Straits. Turkey was given the right to remilitarize the shores. The waters were open in peace time to merchant ships but only a limited tonnage of war vessels could go through to the Black Sea. Turkey could close the waters to belligerents except in upholding League of Nations action. See STRAITS.

morals court. A court the jurisdiction of which includes cases of family troubles and delinquencies of women and girls and sometimes of minors.

moratorium. A period of suspension of normal operations. See MINNESOTA MORTGAGE MORATORIUM; HOOVER MORATORIUM.

Morgan Line. The line of demarcation, set up after World War II in what had been northeastern Italy, between the occupying troops of Yugoslavia on the east and those of the British Commonwealth and the United States on the west, established pending the determination of a new, permanent Italian-Yugoslav boundary. Its name was derived from that of the British representative at the negotiations which resulted in the line, Lieutenant General Sir William Morgan. See FRENCH LINE.

Morley-Minto Constitution. An early constitution for India granted in 1909. It enlarged the advisory legislative councils and made it possible for Indians to become members of the viceroy's council and the councils of the governors of the provinces. Named for Viscount John Morley, secretary of state for India, and the Earl of Minto, viceroy of India.

morning hour. One of the steps in the order of business of the United States House of Representatives. In it committees may call for the consideration of public bills other than financial bills.

Morrill Act. A Federal law of 1862 introduced by Sen. J. S. Morrill of Vermont giving to the states federal lands to be used as an endowment for training in agriculture and the mechanical arts. The states were offered 30,000 acres for each representative and senator. Most of the states in the

Middle West have such "land grant colleges."

Moscow trials. A series of trials from 1936 to 1939 of some of the most famous communist leaders in the USSR for allegedly trying to overthrow the Stalin regime and for dealings with Trotsky or the German army. Most of them pleaded guilty and were executed. At the time the trials were widely criticised as political persecution and as wrecking Soviet leadership, but during World War II it appeared more likely that the trials had weeded out potential Soviet fifth-columnists.

Moslem. See MOHAMMEDANISM.

Moslem League. See ALL-INDIA MOSLEM LEAGUE.

mosque. Mohammedan place of collective worship.

mosquito abatement district. Special governmental district set up solely for the purpose of combatting and eliminating mosquitos.

most-favored-nation clause. The clause in a treaty by which one party or both grant to the other the privileges of the "most favored nation," that is, all privileges granted to any third state. The unconditional form of the clause grants the privileges with no strings attached. In the conditional form, the privileges are granted only in return for a special quid pro quo similar to that given by a third state for the same privilege.

motion. A proposition presented for action to a legislative body by one of its members.

M. P. Member of Parliament in Great Britain, really a member of the House of Commons.

M.R.P. The *Mouvement Républicain Populaire*, or Popular Republican Party, a French political party, which, after World War II, derived its strength from the wartime resistance movement in France. Charles de

Gaulle was at first the active leader, though his leadership later became indirect. The party is one of the moderate left, more conservative than the Socialists. It stands for the guarantee of national independence and for the maintenance of the rights of citizens by means of the co-operation of powers and the separation of functions, hence not giving too much power to the Assembly. It states its position as one reconciling political freedom and social justice. It polled about 25 or 30 per cent in the first postwar elections, about the same number as the Communists and a little more than the Socialists, the two other strongest parties.

muckraker. One who looks for and either charges or exposes corruption in public affairs. It came into popular use following a speech of President Theodore Roosevelt in 1904 when he used the verb form, muckrake.

Mudania Armistice. An armistice of October 11, 1922 closing the fighting between Turkey and Greece following World War I. See LAUSANNE, TREATY OF.

Mudros Armistice. An armistice, dated October 30, 1918 between Turkey and the Allies taking Turkey out of World War I.

mud-slinging. American slang term for the use in a political campaign of remarks derogatory to the character and ability of an opponent.

mufti. Mohammedan teacher of the law and religious leader. See GRAND MUFTI.

mugwump. One who bolted the Republican party in 1884. Term of aspersion for an independent voter. The classical definition is a political bird sitting on the fence, with his mug on one side and his wump on the other.

Mukden Incident. The alleged bombing of the South Manchurian Railway just south of Mukden by Chinese "bandits" on September 18, 1931. The railway zone was under the control of the Japanese army, and on the pretext of pursuing the bandits, the Japanese overran all of Manchuria.

multilateral. Pertaining to several sides or parties. A multilateral treaty is one signed by several or many states.

multi-national. A term used to describe a state which has in it more than one nationality in terms of cultural background, such as Switzerland, which is a composite of French, German and Italian elements.

multi-partite. Having many parties or signatories. For example, used to describe a treaty.

multi-party system. A party system where there are several major parties and several minor ones. It has what Americans and British look upon as a disadvantage in the fact that a majority is rarely if ever commanded by one party. Hence the support of the administration must come from two or more parties and is likely to be unstable because they may disagree among themselves.

Munich Accord. One of the major events leading up to World War II. An agreement between Hitler, Mussolini, French premier Daladier and British prime minister Neville Chamberlain at Munich on September 30, 1938 by which Germany received the German-inhabited sections of Western Czechoslovakia known as Sudetenland. The conference was preceded by a tense situation caused by Hitler's threat to go to war against Czechoslovakia if the Sudetenland were not surrendered by October 1, and by the mobilization of the German, Czech and French armies and the British fleet. The accord followed closely the ultimatum given Chamberlain by Hitler at Godesberg on September 23. The Czechs were not consulted at

Munich but were forced to accept. They lost not only the Sudetenland but also their fortified line of defense against Germany in the Bohemian mountains, and were powerless to resist further German encroachments. It was also followed by Polish and Hungarian territorial claims which the Czechs were forced to accept. Germany occupied Czechoslovakia the following March.

municipal. 1. Pertaining to a city or municipality. 2. Internal. For example, as opposed to international law, the national laws of a country are called municipal law.

municipal law. The internal law of a country, as distinguished from international law.

municipal ownership. Ownership and operation of some public service such as an electric power plant by a municipality.

municipality. A city with its own government.

munitions. Arms, ammunition, and such instruments and machines as are primarily of use in war.

Munitions Assignment Board. A joint United States-British board, set up January 26, 1942, the function of which was to collect and provide to the Combined Chiefs of Staff information on the munitions resources of the two countries, to recommend providing for such materials, and to allocate them to the different United Nations.

munitions industry. Various branches of industry making arms and ammunition.

Murmansk route. In World War II vessels routed through the area outlined by the north British Isles, Iceland, the northern tip of Norway and Finland, to the ports of Murmansk and Archangel in the Soviet Union were said to travel the Murmansk route, although their actual paths differed. The most critical part of the route was that off the northern coast of Norway and Finland where Allied ships were under almost constant attack from underwater, surface and air operations by the Nazis.

Muscle Shoals. An electric power project in the Tennessee Valley authorized in 1918 to furnish power for the production of nitrates. It was discontinued at the end of the war and later turned over in 1933 to the Tennessee Valley Authority.

mutiny. Concerted refusal to obey the orders of army or navy officers or of officers of a merchant vessel.

mutual aid. Canadian equivalent for lend-lease during World War II.

mutual assistance pact. A treaty by which two states promise to give assistance to each other if either is attacked.

M. V. O. See ROYAL VICTORIAN ORDER.

N

N

N

N

N

N

N

N

N

N

N

N

N. A. M. National Association of Manufacturers. The manufacturers' organization of the United States. Because of the susceptibility of manufacturing to regulation and tariff protection this organization is naturally interested in politics, and because of its great economic weight it is influential as a conservative pressure group.

Nansen passport. Passport issued under the authority of the League of Nations permitting freedom of movement for refugees after World War I. So called from the name of Fridtjof Nansen who began the League work for refugees.

Napoleonic code. A series of five legal codes drawn up by a commission of jurists under the direction of Napoleon and promulgated between 1804 and 1810. They included civil, commercial and penal codes and codes of civil and criminal procedure. They have been widely drawn upon in the codes of other continental European countries, Japan, and the states of Latin America. Also, they were the basis of the civil code of Louisiana, adopted in 1824, revised in 1870.

narrow seas. Narrow waterways about Great Britain such as Bristol Channel, the Irish Sea, and North Channel, which the British used to claim as territorial waters.

nation. A large group of people who generally form a state and who are welded together by common traditions and culture and usually by a common language. A nation regards itself and is regarded by others as distinct from other nations. Today we usually consider a nation as being identical with a state because we regard a state as being formed by the people who belong to a single nation, the so-called nation-state. Many nations, however, may form a state, particularly if the state is a federation such as Soviet Russia, which is composed of many nations: Russians, Ukrainians, White Russians, Georgians, Armenians, etc. Typical nation-states are France, Sweden, and Portugal. Switzerland is a multi-national state in which three nationalities (German, French, Italian) have been united through history into one nation. Loyalty to the nation can be distinguished from loyalty to the government in power.

nation-state. The modern state in which the state boundaries fairly well coincide with the limits of the more or less homogeneous group of inhabitants, as opposed to older empires in which there was a definite absence of such relation between boundaries and homogeneity of inhabitants. See NATION.

national. Pertaining to the whole nation. The term is used to refer to matters concerning the state, such as the national debt, national government, national legislation, national elections, etc. It is also used for things which concern the whole nation and which are parts of their nationhood, such as the national anthem, national history, national folklore, national flag, etc. In international law "national" is used in yet another sense. It is almost synonymous with "citizen" or "subject" but broader; that is, a national, for example an inhabitant of an overseas possession, owes allegiance to a state and receives its protection but does not have all the rights of its citizens. See STATE, NATION, NATIONALISM.

National Advisory Committee for Aeronautics. Established by act of Congress March 3, 1915 to "supervise and direct the scientific study of the problems of flight, with a view to their practical solution . . ." and by later amendment to "direct and conduct research and experiment in aeronautics." In time of war the research information is available only by permission of the Army and Navy. In peace time, the information is available generally.

National Assembly. The joint session of the two houses of the French parliament under the Third Republic. This joint session voted amendments to the constitution and elected the president.

national bank. 1. A bank established to do the banking business for a national government, as the Bank of France. 2. In the United States a private bank chartered by the federal government. It carries on regular banking business and must be a member of the Federal Reserve System.

national chairman. In the United States, the chairman of the national committee of a political party. He is the choice of the presidential candidate, and is the director of the political campaign.

National Civil Service Reform League.

A private organization set up in 1881 for the promotion and extension of civil service in the federal government.

national committee. A committee of each major United States political party composed of one man and one woman representative from each state and territory and the District of Columbia, which acts for the party between presidential election years and directs the campaign in those years.

National Committee of Liberation. The first formal organization led by General de Gaulle, set up after the fall of France in 1940, to work for the restoration of the country.

National Compliance Board. One of the divisions of the National Recovery Administration the function of which was to get employers to conform to the regulations.

national convention. Quadrennial meeting of delegates of a major political party from all the states and territories of the United States for the purpose of nominating a candidate for president and drawing up the party platform.

National Council. Lower house of the Swiss parliament.

National Council of Corporations. The overall economic organization in Fascist Italy on which were represented the 22 "corporations" or employer and employee organizations in each of the major economic divisions. It consisted finally of over 500 members whose function was to plan and recommend the economic policy of the country.

national debt. The official governmental debt of a state.

National Federation of Federal Employees. A union of federal employees established in 1917. It withdrew from the American Federation of Labor in 1932. Its membership is about 75,000.

National Gallery of Art. A national art

gallery located in Washington, instituted with gifts of paintings and the gallery itself by Andrew Mellon. It is a bureau of the Smithsonian Institution. See SMITHSONIAN INSTITUTION.

National General Mobilization Act. A Japanese law of April 1, 1938, in which the government was given power to mobilize fully all the manpower, resources, and economic machinery of the country for the prosecution of the war against China.

national government. 1. The government of a national state, as opposed to local or intermediate governments or, in the United States, to the governments of the several states. 2. A coalition government of parties representing varying views set up in order to present a unified national front in an emergency.

National Guard. A part of the armed forces of the United States called up only in emergencies. In peace time it is trained subject to army standards, and given a nominal pay by the federal government, but is organized on a state basis. It is the successor to the militias of the states and is composed of volunteers.

national holiday. A day set aside for national observance for its significance in the history of a state, as for example a day to commemorate the achieving of independence. In the United States such holidays include Washington's Birthday (February 22), Memorial Day (May 30), the Fourth of July, Labor Day (first Monday in September), and Thanksgiving (the fourth Thursday in November).

national honor. A feeling of such high, national self-regard that questions in which it is involved have historically usually required war before it could be satisfied.

National Housing Agency. An emergency war agency set up February 24, 1942 to consolidate the functions of various previous housing agencies. It determined the war housing needs, and aided in providing facilities therefor.

National Industrial Recovery Act. An act passed by Congress on June 16, 1933. Its provisions represented the attempt of President Franklin D. Roosevelt to free the country of the business depression which had resulted in an estimated unemployment figure of eight million. The act was put into effect by the National Recovery Administration, Hugh S. Johnson administrator from June, 1933 to September, 1934. There were ten objectives among which were: the removal of obstructions to the free flow of interstate and foreign commerce; the elimination of unfair competitive practices; increase of purchasing power; improvement of the employment situation; improvement of labor standards; the formulation of codes of fair competition having the effect of law (sec. 3); recognition of the right of employees to organize and bargain collectively through representatives of their own choosing; and the compliance by employers with the maximum hours of labor, minimum rates of pay, etc. The Supreme Court invalidated the act on May 27, 1935. The President officially terminated the National Recovery Administration by executive order December 21, 1935.

National Insurance. See SOCIAL SECURITY, SOCIALIZED MEDICINE, BEVERIDGE PLAN.

National Labor Party. The branch of the British Labor party which, under Ramsay MacDonald, helped to form a coalition government in 1931.

National Labor Relations Act. A law of July 5, 1935, affirming the right of employees to organize and to choose their representatives for purposes of collective bargaining. Also called the

Wagner Act, for Senator Robert F. Wagner of New York, its sponsor.

National Labor Relations Board. A board set up by the National Labor Relations Act in 1935. Its function is to assure freedom of employee organization and bargaining. It has power to investigate, hear and render decisions, and to conduct bargaining elections.

National League of Women Voters. In the United States, a nation-wide women's association, founded 1920, active in promoting good government.

National Mediation Board. A government agency set up June 21, 1934, to settle promptly labor disputes over wages, hours, and conditions and rules of work in railroad, Pullman, express and air lines. Subdivisions are the National Railroad Adjustment Board and the National Railway Labor Panel.

national origins. The principle on which the quotas of immigrants admitted to the United States are based. The total number admitted (about 150,-000) is divided among the different nationalities in the proportions that those nationalities or "national origins" were present in the United States population of 1920. Established by the Immigration Act of 1924.

National Public Works Board. A board set up June 16, 1933, to supervise the Public Works Administration. It had oversight of highway, park, building, housing, bridge, dock and canal improvement and construction, and of navigation, erosion, and water-power control.

National Recovery Administration. See NATIONAL INDUSTRIAL RECOVERY ACT.

national resources. The combined resources of a state, usually thought of in terms of mineral raw materials and water power.

National Resources Board. A government board set up June 30, 1934 to draw up for the president a comprehensive plan for developing the land, water, and other resources of the country. Functions transferred to the National Resources Committee, June 7, 1935.

National Resources Planning Board. A reorganization of the National Resources Committee with the same functions for the planned use of our national resources, functioning from 1939 to 1944.

National Socialist Party. The NSDAP (Nationalsozialistische Deutsche Arbeiterpartei), or National Socialist German Workers party, or Nazi party. Its program was the rebuilding of a strong militaristic Germany which should expand and prosper at the expense of its neighbors. Its methods were most ruthless dictatorship, false propaganda, and force. See NAZISM.

national treatment. Extending, in a treaty, to the citizens or nationals of another state, the same commercial privileges a state gives to its own nationals.

National War Labor Board. An emergency war agency set up January 12, 1942 to handle disputes not settled by negotiation or the Conciliation Commissioners of the Labor Department. It could mediate or arbitrate and its jurisdiction was final. Proposals for increases in wages were submitted to it, and it applied the Little Steel Formula. See LITTLE STEEL FORMULA.

National Youth Administration. An agency set up within the Works Progress Administration June 26, 1935 to provide part-time jobs for needy students in high schools and colleges, and job training for unemployed youths. Liquidated in 1943 after being transferred to two other agencies.

nationalism. A belief which exalts one's own nation over all other nations and places loyalty to one's nation very high on the scale of human values. It consists of a mixture of various sentiments and beliefs, but not all of them are always present in modern nationalistic thinking. Some of them are: attachment to the native soil, pride in the nation's cultural and historical achievements, love of the national language, a striving to safeguard the national heritage within and outside the national frontiers which leads first, to a demand for self-government, if not attained; second, to the desire to expand and to "bring home" national groups living abroad; and third, an effort to assimilate minorities of other nationalities. Nationalism is a modern movement and is closely connected with the rise of the nation-state which followed the decline of feudalism, the breaking up of the mediaeval empire and with the Reformation. The spread of popular sovereignty also meant an increase in nationalism, as loyalty to the monarch or to an aristocracy found a substitute in loyalty to the nation. The French and American revolutions have often been regarded as the first major manifestations of modern nationalism. The 19th century, "the century of nationalism," brought about the establishment of many new nation-states. The age culminated in the Wilsonian idea of "national self-determination," which broke up the remaining European empires (Czarist Russia, Austria-Hungary, Turkey) and created a dozen more small nation-states. In this century nationalism has spread to Asia, resulting in independence movements in India, Indonesia, Indo-China, Arabian countries and elsewhere. In Europe after World War I, nationalism developed in an aggressive direction, bent on expansion and intolerance toward minorities, and often joined forces with racial doctrines. Whereas the earlier liberal nationalism (which still survives in the Western democracies) was a unifying and constructive force in a nation's cultural and political life, the new nationalism led to aggression, dictatorial and totalitarian regimes, nazism and fascism. It did much to destroy international organization and good will. See NATION, STATE, POPULAR SOVEREIGNTY, REPUBLIC, LIBERALISM, WILSONIAN DEMOCRACY, FASCISM, NAZISM, RACE, MILITARISM.

nationality. The attribute which indicates the state of which a person is a member.

nationalize. To take over ownership by a national government. For example, nationalizing the armament industry would mean that a government became the owner of the munitions plant.

native policy. Policy of an empire toward the native inhabitants of its colonies.

native prince. One of the princes of the native states of India. See NATIVE STATES.

native states. The 575 native dependent principalities scattered throughout India. They have their own rulers and are not a part of British India though Great Britain carries on their external relations and furnishes domestic advisers. Plans for reorganization of Indian government indicate their participation. Collectively they include about ninety million people.

natural law. The law intrinsic in the nature of man and in human society, the principles men should always abide by. The term is used in theology, philosophy, political theory and jurisprudence. It is a kind of ideal law, a measuring stick which should be applied to legislation (or positive law). It is timeless and universal. In philosophy the Greeks Plato and Aristotle, the Stoic school, the Roman jurists, the English Hobbes and Locke, the Dutch Spinoza, the Germans Kant and Leibnitz and the Frenchman Rousseau discussed natural law from various angles. The natural-law school is often contrasted with the positive-law school. "Naturalists" believe that natural law is higher than positive law (derived from legislation) and when a conflict between the two exists, natural law should always overrule positive law. "Positivists," however, deny the existence of natural law and call law valid only if it is issued and enforced by a sovereign. The two schools have often clashed in the field of international law. In a sense natural law is based on some sort of belief in God or a God-like nature. It plays a great role in Catholic philosophy: St. Thomas Aquinas made it a cornerstone of his philosophy. See POSITIVE LAW, NATURAL RIGHTS, SOVEREIGNTY, LAW, INTERNATIONAL LAW.

natural resources. Resources provided by nature such as minerals, forests, and water-power.

naturalization. The act or acts by which a state adopts or receives a foreigner into its citizenship. The process may take place with individuals upon application or upon marriage or, for a minor, naturalization of parents. Naturalization may also be collective as when a territory with its inhabitants is transferred from one country to another.

natural rights. The rights with which man is endowed by God or Nature, such as life, liberty, property and the pursuit of happiness. Natural rights are the core of every individualist philosophy, and were rediscovered and formulated by French, English and American philosophers and statesmen in the 18th century. John Locke pictured the state as safe-guarding the natural rights of the individual. And this view laid the basis for English and American liberalism. The earliest constitutional documents enacting natural rights into civil rights were: The Bills of Rights of Virginia and Pennsylvania (1776), the French "Declaration of the Rights of Man and Citizen" (1789), the first ten Amendments of the American Constitution (1791). Collectivist philosophies repudiate many or all these rights. See LIBERALISM, RADICALISM, JEFFERSONIAN DEMOCRACY, FREEDOM, CIVIL LIBERTIES, RIGHTS OF MAN, LAISSEZ FAIRE, DECLARATION OF RIGHTS.

naval base. The harbor from which a naval force operates and upon which it depends for supplies. In addition to sufficient protected anchorage space, a prime requirement is equipment for major repairs.

naval disarmament. The abolition of weapons of naval warfare. This was accomplished between World Wars to only a slight extent; the process is perhaps more properly called limitation of armaments.

naval disarmament conferences. See WASHINGTON CONFERENCE, GENEVA NAVAL CONFERENCE, and LONDON NAVAL CONFERENCE of 1930.

naval ratios. The ratios of tonnages of capital ships established by the Washington Conference (United States 5, Great Britain 5, Japan 3, France 1.67 and Italy 1.67) and of cruisers and destroyers set up by the London Naval Conference of 1930 (approximately United States 10, Great Britain 10 and Japan 7).

Naval War College. An advanced training school of the United States Navy at Newport, R. I.

navigable waters. Rivers, bays, etc. capable of bearing sizeable vessels.

Navy, Department of. One of the ten executive departments of the United

States government. It was established April 30, 1798.

navy second to none. A navy as big as the biggest. This avowed objective of Germany·at the turn of the century was a challenge to British naval supremacy and most likely to bring the two powers into conflict. See TWO-POWER NAVY.

navy yard. Place belonging to a government for building and repair of naval vessels.

Nazi. 1. Pertaining to the National Socialist Party of Germany. **2.** Having characteristics and policies similar to the National Socialists in Germany. **3.** Member of the National Socialist Party. See NAZISM.

Nazism. A German fascist social and political movement founded after World War I whose followers ruled Germany from 1933 to 1945. It was influenced by the example of Italian Fascism, by older German nationalistic creeds, by racist theories and by Prussian militarism. In its methods it was ruthlessly dictatorial and totalitarian, using modern propaganda techniques and developing them to unexcelled perfection. It appealed first to those Germans who were hardest hit by their defeat in World War I and by the policies of the Weimar Republic, later on to those of the middle classes who lost their wealth during the German inflation and to workers who were disappointed with the rival Socialist and Communist parties. Many monarchists, ex-officers, irresponsible adventurers, unemployed workers, and later a large number of businessmen and bankers who were afraid of socialism, rallied behind the Nazis. The Nazis promised social peace, bread and jobs for all, and the re-establishment of Germany as a strong world power. Their nationalistic slogans made the foreign powers, the Marxists, democratic liberals, Catholics and particularly the Jews—who according to the Nazis formed a world-wide conspiracy—responsible for the German defeat in World War I, the "humiliating" Treaty of Versailles and the economic misery of the 1920's. All this had a broad appeal for the masses.

The National Socialist German Workers Party (NSDAP) was founded in a Munich beer hall in 1920 by Adolf Hitler, an Austrian-born painter and ex-soldier. In 1923, with the help of General Ludendorf, he staged an unsuccessful attempt to overthrow the Bavarian Government, the so-called "Beer Hall Putsch," and was sentenced to five years' imprisonment. In prison Hitler began *Mein Kampf* (My Struggle), which became the Nazi Bible. The Party was insignificant in size until the election of 1930, when the economic depression had begun to make itself felt. After that it grew by leaps and bounds, staging violent armed conflicts with its opponents, breaking up their meetings and terrorizing many. Opposed by weak and lukewarm republican governments and divided opposition, the Nazi Party with the help of its uniformed armies, the S.A. (Storm Troopers) and the S.S. (Elite Guard), constituted the largest, most fanatic and optimistic political force in Germany when, in January, 1933 a treacherous group of advisers persuaded President von Hindenburg to appoint Hitler as Chancellor. In a few months the Weimar Republic and all other parties were abolished and the Nazi Party established itself as the only party in Germany. It ruthlessly suppressed criticism, threw opposition leaders into concentration camps or chased them into exile. Nazi theories were now put into practice, and the Party's rule lasted until May,

1945 when it was dissolved by the victorious Allies and its leaders arrested, many of them held for trial at Nuremberg. Hitler reportedly committed suicide in Berlin before the Red Army took the city and was cremated by his guards. See THIRD REICH, FASCISM, TOTALITARIANISM, RACE, ARYAN, NORDIC, ANTI-SEMITIC, IMPERIALISM, MILITARISM, NATIONAL-ISM, WEIMAR REPUBLIC.

Near East. The countries bordering or close to the eastern Mediterranean: Turkey, Syria, the Lebanon, Palestine, Transjordan, Egypt, and Saudi Arabia. The British consider the lower Balkan states and Turkey as the Near East and would class the rest of the above states in the Middle East. See MIDDLE EAST.

necessary and proper clause. See ELASTIC CLAUSE.

negotiate. To discuss directly with a representative of another party, as for example, another state, or another party to a labor dispute, with a view to reaching an agreement.

negotiated peace. A peace in which the terms are arrived at by the loser's bargaining with the winner as opposed to a peace settlement imposed by the winner.

Negro suffrage. Participation of Negroes as qualified voters in elections.

neo-mercantilism. See MERCANTILISM.

NEP. See NEW ECONOMIC POLICY.

nepmen. Those who set up businesses and prospered under the New Economic Policy. See NEW ECONOMIC POLICY.

nepotism. The granting of political favors to relatives.

net income. 1. The income used for tax purposes after certain expenses and other deductions have been allowed. 2. Gross income of a corporation minus operating expenses.

Neuilly, Treaty of. Treaty of peace between the Allies and Bulgaria after World War I, signed November 27, 1919. By this treaty she lost a seaboard on the Aegean; recognized the independence of Yugoslavia, and had to pay reparations, limit the size of her army to 20,000 men and surrender most of her war materials.

neutral. 1. A state which does not participate in a war between other states. For the rules of non-participation, see NEUTRALITY. 2. A national of such a state. 3. Of or pertaining to such a state, as a neutral ship. 4. Pertaining to non-participation in war.

neutrality. The political and legal position of a state (nation) which in time of war abstains from hostilities and is impartial toward the belligerents. The legal concept of neutrality is comparatively new, and developed chiefly on the sea as a result of rapid increase in European sea-borne trade. The Napoleonic wars demonstrated that in any really great war the rights of neutrals to continue their trade were bound to suffer; the United States tried to insist on her rights of neutrality with limited effect. The First and Second Hague Peace Conferences of 1899 and 1907 and the Declaration of London in 1909 formulated the rights and duties of neutral states. According to them a neutral state is obliged not to aid any belligerent and to prevent its citizens from performing certain but not all acts in aid of a belligerent. Neutral territory, including air space above it, is inviolable, belligerents may not move troops or war supplies across it or set up radio stations on it. Belligerent troops entering neutral territory must be interned. No belligerent act is to be performed in neutral waters, but belligerent ships may pass through them and may stay in neutral ports for 24 hours. Neutral governments may not supply belligerents with warships or war material, but private citizens of neutral states may supply the latter. It is doubted whether the concept of "collective security" embodied in the Covenant of the League of Nations and in the Charter of the United Nations is compatible with the idea of neutrality, as members of these international bodies are obliged to take concerted action against aggressors. See NON-INTERVENTION, NON-INTERVENTION COMMITTEE, AGGRESSION, SANCTIONS, INTERNATIONAL LAW, LEAGUE OF NATIONS, UNITED NATIONS.

Neutrality Act. A United States law of August 1935 providing that when the president found a state of war to exist he would embargo the sale to the belligerents of arms, ammunition and instruments of war. On February 29, 1936 loans were added to the forbidden list. April 30, 1937 other changes were made, chiefly the addition of the cash-and-carry principle, which provision was only to remain in force for two years.

neutrality zone. See DECLARATION OF PANAMA.

neutralize. Process or act of creating permanent neutrality. Switzerland was thus declared neutral by the powers in 1815.

New Deal. The domestic program of Franklin D. Roosevelt when he took office March 4, 1933. It included measures for combatting unemployment, reviving industry, agriculture, trade and transportation, reorganization of banking, credit and securities systems, and a broad program of housing and public works. It was inevitable that with the sudden increase of all kinds of regulation only the broad outlines of policy could be laid down by Congress and that a vast amount of rule-making should be done by administrative decree. The phrase came from President Roosevelt's speech accepting the nomination at the Democratic National Convention at Chicago, July 2, 1932, in which he pledged "a new deal for the American people."

New Dealer. Participant in or backer of the New Deal.

New Economic Policy (NEP). A transitional, partly free economic system in force in the Soviet Union between 1921 and 1928. Lenin was not able to introduce a complete communist economy all at once. After the Russian Revolution of November 1917 three periods can be distinguished: (1) a short period preceding the outbreak of the Civil War in July 1918 characterized by the nationalization of certain key industries and by state control hardly more stringent than in capitalist countries during war time; (2) during the Civil War Russian economy was centralized and controlled by a semi-military administration, the nationalization of industries was accelerated and commerce turned into a giant form of government-controlled barter; (3) in 1921 at the end of the Civil War return to more normal conditions was favored in order to win the peasants over. The New Economic Policy ended wartime measures, requisitioning grain from the farmers was abolished, and the free grain trade and free retail and wholesale markets for all kinds of goods were restored. The nationalized industries or trusts became more independent from state control. Private trade was legal though subject to license and rather harsh taxation. Foreign trade remained controlled. Meanwhile through education and propaganda and through the establishment of huge power plants and basic industries Russia was transformed from a backward peasant country into a nation well on the way toward modern industrialism. In 1928 "Gosplan," the economic "brain-trust" of the Soviet Union prepared the first Five Year Plan, which ended the period of NEP and introduced a completely planned and centralized economic system. See COMMUNISM, BOLSHEVISM, COLLECTIVE FARMS.

New Order. Term used by the Germans to refer to their regime in Europe.

New Order in East Asia. Term used by the Japanese to describe their regime in Manchuria, China and southeastern Asia.

night court. Regular sessions of a court, particularly a municipal police court, held in the evening in order to interfere as little as possible with the occupations of those coming before it.

Nilotic Federation. Projected organization of states and territories through which the Nile and its tributaries flow.

Nine Power Treaty. A treaty signed by the United States, Belgium, Great Britain, China, France, Italy, Japan, the Netherlands and Portugal February 6, 1922 at the Washington Conference. In it the signatories agreed to respect the sovereignty, independence, and territorial and administrative integrity of China, and to observe the principle of the Open Door.

Nisei. Literally, second age or generation. Technically it includes only those born to Japanese parents outside Japan; the term in general is used in the United States to mean all American citizens of Japanese descent.

N.K.V.D. Soviet secret police, the Peoples Commissariat for Internal Affairs. Successor to the O.G.P.U.

Nobel Peace Prize. An annual prize given each year under the will of Alfred B. Nobel, Swedish explosives maker, to a person outstanding in the promotion of international friendship and peace and the reduction of armaments. Other prizes are also given in physics, chemistry, medicine, and literature.

nobility. Total body of nobles. See PEERAGE.

no confidence. A vote in the House of Commons, or other legislative body under a parliamentary form of government, against the policy of the cabinet; that is, a vote indicating that the cabinet no longer enjoys the backing or "confidence" of the members of the body. After such a vote the cabinet resigns, and in the British system a new election is held. In other systems a new cabinet is usually formed, involving a realignment of parties.

nominate. To designate a person for election or appointment. For elections the designating is usually done by a nominating convention, caucus, or primary election. See PRIMARY.

nominating convention. Any official meeting for the purpose of nominating candidates for public office. The meetings for nominating candidates for the presidency and vice presidency are usually just called national conventions.

nomination. 1. The choice or designation as candidate in an election or for an appointment. 2. The process of such designation.

non-aggression pact. A treaty in which each party pledges to refrain from attack or other acts of aggression upon the other party or parties.

noncombatant. A person who does not engage in or directly advance the cause of the armed hostilities of his state in time of war. Industrial participation in war has almost robbed the term of its former significance.

non-co-operation. The holding aloof from participation in or collaboration with a government. This has been one of Gandhi's methods of obstructing British rule in India.

nonfeasance. The omission of the performance of some act, particularly by a public official, which should have been performed.

non-intervention. The principle of international law stating that in a state of peace a nation should refrain from interfering with the domestic affairs of another nation. This is based on the principle that all nations are equal and sovereign and have therefore complete freedom to manage their domestic affairs as they please. In war time "non-intervention" is often used as a synonym for neutrality. See NEUTRALITY, NON-INTERVENTION COMMITTEE.

Non-Intervention Committee. An international committee initiated by France and Great Britain in August 1936 to supervise the carrying out of a common policy prohibiting the sending of arms, munitions, war material and airplanes to either side in the Spanish Civil War. Twenty-seven nations adhered to this policy. The last meeting of the Committee was in July 1938. Its failure was believed to be due to its lack of power to prevent governments from openly or disguisedly intervening in the struggle in Spain. Germany and Italy, though members of the Committee, vigorously aided the insurgents under Generalissimo Francisco Franco, while Soviet Russia was known to support the Loyalist Government. Great Britain, France and many smaller nations adhered to their declarations of non-intervention although volunteers from all countries participated in the Spanish Civil War. The United States was not a member of the Non-intervention Committee, and announced that it would follow a "policy of non-interference in the internal affairs of foreign countries." In January 1937 Congress amended the Neutrality Act making it unlawful to export material of war destined for "use of either of

the opposing forces in Spain." See NEUTRALITY, NON-INTERVENTION.

non-justiciable. 1. Pertaining to a dispute which does not lend itself to settlement by a court on a basis of law because one of the grounds of the dispute is the existing law. 2. Pertaining to a "political" dispute.

non-national state. A state which does not have a single dominant cultural nationality, but several, like Switzerland. Also called a multinational state.

non-partisan. 1. Composition, as of a commission or political ticket, without regard to political party affiliations of its members. 2. Free from party domination.

Non-Partisan League, The National. A farmers' pressure group organized in 1915 in North Dakota to break the wheat trade monopoly. By 1918 it dominated the North Dakota government, flourishing there and in nearby states for something over ten years. Its program included state ownership of grain mills, elevators and warehouses, state grain inspection, hail insurance, no taxes on farm improvements, and farm credit banks. Two leaders were A. C. Townley and L. J. Frazier.

non-recognition doctrine. The doctrine that a state should not recognize a change in status of another state brought about by force. Also called the Stimson doctrine.

Nordic. A term meaning northern, applied loosely and without scientific foundation to the people of Scandinavia and North Germany, or those of neighboring countries, who have long heads, fair hair and fair complexions. The racists of Germany, especially the Nazis, asserted that the so-called "Nordic people" constitute the aristocracy of the so-called "Aryan race," and were predestined by Creation to lead and rule the world, being physically, morally and mentally superior to all other peoples. The Nazis believed that there was also a Nordic culture, spirit and mentality which was distinct from, and of a higher order than European, Christian or Western cultures. Scientists have refuted all these beliefs without qualification, proving that "Nordic" characteristics cannot be isolated and that the majority of great men could not possibly be called "Nordic." See RACE, ARYAN, NAZI, ANTI-SEMITISM.

normalcy. A term used by the Republicans and their candidate, Warren G. Harding, in the campaign of 1920. Their slogan was "back to normalcy." The policy involved a return to high protective tariffs, a drastic reduction in income taxes, no government interference with private enterprise and a less co-operative policy in foreign affairs, all as opposed to the policies of President Wilson which were advocated by the Democratic candidate, James M. Cox. The phrase became a key-word of the Harding administration.

Normandy. French peninsula where the allied invasion of the continent took place in June, 1944. It lies across the English Channel opposite the south of England. It was from Normandy that William the Conqueror invaded and conquered England in 1066 A.D.

North. The states of the United States which remained loyal to the Union in the Civil War.

Northwest Ordinance (Ordinance of 1787). A sort of constitution for the Northwest Territory. It promised that every man moving into the territory was to have religious freedom, the right of trial by jury, and a chance for a free education; and prohibited slavery. These ideas became embodied in constitutions of western territories that were acquired later.

The Ordinance provided also for division of the territory into states. From this territory emerged Ohio, Indiana, Illinois, Michigan, Wisconsin, and part of Minnesota.

notary public. A person commissioned by the state to attest facts by signing and affixing the seal of the state to contracts and other documents which require the formality of such a seal.

notice and hearing. Provision that a person affected must be notified, as by public notification, that a certain administrative action is going into effect, and giving him the opportunity to be heard in protest or application.

N.S.D.A.P. See NATIONAL SOCIALIST PARTY, NAZISM.

nuisance. An act or the maintenance of something which is dangerous or offensive to the community. It may be stopped by summary abatement, suit for damages, or injunction.

nuisance tax. A tax, usually on luxuries or amusements, which appears to cause inconvenience out of proportion to the receipts.

nullification. See STATES' RIGHTS.

Number 10. No. 10 Downing Street, the residence of the British prime minister.

nuncio. Diplomatic representative of the Pope, classed as a diplomat of the first class.

Nuremburg Congress. The annual Nazi party congress held formerly in Nuremburg in September.

Nuremburg Laws. German laws of September 1935 prohibiting marriage of Jews and non-Jews, withdrawing citizenship from Jews, and prohibiting any female non-Jew under 45 from working in a Jewish home.

Nuremburg Trials. See WAR CRIMES TRIALS.

N.Y.A. See NATIONAL YOUTH ADMINISTRATION.

O

oath of office. An oath taken by an incoming government official to discharge the duties of his office and to uphold the Federal or State Constitution and the laws.

O. B. E. See ORDER OF THE BRITISH EMPIRE.

obiter dictum. Literally a passing saying or extra statement. A portion of a judicial opinion which does not bear directly upon the issue the judge is called upon to decide. Hence, it is not strictly the law in the sense of the main decision, but it indicates the thinking of the judge and serves as something of a clue to possible future decisions.

obligatory arbitration. See COMPULSORY ARBITRATION.

obstructionist. One who impedes legislation, particularly progressive legislation, by utilizing the technical rules of a legislative body to delay action.

occupation. The act by which a state takes and keeps effective possession of territory which belongs to another state. Usually the act is accompanied by the intention to extend its sovereignty over the occupied territory. A military occupation does not presume the intention to extend sovereignty over the occupied territory. See MILITARY OCCUPATION.

occupational representation. Representation in a legislative body, not on a geographical district basis but on that of business occupations or vocations. This suggestion has been raised on the theory that with the increasing diversity of man's economic activities an individual's interests would be better represented by a person in the same vocation or occupation than by one who merely lives in the same vicinity; also that those in the same occupation throughout a country have more in common than those who live in the same area. An attempt to set up this kind of representation was made in fascist Italy.

O. C. D. See OFFICE OF CIVILIAN DEFENSE.

ochlocracy. Rule by the multitude or the mob.

October Revolution. The Russian Bolshevik revolution of 1917. On November 6 the Bolshevik-lead soldiers, sailors and workers of Petrograd—then the capital of Russia and now called Leningrad—captured the main government buildings and overthrew the Provisional Government of Alexander Kerensky, who escaped and went into exile. A chief cause of the uprising was the popular fear that the reactionary army leaders were plotting to take over the government. The next day the Second All-Russian Congress of Soviets, minus the moderate socialist members, voted to approve of the Revolution, and the Bolsheviks have ruled Russia ever since. According to the Russian calendar the dates were October 24 and 25, hence the name.

Octobrists. 1. A youth organization in the Soviet Union for children in their teens, the name deriving from the October Revolution of 1917. See OCTOBER REVOLUTION. 2. Members of a moderately liberal Russian political party whose reform program and constitutional principles were in general adopted by the Czar in his manifesto of October during the Revolution of 1905.

octroi. French word for a grant, privilege or concession, especially a commercial concession, granted by a sovereign as a monopoly.

O. D. T. See OFFICE OF DEFENSE TRANSPORTATION.

O. E. M. See OFFICE OF EMERGENCY MANAGEMENT.

O. E. S. See OFFICE OF ECONOMIC STABILIZATION.

"Of the people, by the people, and for the people." A description of the United States government given by President Lincoln in his address delivered November 19, 1863 at the dedication of the national cemetery at Gettysburg, Pa.

off year. A year between election years in which there is no election. In terms of United States national politics, the off years are the odd years, as 1947, 1949, 1951.

office group ballot. See MASSACHUSETTS BALLOT.

Office of Censorship. An emergency war agency set up December 19, 1941 to censor all communications in and out of the United States.

Office of Civilian Defense. An emergency war agency set up May 20, 1941 to co-ordinate state and federal measures for protection of civilians in case of war emergency. Its two branches supervised protective functions such as blackouts and special fire protection and "war service"

functions such as child care, health, housing, and transportation.

Office of Defense Transportation. An agency set up December 18, 1941 to analyze and provide for wartime traffic needs and co-ordinate efficiently the nation's military and civilian transportation. Under its jurisdiction were railroads, trucking, inland waterways, pipe lines, air transport and coastwise and intercoastal shipping.

Office of Economic Stabilization. An emergency war agency set up October 3, 1942 within the Office of Emergency Management for controlling purchasing power, prices, rents, wages and the migration of labor in an attempt to keep living costs from rising excessively. Its powers were transferred on December 12, 1946 to the Office of Temporary Controls for liquidation.

Office of Education. An office set up March 2, 1867 and long a branch of the Interior Department, which has been transferred to the Federal Security Agency. Its functions are to carry on research and collect facts on education throughout the country which are made available to public schools and colleges. It also administers grants-in-aid for educational purposes.

Office of Emergency Management. An over-all government agency set up May 25, 1940 to co-ordinate the efforts of some of the civilian war agencies such as the War Labor Board, Office of Civilian Defense, Office of Defense Transportation, Office of Economic Stabilization, Office of War Information, Office of War Mobilization, War Manpower Commission and War Production Board.

Office of Land Utilization. An office set up in the Interior Department, April 15, 1940 co-ordinating the various efforts of the department relative to land utilization, conservation, and forestry.

Office of Price Administration. An agency set up August 28, 1941 for the purpose of stabilizing prices and preventing profiteering through various types of rationing and price control. On December 12, 1946 its powers were transferred to the Office of Temporary Controls.

Office of Production Management. A government agency set up January 7, 1941 to recommend a policy for the regulation of defense materials and plant facilities for emergency war production. Its functions were transferred to the War Production Board, January 24, 1942.

Office of Strategic Services. An agency set up June 13, 1942 under the Joint Chiefs of Staff to collect and analyze strategic information for them, and other information specially helpful to other government agencies. Formerly performing these functions were the Office of War Information and the Office of Facts and Figures.

Office of Temporary Controls. An agency created by President Truman December 12, 1946, to liquidate the functions of the Office of Price Administration, Civilian Production Administration, Office of War Mobilization and Reconstruction and the Office of Economic Security.

Office of War Information. A government agency set up June 13, 1942 for the purpose of facilitating the flow of war news to the public, both at home and abroad for aiding in an understanding of the progress of the war effort, to advise the other government agencies in these matters, and to approve government-sponsored radio programs and moving pictures.

Office of War Mobilization. A government agency set up May 27, 1943 for the purpose of mobilizing the industrial and natural resources and civil-

ian manpower of the country for the war effort, to adjust and stabilize the civilian economy, and to co-ordinate the production and distribution efforts of the various other government agencies.

Office of War Mobilization and Reconversion. The successor, in 1944, of the Office of War Mobilization. Its function was to plan the most economical use of manpower and resources in the return to a peace time economy. On December 12, 1946 its powers were transferred to the office of Temporary Controls for liquidation.

Ogdensburg Agreement. A United States-Canadian agreement of August 18, 1940 to set up a permanent joint defense board for the consideration of common defense problems.

O.G.P.U. Abbreviation of the Russian words meaning United State Political Department, an agency known as the Cheka from 1919 to 1922 when it was made an organ of the Soviet government. It dealt with political offenders and its powers included arrest without warrant, secret trial and punishment. Some of its trials were staged in public, however, as that of the British engineers in 1933. It was a bulwark of the Communist regime in Russia until its police powers were turned over to the new Commissariat for Internal Affairs (N.K.V.D.) and its judicial powers to the courts, in 1934.

Ohio gang. A term of disapproval applied to the groups of Ohio politicians lead by Mark Hanna in the administrations of President McKinley and by Attorney General Harry M. Daugherty in that of President Harding.

okies. Refugees, in California particularly, from the dustbowl area in the middle 1930's. Many were from Oklahoma, whence the name.

old-age insurance. A form of insurance

which provides payments to persons in old age. Such insurance has been of growing importance in state and federal social policies. See SOCIAL SECURITY.

Old Bailey. The old central criminal court for metropolitan London and its adjoining prison. The name comes from the fact that it is located in a "bailey," the space between the inner and outer walls of an old fortress.

Old Guard. Veteran political figures, usually thought of as on the conservative side.

Old Lady of Threadneedle Street. Popular English name for the Bank of England. See BANK OF ENGLAND.

oligarchy. 1. Literally rule by a few, hence a state or government in which all governmental power is concentrated in a small group of individuals. 2. The small group controlling such a state or government.

O. M. See ORDER OF MERIT.

O. P. A. See OFFICE OF PRICE ADMINISTRATION.

open city *or* **town.** An unfortified and undefended city or town. Traditionally it was forbidden by international law to bombard such a place, but the locations of munitions factories in them and the attack of such factories by air has wrecked this rule.

"open covenants openly arrived at." The first of President Wilson's Fourteen Points, aimed at abolishing secret treaties and agreements and secret diplomacy. See FOURTEEN POINTS, SECRET TREATIES.

open diplomacy. The publication of international agreements and of pertinent information in the negotiation thereof, as opposed to secret diplomacy.

Open Door. Access to the economic opportunities within a country on a basis of equality of all other states and the citizens thereof. It follows that no special concessions would be granted any state and there would be no discrimination against any foreigners desiring to do business within the state. The Open Door in China has been one of the cornerstones of United States foreign policy in the Far East since it was first stated by John Hay in 1899.

open primary. A primary in which there is no restriction that the members of a party must vote for the candidates of that party, but all voters are free to vote for the candidates of either party. See CLOSED PRIMARY.

open sea. See HIGH SEAS.

open shop. A factory or other place of business in which some of the employees do not belong to a union.

Opinions of the Attorney General. The compilation of the opinions of the United States attorney general issued by him to the president and other important government officials in interpretation of the laws.

Opium Wars. Two wars with China, the first by Great Britain in 1839–42 and the second by Great Britain and France in 1857–58, which opened up China to foreign trade and in particular permitted the importation of opium into China.

O. P. M. See OFFICE OF PRODUCTION MANAGEMENT.

opportunism. The practice of basing the activities of government on temporary conditions or opportunities as they occur rather than on a long-run policy.

opportunist. A person who follows the line of least resistance in seizing temporary advantages and easy choices rather than hewing to a line of principle and long-run policy.

opposition. The party or parties composing that portion of a legislative body which is against the "government," or the party or parties in control.

opposition bench. The benches in the

House of Commons occupied by the leaders of the opposition. See OPPOSITION, FRONT BENCH.

opt. To choose or vote for. Used particularly in connection with the choice of nationality which a person desires, as the Hungarians in Transylvania after World War I, who could become Romanians or opt for Hungarian citizenship.

optant. One who chooses or exercises an option in nationality. See OPT, HUNGARIAN OPTANTS.

optional charter plan. A plan for providing charters for cities in which the state by law offers several forms of charters and the cities are permitted to choose the one they want, that is, one with a mayor-council plan, a commission plan or a manager plan, whichever they may prefer.

Optional Clause. An optional annex to the protocol of signature of December 16, 1920 of the World Court Statute. It provided that, by separately signing this annex, the signatories promised to accept as compulsory the jurisdiction of the World Court as stated in Article 36 of the Statute, namely in interpretation of treaties, questions of international law, facts constituting breaches of international obligations and reparations for breaches of international obligations.

order, administrative. See ADMINISTRATIVE ORDER.

Order-in-Council. A British administrative order issued by a government department (formerly by the privy council) in pursuance of authority established by an act of parliament.

order of business. The arrangement of items to be taken up, as for example, in a day's work of a legislative body.

Order of Merit. A high British honor given to distinguished men and women. It ranks after the first class of the Order of the Bath, but is not itself an order of knighthood. See ORDERS OF KNIGHTHOOD.

Order of St. Michael and St. George. The Most Distinguished Order of St. Michael and St. George, one of the British orders of knighthood composed of outstanding inhabitants of the Empire and those who have rendered the crown special services in foreign or colonial affairs. Founded in 1818. The classes are Knights Grand Cross (G.C.M.G.), Knights Commanders, (K.C.M.G.), and Companions (C.M.G.).

Order of St. Patrick. The Most Illustrious Order of St. Patrick, the ranking Irish order of the British knighthood. Its members are designated K.P. Founded in 1783.

Order of the Bath. The Most Honourable Order of the Bath, a high ranking order of the British knighthood granted for special military or civilian service, founded in 1725. Its 1500-odd members are divided into three classes in order of precedence: Knights Grand Cross (G.C.B.), Knights Commanders (K.C.B.), and Companions (C.B.).

Order of the British Empire. A British order of knighthood granted for service to the Empire, established in 1917. Its classes are Knights Grand Cross (G.B.E.), Knights Commanders (K.B.E.), Commanders (C.B.E.), Officers (O.B.E.), and Members (M. B.E.).

Order of the Garter. The Most Noble Order of the Garter, the oldest and highest ranking British order of knighthood, founded in 1348. It is composed of only twenty-five regular members or companions, rarely other than members of the peerage, who have rendered very distinguished service to the crown, plus the members of the royal family and certain members of foreign royalty. The members are designated K.G.

Order of the Indian Empire. The Most
Eminent Order of the Indian Empire,
one of the British orders composed
of those who have served the crown
in India. There are three classes:
first, the Knights Grand Commanders (G.C.I.E.); second, Knights Commanders (K.C.I.E.); and third, Companions (C.I.E.).

Order of the Star of India. The Most
Exalted Order of the Star of India, an
order of British knighthood granted
to certain Indian native princes and
to Britons who have rendered special
service to the crown in India. Founded in 1861. There are three classes:
Grand Commanders (G.C.S.I.),
Knights Commanders (K.C.S.I.), and
Companions (C.S.I.).

Order of the Thistle. The Most Ancient
and Most Noble Order of the Thistle,
the ranking Scottish order of knighthood. Its members are designated
K.T. Founded in 1540.

Orders of Knighthood. Formerly spec-
ial organization of knights, but now,
various ranks of knighthood con-
ferred for different forms of service
to the sovereign. See ORDER OF THE
GARTER, ORDER OF THE THISTLE,
ORDER OF ST. PATRICK, ORDER OF THE
BATH, ORDER OF THE STAR OF INDIA,
ORDER OF ST. MICHAEL AND ST. GEO-
RGE, ORDER OF INDIAN EMPIRE, ROYAL
VICTORIAN ORDER, ORDER OF THE
BRITISH EMPIRE.

ordinance. A law passed by a municipal legislative authority.

ordinance power. The power of administrative officials to fill in the gaps and
details in the administration of a law
by administrative orders.

organismic theory. The political theory
that the state is a real physical organ-
ism or being, a personality distinct
from the people who compose it.

organization. The core of the party
machinery made up of the most dependable party regulars.

Orgbureau. The organization bureau of
the Russian communist party central
committee. It has such organizational
functions as membership, conventions, and propaganda. See POLIT-
BUREAU.

original jurisdiction. The jurisdiction
which a court possesses over the class
of cases which are heard for the first
time in that court. See APPELLATE
JURISDICTION.

original package doctrine. A doctrine
which arose in the development of the
interpretations of interstate commerce to the effect that goods within
a state were considered still in interstate commerce and subject to its
regulation as long as they were in the
original package, i. e., the container
in which they had entered the state.

Oslo Convention. A treaty signed in
Oslo December 22, 1930 by Belgium,
Denmark, Luxemburg, Netherlands,
Norway, and Sweden promising not
to increase tariffs, and indicating a
willingness to negotiate further on economic problems and tariff reduction.

O. S. S. See OFFICE OF STRATEGIC
SERVICES.

Ostmark. Nazi German title for Austria after its annexation in March,
1938.

Ottawa Conference. An economic conference of Great Britain, the Dominions, and India, held in Ottawa,
Canada, July 21–August 20, 1932.
The agreements concluded there provided for a system of intra-imperial
tariff preferences, by limiting British
tariffs, as regards the Dominions, and
raising them for other countries, thus
giving the Dominions a larger share
of British trade. The Dominions in
turn promised to keep their protective tariffs down for British goods.

Ottoman. Turkish.

outcasts. A new and less harsh term
for India's Untouchables. See UN-
TOUCHABLES.

outdoor relief. Relief administered outside of regular institutions or offices, that is, in the homes of the recipients.

outlaw. A person, usually wanted for crime, to whom the protection of the law has been denied and for whom often a reward is offered for bringing him in dead or alive.

outlawry of war. The effort to make war an illegal instead of legal method of settling international disputes. Non-aggression pacts were a method

used among a few states, but the chief attempt was the Pact of Paris of 1928, also known as the Kellogg Pact. See PARIS, PACT OF.

O.V.R.A. Italian Fascist secret police, as repressive and arbitrary as the other totalitarian police systems.

O. W. I. See OFFICE OF WAR INFORMATION.

O. W. M. See OFFICE OF WAR MOBILIZATION.

O. W. M. R. See OFFICE OF WAR MOBILIZATION AND RECONVERSION.

P

P. A. C. See POLITICAL ACTION COMMITTEE.

pacific blockade. A blockade of the ports of a state in time of peace by another state without the intention of making war. In addition it differs further from a belligerent blockade in that in general it does not apply to the vessels of third states, and that ships caught attempting to run the blockade are sequestered, not confiscated. See BLOCKADE.

pacific settlement. The peaceful settlement of an international dispute, usually thought of as brought about by some established means such as arbitration or adjudication.

Pacific War Council. An international body set up in Washington, March 30, 1942 to discuss matters of policy in regard to the joint prosecution of the war by the United Nations in the Pacific area. Represented thereon were the United States, Great Brit-

ain, China, Australia, Canada, the Netherlands, New Zealand, and the Philippines.

pacifist. A person opposed entirely to resorting to war for the settlement of international disputes or to participating in war.

pack. To fill with persons favorable to a particular faction, state, or point of view, as in a caucus or convention. See also COURT-PACKING PROPOSALS.

pact. Term used for an international agreement, especially a solemn political agreement.

Pact of Paris. See PARIS, PACT OF.

Pact of Saadabad. See MIDDLE-EASTERN PACT.

pacta sunt servanda (PAK-tuh soont ser-VAN-duh). Literally, pacts ought to be observed. The fundamental assumption underlying the binding force of treaties in international law.

pair. To agree with another member of a legislative body, who is going to vote the opposite way on a measure, that if either is absent the other will refrain from voting. This makes possible necessary absence without causing the loss of a vote.

Pakistan. New state proposed by the leaders of the All-India Moslem League to be formed of those parts of India in which Mohammedans predominate.

palace guard. Originally the king's bodyguard. Recently used to describe the body of close friends and advisers to the head of the state or government, as for example the close advisers of the president of the United States.

Palazzo Venezia. Palace in Rome from which Mussolini used to address the Italian populace and in which his office was located, on the Piazza Venezia.

Pan Africanism. A movement to draw closer together politically all the peoples of Africa. It has not as yet exerted very much weight.

Pan American Conferences. See PAN AMERICAN UNION; BUENOS AIRES CONFERENCE; LIMA CONFERENCE; MONTEVIDEO CONFERENCE.

Pan American Defense Board. The Inter-American Defense Board; it met in Washington and was composed of military and naval representatives of the American republics for the purpose of formulating and recommending joint defense measures. It was established by a resolution of the meeting of the foreign ministers of the American republics at Rio de Janeiro in January, 1942.

Pan American Highway. See ALL-AMERICAN HIGHWAY.

Pan American Union. An organization of the 21 American Republics. Regular conferences are held every five years and in recent years there have been several special conferences for strengthening inter-American solidarity in the face of threats of aggression from abroad. Its first conference was held in 1889. Its headquarters are in Washington, where the governing board is made up of the United States secretary of state and the diplomatic representatives at Washington from the other member countries.

Pan Americanism. A movement for closer co-operation among the American republics. It is greatly aided by the Pan American Union.

Pan Arab Movement. A movement for uniting the Arab peoples more closely, as into a federation or confederation. See ARAB LEAGUE.

Pan Europe. A term for a European federation or a so-called United States of Europe.

Pan Germanism. A pre-1914 movement among the Germans advocating annexation of all nearby territory inhabited by German-speaking people, in other words bringing all Germans into the German state. Nazism incorporated most of these ideas.

Pan Islamism. A movement to unite all or almost all the Mohammedans into a single political unit. It is weak because of the lack of a caliph, the head of the religion, and the great geographical scattering of the Moslems.

Pan Slavism. A movement to unite all the Slavs. Usually this stems from Russia, but it has had enthusiastic adherents in some of the other Slavic countries, especially Bulgaria and Yugoslavia.

Panama Canal Zone. A strip of United States territory running across the Isthmus and Republic of Panama in which is located the Panama Canal. It is administered by a governor appointed by the president of the United States. The grant for the territory was made in perpetuity, but the United States makes an annual payment to the Republic of Panama on a kind of lease basis.

Panama, Declaration of. A declaration by the American republics, agreed to at Panama, October 3, 1939 that belligerents should not commit hostile acts within a zone at least 300 miles from the American shores. The belligerents of World War II refused to observe it.

Panay incident. The unwarranted and deliberate attack on, and sinking of, the United States gunboat *Panay* on the Yangtze River above Nanking, December 12, 1937. The Japanese apologized immediately, and later sent a second apology and paid about $2,000,000 damages. The Japanese were evidently testing out the American reaction to that kind of treatment.

panic. Pre-1914 term for a business depression presumably induced, at least in part, from widespread apprehension regarding business conditions.

papacy. Office of the pope. See POPE.

Papal Guarantees, Law of. Italian law of 1871 guaranteeing the Pope free exercise of his office, including the sending and receiving of diplomats, assuring his free use of Vatican City, and the payment to him of a sizeable annuity. Cordial relations with the papacy, however, were not established until after 1900. See LATERAN ACCORD.

paper blockade. A blockade which has been only proclaimed, i. e., exists on paper but is not backed or made effective by sufficient naval strength. See BLOCKADE.

pardon. 1. To free a person from the penalties of committing a crime. 2. The power of a chief executive to free a person from the penalties of committing a crime.

Paris, Declaration of. See DECLARATION OF PARIS.

Paris, Pact of. An international agreement of August 27, 1928 entered into by almost all the countries of the world, condemning recourse to war and renouncing it as an instrument of national policy. The parties further agreed that they would not settle their international disputes by other than pacific means. Also known as the Kellogg, or Kellogg-Briand, Pact.

Paris Peace Conference. The peace conference after World War I which met in Paris during the first six months of 1919. It drew up treaties with the various enemy states named after different Paris suburbs where they were signed. See TREATIES OF VERSAILLES, ST. GERMAIN, TRIANON, NEUILLY, SÈVRES.

parish. Unit of local government in Louisiana similar to the county in other states.

parity. Equality, applied to national demands, as for example of naval tonnage or military strength.

parliament. The name first given to the supreme legislature of Great Britain and adopted by many legislative assemblies in Europe, Latin America, and elsewhere. The English Parliament, often called "the mother of parliaments," dates back to 1275 and consists of two chambers: the House of Commons and the House of Lords. The House of Commons is by far the more important of the two and is elected much like the American House of Representatives, which is largely modelled on it. The House of Lords is an assembly of the heads of aristocratic families (called the Peers of the Realm), of the Bishops of the Church of England, and Britain's highest judges. See PARLIAMENTARY SYSTEM.

parliamentary flag. A flag of truce.

parliamentary law. The rules governing the order and methods of carrying on business in a legislative body, which can also be used by any assembly.

parliamentary procedure. The customary order and methods of carrying on the business of a legislative body.

parliamentary system. A system of government where the executive part of the government is responsible for its actions to the legislative branch, namely to parliament. In this system the chief executive or head of the government (prime minister, premier) and the other members of the cabinet are also members of parliament and their position depends upon the confidence of the majority of members of parliament. Once this confidence is withdrawn and the government is voted down on an important issue, the government is obliged either to submit its resignation to the head of the state (king, president, etc.) or to ask the head of the state to dissolve parliament and to let the people elect a new parliament, which in turn expresses its stand toward the government. If this newly elected parliament again votes against the government, the prime minister and his cabinet hand in their resignations at once and the leader of the opposition is asked by the head of the state to form a new government. In the parliamentary system the members of the cabinet usually initiate legislative measures and act in a sense like a central committee of the legislature. Great Britain, the British Dominions, most European democracies and a number of Latin American countries have adopted this system. In the United States the three branches of government (executive, legislative, and judiciary) are separate and there is no way for the legislature to remove the chief executive if unsatisfied with his actions, except by impeachment in case of proved violation of the constitution. See PAR-LIAMENT.

parliamentary undersecretary. The cabinet member, found especially in British governments, representing a department in which he ranks next to the secretary or minister. Like his superior, he is a member of parliament and may represent the cabinet therein, and loses office when the cabinet resigns.

parole. 1. To liberate a prisoner before his term has expired, or one serving an indeterminate sentence, on certain conditions, for example, that he refrain from wrongdoing. 2. The liberation of a prisoner as above.

Parteitag (pahr-TIE-takh). Literally, the party day. The Nazi Party Congress which was held annually in September at Nuremberg.

partial succession. The transfer of part of the rights of a state to another state, as when the second state acquires part of the territory of the first, or as when the second loses or gains a part of the sovereignty of the first as in the establishment or dissolution of a protectorate.

partisan. 1. Adhering to one party or another in a dispute; not impartial. 2. One of a body of troops detached from the main forces and carrying on hostilities behind enemy lines. 3. Members of bands of Yugoslav irregulars, which fought the Axis in Yugoslavia after that country fell to the Germans in April, 1941. Their leader was Josip Broz, later known as Marshal Tito. During the war they formed a political organization and set up a provisional government which enjoyed the increasing favor of the Allies until the Partisans finally gained control of the whole country at the expense of the Chetniks. The Partisans had a wide representation throughout Yugoslavia and favored diminished influence of the Serbs and a greater influence for the other parts of the country, to be worked out in a federal form of government. See CHETNIK.

partition. The division of a country into parts. Such a solution was suggested by the British for Palestine in 1937. See PARTITIONS OF POLAND.

Partitions of Poland. Three divisions of Poland among Austria, Prussia, and Russia, in 1772, 1793, and 1795 ending with its entire absorption by those three countries. The advance of the Russian boundary in 1944 to the Curzon Line is sometimes referred to as a fourth partition.

party. 1. A political organization which, at election time, presents the voters with a list of candidates for public office who presumably favor the platform or list of principles which the organization advocates. 2. One of the states participating in an international agreement.

party circle. A circle (or square) at the top of the columns in a party-column, or Indiana, ballot in which the voter may place a cross, thus voting for all the candidates of that party and no one else.

party-column ballot. See INDIANA BALLOT.

party line. The policy or interpretation of policy laid down by a party. The term is commonly used in connection with the communist party.

party lines. Strict division, as in a vote in a legislative body, of the members according to party affiliation.

party square. See PARTY CIRCLE.

pass examination. An examination by which a person qualifies for a government position under Civil Service, not by being the highest, or one of the three highest of the examinees, but merely by passing, or receiving higher than a minimum grade.

passive obedience. The idea brought forth by many political philosophers that no matter how bad a king was he still deserved to be obeyed without resistance, as his appointment came from God. See DIVINE RIGHT OF KINGS; RIGHT OF RESISTANCE.

passive resistance. The non-violent hindrance of the operation of British rule in India by the Nationalists, such as by having large numbers of people sit on train tracks to prevent the movement of trains.

passport. A document identifying the bearer and issued by a government authority, used for travel in a foreign country. In the United States passports are issued by the State Department and must often be stamped with a visa by the diplomatic or consular representative of the country in which the bearer plans to travel. They have also been used in many countries for internal travel, and there are special passports for diplomatic agents, ship captains and in wartime for travel in a war zone. See VISA.

patent. 1. An exclusive right granted by a state to an inventor or a corporation to exploit an invention for a limited number of years. 2. The instrument which conveys title to public land.

Patent Office. An agency in the United States Department of Commerce, headed by the Commissioner of Patents, which receives and grants applications for patents and trade marks. Established in 1802 as part of the State Department, transferred to the Department of the Interior in 1849 and to Commerce in 1925.

paternalistic. Pertaining to a state which treats its citizens somewhat in the manner a father treats his children, that is, by closely controlling their private affairs.

patriarch. An honorary title given to the most important bishops of the early Christian Church, notably those of Rome, Constantinople, Alexandria, Antioch and Jerusalem. Later it often was given to the bishop with jurisdiction over all the bishops of a country, as in Russia.

patriarchy. An organization of society

in which the male head of the family or clan dominates its family and religious life.

patriotism. Devotion to one's country.

patronage. Appointive offices and public jobs which are available for political appointments when a party comes into power.

pauper. A person who does not support himself and is entirely dependent upon public support.

pay-as-you-go taxation. The United States system of income taxation instituted by the law of June 9, 1943 whereby persons pay their taxes in the year they earn them instead of the year after, as was the case prior to 1943. The change was made possible by an abatement or "forgiveness" of 75 per cent of the person's tax for either 1942 or 1943, the balance to be paid in addition to the regular tax for the other year, thus bringing the person up to date by 1944. See WITH-HOLDING TAX.

pay-roll tax. A tax on the total amount of a firm's payroll. Two such federal taxes have been in effect to provide money for unemployment benefits (3%) and old-age insurance (1%). See WITHHOLDING TAX.

peace. 1. Absence of or freedom from war. 2. A treaty of peace. 3. Public order and tranquility.

peace aims. Statement of the objectives of a state in regard to the details of the peace settlement which should follow a war.

peace at any price. Refusal to fight under any consideration.

Peace Ballot. A vote held in Great Britain on various peace questions, the results of which were announced June 27, 1935. About 12,000,000 voters (almost 40 per cent of the nation's total) participated. The votes were as follows: favoring British membership in the League of Nations, 95 per cent; favoring reduction of armaments, 90 per cent; favoring abolition of military aircraft, 82 per cent; favoring prohibiting private arms manufacture, 90 per cent; favoring non-military sanctions, 86 per cent; favoring military sanctions against an aggressor, 58 per cent.

peace conference. An international conference to re-establish or maintain peace. In the first case the parties have recently been at war and their representatives meet to negotiate a peace treaty. In the second case the conference is held with the purpose of preventing, postponing, or mitigating war, as the Hague Peace Conferences.

"peace for our time." From the statement of Prime Minister Neville Chamberlain of Great Britain on the results of the Munich Conference in September, 1938. World War II started less than one year later. See MUNICH ACCORD.

peace movement. The movement to establish international peace and to prevent future war, chiefly by an insistence on the peaceable settlement of international disputes and a growing reliance on the organs of international organization and government.

peace of the port. The general standard of law and order in a port city. If crimes committed on vessels in port are so serious as to disturb this standard of law and order, they are under the jurisdiction of the authorities in the city rather than that of the captain of the vessel, as is the case in minor disturbances.

Peace Palace. A large building at The Hague, the Netherlands, which is the seat of the Permanent Court of Arbitration and was the seat of the Permanent Court of International Justice. It was built through the generosity of Andrew Carnegie and dedicated in 1913.

"peace without victory." A phrase from a speech by President Wilson before the United States Senate, January 22, 1917 to describe the kind of peace he thought should follow World War I.

peaceful change. The process of modifying by international agreement the rules of international law so as to conform to changing conditions. It is obvious that there is a need for law to keep abreast of the times, while avoiding modifications by forceful unilateral action. This need was recognized and provided for in Article 19 of the League of Nations Covenant, but this provision was never put into effect.

peanut politics. American slang term for the pursuit of minor matters of political advantage.

Pearl Harbor. The harbor and United States naval base in the Hawaiian Islands attacked by Japanese planes on December 7, 1941 and hence a term for the date upon which hostilities commenced for the United States in World War II.

peer. 1. An equal, as in a jury of one's peers. 2. Members of the peerage. See PEERAGE.

peerage. The nobility, or body of peers. In Britain the peerage is composed of five classes, whose rank and approximate numbers are as follows: dukes, 26; marquesses, 38; earls, 195; viscounts,111; barons, 544. Members of the peerage have seats in the House of Lords and their titles are hereditary. See each of the titles listed separately.

penal. Pertaining to punishment for public offenses.

penal colony. A penal institution, usually established in an overseas colony, to which were transported prisoners sentenced in the mother country. Examples were the French colony at Devil's Island in French Guiana and the former British colonies in Australia and Tasmania. They were fa-mous for their brutality and are now considered outmoded as a method of confinement.

Pendleton Act. The Federal law of 1883 establishing the federal civil service.

penitentiary. Institution for the confinement of convicted criminals.

pension. A regular payment, usually monthly, paid to persons in consideration of certain past military or civil service to the government, or service to a private agency or corporation. The person may or may not have contributed financially while in service to the fund from which the payments are drawn.

peonage. A state of involuntary servitude growing out of payment in work for debts. It lasts as long as the debt remains unpaid. The word comes from the Spanish *peon* meaning foot soldier, and has been applied mainly to Indian and mestizo (half-breed) laborers in Latin America and the Philippines. Peonage was abolished in Mexico in 1917 and until then one third of the Mexican people were legally held in debt bondage. In the Philippines in 1928 twenty per cent of the people were held in peonage, but the Bill of Rights of the Philippine Commonwealth (1935) made all involuntary servitude illegal. In America the Thirteenth and Fourteenth Amendments to the Constitution and special anti-peonage legislation in 1875 abolished all involuntary servitude. In some states, however, isolated cases of peonage continued to occur. The United States Supreme Court in 1910 declared state laws tolerating peonage unconstitutional. The League of Nations and the International Labor Organization have also come out against all cases of involuntary servitude. See SLAVERY.

People's Court. A Nazi court set up in Germany in 1936 to hear cases of subversive activities against the Nazi regime. It was a political tribunal with practically no safeguards for the defendant.

per capita. Per person, literally per head. A kind of common denominator to which factors affecting groups of various sizes, such as costs of government, may be reduced.

perjury. Knowingly telling an untruth or less than the whole truth after having sworn to tell the whole truth.

permanent appropriation. A form of appropriation found in Great Britain and one or two states of the United States in which appropriations are repeated at each session of the legislative body until the repeal of the law authorizing them.

Permanent Court of Arbitration. A panel of arbitrators set up by the first Hague Peace Conference (1899) from which members could be drawn to settle international disputes.

Permanent Court of International Justice. The so-called World Court set up by the League of Nations, the first real world court. It first met in 1922, and until 1939 handed down about 75 decisions and advisory opinions on all kinds of justiciable internaional questions. Membership was separate from the League of Nations but the two membership groups largely coincided. The League Council and Assembly picked the judges, the varying number of which was about 15. Its jurisdiction covered all matters submitted to it, but particularly treaty interpretation and questions of international law. It has been supplanted under the United Nations by the International Court of Justice. See OPTIONAL CLAUSE.

Permanent Joint Board on Defense. A United States-Canadian board set up August 17, 1940 to consider the joint problems of defending the two countries.

permanent registration. A system of voter registration in which a person registers only once and his registration is kept in force as long as he does not change residence. In some states the registration is maintained permanently only if the voter votes at stated intervals.

permanent undersecretary. The highest civil servant or permanent member of a British government department, such as the foreign office. He ranks next to the secretary and parliamentary undersecretary, but when they go out of office with a change of government the permanent undersecretary stays on.

permissive powers of Congress. Powers which Congress may or may not exercise as it sees fit. The power to pass national bankruptcy laws, for example, was not used by Congress for over one hundred years after the establishment of the Constitution.

permit. An official authorization to perform a certain act or to carry on a given activity, such as hold a meeting or build a certain kind of building. Often used as a synonym for license, though license often carries the idea of annual renewal for a continuing activity.

perquisites. Matters of profit gained incidental to public office and in addition to the regular salary thereof, such as fees, patronage, contracts, and minor graft.

person. An entity which is subject to the legal rights and duties imposed by a state. Usually thought of as an individual human being, but under United States law includes groups of people legally formed into a corporation, sometimes called an "artificial" person as opposed to a "natural" person.

personna grata (pur-SO-nuh GRAH-tuh). A person who is acceptable on political or personal grounds. This term is applied chiefly to diplomatic agents to indicate that they personally are satisfactory to the receiving state.

persona non grata (pur-SO-nuh NAHN GRAH-tuh). A person not acceptable. See PERSONA GRATA.

personal liberty. The freedom of persons to speak, write, and assemble peaceably and to move freely from place to place.

personal property. See PROPERTY.

personal union. The relation of two states connected only by having the same ruler. Examples have been England and Hanover, the Netherlands and Luxemburg, and Belgium and the Congo Free State. See REAL UNION.

personation. The impersonating of another person in order to cast a vote in his name illegally.

personnel administration. The processes of recruitment, classification, grading, discipline, promotion, and retirement of public employees.

petition, right of. The right which a person enjoys in free countries to request his government to take some specified action.

petit jury. See TRIAL JURY.

Petroleum Administration for War. An emergency war agency set up December 2, 1942, under the Secretary of the Interior to secure the most efficient use of our petroleum supplies and facilities for the war effort.

Philippine Independence Act. Law of March 24, 1934 providing for Philippine independence after a ten year transitional period, on July 4, 1946. During this time the United States tariff was to be increasingly applicable to Philippine goods. The Filipinos had refused this general plan the year before, but accepted it with minor changes when offered the second time.

phobia. Used as a suffix after the name of a state to indicate intense dislike of that state and things pertaining to it, as Anglophobia, Russophobia, hatred of England, Russia.

phony war. A slang term to describe the western front in the period of World War II between the fall of Poland in the autumn of 1939 and the German attack on Denmark and Norway in the spring of 1940. Also called the "sitzkrieg." During that time there were intermittent and desultory attacks on each side and it appeared to many that neither side was really trying to reach a decision and win the war along that front. Critics claimed this war was mere pretense on the part of Great Britain and France as a gesture in the direction of their commitments to Poland, and on the part of Germany because Hitler had no real disagreement with Britain and France.

P.I.C.A.O. See PROVISIONAL INTERNATIONAL CIVIL AVIATION ORGANIZATION.

picket. To stand or walk around the entrance to a building, grounds, or other place of employment and try to prevent employees from going in to work during a strike. Or, the same tactics as a form of protest against the words or actions of an individual or organization.

pigeonhole. To put legislation aside indefinitely.

pillage. 1. Personal and unauthorized looting by members of armed forces, as distinguished from the requisitions which may be made in an occupied territory for military needs or administrative purposes. 2. To loot as above.

pilotage. Fee for the services of a marine pilot.

pineapple primary. Slang term for the state primary of 1928 in Chicago, so-called because of the occasional use during the campaign of bombs, referred to at the time as "pineapples."

piracy. An act of violence, usually robbery, committed on the high seas by persons sailing a private vessel without the authorization of any state or political organization and without political motive.

place in the sun. A euphemistic phrase meaning a place of importance in world affairs, primarily as a colonial empire.

plaintiff. A person who is complaining or bringing a law-suit.

plank. Term for each item, clause, or principle in a party platform.

planned economy. An economic system in which the fulfillment of needs is not left to supply and demand but production is deliberately set at figures calculated to fulfill certain demands and end the problems of waste and want. Russia has tried this under the five year plans, and the other major belligerents planned production for war needs in somewhat the same way in World War II.

platform. A statement of principles advocated by a party or candidate at election time, presumably to be incorporated into public policy if the party or candidate is elected.

Platt Amendment. An amendment to the U. S. army appropriation act of 1901 limiting the treaty-making and financial powers of the new Republic of Cuba, and providing that the United States could intervene therein for the protection of life, property, and liberty. These provisions were included in a United States-Cuban treaty of May 22, 1903, and in the Cuban constitution of the same year. The amendment was abrogated by a new treaty between the two states May 29, 1934, one of the first concrete examples of the Good Neighbor Policy.

plebiscite. A vote taken among the people of a territory to determine whether the territory should be annexed to a state or whether some

other disposition should be made of it. Usually includes a choice between two states. Occasionally, as in the Saar in 1935, there is some other alternative, in that case remaining under the control of the League of Nations.

plenary session. A full session of all members of an international conference or assembly.

plenipotentiary. Literally, with full powers; applied, for example, to a diplomatic officer.

plump. Slang term meaning to give all the votes of a group or delegation in a political convention to a single candidate. Usually used as "to plump for."

plunderbund. Slang term for a group of grafting politicians.

pluralism. The political theory that a person's interests are not single but plural, and that other interests than political—usually economic—should be represented in the policy-making of the community.

plural voting. Voting for more than one candidate in a given election. For example, in Great Britain the graduates of each of the older universities elect one or two members of Commons to represent the universities, in addition to voting on candidates in the districts in which they live.

plurality. 1. The largest number of votes of three or more candidates when no one of them obtains a majority. 2. The excess of votes for such a successful candidate over those of next highest.

plutocracy. 1. Government by the wealthiest class in the state. 2. The wealthiest class in a state.

pocket battleship. A war vessel of 10,-000 tons carrying guns larger than eight inches. This was the largest war vessel permitted to Germany under the Treaty of Versailles.

pocket borough. An election district

controlled by one man, that is, in his pocket. See ROTTEN BOROUGH.

pocket veto. The process by which a chief executive prevents a bill from becoming law by refraining from signing it. Usually a bill becomes a law after a certain number of days (ten, excepting Sundays, in Congress) if the legislative body is still in session. But if, for example, the Congress adjourns before the ten days are up, the bill dies unless the president signs it. Hence the president can kill any bill sent him in the last ten days of the session by refraining from signing it or, as it were, by keeping it in his pocket. He does not have to give his reasons, as in an ordinary veto, and the bill cannot be passed over this veto by a two-thirds majority. A similar power is granted to the governor in about half the states.

pogrom. A Russian word meaning devastation, applied to organized massacres of helpless people, usually Jews and usually with unofficial government sanction. It was used originally to mean such massacres under Czarist rule in Russia; now applied to any such massacre any place.

point of order. In parliamentary law a question raised by a member as to whether the action being taken is appropriate under the rules.

poison gas. Gases which are poisonous or harmful to human beings, and used for military purposes. Efforts have been made to outlaw their use in war, but these have not been accepted by all states, the United States and Japan being two of the most reluctant.

police. 1. A group of persons specifically commissioned for the maintenance of law and order, the investigation of crime and the apprehension of criminals and suspects. 2. To patrol or keep order.

police court. Lower municipal criminal court.

police power. The power of a state to regulate the activities of individuals for the protection of public safety, morals, health, and general welfare. This is a very broad power, and is reserved to the states in the United States as it is not granted to the federal government by the Constitution.

police state. A state in which ultimate governmental administration and enforcement is not carried out by the regular administrative and judicial organs of the government so much as by the arbitrary power of the police of the state, particularly including the secret police. The term has been applied to dictatorships which have been distinguished by the wide activity of the secret police.

policy. A series of objectives which a governmental body strives to attain and the means which it consciously plans to use in the pursuit of those objectives.

Polish Corridor. A strip of territory between Prussia and East Prussia granted by the Treaty of Versailles to Poland providing access to and a frontage on the Baltic Sea. It was particularly irritating to the Germans because it separated East Prussia from the rest of Germany. Abolished after World War II when East Prussia was divided between Poland and the U.S.S.R.

Polish Legion. Organized units of Polish soldiers fighting in the allied armies in the two World Wars.

Politbureau. The political bureau of the central committee of the communist party in the U.S.S.R. It is the policy-forming branch. See ORGBUREAU.

political. 1. In general, anything pertaining to state or government, as political interests or political office. 2. More specifically, pertaining to policy making, as a political decision, as opposed to a legal one.

Political Action Committee. The political organization of the Congress of Industrial Organizations. It first appeared as an organized pressure group in this form in the election of 1944, under the chairmanship of Sidney Hillman, and in support of President Franklin D. Roosevelt.

political assessment. A compulsory contribution to the party treasury by those put in office by the party. Usually the contribution is a percentage of the office-holder's salary.

political club. A social organization of people with common party interests.

political economy. A more or less obsolete term for economics.

political offense. An offense committed with a political end in view, for instance a change in the form of composition of the government by extralegal means.

political prisoner. A person who is confined by the government for holding political views not acceptable to the government.

political refugee. A person who has had to flee from his homeland because he holds political opinions not acceptable to the government of his home state.

political science. The study of the formation, forms, and processes of the state and government.

political theory. The study of the philosophy of the state and government or a particular idea thereof.

politician. A person with a direct interest in politics either as a successful or unsuccessful aspirant for public office or as one of the workers in a party organization.

politics. 1. The processes of government, particularly those related to elections. 2. The study of governmental forms and processes, that is, political science.

polity. 1. The form or constitution of the civil government of a state. 2. A state.

poll. 1. A vote, either the process or the count. 2. To take a vote. 3. Polls. See POLLING PLACE.

poll tax. A head tax, or flat tax on every person. Often used as a requirement for voting, as in the United States where the number of states requiring it had been reduced by 1946 to seven, namely: Alabama, Arkansas, Mississippi, South Carolina, Tennessee, Texas, and Virginia.

poll watcher. A person designated by a political party to watch a particular voting place to report illegal voting.

polling place. The place where the voters come on the proper days to cast their ballots in a popular election.

poorhouse *or* **poor farm.** A governmental institution providing a residence for paupers. Usually it is established by the county.

poor laws. Legislation to provide for the poor from public funds. It had its origin in the breaking up of the feudal society in which the lords were obliged to take care of their serfs. In European countries where the Church was powerful, poor relief lay in the hands of the ecclesiastical authorities. A national system of poor relief was first developed in England and Scotland. Poor laws were at first to control begging and vagrancy and to regulate almsgiving. The Poor Relief Act of 1601 was the first which recognized the responsibility of the state for the poor by providing that each parish levy a tax for such relief, and provide work for the poor, apprenticeship for children and care for the infirm. These laws were followed by more humanitarian legislation at the end of the 18th century and beginning of the 19th. In the United States, because of the absence of federal provisions, various types of poor relief exist in the different states, many of them based on the Elizabethan law of 1601. In New England the township is the unit of administration, while in other states the counties or State Boards of Charities administer poor relief. In the 20th century poor laws have been generally superseded by modern systems of social security and community welfare. See SOCIAL SECURITY, SOCIALIZED MEDICINE, PUBLIC HEALTH, BEVERIDGE PLAN.

poor relief. See POOR LAWS, SOCIAL SECURITY, BEVERIDGE PLAN.

pope. The spiritual head of the Roman Catholic Church and the temporal head of Vatican City.

Popolo d'Italia, Il (eel-POH-poh-loh dee-TAH-lee-ah). Mussolini's own newspaper in Milan, founded in 1914. At first socialist, it later developed into a leading organ of Italian Fascism.

popular. Pertaining to the people or that which is representative of most of the people.

Popular Front. A combination of reformist parties in France which from 1936 to 1939 formed a coalition government. The Front was created in face of severe international and internal economic and political crises and appeared in the French elections in 1936 which strengthened the Socialists and Communists and weakened the middle-of-the-road parties. The leader of the strongest party, the Socialist Léon Blum formed a popular front (*Front Populaire*) government, together with the Radical-Socialists and several smaller parties, but without the Communists, who however, gave it support. Its policy was neither Marxist nor Socialist but one favoring strong social reforms and improving working conditions. It was unable to deal with the mounting financial and economic difficulties and was followed in 1939 by a government consisting of representatives of the Radical-Socialists and center parties, but not the Socialists.

The idea of "popular front" governments has been furthered in many countries by Communist and Socialist parties in the 1930's as a means of self-defense against spreading fascism and Nazism. The Spanish loyalists during the Civil War constituted such a front reaching from Moderate Liberals to Communists and Trotskyites. See SOCIALISM, MARXISM, COMMUNISM, LEFT.

popular sovereignty. The system of government in which sovereignty rests in the people itself. Sovereignty being the supreme power in the state, the people rule themselves through their representatives. The idea of the rule of the will of the people was born in France in the 18th century and was expounded by Jean Jacques Rousseau. Jefferson was its American apostle; he created the basic American political philosophy that the will of the people is the only true source of governmental power. America being a federal republic, this basic doctrine was not easy to put into practice, as certain elements of political power remained with the states. Many conflicts ensued between the Federal government and the states, or groups of states. One of the hottest conflicts preparing the ground for the Civil War was the question which preoccupied the public in the 1850's, whether the people in the Territories (Kansas, Nebraska, etc.) had the right to decide for themselves the question of slavery. Abraham Lincoln was an outstanding defender of popular sovereignty and his Gettysburg Address became its classic formulation. See SOVEREIGNTY, STATE RIGHTS, REPUBLIC, NATION, NATIONALISM.

population pressure. The pressure of the

numbers of the people of a state upon their sources of subsistence. If the sources of subsistence are relatively limited for the number of people, it is said to increase the population pressure.

Populist Party. A third party formed in the United States in 1890 by discontented farmers and laborers chiefly in the Middle West, but active to some extent also in the South. It showed considerable strength in 1892, then waned and disappeared after 1908. It condemned the capitalistic interests and demanded public ownership of railroads and telegraphs, increase of paper money and the free coinage of silver. James B. Weaver was an important leader. William Jennings Bryan was the presidential candidate in 1896, 1900, and 1908.

pork. American slang expression meaning something from the pork barrel. See PORK BARREL.

pork barrel. Those federal or state appropriations for local improvements which are looked upon as political favors to the local politicians or their communities rather than as fulfilling real local needs.

portal to portal pay. A daily wage based not on the actual time that a person spends working, but based rather on the time he spends from the moment he enters the "portal" or gate of the mine or factory until he leaves the property after his day's work. The principle was accepted by the United States Supreme Court, March 27, 1944 in iron ore mining, in which the time the miners spent being transported from the entrance of the mine to the "working face" was considered part of their working day, on the theory that it was time required of the miners as part of their job. Within the following fourteen months the principle had been extended to soft and hard coal mining in new union

contracts. In 1946 in the Mount Clemens Pottery Company case the principle was extended to factory work, but the court decided that the amount of time spent between the portal and the place of work was in this case not of sufficient consequence to warrant a readjustment of the daily wage.

port authority. A governmental body administering the regulations for movement of goods and people to, from, and within a sea, lake, or river port. The Port of New York Authority also builds and controls such structures as the George Washington Memorial Bridge and the Holland Tunnel.

Porte. See SUBLIME PORTE.

portfolio. Term sometimes used to refer to a government department or ministry. In certain countries ministers are added to the cabinet as general advisers without being placed at the head of a government department. Such persons are called ministers without portfolio.

Portsmouth, Treaty of. Peace treaty following the Russo-Japanese War signed at Portsmouth, New Hampshire, due to the influence of Theodore Roosevelt, on September 5, 1905. By it Japan secured the southern part of Sakhalin Island, Russian rights to the South Manchurian Railway, and mining rights in south Manchuria and Russia's leasehold at Port Arthur.

posse. See POSSE COMITATUS.

posse comitatus (POH-say kah-mi-TAH-tus). Literally the power of the county. The adult males of a county who are liable to calls for assistance from the sheriff, or the ones so called upon. Usually a small group of armed citizens temporarily called upon to catch a particular criminal.

positive law. A body of rules created and enforced by a sovereign political authority (King, Leader, People). The laws enacted by a Congress or Parliament, the elected representatives of the sovereign people, and enforced by the officials of the people constitute positive law in a democracy. This law is distinguished from the law of God, from natural law, international law, etc., which have different origins and the enforcement of which is often not clearly defined. The so-called "positive law school" maintains that positive law is the only true law. Opponents of this school, however, fear that eliminating all other laws may easily lead to tyranny, in which the sovereign would be able to make and enforce any kind of unjust law which may be completely against the traditions and beliefs of a nation and against the sense of justice and decency rooted in its citizens. In case the sovereign is a king or dictator, the whole people may suffer from the exclusive rule of positive law. In case the people itself is the sovereign, the exclusive rule of positive law may result in the oppression of racial, religious, political or national minorities. Positive law is also called Statutory Law, as it is formulated in so-called Statutes containing Acts of Legislation. See LAW, SOVEREIGN, STATUTES, COMMON LAW, INTERNATIONAL LAW.

Post Office. The governmental department whose function it is to collect and distribute mail. In the United States, the Department also has certain banking functions such as the transmission of money by "money orders" and collection of savings deposits.

post road. A road over which mail was transported, originally one equipped with post houses for changing horses.

postal money order. A method of transmitting funds by an order for a certain amount, bought at a post office for a small fee, payable to a certain person who then cashes it, on its receipt, for the face value.

postal savings. A savings deposit system established within the United States Post Office Department in 1911. A similar and very popular system was begun in England in 1861.

postmaster. Official at the head of a local post office.

Postmaster General. In the United States government, the member of the cabinet in charge of the Post Office Department. He is often chairman of his party's National Committee.

Potsdam Agreement. An agreement between President Truman, Prime Minister Atlee and Generalissimo Stalin, after a conference held July 17 to August 2, 1945. It included the establishment of a Council of Foreign Ministers, and the control, reparations, disarmament, and eastern boundaries of Germany. There was further discussion also of Austria and other German satellites, European transportation, Iran, Tangier, and the Straits.

pourparler (poor-pahr-LEY). French term meaning an informal discussion, as before drawing up a treaty.

POW. See PRISONERS OF WAR.

power. 1. The authority or right of a government or state to act. 2. The ability to compel compliance. 3. Synonym for state, for example, a great power.

power politics. International political relations in which states pursue the enlargement of their own power as an end in itself, and in which they stand ready to use their power, ultimately measured by the threat or use of military force, as the chief means for enlarging that power.

P. R. See PROPORTIONAL REPRESENTATION.

Pravda (Truth). Official Russian Communist Party newspaper in the U.S.S.R., published in Moscow.

preamble. An introduction or preface to a law or constitution giving its purposes.

precinct. Small governmental district or subdivision, such as a voting district within a ward or an urban unit for police administration.

precedent. Any governmental action of sufficient validity to be followed in later cases of exactly the same kind. Particularly important in legal decisions and administrative rulings which thus come to have the force of law.

prefect. The administrative head of the French *département*. He is a key person as the regional head of the national administration and the chief supervisor of the local functions of the *département*. Italy and Japan have similar officials with the same title. The name is descended from a Roman title held by various types of high officials.

prefecture. The office of the prefect.

preferential voting. A system of proportional voting in which the voter votes for several candidates indicating his first, second, and other preferences. See HARE PLAN.

premier. Head of a cabinet; prime minister.

preparedness. State of readiness of the armed forces to repel an attack. The term is purely relative, as the degree of preparation necessary to defeat one aggressor might be quite inadequate for another.

pre-primary convention. A convention of a political party prior to a primary for the purpose of securing solid party backing for a certain list of candidates. Sometimes used as a method of circumventing a non-partisan primary.

prerogative. Originally a special right or privilege inherent in a king, hence special exclusive powers, as, for example, the powers of a chief executive as opposed to the powers of the legislative branch of government. In constitutional monarchies the king's official prerogatives are exercised on the advice of his ministers.

prescription. The establishment by a state of title to a territory as a result of prolonged and continuous control over it.

presentment. Statement by a grand jury that certain facts warrant a criminal trial of some person. It differs from an indictment in that it originates with the grand jury itself and not with the prosecutor.

presidency. 1. The office of a president. 2. Title for each of the three major provinces in British India: Bengal, Bombay, and Madras.

president. 1. The chief executive in a number of republics, largest of which is the United States. 2. An officer who presides over or is chairman of a legislative body. For example, the vice-president of the United States is the president of the Senate.

presidential government. A form of government in which the head of the government (the president) is chosen directly by the electorate and is responsible to it rather than chosen by the legislative body and responsible to it. The president's term is fixed and he cannot be turned out of office by an adverse vote in the legislative body as can a prime minister. The president and the legislative body form two equal and co-ordinate divisions of the government.

presidential primary. A primary election held in the spring or summer of election years in many of the United States in which the voters indicate their choices for presidential candidates. The choice is binding on the convention delegates to different degrees in different states. These primaries are closely scrutinized for indications as to the strength of a given candidate.

presidential succession. The order in which officials assume the office of president in case it becomes vacant or in case the president is unable to discharge his duties. In the United States the first to succeed to the office is the vice-president, as provided by the Constitution. By statute the next persons are the Secretary of State, Secretary of the Treasury, Secretary of War, and the other cabinet members in order of the establishment of their respective departments. The law perpetuates an inaccuracy, as the War Department is older than the Treasury.

president's annual message. See ANNUAL MESSAGE.

Presidium. A kind of executive committee of the Supreme Soviet of the U.S.S.R. It convenes and dissolves the Supreme Soviet, acts for it between sessions and sees that the individual republics in the union and the Council of People's Ministers follow the laws. It has the power of pardon and appoints the army high command.

press, freedom of. See FREEDOM OF THE PRESS.

pressure group. An organization not directly affiliated with any political party, which actively seeks to further its own ends, most often economic, by a more or less continuous and organized campaign to elect candidates of either party to office who will back its program, and to keep a continuous pressure on elected officials to favor its ends. This is done by paid lobbying and threatening political punishment at the next election.

pressure politics. The pursuit of political objectives by means of pressure groups. See PRESSURE GROUPS.

pretender. One who claims a throne but is not able to make his claim effective. Examples are the Old Pretender, James Francis Edward Stuart (1688–

1766) and the Young Pretender, Charles Francis Stuart (1720–1788), also known as Bonnie Prince Charlie, who successively claimed the throne of Great Britain after the expulsion of the Stuarts in 1689.

preventive justice. The maintenance of justice by preventing an act which would work an injustice, as by the use of an injunction. See INJUNCTION.

preventive war. A war begun by a country when it is in a state of preparedness, against another country which it is believed will attack the first country when it, too, has reached a state of preparedness for war. In other words, a war begun to prevent another war which would probably have much less favorable results.

previous question. A motion in parliamentary law which, if voted, closes debate on the main question under consideration and brings it up to an immediate vote.

price ceiling. Maximum price for a commodity established by a government agency, as in the United States by the Office of Price Administration during and after World War II.

Price Control Act. Law of January 30, 1942 setting up the Office of Price Administration. See OFFICE OF PRICE ADMINISTRATION.

price-fixing. 1. The process of determining prices to prevent undue rise and fluctuation. 2. Process of agreement among dealers on a given price for a product to prevent the normal effects of competition.

price stabilization. The process of setting a whole scale of maximum prices to prevent all from rising, and to maintain the fairness of prices in relation one to another.

primary. A method of nominating party candidates for public office by a popular election. Usually a voter may vote only in the primary of his own party. See CLOSED PRIMARY and

OPEN PRIMARY. Primaries are usually held at the regular polling places and are supervised much as are regular elections. More accurately called a direct primary election.

prime minister. The first minister or head of the cabinet. In Great Britain he is referred to as first among equals.

primogeniture. The rule that the oldest son inherits the entire estate of his father. In England it was particularly applied to real property. In America it has been abolished in favor of "free inheritance" since 1798.

Primrose League. British Conservative political organization, founded in 1883, named for the favorite flower of Benjamin Disraeli who was a great leader of the Conservatives.

prince. A European title descended from the Latin word *princeps*, meaning chief or first. 1. Title of a ruler, often independent, as the Prince of Monaco, or subject to a king or emperor, when he is about the equivalent of duke. The German word is *prinz* or *fuerst*, the Russian *knez*. 2. Son of a king or member of a royal family. In Britain used as a courtesy title for royal dukes or earls.

prince consort. Husband of a queen who has inherited a throne in her own right. He does not share her power or prerogatives. Example: Prince Albert of Saxe-Coburg, Prince Consort of Queen Victoria of Great Britain.

Prince of Wales. Title conferred on the oldest son of the monarch of Great Britain. First granted in 1301 by Edward I to his son, afterwards King Edward II.

princess. Daughter or grandaughter of a monarch, or wife of a prince, or a female member of a royal family. See PRINCE.

princess royal. In Britain, the oldest daughter of the reigning sovereign.

priority. A privileged position granting precedence. During World War II many scarce goods and services were allocated on a system of priorities, in which important military needs were granted highly preferential treatment while unessential civilian needs were granted none. After the war, servicemen were granted somewhat similar precedence in certain instances, such as in procuring home-building permits and government-surplus supplies.

Pripet Marshes. Marshy land lying near the center of the pre-1939 Polish-Russian frontier. Generally considered previously as an important military barrier.

prisoners of war. Members of the armed forces of a state captured during war by the enemy. Their treatment is regulated by a number of international agreements, notably the Geneva Convention of 1929.

private bill. In the United States Congress a bill of only limited application or operation, such as to pay a personal claim or build a section of a highway.

Private Calendar. In the United States House of Representatives the Calendar of the Committee of the Whole House; a calendar for special or private bills. See HOUSE CALENDARS.

private enterprise. Business conducted freely by private individuals as opposed to business owned and operated by government.

private international law. Rules governing the relations of individuals who belong to different states. See INTERNATIONAL LAW.

private international unions. Organizations composed of representatives of different countries who do not represent their governments, as the Rotary International or the International Chamber of Commerce.

private law. The rules defining the rights, duties, and relationships of two persons within the state in regard to each other. See PUBLIC LAW.

private member's bill. A bill introduced into the British parliament by an ordinary member, not a cabinet member, and therefore not a "government bill."

private property. See PROPERTY.

privateer. 1. A ship that is privately owned and operated but which is commissioned by a state to participate in hostilities. See LETTERS OF MARQUE AND REPRISAL. 2. To carry on active hostilities against the merchant shipping of an enemy state with a private vessel commissioned for the purpose. Abolished by the Declaration of Paris, 1856.

privilege, parliamentary. The right of a member of a legislative body not to be held accountable outside that body for any statements made therein.

privilege tax. A tax levied on the privilege to engage in a particular kind of activity, profession or business.

privileged question. In parliamentary practice a motion which takes precedence over other motions.

privileges and immunities. Exceptions to the ordinary operations of the laws. See DIPLOMATIC PRIVILEGES AND IMMUNITIES.

Privy Council. In Great Britain a large group of advisers to the king made up of all present and past cabinet members and a few other persons outstanding in public affairs. It meets only at coronations, but functions through the cabinet, which is a part of it. Theoretically it issues the orders in council. In Japan the Privy Council was a similar though smaller advisory group which rendered real advice on laws and treaties.

prize. An enemy or neutral merchant vessel seized by a belligerent during war. Almost any enemy vessel is liable to confiscation but a neutral vessel is liable only if taken in certain circumstances such as blockade-running or resisting visit and search by the belligerent.

prize court. A court set up by a belligerent to decide upon the legality of captures of vessels and goods at sea, and their consequent liability to confiscation.

prize crew. The crew put on a prize by the capturing vessel. This crew takes the prize to a port where there is a prize court for condemnation proceedings.

probate court. A county court which has jurisdiction over the estates of deceased persons and matters in relation to the care of minors.

probate judge. The judge of a probate court. See PROBATE COURT.

probation. Freedom granted to a person convicted of crime before he has served his sentence on condition that he reports to a specified official at stated intervals and refrains from committing other crimes.

probe. 1. Popular expression meaning an investigation. 2. To investigate.

processing tax. A tax on the preparation or processing of food products under the Agricultural Adjustment Administration.

procès verbal. The official minutes or proceedings of an international conference.

proclamation. An official public executive announcement regarding some governmental act or order.

progressive. A person who favors gradual, legally-instituted improvements in the structure and functioning of the state.

Progressive. A member of the Progressive Party.

Progressive Citizens of America. A liberal group formed on December 29, 1946 chiefly by an amalgamation of the National Citizens Political Action Committee, headed by Dr. Frank Kingdon, and the Independent Citizens Committee of the Arts, Sciences and Professions, headed by Jo Davidson. It differs from the otherwise comparable Americans for Democratic Action in that it has not specifically aligned itself against Communism. Its program is in most respects a continuation of that of the late President Franklin D. Roosevelt. Kingdon and Davidson were named co-chairmen.

Progressive Party. A party originating with the split of liberal elements from the Republican Party in 1912 under Theodore Roosevelt. Its influence continued through the election of 1924, when Robert M. La Follette, Sr. was its presidential candidate. It favored the stricter regulation of big business, woman's suffrage, and other extensions of the democratic controls of government.

progressive tax. See TAX.

prohibition. In a wide sense the prohibition by law of the manufacture, sale and use of certain foods, clothes and other articles deemed harmful to the physicial and moral wellbeing of the population. Generally applied to the prohibition of alcoholic beverages.

The most outstanding case of a complete prohibition of the manufacture, transportation and sale of intoxicating beverages, containing 0.5 per cent or more of alcohol, was the Eighteenth Amendment to the United States Constitution which was in force from January 1920 until December 1933. It was preceded by restrictions and prohibitions on a local scale since colonial times but was intensified with the spreading of organized temperance movements in the 19th century. Complete prohibition was sponsored by various Temperance Societies, the Anti-Saloon League and church groups, and had far greater backing in rural regions than in large cities. The National

Prohibition Act of 1920 provided severe penalties for violating the Eighteenth Amendment but the enforcement of the Act was not entirely successful. A large part of the public was hostile to the Act, and violators such as bootleggers, speakeasies, roadhouses, etc., were patronized and concealed from the authorities against a background of crime, violence and bribery. Opponents of prohibition increased in numbers and the Democratic Party proposed its repeal in the platform in 1932. Following the election of President Roosevelt the Eighteenth Amendment was repealed. Prohibition continued in a few States and in many districts local option prevails.

Complete prohibition of alcoholic beverages was in force in Finland from 1919–1932. Norway and Iceland also have enacted national prohibition, while Sweden and Denmark favor local prohibition and restrictions. Canada introduced prohibition during the first World War but it was gradually abolished during the 1920's. In Russia the sale of vodka was prohibited during the first World War, but government monopoly of manufacturing vodka was restored in 1925. The sale of extremely deleterious liquor such as absinthe is forbidden in France, the Low Countries, Switzerland and Italy. Licensing of stores, saloons, etc., selling alcoholic beverages, and restricting the hours of sale is in force in most civilized countries.

Prohibition Party. A minor political party organized in 1869, the chief aim of which was to secure prohibition. See PROHIBITION.

projet de loi (praw-ZHAY duh LWAH). Literally a project of law, the French term for a bill sponsored by the cabinet. See PROPOSITION DE LOI.

proletariat. The name for a class of

workers who are free to sell their labor to employers for a definite period of time. They are thereby distinguished from slaves and serfs. They also differ from artisans or farmers, inasmuch as they do not own their tools and machines as the former do. Proletariat, or proletarians, is a Marxist term generally used in Europe by both Marxists and non-Marxists, but not used in colloquial American. Public opinion polls in the United States have shown that the overwhelming majority of workers regard themselves as belonging to the middle classes, not to the lower classes which according to Marx form the proletariat. See MARXISM, COMMUNISM, SOCIALISM, CLASS STRUGGLE, BOLSHEVISM.

promulgate. 1. To publish or declare a law or decree. 2. To put into effect a law or decree by publication.

propaganda. The name for various methods intended to influence public opinion and actions. It may take spoken, written, pictorial or musical form, and sometimes political acts themselves are designed to influence the public mind. Propaganda is as old as mankind, but its techniques have developed enormously during the last generation. This is partly due to technological progress (radio, motion pictures, wide distribution of newspapers, magazines, posters), partly to the spreading of literacy making it possible to reach the broadest masses through the written word and partly to a development of mass psychology. In wartime, propaganda directed by governments becomes an important factor in strengthening the morale of the home front and of the armed forces and in undermining the fighting spirit of the enemy. This has also been called "psychological warfare." Democracies in peace time resent government propaganda, while totalitarian countries continue their efforts to persuade their own people and foreign nations of the supremacy of their principles, achievements and policies. In totalitarian countries there is virtually no distinction between education and propaganda. In nongovernmental spheres propaganda flourishes in democracies. It is used for advocating and publicizing religious beliefs, political and social movements, all kinds of goods and services including entertainments, education, etc. Advertising and public relations are all branches of propaganda activities. They are especially highly developed in America. Propaganda in itself is a tool and is neither moral nor immoral. Liberal democracy usually believes in exposing the individual to all kinds of propaganda-influences and providing him with enough education to enable him to evaluate freely the outpouring of propaganda reaching him daily, and to make his choice according to his own judgment.

property. Everything a person, or group, or state rightfully owns. Right to property is recognized in every society, even among aboriginal tribes. Equally recognized is the right to use, sell, and dispose of property, be it land, jewels, interest on a loan, or one's share in a common pasture. Different societies treat property differently: almost all of it is commonly owned in most primitive societies or in modern communist states; much of it is linked to obligations and rights in the mediaeval feudal societies, most of it is owned by individuals in early capitalistic societies while in more highly developed capitalism more and more property is transferred into the hands of corporations. In modern democratic capitalistic society property has increased in importance and its possession and use occupies a far greater place in human activities than in other societies. Our political ideas are partly based on the natural right of the individual to "life, liberty and property," though Locke, who coined this phrase, added that property should belong rightfully only to a person who "mixes his labor with and joins it to something that is his own." Jefferson transformed Locke's phrase into "life, liberty and the pursuit of happiness" in the Declaration of Independence. Our middle class society believes, as did Aristotle in ancient Greece, that property makes a person more responsible and a better citizen. Marxism, however, divides the "means of production" (factories, machines, transportation, banking, etc.) from the rest of property and transfers them to the ownership of the state or the people as a whole; in the U.S.S.R. land and industries are owned by the state.

From a legal point of view one may speak of private property and public property, the first belonging to private persons or groups (corporations, free associates, families, etc.), the latter to the state, county, city, township, or even to the United Nations.

Law divides property into personal and real property. The former is generally, though not always, identical with movable property, the latter with immovable property. Taxes are levied on property; its sale, inheritance and use is regulated by law in every detail. More and more property is no longer managed by its owners (as it usually was a hundred years ago), but by trustees, managers, lawyers, banks. See LAISSEZ FAIRE, TAX, PUBLIC LAND POLICIES, PUBLIC UTILITIES.

property qualification. The requirement that a person own a certain amount of property in order to vote. Although prevalent in the late 18th and early 19th centuries, this requirement has been removed in most democracies.

proportional representation. A system of elections for legislative bodies in which an attempt is made to secure the representation of all parties or points of view in approximately the same proportions as their supporters exist in the community. Provision is made for several representatives per district, and for securing representatives for minorities. See BADEN SYSTEM; CUMULATIVE VOTING; HARE PLAN; D'HONDT SYSTEM; LIST SYSTEM.

proportional taxation. A system of taxes in which the rate of the tax is the same regardless of the size of the tax base, or amount to be taxed. Thus the size of the tax is always proportional to the amount which is taxed.

proposition de loi (praw-paw-zee-SYOHNG duh LWAH). The French term for a bill sponsored, not by the cabinet, but by a private member of parliament. See PROJET DE LOI.

prorogation. The act by which the British king ends a session of Parliament. It ends the life of all bills still under consideration and they must be entered all over again at the next session.

prorogue. See PROROGATION.

prosecuting attorney. An official, usually of a county, in charge of beginning and carrying through lawsuits, usually criminal, on behalf of the government.

prosecutor, public. See PROSECUTING ATTORNEY.

protection. 1. Total or partial immunity from competition from foreign goods secured by making their importation difficult by the establishment of a tariff or similar restriction. 2. Freedom from arrest which lawbreakers such as gambling-house keepers enjoy because of money paid to police or their political superiors. 3. Freedom of attacks by racketeers received by paying them for this immunity. 4. See DIPLOMATIC PROTECTION.

protective custody. Detention of an individual, presumably to see that no harm befalls him, often used in Nazi Germany but without any element of protection.

protective tariff. See TARIFF, MERCANTILISM, FREE TRADE.

protectorate. A state not fully independent for which certain sovereign rights are held and exercised by a stronger, independent state. The rights usually held by the independent state are those of foreign relations and defense, that is, the stronger "protects" the weaker. Most protectorates are set up by a treaty which defines the rights of the protecting state. Other rights are usually presumed to remain in the hands of the protectorate itself. See VASSAL STATE.

pro tempore *or* **pro tem.** Literally, for the time, that is, temporarily. Used particularly of a temporary presiding officer in a legislative body.

prothonotary. Title for the clerk of court or chief clerk of court in certain of the United States.

protocol. 1. An international agreement, usually less comprehensive than a treaty. 2. A draft agreement, before acceptance in final form. 3. Diplomatic manners such as proper dress, seating at formal dinners, and arrangements for conferences. 4. (Plural) The official proceedings of an international conference.

province. Term widely used outside the United States and a few other countries for one of the major subdivisions of the state.

provisional government. A temporary government holding office with the understanding that a permanent government will soon replace it.

Provisional International Civil Aviation Organization. A temporary organization set up at an international conference in Chicago which opened November 1, 1944. Until a more permanent control body can be established, it is to encourage civil aviation, promote its safety and bring some agreement in its rules. Its members form an Assembly which meets annually, and it has a kind of executive committee called a Council. See FIVE FREEDOMS.

provisional orders. Administrative orders issued in Great Britain by government departments or even local government authorities subject to subsequent authorization or veto by Parliament.

public. 1. Anything pertaining to the state or one of its subdivisions. 2. The general run of the population. 3. Pertaining to the general population.

public administration. The management and control of the non-policy-making personnel employed by a state and the physical things which must be used in the functioning of a state.

public bill. A measure submitted to a legislative body which is of broad general application. See PRIVATE BILL.

public crib. American slang expression for the public treasury. "To feed at the public crib" means to live off the public treasury, as, for example, by public employment.

public debt. The debt of the state or one of its subdivisions.

public defender. Attorney provided by a governmental unit, such as a county, to defend persons who cannot afford to hire their own lawyer in trials in which they are accused of committing a crime.

public domain. See PUBLIC LAND POLICIES.

public employee. A person employed by the state or one of its subdivisions.

The term does not include policy-making officials.

public finance. 1. The various processes involved in the financial life of a state —securing of income, expenditures, borrowing, and administration of funds. 2. The formal study of the above processes.

public health. The science of disease prevention and of promoting physical health through community sanitation, control of infections and epidemics, education of the people in principles of hygiene, organization of medical and nursing services, and recognition that maintenance of health is dependent on living standards.

The modern public health movement started at the end of the last century when it was discovered that many diseases can be prevented through sanitation and education. The rapid development of public health in civilized countries resulted in virtual extinction of communicable diseases such as cholera, plague, typhoid and smallpox and in the control of diphteria. Pasteurization of milk lessened tuberculosis; infant mortality decreased to a remarkable extent.

Some of the methods of public health are: high standards in water supply and waste disposal, compulsory vaccination of children, compulsory medical examination of school children and for applicants for marriage licenses. Public health is also concerned with better housing, zoning laws, systems of transportation, sanitary and protective conditions in factories, improvements in agriculture and in handling of food, combatting malnutrition, etc.

In America the United States Public Health Service and public health departments of most states and cities are charged with public health. The League of Nations' health organization functioned effectively. Questions of international public health are discussed by the International Labor Office and the International Institute of Agriculture. The United Nations Social, Humanitarian and Cultural Commission drew up a constitution for a new World Health Organization in 1946, to be approved by the member nations. See SOCIAL SECURITY, SOCIALIZED MEDICINE, BEVERIDGE PLAN.

Public Health, International Office of. An office set up by international agreement in 1907 for the collection and publication of health information. It is directed by a committee of representatives of the various participating states. Since 1923 it has worked very closely with the health section of the League of Nations.

Public Health Service. A government agency set up for marine hospital service in 1798 and after some changes in name finally transferred from the Treasury Department to the Federal Security Agency in 1939. Its function is to guard and improve the public health through research and co-operation with state and local agencies in disease prevention and control.

public industry. Manufacturing plants owned by the state or a subdivision of a state, such as a city-owned plant.

public international law. See INTERNATIONAL LAW.

public international union. An association, of which the members are states, established to perform some more or less non-political function for the states of the world as a whole. Examples are the Universal Postal Union, the International Institute of Agriculture, and the International Bureau of Weights and Measures.

public land. Land, usually thought of as large in amount and undeveloped, which belongs to the state or a subdivision thereof.

public land policies. Public land or public domain are names for land owned by the state. Publicly owned land is a far older institution than privately owned land. In civilized societies disposal of publicly owned land has always been a controversial question, particularly in new countries which are to a large extent completely unsettled and where the state owns all land intending to distribute it among prospective settlers. The first step in colonies was usually to transfer the land from the natives to the colonial power through conquest, treaty, or purchase.

The public land of the United States grew through a number of huge acquisitions to the thirteen original states: the territories of Louisiana, Florida and parts of Texas, the establishment of a title to Oregon, the conquest of large lands from Mexico, and finally the purchase of Alaska. The disposal of these territories did not follow any conscious coherent public land policy. In the beginning the United States was poor and its chief asset was land. Land grants were made for cash payment or as rewards to deserving individuals, corporations or institutions. Land was a good source of revenue and the making of land grants was urged therefore by the East while the West demanded it under pressure from new settlers. Grants were given as military bounty, for educational purposes, to encourage improvements such as building of railroads, to erect public buildings and institutions, etc. According to the Homestead Act of 1862 settlers could acquire farms of one hundred sixty acres free of all charges provided the prospective owners lived on the land for at least five years. Different regulations exist for different kinds of public land: desert land, timber land,

mining areas, etc. Some lands are reserved by law: forests, national parks, Indian reservations, public water reservoirs, power site reserves, military reservations, bird and game reserves, etc. In the United States such reserved lands total over a quarter of a billion acres (over a fifth of the original public domain). What still remains of unreserved public land mainly consists of land too rough for croppers or grazing. In Alaska there is still space for settlers. In the U.S.S.R. public land policy is completely different; there most of the land is owned by the state in trust for the people. In European countries land has often been expropriated from great landowners and distributed among peasants: this was called land or agrarian reform. This policy was carried out by the great French Revolution, in Denmark and recently in Poland and Hungary. See PROPERTY.

public law. The rules defining the rights, duties, and relations of the individual and the state in regard to each other. See PRIVATE LAW.

Public Law 16. The law providing financial assistance for the vocational rehabilitation of veterans of World War II who suffered disabilities incurred or aggravated while in the service. Many kinds of training and education are paid for by this law, the financial provisions of which are more liberal for such training than the regular G. I. Bill of Rights. See G. I. BILL OF RIGHTS.

public office. Used to refer to any high appointive position or any elective post in the service of the state or its subdivisions.

public opinion. An attitude on some question of general interest held by the people or a considerable part thereof.

public ownership. Ownership, and usually operation also, of some business enterprise, such as a street railway, by a state or subdivision thereof. See PROPERTY, SOCIALISM, STATE SOCIALISM, COMMUNISM, MARXISM.

public prosecutor. See PROSECUTING ATTORNEY.

public revenue. The income of the state.

Public Roads Administration. A government agency set up in the Agriculture Department in 1894, transferred to the Federal Works Agency in 1939. Its chief function is to cooperate with the state highway departments in building and maintaining a satisfactory network of highways throughout the country.

public safety. The protection of the local community as a whole, chiefly performed by the police and fire departments. Often cities combine these two services under a single administrative official entitled the Director of Public Safety.

public utilities. Industries which supply electricity, gas, water, communications (telephone, telegraph, broadcasting), municipal transportation (streetcar, bus, subway, ferryboats) or some other such service available to the general public. More recently industries supplying water and electricity for a large agricultural area (i. e., TVA) have been added to this group. Public utilities may be publicly or privately owned: they always operate under licenses or charters and follow special regulations. Public utilities by their nature are seldom competitive. Special regulations for public utilities are due to this and to the fact that their services, unlike other branches of industry, are more or less indispensable. This situation is described by the phrase "affected with a public interest" coined by Chief Justice Waite of the U. S. Supreme Court in 1876. Government regulations throughout the world aim to limit rates of profit

and prevent exploitation of the monopolistic position. Public utilities are obligated under the law to serve all without discrimination, and have to render reasonably good service. Customers of public utilities also are bound by obligation to the companies unusual in other business transactions. In America public utility rates are fixed by direct legislation, and are controlled by regulatory commissions. Federal control over interstate operation of utilities is exercised in varying degree by the Interstate Commerce Commission, Maritime Commission, Federal Power Commission, Securities and Exchange Commission and the Federal Communications Commission. Another device to make public utilities available to more people and to keep rates down in rural regions is the public corporation, or government agency, which acts as a "measuring stick" while providing huge areas with power, water, irrigation, etc. (Tennessee Valley Authority, Rural Electrification Administration). In Britain public utilities are regulated by special acts of Parliament; the present socialist government has nationalized all public utilities and railways. In Europe certain public utilities have been state property for a long time (railways, telephone, telegraph, broadcasting); others are mostly municipal property (gas, city transportation, water, electricity).

public works. Construction projects for public use such as bridges and roads.

Public Works Administration. A government agency set up by the National Recovery Act of June 16, 1933. Its function was to aid the capital goods and construction industries and increase employment thereby. It was permitted to provide army and navy equipment, railroad loans and various state and municipal public work projects.

publicist. Person who writes in the field of public affairs.

publicity laws. Laws requiring the publication of campaign expenditures and the sources thereof, such as the United States Corrupt Practices Act of 1925.

publicity pamphlet. Publicly prepared booklet sent to the voters in certain states including information of interest to the voters regarding the principles of the parties and the qualifications of the candidates.

pull. American slang term for the ability to obtain office, public business, or other favors because of personal acquaintance and friendship with the person who is in a position to bestow them.

pump priming. The process of putting public money into a public works program on the theory that the expenditures therefor in wages and materials will improve the general economy of the country.

puppet government *or* **state.** A term for a government or state having its policies dictated by, and usually owning its existence to, another state. For example, Manchukuo was a puppet state of Japan, and Germany controlled a puppet government in Romania during World War II.

Pure Food and Drug Acts. Federal laws aimed at certain practices in the manufacture, labelling and advertising of foods and drugs when sold in interstate commerce. President Theodore Roosevelt sponsored the first two in 1906. The Meat Inspection Law required the federal inspection of meats, the Pure Food and Drug Act required that patent medicines bear labels giving the amount of narcotics or harmful ingredients they contain, prohibited the sale of poisonous or adulterated foods and regulated statements concerning the contents of packaged foods. These powers were extended in amendments passed in 1912, 1913 and 1925. The Wheeler-Lea Act of 1938 banned false advertising claims for foods, drugs, cosmetics and therapeutic devices. Under this law, advertising claims are under the scrutiny of the Federal Trade Commission and false branding is under the Food and Drug Administration.

purge. 1. To clean out unfaithful members of a party or state. Used particularly of the Russian execution of large numbers of people who were considered traitors. 2. A house-cleaning of party members or citizens considered traitors.

putsch (POOCH). German term for an unsuccessful attempt at revolt.

PW. See PRISONERS OF WAR.

Pyrrhic victory. A victory in which the cost is out of all proportion to the gains therefrom. Pyrrhus, king of Epirus, defeated the Romans in 279 B. C., but in so doing lost a large part of his army.

Q

Quadrilateral. 1. The four-sided strip of territory between the Danube and the Black Sea comprising the southern part of the Dobrudja, which Romania acquired from Bulgaria after the Second Balkan War. A large number of Bulgarians live there and Bulgaria demanded and, thanks to the Axis, regained it in 1940 and retained it in the 1946 peace treaties. 2. A fortified area based upon four fortifications or fortified cities. The two most usually referred to were Verona, Legnago, Mantua and Peschiera, which gave Austria its hold on northeastern Italy in the 19th century, and the Polish cities of Warsaw, Ivangorod, Novogeorgievsk and Brest-Litovsk in World War I.

Quadruple Alliance. The European Alliance of November 20, 1815, composed of the powers of the Holy Alliance—Austria, Prussia, and Russia—plus England. See QUINTUPLE ALLIANCE, HOLY ALLIANCE.

Quai d'Orsay. The embankment along the Seine River in Paris on which is located the French foreign ministry, hence the French foreign ministry itself.

qualified status. The position in international law of a state which is not entirely independent, as, for example a protectorate.

quarantine. 1. To detain persons or ships temporarily to prevent the spread of disease. 2. The temporary confinement of persons to a residence or part of a hospital, or of ships within a port, to prevent the spread of disease. Usually the detention lasts for a period of time or until examination indicates there appears to be no danger of contagion.

Quarantine Speech. Speech by President Franklin D. Roosevelt, October 5, 1937 at the opening of the Outer Drive bridge in Chicago. He pointed out that an epidemic of world lawlessness was spreading; that epidemics of disease require a quarantine to protect the community against the spread of the disease; that with the danger of war spreading, the United States would endeavor to keep out, but that there is no complete protection in a world of disorder; and that the nations' will for peace must express itself so that nations tempted to violate their agreements will desist.

"Quart of milk for every Hottentot." W. T. Witherow, president of the National Association of Manufacturers, speaking at a war conference of American industries in December, 1942 said, "I am not fighting for a quart of milk for every Hottentot . . ." He was alluding to a passage in a speech by Henry A. Wallace, then vice-president of the United States, on May 8, 1942 in which he said, "Half in fun and half seriously I said the other day to Madame Litvinov 'The object of this war is to make sure that everybody in the world has the privilege of drinking a quart of milk a day.' "

quarter. Mercy to, or refraining from killing, those who surrender in battle. It is a generally accepted rule of international law that a declaration that no quarter will be given is forbidden.

quarter sessions, court of. An intermediate criminal court in Great Britain, so called because it sits quarterly. It is a kind of county court of appeal, to which cases are taken from the court of petty sessions which handles lesser crimes. The court is composed of all the county judges who attend. See ASSIZES.

quarter-sphere defense. The pre-Pearl Harbor suggestion for United States defense which assumed it was impossible to defend the whole western hemisphere from possible invasion, and which contracted the area which the United States would consider its defensive zone to the territory lying north of the easternmost part of Brazil. This included about the northern half of the western hemisphere, or about a "quarter-sphere."

queen. Female ruler of a kingdom, or wife of a king.

queen consort. A queen who receives the title as the wife of a king, and not because she herself inherited the crown. See PRINCE CONSORT.

queen mother. Mother of the ruling king.

question hour (*or* **time**). The part of the legislative day in the House of Commons devoted to the answers by the cabinet to questions asked by members at least one day in advance. Often the questions are critical and the ministers are thus made to defend their policies before the house at frequent intervals.

Quintuple Alliance. The Quadruple Alliance plus France, who joined in 1818. It was an alliance of the great powers of Europe for the purpose of preventing revolution and maintaining the status quo. England soon withdrew. See QUADRUPLE ALLIANCE, HOLY ALLIANCE.

Quirinal. One of the seven hills of Rome on which is located the palace of the former King of Italy, hence a term formerly used for the Italian government.

quisling. Synonym for traitor. Term comes from the name of Vidkun Quisling, head of the Norwegian Nazis, who was instrumental in expediting the Nazi seizure of Norway and was made head of the first puppet government in Norway. He was executed October 24, 1945.

quorum. The number of members, for example, of a legislative body, required to be present in order that the body may discharge its functions.

quota. A number or amount which is a portion of a larger whole. The United States immigration laws distribute quotas or parts of the whole number admitted among various countries. Some countries restrict imports by similarly fixing certain amounts which will be received from certain other countries.

R

race. A large group of people of common origin with clearly distinguishable physicial similarities. There are very few pure races today. Particularly the various branches of the white or Caucasian race have been so intermingled through the countless invasions, emigrations, interchanges, etc., that individuals who could be called "pure" representatives of the Nordic, Alpine or Mediterrenean race are in a distinct minority. Anthropologists and biologists generally deny that mere membership in a particular race results in the inheritance of other than physical characteristics, or that belonging to a race determines biologically the mental or moral make-up of an individual. They also deny that any race as a race is mentally or morally superior to any other race. Such differences existing between members of different races have historical, environmental, or social and not simply racial reasons. The so-called "racists," however, believe that the domination of one group over another can be justified by their superior racial qualifications. See ARYANISM, NAZISM, NORDIC.

racism. See ARYANISM, NORDIC, RACE.

racket. Extortion by means of threatening violence to a person or his business.

racketeer. Extortionist whose weapon is the threat of violence.

radical. One inclined to be unsatisfied with, and even indignant about, existing political and social institutions. Radicalism is a term containing a large number of beliefs, all desiring social change and systematic destruction of the present, and establishment of more favorable social, political and economic institutions. In modern society radicals are usually those who desire certain fundamental reforms in order to better the economic, social and political position of the masses. Radicals would fight for the propertyless underprivileged against those who own property and occupy high social positions. Modern radicalism was born in the late 18th century in France and England and was advocated in America particularly by Thomas Paine. In England the extremists of the Liberal or Whig Party, under James Fox, were called "radicals." In America today radical is often identified with socialist or communist, while in Europe it is used as a label for the reformist groups among fairly moderate, liberal middle class parties, such as the French Radical-Socialists, or the Beveridge wing of the British Liberal Party. In Yugoslavia the Radical Party today is one of the most conservative parties and is called "reactionary" by Marshal Tito's followers. See LEFT, LIBERAL, REPUBLIC, UTILITARIANISM.

radicalism. See RADICAL.

railroad. To rush a bill through a legislative body intentionally, thus not allowing full consideration or permitting those who might oppose the bill to organize to defeat it.

Railroad Brotherhoods. The Grand International Brotherhood of Locomotive Engineers (1863), the Order of Railway Conductors of America (1868), the Brotherhood of Locomotive Firemen (1873), the Brotherhood of Railway Trainmen (1883), the Order of Railroad Telegraphers (1886) are referred to in the trade-union world as the great railroad brotherhoods. They were organized as mutual insurance or benefit societies but became the labor unions of the respective groups.

Railroad Retirement Board. A board of three appointive members set up by an act of August 29, 1935. It administers the annuity, pension, and unemployment benefit provisions of the retirement system of the railroads.

rajah. Prince or ruler of one of the native states of India.

rally. Political mass meeting held during an election campaign for the purpose of arousing enthusiasm for a party or candidate.

ranger. In the United States a term used for the state police, particularly in Texas and the Northwest.

rank and file. Term borrowed from military usage meaning the total membership of a political party, exclusive of the leaders.

ranking member. Next to the chairman of a Congressional committee, the member who has the greatest seniority in the committee. The ranking member of the minority is the minority member with greatest seniority.

Rapallo, Treaty of. Treaty of April 16, 1922, between Germany and Russia in which they agreed to re-establish diplomatic and trade relations, and drop their mutual reparations claims.

rapporteur (ra-pawr-TEWR). A reporter of a committee in the French parliament who directs the debate on and defends the measure. He is not the chairman of the committee nor a cabinet member. Similarly a reporter or secretary of a committee at an international conference or at the United Nations.

rapprochement (rah-prawsh-MAHNG).

The establishment or, more correctly, the re-establishment of friendly relations.

rate. 1. Charge made for a unit of service rendered, as by a public utility. 2. The proportion of a tax to the tax base, or amount taxed. 3. (Plural) British term for local taxes.

rate of exchange. The amount of one country's money which at any given time may be obtained for a fixed amount in another country's money, for example the number of francs per dollar.

ratification. An act, usually by the head of the state, confirming the signature of a treaty. In the United States the president can ratify treaties only if two-thirds of the Senate concur.

ratify. To confirm a treaty signature.

ration. To allot to an individual a share or limited amount of a commodity because the total amount of that item is limited, and individuals cannot all be treated fairly if some are permitted to buy unlimited amounts.

rationalization. The streamlining and co-ordination of industry by means of increased standardization, more efficient management, and reduction of competition. Often referred to as the process which put Germany back on its feet in the 1920's.

ration board. In the United States a local group of citizens which locally administered the rationing program of the O. P. A. in World War II. It issued the ration books, gasoline coupons, and permits to purchase tires.

ration book. In the United States one of the books of coupons issued to each person during World War II. The coupons were turned in upon purchase of various rationed articles such as shoes, sugar, meats, and canned goods. The two kinds of coupons, stamps or "points," most referred to were the red points for meats and fats, and the blue points for processed, chiefly canned, foods.

raw materials. Substances of value in manufacturing produced by nature, such as ores or vegetable fibers, prior to their processing into finished goods. Of political significance because their distribution over the earth is unequal, and a desire to control the source of such materials has been used by some states to add a further excuse to a policy of imperialism.

reactionary. A person, political or economic point of view or a movement favoring a return to an earlier, more conservative social or economic or political order. The reactionary is more negative than the conservative; he concentrates on tearing down recent changes. See COUNTER-REVOLUTION, CONSERVATIVE, AUTHORITARIAN.

reading. In legislative bodies bills are read several times before final action upon them. In the Congress of the United States, for example, there are three readings. The first is merely publication of the title; the second is a real reading with opportunity for amendment. The third reading is only a reading of the title unless there is a demand that the bill be read in full. After the third reading the bill is engrossed and then finally comes the vote on the bill. See ENGROSSED BILL.

realist. 1. A person who takes into account as far as possible the factual factors which help determine a course of action. 2. More often, a person who says he does.

Realpolitik (RAY-ahl-poh-lee-TEEK). German term for power politics. See POWER POLITICS.

real property. See PROPERTY.

real union. A combination of two or more states which share certain governmental functions, as for example, Austria and Hungary which shared the sovereign, the defense forces, and the foreign office. In such cases, where foreign affairs in one office represent the component parts, from the point of view of international law the union is one state. See UNION.

reapportionment. The re-assignment of the number of representatives to a given area, as for example, a re-assignment of the number of members of the House of Representatives to the various states.

reason of state. Some compelling official reason regarding the welfare of a country which usually at the time cannot be made public.

rebate. 1. The return of part of a payment made, as of a tax. 2. To return part of a payment.

rebel. 1. A person who takes up arms against his country. 2. To take up arms against one's country.

rebellion. An armed rising against a state by the citizens thereof.

rebus sic stantibus (REE-bus sik STAN-ti-bus). Literally, things remaining as they were. Often referred to as a basic assumption for the continuing validity of a treaty. It may not be invoked, however, for the unilateral denunciation of a treaty.

recall. A special election to determine whether an official shall be removed from his office before his term expires. The process most often applies to elected administrative officials, though in some states it may be used against judges and appointed officials. The first step is usually a petition for removal of the official and if this is completed the election is set.

recapture clause. A provision in the laws regulating railroads, in effect from 1920 to 1933, that roads had to turn over to the government half of their earnings over six per cent. This share formed a loan fund for the less successful roads. The provision was an effort to equalize for all roads the return from the same rates.

receiver. A person appointed by a court to conduct the business of a person who has filed a bankruptcy petition until the petition is dismissed or a trustee appointed to continue to carry on the business.

recess appointment. An appointment made by the president while Congress is not in session, hence when it is impossible to have it confirmed by the Senate. Such an appointment is terminated if not confirmed in the next session. Usually there are similar provisions in the states of the United States where senatorial confirmation of appointments is required.

recession. The recurrence, in 1937, of the 1933 depression in the United States.

reciprocal trade agreement. An international trade agreement providing mutual tariff or trade concessions. Such agreements have been basic in the United States international economic relations since 1934.

Reciprocal Trade Agreements Act. A law of June 12, 1934, giving the president authority for three years (since extended) to conclude with other states trade treaties including mutual tariff reductions up to 50 per cent and a most-favored-nation provision. He was also given the power not to extend such concessions to states discriminating against the United States.

reciprocity. A situation in which special concessions made by one party, as for example in international trade, are balanced by similar concessions by the other party.

recision. Cancellation, particularly as applied to World War II contracts after the end of the war.

reclamation. Process of saving and restoring to its original condition something, such as land, which has gone to waste.

Reclamation, Bureau of. A bureau in the Interior Department the function of which is the administration of the water conservation program and irrigation programs, and power plant maintenance in such projects as Boulder Dam, Columbia River project, etc.

recognition. 1. The process of acknowledging the independence and equality of a state and its right to be admitted into the family of nations. It may be by one state or several at a time. *De jure* (legal) recognition is full legal recognition including the exchange of diplomats. *De facto* (in fact) recognition is less than full legal recognition. 2. The act of a presiding officer in granting the floor to a member of a legislative body.

recommit. To send a matter back to a committee.

reconsider. To reopen the debate and re-vote on a law which has been voted upon.

reconstruction. The rebuilding of a country after the catastrophe of war. In the United States applied particularly to the post-Civil War period.

Reconstruction Finance Corporation. A governmental agency created January 22, 1932, and transferred to the Commerce Department February 24, 1942. Its function is to provide loans for banks, insurance companies, railroads, industries and agriculture. During World War II it functioned in part through such subsidiaries as the Defense Plant Corporation, Rubber Reserve Company and Metals Reserve Company.

reconversion. The process of changing industry from war production back to production for peace time use.

recorder. A county official in some states whose function is to keep the records of the county.

recredential. The letter of appreciation and credential for departure given a diplomat who is leaving his post by the head of the state to which he has been accredited. See LETTER OF CREDENCE.

recount. The process of counting the ballots a second time to verify the results of a given election in certain districts on the ground that the first count was not fair and accurate. This process is usually instituted by a defeated candidate, who has to make a deposit in order to prevent such demands for nuisance purposes. If there is a substantial change, usually a stated percentage, in the recount, the deposit is refunded.

red. Term used to refer to anything Russian or extreme left-wing politically, as socialism or communism.

Red Army. Army of the U.S.S.R.

Red Cross. The Red Cross has for its functions the improvement of health and the relief of suffering throughout the world. Its organization is unique. It is a private international union, the League of Red Cross Societies, which functions through a Board of Delegates, an International Conference, and a Standing Commission. The individual national societies, however, hold a special place within their respective states; in the United States, for example, the society was chartered by Congress in 1905. National societies, moreover, are recognized only in states which have adopted the Geneva Red Cross Convention. The Red Cross insignia became identified with army sanitary services by the Geneva Convention of 1864 regarding the treatment of wounded in time of war.

red points. See RATION BOOK.

Red Revolution. The Bolshevik revolution in Russia in November, 1917. See OCTOBER REVOLUTION.

red scare. Widespread excitement about and fear of communism.

Red Star (Krasnaya Svezda). Publication of the Russian army.

red tape. The delay of official business by administrative technicalities.

Red Terror. The Bolshevik revolution in Russia in November, 1917. See OCTOBER REVOLUTION.

redeem. To discharge an obligation by full payment, as of bank notes or bonds.

redistrict. To redraw the boundary lines of electoral districts, necessitated by the need of increasing, decreasing, or equalizing the districts.

redress of grievances. Relief from injustices imposed by government. The right to petition for such relief is included in the first amendment to the United States Constitution.

re-entry permit. Document signifying permission for an alien to re-enter the United States.

refer. To turn a matter over to a committee.

referee. Person appointed by a court to represent it in bankruptcy proceedings.

referendum. The process by which the electorate in certain states may vote upon laws passed by the legislature. In some cases the legislature may present the law to the people to uphold or reject at an election. In others the people may petition to have a certain law submitted to the voters and if the petition is completed an election is held to determine whether the law shall remain or not.

reforestation. The planting of trees, particularly in formerly wooded areas as a conservation measure. See CONSERVATION.

reformatory. Institution for the confinement of juvenile lawbreakers.

refugee. A person who seeks safety by fleeing from his own country to another.

refunding. Process of replacing one set of bonds with another, often at a lower rate of interest.

regalia. The emblems or special apparel of office.

regency. A group of men (regents) exercising the essential powers of a monarch because the ruler is a minor, absent, or incapacitated. Occasionally there is a single regent.

regent. One person or one of a group of persons exercising the powers of a monarch while the ruler is a minor, absent, or incapacitated.

regents, board of. Board charged with the oversight of a state university or department of education, as in New York State.

regicide. 1. The murder of a king. 2. Murderer of a king.

regime. Governmental rule, system, or administration.

regional. Pertaining to a geographical area, usually one of intermediate size.

regional arrangements. See UNITED NATIONS, and Charter of the United Nations, Article 52–54, Appendix.

regional planning. The establishment of a program for the most efficient and productive use of the resources and facilities of a contiguous part of the country.

regionalism. A principle which recognizes the distinct features of a geographical region within a country, sometimes by investing it with powers of local government and cultural autonomy. It involves sentiments such as love of one's own region, the desire of reviving a glorious past, fear of a strong central government and a belief that regional self-government is more efficient and develops greater civic loyalty in the people. Regionalism, however, recognizes the national authority and unity as more important than regional loyalty. Regionalism is based more on historical, ethnic, national, linguistic, and cultural peculiarities, while sectionalism is based on different economic conditions. Areas in which regionalism has been an important issue include: Catalonia and the Basque country in Spain; Brittany in France; Scotland and Wales in Great Britain; Sicily in Italy. The federal structures of the Soviet Union, Czechoslovakia and Yugoslavia are in large part recognitions of regional movements. In the United States sectionalism has been a greater force. In recent years in the United States considerable attention has been given to functional units, as in the great metropolitan regions. In the United Nations provision is made for international regional arrangements, such as the Pan-American Union. See SEPARATISM, AUTONOMY, STATES' RIGHTS.

register of deeds. County official in some states who keeps the records of real estate ownership.

registered mail. Mail which is literally registered or listed with the post office, for an extra charge, for the purpose of identification and special handling, thus providing special security for unusually valuable mail.

registration. The process by which an individual gets his name upon the official list of voters. Usually the prospective voter applies in person before election officials to be placed on the list and indicates that his qualifications are satisfactory. The process is intended to insure that only qualified voters vote and those only once per election. It is obvious that mismanagement in the registration can lead to voting irregularities.

règlement(reg-luh-MAHNG).1.French for regulation, rule, or law. 2. Manual of rules for each of the two houses of the French parliament.

regressive tax. See TAX.

regular. 1. Pertaining to a political organization that consistently bears the official party label. 2. A person who always adheres to the organization bearing the official party label.

regulatory commission. An administrative commission which is empowered to regulate or control a particular service, as for example, the Interstate Commerce Commission which fixes rates and establishes certain standards of safety on railroads.

rehabilitation. Social and economic reestablishment.

rehearing. A second hearing.

Reich. German word for the German state or realm.

Reich Citizenship Law. German law of 1935 withdrawing citizenship from Jewish citizens of Germany.

Reichsbank (RIKES-bahnk). National bank of Germany.

Reichsrat (RIKES-raht). The upper house of the German parliament. It was not of equal powers but had a kind of provisional veto over laws which could be overridden. It represented the German states rather than the people directly. It was abolished by the Nazis.

Reichstag (RIKES-tahg). The lower and really legislative body of the German parliament. It became a mere rubber stamp under Hitler.

Reichstag fire. On the night of February 26, 1933 the Reichstag building in Berlin was destroyed by fire. Late in the year the Nazis brought to trial a young Dutch communist found at the fire. He was mentally unbalanced, but was tried and executed January 10, 1934. In 1946 evidence in Nazi files revealed that Hermann Goering planned and directed the fire as a plant to discredit communists and social democrat members of the Reichstag.

Reichswehr (RIKES-vayr). German regular army.

Reinsurance Treaty. A Russo-German treaty of June 18, 1887, in which each party promised to remain neutral if the other were at war, Germany thereby giving Russia something of a free hand in the Balkans if she didn't clash with Austria. The treaty was for only three years and was not renewed.

relief. Assistance given to persons who are not self-supporting, in the form of financial aid, goods, or jobs created for the specific purpose.

religious freedom. The right to worship as one sees fit.

Relocation Authority. See WAR RELOCATION AUTHORITY.

"Remember Pearl Harbor." An American slogan in the early days of World War II. See PEARL HARBOR.

"Remember the Alamo." Battle-cry of the Texans at the battle of San Jacinto, April 21, 1836 in which Sam Houston led his men to victory over Santa Anna who, on the preceding March 6, had finally succeeded in overcoming the garrison of San Antonio and killing them all. The Alamo Mission, or mission of San Antonio de Valero, was the site of the massacre in March.

"Remember the Maine." American battle-cry in the Spanish-American War. The mysterious explosion and sinking of the United States battleship Maine in Havana Harbor February 15, 1898 was an important contributing factor in the outbreak of the war.

remilitarize. To place troops in and fortify an area again after a period in which there were no troops or fortifications in the area. The Rhineland was thus remilitarized in March, 1936.

remit. 1. To cancel, as a tax. 2. To send a case back to a lower court for further consideration.

removal. Expulsion of an official from office as by impeachment or by action of the appointing officer.

rendition. The turning over by one state of the United States to another state of persons accused of crime in the latter state. The request is made by one governor to another. The process is somewhat similar to international extradition, but rendition is established by the Constitution rather than by interstate agreement, states usually give up their own citizens as well as those of other states, and a person may be tried for a different crime than the one cited in the request for rendition. See EXTRADITION.

renegotiation. The repetition of the negotiation of a contract between the government and a business firm revising the original terms on the ground that under the original contract the firm was making excessive profits.

Rentenmark. A new German mark established in 1923 after the inflation and after the old mark had lost its value. The new paper mark was given the value of the old gold mark but was unsecured by gold. A limited number were printed and this, together with other economic measures such as balancing the budget, enabled the new mark to maintain its value.

rentier (rahng-TYAY). A person whose income is derived to a considerable extent from bonds, annuities, and similar investments.

reparations. Charges assessed against a loser in a war by the winner as repayment for the damage done by the former to the territory and property of the latter. Sometimes paid in cash over a period of years, or in manufactured goods, machinery or raw materials. See ARTICLE 231.

Reparations Commission. A commission set up by the Treaty of Versailles to determine the size of the reparations to be demanded of Germany and her satellites. It reported on April 28, 1921, that the German figure was 132,000,000,000 gold marks, about $32,000,000,000, plus reparations in kind. See REPARATIONS; REPARATIONS IN KIND.

reparations in kind. Charges in goods as repayment for damaged goods, such as coal, railroad equipment, or live stock. See REPARATIONS.

repatriation. Process of returning persons to the state of their former allegiance.

Repeal Amendment. The twenty-first amendment to the United States Constitution which repealed the eighteenth or prohibition amendment, thus removing the federal restrictions on the manufacture and sale of intoxicating liquor.

repeater. A person who votes more than once at an election.

representative. 1. A person who represents other citizens, particularly in a legislative body. 2. Pertaining to the process by which one person represents a number of others.

representative government. A governmental system in which the people rule themselves through their duly elected and authorized agents or representatives.

reprieve. The delay or postponement of the execution of a sentence.

reprisal. An act of a state bringing pressure to bear upon another state by some illegal means such as intervention, occupation of part of the latter's territory, or seizure of its ships.

republic. A state in which the sovereign (or supreme) power rests in the people, who govern through their elected representatives. Usually the head of a republic is called a president and is elected either by the people or indirectly by the people's representatives (Assembly, Electoral College, etc.). Republicanism implies a belief that the will of the people should prevail and that every free citizen should have the right to participate in matters of state and should not, if qualified, be prevented from ascending to the highest offices of state. Republicanism and political democracy have become closely connected conceptions, in principle if not always in fact. See STATE, SOVEREIGNTY.

republican. 1. Pertaining to a republic. See REPUBLIC. 2. One who advocates a republic as a form of government.

Republican. A member of the Republican Party.

Republican Party. One of the two major United States political parties. It was organized in 1854 as an anti-slavery party. Lincoln was its first great leader. It has had a dominant position much of the time since the Civil War as the party of conservatism generally, sound money, and a high protective tariff.

repudiation. The refusal to accept, as for example, a debt.

requisition. 1. The right of a belligerent to seize such enemy property as is not subject to confiscation upon payment or upon acknowledgment of the obligation by giving a receipt. See CONFISCATION. 2. To seize enemy goods as in 1. 3. An order or request, as for supplies, drawn upon a government store-room or supply house. 4. A form for such orders. 5. To order or request as in 3.

res adjudicata (REEZ uh-joo-di-KAY-tuh). Literally, a thing which has been adjudicated. A final decision of a court upon a matter within its jurisdiction.

reservation. 1. An exception to full acceptance, as for example, the Senate may approve a treaty with reservations. 2. A certain area set aside for special purposes as for forests or a domicile for Indians.

reserved powers. Governmental powers not granted to Congress but retained by the states, such as general criminal jurisdiction.

Resettlement Administration. A government agency set up April 30, 1935, to supervise provisions for the resettle-

ment of families with low incomes. It was transferred to the Farm Security Administration January 1, 1937.

residence. The length of time lived in a certain place.

residual powers. Powers which remain as those left after certain powers have been specifically enumerated. In the Constitution such powers are left with the states and the people, not with the federal government.

resistance movement. See UNDERGROUND.

res nullius (REEZ NUL-ee-us). Literally a thing of, or belonging to, nobody. Territory previously unoccupied by any state of European civilization.

resolution. A formal statement of the will or opinion of a legislative body as determined by vote. It begins with the clause, "Be it resolved . . ." In Congress a joint resolution when passed is law. See ACT; CONCURRENT RESOLUTION.

responsible government. A government in which the executive depends for the tenure of his office upon the support of a majority in one house or both houses of the legislative body. The legislative may in turn, as in Great Britain, be responsible to the voters, that is, if it repudiates the executive he may dissolve parliament and call a new election. The new majority, responsible to the voters, would then pick a new executive in turn responsible to the new legislative body.

restoration. 1. The return to control by the emperor in Japan in 1868. See SHOGUN. 2. Stuart Restoration of 1660. Return to the English throne of the Stuart family (Charles II) after the Protectorate. 3. Bourbon Restorations. Return to the French throne of Louis XVIII in 1814, after the abdication of Napoleon, and again in 1815, after the Hundred Days of

Napoleon. Other restorations following Napoleon's abdication were: Bourbon kings in Spain and Naples; former rulers to the Papal States, Tuscany, Sardinia, and some of the German states.

restraining order. A temporary court order issued to prevent a certain action while the court decides whether to issue an injunction.

restraint of trade (or restraint of competition). A term meaning any interference with free competition by one, few or all of the competitors. Originally it referred usually to contracts in which employees promised not to go into trade on their own and compete with their employers after having left their service. Sometimes this was a guarantee for preserving trade secrets, sometimes mainly to satisfy the employers' desire to monopolize a rather restricted market. Later, all combinations between corporations, such as trusts, cartels, or monopolies designed to eliminate competition became known as restraints of trade. Legislation in many countries has tried to counteract combinations and their harmful effects on free competition and on the public. See LAISSEZ FAIRE, UNFAIR COMPETITION, SHERMAN ANTI-TRUST ACT.

resulting powers. Powers of Congress not specifically granted by the Constitution but derived from powers which are specifically granted. An example is the power to establish federal prisons for the punishment of counterfeiting, piracy, etc., which are provided for explicitly in the Constitution.

retire. 1. To conclude permanently one's career in public employment. 2. To withdraw from, as, for example, elective office or a political contest.

retorsion. An act of a state bringing pressure to bear upon another state by unfriendly but not illegal means, such as a boycott or discriminatory tariff.

retrenchment. A reduction, as, for example, in the functions or expenses of government.

retroactive. Having an effect over acts committed previously.

retroactive legislation. Laws which have an effect over a period in the past as for example one changing the rate of tax due on last year's income. In general retroactive criminal laws are *ex post facto* laws and prohibited by the Constitution. See *EX POST FACTO*.

return. Statement of tax liability.

returns. Election results.

revanche (ruh-VAHNGSH). Literally, revenge. Policy of retaliation for previous wrongs or military defeat. For example, this was an important element in the French attitude toward Germany after the end of the Franco-Prussian War in 1871.

revenue. Government income, as from taxes and other sources.

reverse lend lease. Furnishing of goods and services by an ally to the United States in World War II on a lend-lease basis. See LEND-LEASE ACT.

revisionist. 1. Pertaining to a policy of desiring to change the terms of a treaty. 2. A person wanting to change treaty terms.

revolt. 1. To attempt, successfully or unsuccessfully, to seize by force the control of one's own state or part thereof. 2. An attempt so to seize control.

revolution. A sudden change in the character of the government of a state, usually brought about by force.

Revolutionary War. The war which the American colonies fought against England to secure the independence they declared July 4, 1776. The fighting ended in 1781 with the surrender of Cornwallis at Yorktown. The peace was signed at Paris in 1783, the colonies retaining their independence.

Many other questions such as boundaries were left unsolved. See JAY TREATY.

revolving fund. A fund set up which is never entirely expended as repayments into it make further loans possible, etc.

R. F. C. See RECONSTRUCTION FINANCE CORPORATION.

R. F. D. Rural Free Delivery. The free delivery of mail by the Post Office Department in the rural areas of the United States as part of its regular service. Such delivery is sent out from local post offices along "rural routes," and a person's postal address is given, for example as R. F. D. No. 1, or R. R. No. 1.

Rhineland remilitarization. The re-entry of armed Germans into the territory along the Rhine March 7, 1936 in violation of the Treaty of Versailles. This territory, which had been demilitarized, included the area on the left or west side of the river which lay within Germany, and a strip 50 km. (about 30 miles) wide on the right or east bank from Switzerland to Holland.

rider. An amendment or change in a bill added on as an extra part.

Riga, Treaty of. Treaty of March 18, 1921 between Russia and Poland after they had been at war about a year over their boundary. The treaty set the new boundary which existed until 1939. It was west of the old Polish boundary of 1772, which the Poles would have liked, but far enough east to include several million White Russians and Ukrainians in Poland. It was also considerably east of the Curzon Line. See CURZON LINE.

right. An expression embracing conservatives, reactionaries, authoritarians, traditionalists, Fascists and Nazis. It originated in the European parliamentary practice by which parties sit in a semi-circle in the assembly room, the conservatives and Fascists on the right, the liberals, radicals, socialists and communists on the left and the middle-of-the-road parties in the center. A "rightist" is one who embraces the belief of any of the above mentioned "right" groups. The expression is even vaguer than the term "leftist," as many a conservative is as violently opposed to Fascist or Nazi revolution as any member of the "left." See LEFT, FASCISM, NAZISM, CONSERVATIVE, AUTHORITARIAN, REACTIONARY.

right of assembly. The right of people to meet peaceably for whatever purposes they desire.

right of resistance. The theoretical right, advocated by some political philosophers and denied by others, to resist and throw off the rule of a king if he should be unjust. Underlying this was the idea that the king derived his power from the people rather than from God. It is quite evident that this was not a right to be found on the statute books and enforced by the government. See PASSIVE OBEDIENCE; DIVINE RIGHT OF KINGS.

right of way. 1. The right to move across another's property. 2. A strip of land through other persons' property which has been secured, as by the state or a railroad company, through which to pass a road or railroad.

rights of man. Certain rights with which all men "are endowed by their Creator," as the Declaration of Independence says. They are the natural rights of the individual re-discovered and formulated by French, English and American philosophers and statesmen in the 18th century and incorporated in such documents as the French "Declaration of the Rights of Man and Citizen" (1789) and in the Bills of Rights of American state Constitutions and the first ten amendments of the Constitution of the United States. They are also called civil liberties. See NATURAL RIGHTS, CIVIL LIBERTIES, LIBERALISM, RADICALISM, INDIVIDUALISM, LAISSEZ FAIRE, JEFFERSONIAN DEMOCRACY, DECLARATION OF RIGHTS.

rigid constitution. A constitution which is very difficult to amend and hence hard to change. See FLEXIBLE CONSTITUTION.

ring. 1. A corrupt political boss and his henchmen, as the Tweed ring. 2. A group of candidates. The phrase "to throw one's hat in the ring," is often used to mean that one is entering a contest as a candidate for office.

Riom trial. The trial by the Vichy government of the leaders of the French Third Republic during its last years —Daladier and Blum, premiers; Pierre Cot and Guy La Chambre, air ministers; General Gamelin; and, later, P. Jacomet, secretary general of the war ministry. They were indicted in October, 1940 charged with having declared war on Germany without reason, thus provoking war with Germany. Later this charge was changed to having inadequately prepared France for war. Over a year was spent by the court in preparation and arguing the matter of procedure. The first public hearing was not held until February 19, 1942. Over twenty hearings followed. The court then adjourned for Easter and later suspended the hearings April 14. This practically ended the trial with neither conviction nor acquittal of the accused.

riot. The infraction of general law and order by a group of persons.

riparian. Pertaining to the banks of a river or lake. Used, for example, to refer to the countries bordered by a river.

ripper law. 1. A law changing a governmental agency or a municipal ad-ministration so that the incumbents are thrown out and members of the opposite party receive the offices. 2. Abolishing an agency for the political purpose of getting political opponents out of public office.

rise. To adjourn, as a legislative session or committee meeting.

Rising Sun. The symbol on the Japanese flag, hence pertaining to Japan.

Risorgimento (ree-sawr-ji-MEN-toh). Literally the Italian word for revival or renaissance. The term is used for the rebirth of Italy in the middle 19th century, leading to its emergence as a unified, independent state.

riverain. Pertaining to, or located on, the bank of a river.

Rogers Act. Law of May 24, 1924 merging the former consular and diplomatic services into the Foreign Service of the United States. It also provided that except for the top posts the Foreign Service should run on civil service principles, with recruitment by competitive examinations and promotion based on efficiency ratings.

roll-call. The alphabetical calling of the names of the members in a legislative body to obtain a vote or to determine whether a quorum is present.

Rome-Berlin Axis. The German-Italian understanding and agreement to consult and co-operate which merged finally into a military alliance. The term Berlin-Rome Axis was first used by Mussolini in a speech of November 1, 1936, to describe the agreement reached by Count Ciano and von Neurath, the Italian and German foreign ministers, the week before, providing for German recognition of the Italian annexation of Ethiopia and consultation in the common pursuit of peace. It was further cemented by a trip of Mussolini to Hitler in late September 1937, and of Hitler to Mussolini in early May, 1938. The treaty of military alliance was signed May 22, 1939. See ROME-BERLIN-TOKYO TRIANGLE; ANTI-COMINTERN PACT.

Rome, Berlin, Tokyo Triangle. The ultimate combination of the Berlin-Tokyo anti-Comintern pact and the Rome-Berlin Axis, plus the later satellites. See ANTI-COMINTERN PACT, ROME-BERLIN AXIS.

Rome, Pact of. See LAVAL-MUSSOLINI ACCORD.

Rome Protocols. 1. Three agreements between Italy, Austria, and Hungary concluded March 17, 1934. They provided for the establishment of a common policy on their common problems and for consultation when that seemed opportune; increase of reciprocal export facilities and the building of complementary economies as well as development of traffic through the Adriatic ports; and a new Italian-Austrian economic agreement to include preferential treatment for Austrian products by Italy. **2.** Another trio of protocols was agreed to by the same powers March 23, 1936. These reaffirmed the earlier protocols, set up a permanent consultative organization of the three foreign ministers, and stated that no signatory should hold political consultations regarding the Danube area without contacting the other two signatories.

Romanov, House of (also Romanoff). The imperial dynasty which ruled Russia from 1613 to 1917. Its great achievements were the creation of a European state from a semi-Asiatic one following the expulsion of the Tartars and the expansion of territorial Russia to its natural geographic limits. The great Romanovs were Peter the Great (1682–1725), Catherine II, (1762–1796) and Alexander I (1801–1825). In the 19th and 20th centuries the dynasty became increasingly involved in a system of re-

pression at home and abroad. The March Revolution of 1917, during World War I, caused the abdication of the last of the Romanovs, Czar Nicholas II. In July, 1917 he and his entire immediate family were executed by the Bolsheviks at Ekaterinburg.

Roosevelt Corollary. See MONROE DOCTRINE.

rooster. In the United States, the emblem of the Democratic party often appearing in party-column ballots and formerly used in party newspapers. Said to have originated with the Indianapolis Sentinel in 1842, it was crowing over a Democratic victory after previously having been charged with crowing too soon.

Root formula. A compromise plan suggested by Elihu Root and accepted by the League of Nations in 1929 by which it was hoped the power of the World Court to give advisory opinions could be accommodated to the views of the United States Senate. Essentially the plan was to ask if the United States would object in each case where an opinion might be requested on some matter in which the United States might be interested. The Senate postponed action, pigeonholed the matter, stalled, reserved, and finally voted down membership in the World Court six years later.

Root-Takahira Agreement. A United States-Japanese agreement of November 30, 1908, in which the two powers agreed to maintain the status quo and respect each other's territories in the Pacific region and to respect the independence of China and maintain the Open Door there.

rotation in office. The principle that there should be periodic turnovers in the persons in public office, particularly in the administrative branch. The theory has been advanced that this is more democratic and responsive to the people and avoids the corruption of long-continued holding of office. In fact, however, the principle has played into the hands of the spoils system and denied the function of the expert administrator.

rotten *or* **pocket boroughs.** From the 16th century to 1832 in England there were boroughs with less than one hundred voters electing representatives to the House of Commons. Either these voters were bribed at each election, or were controlled by a neighboring landowner through influence or power as landlord. The number increased during the 18th century due to increased manufacturing which caused a shift in population to the cities. The reform bill of 1832 abolished some of the boroughs as political units, cut down the number of representatives allowed others, and redistributed those seats to towns and counties not adequately represented. The reform bill of 1867 abolished the last of these boroughs.

Roundtable Conferences. See LONDON ROUNDTABLE CONFERENCES.

royal. Pertaining to the person or government of a king or queen.

royal prerogative. See PREROGATIVE.

royal succession. The line of inheritance of the title of king, as for example, to the oldest child or the next oldest brother.

Royal Victorian Order. A British order of knighthood granted for special service to Queen Victoria or her descendants. The five classes are Knights Grand Cross (G.C.V.O.), Knights Commanders (K.C.V.O.), Commanders (C.V.O.), and Members of the Fourth and Fifth Classes (M.V.O.).

Rubber Reserve Company. A subsidiary of the Reconstruction Finance Corporation, first set up June 28, 1940 and transferred to the Commerce Department February 24, 1942. Its func-

tion was to procure natural, synthetic, and scrap rubber for defense purposes.

rubber stamp. An approval given on request without much consideration and with no possibility of refusal.

rugged individualism. A term popularized, if not coined, by Herbert Hoover to indicate the American way of fighting for one's own rights and standing or falling upon one's own ability to perform his job. See INDIVIDUALISM.

Ruhr occupation. Occupation by the French army of the Ruhr valley, the heart of the German industry in northwest Germany, on January 11, 1923, because of the German default on reparations. The French withdrew after the acceptance of the Dawes Plan the following year. See REPARATIONS, DAWES PLAN.

rule of the majority. The principle that the policies of a country shall be determined by the choice of a majority of the people, usually in fact registered by a majority of elected representatives chosen by a majority of voters. It is one of the fundamental bases of democracy.

rule of reason. In the United States the interpretation of the Sherman Act by the Supreme Court in 1911, in cases involving the Standard Oil Company and the American Tobacco Company, that, to be an infraction of the law, a monopoly must be an "unreasonable" restraint of trade.

rules, committee on. The committee of a legislative body which determines the special rules for expediting business. Particularly in a large body where some such system is necessary if anything is to be accomplished, such a committee has a considerable control over legislation as, for example, by limiting debate and amendments.

ruling. A decision or interpretation by

a court or administrative body which has the force of the law or order being interpreted.

"Rum, Romanism, and Rebellion." In the United States a term first used in a critical sense by Rev. S. D. Burchard to refer to the bases of the Democratic party in the campaign of 1884. In part its result was to keep many of the Irish in the Democratic Party and defeat James G. Blaine.

Runciman mission. The visit of Lord Runciman to Prague, Czechoslovakia in August and September of 1938 just prior to the Munich crisis. He was sent by Prime Minister Chamberlain ostensibly to get the facts in the situation; in reality he appeared to be sent to get the Czechs to accede to the German demands.

runoff. A second election or primary which is held because the first is not conclusive. It is usually held because of a requirement that a successful candidate should have a majority of the votes. If no one gets a majority on the first round, a second contest is held between the two highest of the first round.

Rural Electrification Administration. An agency set up May 11, 1935 and transferred to the Agriculture Department July 1, 1939. Its function is to finance rural electrification, including wiring and appliances, by self-liquidating loans.

Russo-Japanese War. The war fought in 1904–5 between Russia and Japan, chiefly in Manchuria, over the conflict of interests there. See PORTSMOUTH, TREATY OF.

Ruthenia. See CARPATHO-UKRAINE.

S

S. Senate Bill.

S. A. *or* **Sturmabteilung.** See STORM TROOPS.

Saad-Abad, Pact of. See MIDDLE EASTERN PACT.

Saar Territory. A small area, in western Germany before 1914, governed by the League of Nations through a commission from 1920 to 1935. The mines of the territory were given to France and the French customs frontier included the area. In 1935 a plebiscite was held as provided when the League administration was set up, offering the population the choice of staying under the League, joining France, or joining Germany. The vote favored Germany.

sabotage. 1. Interference with or prevention of production, usually thought of as industrial production, by intentionally disabling the processes of production, as for example, by rendering the machinery unfit for use. The word comes from the French word for wooden shoe, *sabot*, and means literally to throw a wooden shoe in the machinery. 2. To interfere with production as in 1.

saboteur. A person who carries out or tries to carry out an act of sabotage. See SABOTAGE.

Sachem. One of the leaders of the Tammany Society. The head is the Grand Sachem. See TAMMANY HALL.

safe-conduct. Special permit allowing a person to move through a certain area, as for example, permission by a military commander for an enemy to pass through the territory the commander controls.

Safety Appliance Acts. A series of laws, the first of which was passed March 2, 1893, requiring a standard of safety in such railroad equipment as brakes, couplers, handles, and ladders. They were based on the power of Congress to regulate interstate commerce.

safety belt. See DECLARATION OF PANAMA.

sage-brush states. A term used in the United States to refer to the Rocky Mountain states and those immediately adjoining on the east, presumably more covered with sagebrush than with people.

St. Cyr-l'École. A village in France near Versailles in which is located the French military school, hence the "French West Point."

St. Germain, Treaty of. The peace treaty following World War I between Austria and the Allies, signed September 10, 1919. It gave a considerable amount of territory to Italy, Czechoslovakia, Poland, and Yugoslavia; practically disarmed the country; and made it liable for reparations.

St. Jean de Maurienne Agreement. One of the secret treaties of World War I. Its signatories were France, Great Britain, and Italy, and it defined in more detail the Italian sphere of control to be set up in southern Turkey. It was signed April 17, 1917 but was never carried out.

St. Lawrence Waterway. A project for a series of dams and locks in the St. Lawrence River to make possible the navigation of the Great Lakes by ocean vessels, and from which would also be obtained electric power. A United States-Canadian treaty for the purpose of joint participation in the project was signed January 10, 1934 and defeated in the Senate March 14 of the same year. However, the treaty continued to have the support of the Roosevelt and Truman administrations.

sales tax. See TAX.

Salonica, Treaty of. An agreement signed at Salonica, Greece, July 31, 1938 by the president of the Balkan Entente and Bulgaria, that the states involved engaged to abstain from a resort to force in their mutual relations and agreed as far as they were concerned to renounce the application of the provisions of the Treaty of Neuilly regarding the disarmament of Bulgaria. See BALKAN PACT.

salt tax. A tax on salt. Occasionally used in poor countries as a sales tax of wide distribution. Gandhi has attacked the one in India as being an outstanding example of British imperialist policy.

sample ballot. A facsimile of the official ballot, though clearly marked as a sample, or not official, circulated prior to an election to acquaint the voter with the ballot in order to minimize mistakes.

samurai. The Japanese feudal class composed of warriors and lower nobility. They were subject to the code of the bushido, privileged to wear two swords and had the power of life and death over the common people. Later the word was used to mean the entire feudal regime, and finally it was loosely applied to all Japanese army officers. The original samurai were abolished in 1871, but the members of the class and their descendants were influential in the imperialist expansion of Japan in World War II. See BUSHIDO.

sanctions. In a wide sense the penalties which are applied against those who violate written or unwritten law. Legal sanctions are provided by law while social sanctions are informally applied against those who break social customs. National law has developed everywhere a machinery of enforcement, or sanctions, against lawbreakers.

In a narrow sense we usually speak of sanctions as used against violators of international law and obligations. The League of Nations attempted to make use of sanctions, and Article XVI of its Covenant dealt with sanctions to be imposed against member states resorting to war without submitting their dispute to the League, or waging war against member states who complied with an award or judgment by the World Court or with a recommendation of the League Council. All member states were supposed to sever all trade and financial relations between themselves and an offending member state and in grave cases to participate in concerted armed action against the violator. This was put to a test against Italy in 1935 but most nations were on the whole unwilling to impose sanctions fast and strong enough to prevent or stop Mussolini from conquering Ethiopia. Chapter VII of the United Nations charges the Security Council with determining what sanctions should be taken against states threatening or breaking the peace, or acting as aggressors. See INTERNATIONAL LAW, LEAGUE OF NATIONS, UNITED NATIONS.

Sandhurst. Site of the British Royal Military College and Staff College, 35 miles southwest of London, and hence the "British West Point."

San Francisco Conference. The United Nations Conference on International Organization (UNCIO) which met at San Francisco April 25–June 26, 1945, at which was drawn up the charter of the United Nations. See UNITED NATIONS.

sanitary district. A unit of local government set up for the purposes of sewage disposal, usually overlapping the ordinary jurisdictions, such as several towns or cities in the same county or adjoining counties.

sanjak. An administrative district of the Turkish Empire. Certain ones have been of special historical importance, such as the Sanjak of Novibazar in the Balkans, annexed by Austria in 1908, and the Sanjak of Alexandretta, now called Hatay, at the northeast corner of the Mediterranean, which enjoyed a special regime within the Syrian mandated territory and was annexed to Turkey in 1938.

San Stefano, Treaty of. The first of two peace treaties following the Russo-Turkish War of 1877–78, signed March 3, 1878. It provided for the independence of Romania, Serbia, and Montenegro, and the establishment of a large semi-independent Bulgarian principality extending from the Danube to the Aegean. This was revised by the Treaty of Berlin. See BERLIN, TREATY OF.

Sarajevo assassinations. The assassination June 28, 1914 of the Austrian Archduke Franz Ferdinand and his wife at Sarajevo, Bosnia, by Gavrilo Princep, a member of a Serbian terrorist group. The murder was the occasion for the subsequent ultimatum sent by Austria-Hungary to Serbia and hence one of the factors contributing to the outbreak of World War I.

satellite nation. A small state that is more or less dependent upon, and which ties its policies to those of, a larger power.

Savoy, House of. Former ruling house of Italy. The line was founded around

1000 A.D. when Humbert became count of Savoy. Later they became dukes of Savoy, and in 1718 kings of Sardinia, also ruling Piedmont, Savoy, and Nice. In 1861 Victor Emmanuel II became king of united Italy. Following Italy's unconditional surrender to the Allies in World War II, King Victor Emmanuel III resigned all royal authority to his son, Crown Prince Humbert, who became Lieutenant General of the Realm in April, 1944. In a referendum held June 2–3, 1946 the monarchy was defeated in favor of a republic, and Humbert went into exile.

scalawag. American slang term for a southerner who co-operated with the carpetbaggers after the Civil War. See CARPETBAGGER.

Scandinavia. Collective term used for Sweden, Norway, and Denmark.

S.C.A.P. Supreme Commander Allied Powers in Japan, General MacArthur. He and his staff administer allied power in Japan.

S. Con. Res. Senate Concurrent Resolution.

schedule. An additional detailed statement, as of rates, supplementing a law or other document.

scheduled classes. A new and less harsh term for Untouchables. See UNTOUCHABLES.

Schleswig-Holstein. Two Danish-German districts between the North Sea and the Baltic which figured prominently in 19th century history. Up to 1848 both owed vague allegiance to Denmark, but in that year their inhabitants appealed to Prussia for aid against Danish annexation, and war followed. Prussia soon abandoned the war and Denmark kept the districts, but in 1865 Bismarck used them as pawns in his struggle to drive Austria from the German Confederation. Both Prussia and Austria went to war against Denmark over the two regions

and the latter was easily defeated, Austria getting Schleswig and Prussia getting Holstein. The next year (1866) Austrian Schleswig was an immediate cause of the Seven Weeks War in which Austria was crushed by Prussia and both Schleswig and Holstein were annexed to Prussia. In 1919, under the terms of the Versailles Treaty, a plebiscite was held in northern Schleswig, and the part nearest Denmark voted to join that country while the rest voted for Germany.

Schlieffen plan. The German strategic plan for World War I drawn up originally by Count von Schlieffen, chief of staff from 1891–1906. It had two main parts, namely, first a holding action against Russia until France was disposed of and then an all-out attack on Russia; and second, a plan of attack on France involving a holding action along the Rhine and a hinge movement through Belgium and northern France towards Paris, the hinge to be at the southeast corner of Belgium. In addition there were involved, prior to the war, certain military zones in Germany partially mobilized in varying degrees.

Schneider-Creusot. Armament firm founded and directed by members of the Schneider family whose first plant was at Le Creusot, France. It developed tremendous power in this field; by 1935 it was said to control almost 200 French, and over 200 non-French, armament and allied concerns either directly or through a holding company.

school district. An administrative district used as the basis for taxation and attendance for a public school or school system.

Schrecklichkeit (SHREK - lish - kite). German word meaning frightfulness. A Nazi policy of discouraging opposition by the studied application of atrocities against those who opposed their regime.

Schutzstaffel (SHOOTS-shtah-ful). The elite black-uniformed special guard of the Nazi party. They formed the body-guard of top Nazi leaders and were given a place of favor at special occasions. Certain groups were organized into special military units in World War II. Popularly called S.S.

Schwarze Korps (SHVAHR - tsuh KOHR). Literally the black corps. See SCHUTZSTAFFEL.

Scientific Research and Development, Office of. An agency established within the Office of Emergency Management, June 28, 1941. Its function was to see that research was pursued on scientific and medical problems which were related to national defense. This involved securing personnel, and effecting co-operation between government departments and with private industry.

Scottish representative peers. Before the convening of a new parliament the Scottish peers meet in Edinburgh and elect 16 of their number to represent them in the forthcoming sessions of the House of Lords.

scratch. To vote other than a straight ticket by voting for one or more candidates of another party. See STRAIGHT TICKET.

Scrutin de liste (skryoo-TANG duh LEEST). A French electoral system used from time to time under the Third Republic by which members of the Chamber of Deputies were chosen by groups from each *département* or large electoral district. The alternative plan, which was also used, is the *scrutin d'arrondisement*, by which one member is chosen from each *arrondisement* or small district. *Scrutin de liste* is often used with proportional representation.

sealer. City official who inspects and

seals certain devices to insure that they conform to regulations, as for example, the scales in retail and wholesale stores.

search and seizure. See VISIT AND SEARCH.

secession. See STATES' RIGHTS.

Second Bank of United States. See BANKS OF THE UNITED STATES.

second chamber. In many parliamentary bodies the essential legislative responsibilities are discharged more largely in one of the houses, rather than being almost exactly equally divided between the two houses. In such a case the chamber which is less essential to the legislative process, as for example, the French Senate was called the second chamber.

Second Empire. The French empire established by Louis-Napoleon Bonaparte in 1852, following his seizure of dictatorial power the year before while president of the Second Republic. He took the title of Napoleon III. His reign was marked by an active foreign policy, including participation in the Crimean War against Russia, a victorious war against Austria in Italy, and a futile attempt to create a French-supported empire in Mexico. The empire fell when Napoleon III was defeated and captured at Sedan in the Franco-Prussian War of 1870. Napoleon fled to England and the Third Republic was proclaimed.

Second International. See INTERNATIONAL.

second papers. Petition filed by an alien applying for admission to United States citizenship. This step is taken between two and seven years after the alien's declaration of intention to become a citizen. In support of this petition he must prove the place, date, and method of reaching the United States, and must present two character witnesses who know he has resided in the United States at least five years. See DECLARATION OF INTENTION.

Second Reich. The German empire which existed between 1870 and 1918, under Hohenzollern rule. The term was used to denote the empire as a sort of a successor of the medieval "empire of the German nation," or Holy Roman Empire. It was created out of the many states which had made up the German Confederation, after the Franco-Prussian War, largely through the diplomatic skill of the Prussian statesman, Bismarck. King William I of Prussia became Emperor William I of Germany. The new state launched on a career of industrial and imperialistic expansion, and after Bismarck retired in 1890, this was continued and intensified under William II. The government was dominated by an alliance of Prussian land owners and militarists and the great industrialists, in opposition to the growing strength of the democratic and working-class movements, notably the Social Democratic Party. The emperor's foreign policy lead to the Triple Alliance of Germany, Austria-Hungary and Italy on one side and the Triple Entente of Britain, France and Russia on the other, and eventually to the outbreak of World War I in 1914. The defeat of Germany and her allies lead to the abdication of William II in November, 1918 and the formation of the Weimar Republic.

Second Republic. The French regime between 1848 and 1852. It began with the overthrow of the Orleans monarchy of King Louis Philippe in February, 1848 and was marked by the adoption of a republican constitution and the election of Louis Napoleon Bonaparte as president in December. He took advantage of a conservative, mostly rural, reaction to the revolutionary activities of the Paris workers

to organize a coup d'état in December, 1851 which virtually ended the Second Republic. A year later Bonaparte became Emperor Napoleon III, beginning the Second Empire.

secretariat. 1. The office and staff of a secretary. 2. The administrative service and secretarial force in any international organization, as for example, the League of Nations or the United Nations. 3. The office of the secretary to the British cabinet. 4. Often used outside the United States as a synonym for ministry or government department. See UNITED NATIONS and Charter of the United Nations, Articles 97–101, Appendix.

secretary. 1. Head of a United States government executive department, as the Secretary of State. 2. Person who is responsible for keeping the records and carrying on the correspondence of a governmental body.

secretary-general. The chief administrative officer and head of the secretariat of an international organization such as the League of Nations or the United Nations. He is responsible for the record-keeping and publications of the organization and for making arrangements for its various meetings.

secret diplomacy. The carrying on of important political negotiations and particularly treaties of military alliance, concerning which the public was kept entirely in the dark. See SECRET TREATIES.

Secret Service. A branch of the Treasury Department set up in 1860 to prevent counterfeiting. Its functions have been enlarged to include the protection of the president and policing of the White House, and for investigations of violations of tax and loan laws.

secret session. A legislative session to which the public is not admitted and the business of which the members

are supposed to keep secret. See EX-
ECUTIVE SESSION.

Secret Treaties. Applied especially to
the secret agreements between the
Allies during World War I in regard
to the disposition of the territories of
the Central Powers, notably Turkey
and Austria-Hungary, when victory
was won. See SECRET TREATY OF
LONDON; CONSTANTINOPLE AGREE-
MENT; ST. JEAN DE MAURIENNE AGREE-
MENT; HUSSEIN-MACMAHON AGREEMENT
and SYKES-PICOT AGREEMENT.

Section 7A. Probably the most famous
section of the National Industrial
Recovery Act of 1933. It provided
that employees could organize and
bargain collectively through freely-
chosen representatives, that no employee could be forced to join or leave
a union, and that employers were to
observe the maximum hours, minimum wages, and other working conditions set up for the industry.

sectionalism. See REGIONALISM.

sectional trading. A term which appeared during the 79th Congress
which referred to the trading of votes
by representatives from two different
sections of the country. A more
pleasant term for log-rolling.

Securities and Exchange Commission.
A United States government agency
set up June 6, 1934, to control,
chiefly by registration of securities,
the securities market and prevent the
excessive fluctuation thereof.

Security Council. The organ of the
United Nations which has been given
the "primary responsibility for the
maintenance of international peace
and security." In discharging this
responsibility it has the power to
settle international disputes and to
enforce its decisions, by force, if
necessary through the direction of the
subsidiary Military Staff Committee.
It is a permanent body, meeting in
more or less continuous session. There

are eleven members; the five great
powers are permanent members, while
the other six are elected, three each
year. Each member has one vote. Procedural matters are settled by an
affirmative vote of seven, while decisions on substantive matters require an affirmative vote of seven
including the votes of the five permanent members. This requirement of
unanimity among the great powers in
non-procedural matters in the Security Council, which makes it possible
for any one great power to block such
matters, is known as the so-called
"veto." See UNITED NATIONS Appendix: Charter of the United Nations
Organization, Articles 23–32.

sedition acts. See ALIEN AND SEDITION
ACTS.

seditious libel. Libelous statements
about the Constitution and laws or
persons holding public office, published with the intention to stir up
disorder.

Seiyukai Party. One of the two major
political parties in Japan prior to
World War II, the other being the
Minseito Party. The Seiyukai, which
under other names dates back to
1881, was usually the more powerful
of the two, the more conservative and
imperialistic. Its leaders, however,
attacked the army and fascism. Its
strength lay in the country districts,
but like the Minseito it never truly
represented the people of Japan and
was in fact an alliance between politicians, land owners and industrialists. When it was the dominant party
it merely shared power with the ruling
Japanese oligarchy. After the outbreak of World War II the Seiyukai
was eclipsed by the fascist Imperial
Rule Assistance Association. See
MINSEITO PARTY.

Sejm (SAYM). National legislature of
Poland; from the reconstitution of
Poland in 1923 until 1935 when it was

reduced in numbers, the democratic parliamentary body of the Polish Republic. All real authority, however, was vested in the president who appointed his own successor.

Selective Service. Military service, based on the conscription of the physically fit. At first names are drawn by lot, but the ultimate tendency is to draft all who are fit.

Selective Training and Service Act. A U. S. law of September 16, 1940, providing for the selection by draft of recruits, 900,000 at first, for the army. In addition it provided for the return of these men to their jobs, treatment of conscientious objectors, and pay of men in the service.

selectmen. Administrative officials in the government of the New England towns.

self-defense. 1. The protection by a state of its own rights and domain by its own armed forces. 2. The forceful protection by an individual of his own person.

self-determination. A term used since World War I to denote the right of every people to choose freely the form of government and other institutions it wants to have. It was used as a wartime slogan by the Allies, chiefly for propaganda purposes among the nationalities of Central Europe, the Balkans and Middle East who were subject to the Central Powers, and it was one of President Wilson's Fourteen Points, issued in 1918. The principle was restated in the Atlantic Charter of August 14, 1941 as one of the policies of the United States and Great Britain.

self-government. The process in which a group of people exercise for themselves all the essential functions of government.

self-help. A method of settling international disputes in which a nation tries to reach a decision by reliance upon the threat or use of its own force, as for example, in retortion, reprisal, or war.

self-sufficiency. The condition of a state which possesses such an adequate supply of essential raw materials that it is independent of foreign sources in the building of an industry capable of waging modern war. In this sense no state is literally self-sufficient, or can now attain self-sufficiency; it can achieve only relative self-sufficiency.

semi-sovereign. Pertaining to a state having certain of the powers of sovereignty but not all of them. In the strict sense of positive law, sovereignty may not be divided, but in international law cases of division of sovereignty are found, as for example in protectorates and vassal states, where usually the right to control foreign relations resides in a larger outside nation.

senate. A legislative body, usually called the "upper" of two which form the legislature of a government. The name derives from the Roman Senate, a body of 300 to 600 wealthy and prominent men, the most important organ in the government of the Roman Republic. Modern senates are usually designed to act as a brake on the more democratically chosen members of the "lower" house. The United States Senate is composed of two members from each state, and has the power to approve important presidential appointments and to approve treaties by a two-thirds majority. State senates are usually smaller in size than the lower house, though normally apportioned according to population. Canadian senators are named by the prime minister, roughly according to the population of each province, but the body has limited influence. In Australia the senate contains six members elected from each state. In South Africa they are chosen by provincial assemblies and in the French Third Republic were elected indirectly from each *département*. Most Latin American countries have senates modelled after that of the United States.

senator. Member of a senate.

senatorial courtesy. The special deference given by the United States Senate to nominations for appointive offices in the various states brought forward by senators of those states. In such cases if there is a conflict between the president and a senator as to an appointment in the senator's state, the senate will be inclined to confirm the choice of the senator.

seniority rule. The rule that promotions or committee chairmanships shall be granted to that person among those eligible who has the longest record of service. This rule obviously does not guarantee that the best qualified person gets the position.

sentence. The statement of punishment meted out by a court to a person found guilty of crime.

separation of powers. The principle that the legislative, executive and judicial powers of a state should be exercised by three different branches of the government. It was formulated in the 18th century by the French philosopher Montesquieu, and particularly appealed to the Founding Fathers of the United States. The principle originates in the fear that a government in which all powers are held in one hand or in the hands of one group, branch or organ, would become too powerful. The Constitution of the United States and the American system of government is the foremost example today of the separation of powers. The President holds the executive power, which he exercises through his Cabinet and his executive departments and agencies; Congress holds the legislative power; and the Supreme Court and other Federal Courts exercise the judicial power. Legislation passed by Congress can be vetoed by the President (though only if it is not passed again by a two-thirds vote), Congress may impeach the President or any other high executive or judicial official; the President may recommend legislation; the Senate approves appointments of high executive and judicial officials; the federal courts may declare any legislation passed by Congress or any act of the executive unconstitutional if not conforming with the Constitution. These are the main "checks and balances" which are destined to prevent domination by one branch of government over the other two. Today the executive branch of government has grown more influential than the other two branches, but even so the President frequently is unable to get Congress to act on his recommendations. In the parliamentary system legislative and executive powers are united in parliament. See POPULAR SOVEREIGNTY, REPUBLIC, PARLIAMENTARY SYSTEM.

separatism. A movement to break away a part of a country, or political party, or of a religious or social organization from the main body. The reason for this is usually either a disagreement regarding the political or religious principles advanced by the majority; or in the case of a country a feeling that the part desiring to become "separate" is distinct in nationality, religion, history, etc., from the main body of the country, within which it cannot maintain these distinctions. The term was first used at the time of Queen Mary of England when Protestants refused to hold Catholic Church services.

In the political sphere an important Separatist movement took place in the French and Belgian occupied

German Rhineland after the first World War (1914–1918) which tried to establish an independent Rhineland Republic, separating itself from the German Reich. A movement to separate Catalonia with its capital, Barcelona, from Spain was active and briefly successful in the 1920's and early 1930's. It is interesting that the term has only been used for a few movements and more often it has been said that a part of a nation wishes to secede to join another nation, or to become autonomous, or independent. See SECESSION, AUTONOMY, REGIONALISM.

sequestration. The act of holding (sometimes seizing and holding) property pending a future disposition. It does not necessarily imply appropriation; certain property may be restored, as at the end of a war, while other property may be held pending a special decision upon it.

sergeant-at-arms. An official employed by a legislative body whose main function is to maintain order, but who also brings in witnesses and otherwise aids the body in carrying on its business.

serial bonds. A bond issue retired in installments extending over a stated period of years.

servitude. In international law the permanent right of one state to use the territory of another state for some special purpose, such as the use of port or airdrome facilities or the passage of troops.

session. The convening of a legislative or judicial body, either for a single day or over a longer period of time, terminated either by a set date or the completion of pending business and adjournment.

session laws. Laws passed by each session of Congress prior to 1937. The Statutes at Large are now brought up to date after the end of each session.

Sèvres, Treaty of. The first Turkish peace treaty after World War I, signed August 10, 1920. In it large areas of the former Turkish Empire were given not only to the Arabs, but to the Greeks, Armenians and Kurds. It was not accepted by the new government and was replaced by the Treaty of Lausanne. See LAUSANNE, TREATIES OF.

S.H.A.E.F. Supreme Headquarters of the Allied Expeditionary Force, that is, General Dwight D. Eisenhower's headquarters in World War II.

Shangri-la. Mythical state in James Hilton's novel, *Lost Horizon.* Humorously referred to by President Franklin D. Roosevelt as the base for the United States planes under General Doolittle which first bombed Japan in World War II, April 18, 1942. Now the name of a United States aircraft carrier.

share-cropper. A landless agricultural laborer in the South, paid for his work by a share of the crop he grows. His income rarely enables him to better his condition and he is usually dependent upon his employer for his inadequate housing. One of the most neglected and underprivileged classes in the country.

share-the-wealth movement. Huey Long's plan for the equalization of wealth and the attainment of his slogan, "Every Man a King." He advocated such means as limitation of incomes, 100 per cent inheritance taxes, a high tax on large fortunes, higher wages and shorter working hours. The movement spread over part of the Middle West and at one time threatened to become such a large faction of the Democratic party as to influence party policies.

Sheria. Sacred Moslem law, including the teachings of the Koran and the sayings of Mohammed. Also Sheriat, Shariah.

sheriff. In the United States the chief police officer of a county, who also aids the county courts by serving papers and carrying out judgments and sentences. The name derives from the English word for the king's steward in each shire (shire-reeve).

Sherman Antitrust Act. A law of July 2, 1890, which endeavored to protect free competition in interstate commerce from monopolies by making illegal any combination in restraint of trade. It is an early landmark of the federal regulation of business.

Shiah *or* **Shiite.** 1. Pertaining to a Mohammedan sect strongly at odds with the orthodox majority due to a difference of opinion about the succession of the Caliphs after Mohammed. See SUNNI. 2. A person adhering to the Shiah doctrine. Most Shiahs live in Iran (Persia) and Iraq.

Shimonoseki, Treaty of. Treaty of peace of April 17, 1895, between China and Japan following the war which started the year before. By the treaty China gave Japan Formosa and the Pescadores Islands, paid an indemnity, and recognized the independence of Korea.

Shintoism. The former Japanese state religion until it was deprived of state support and a place in the curriculum of schools by a directive of Gen. MacArthur in December, 1945. Originally it was a primitive worship of the forces of nature and the gods and goddesses of Japanese mythology, notably of the sun-goddess, Amaterasu, from whom the emperors formerly claimed descent. Buddhist influences in the 6th century added the element of ancestor worship, among others. After the imperial restoration of 1868 worship of the emperor, the divinity of Japan, its people and its aims were increasingly stressed, with emphasis upon obedience and sacrifice for the nation on the part of the people. In this form it was a powerful support for the imperialist groups which led Japan into World War II. In his New Year's Rescript, January 1, 1946 Emperor Hirohito denied his alleged divinity, thereby destroying one of the major tenets of the religion. It still lives in a form somewhat similar to its original character, plus the Buddhist additions.

Shipping Board. The United States Shipping Board, an independent agency set up by an act of September 7, 1916. Its function was to build up a merchant marine during World War I and its success may in part be measured by the fact that by the end of the war it had almost 1200 ships under its control.

shipping subsidy. A subsidy granted by a government to a steamship line to build the merchant fleet flying the flag of that government, so that in case of war, for example, the state will have sufficient ships of its own. These subsidies may take such forms as help in construction, grants for operation, or special contracts for carrying mail.

ship's papers. The documents carried on a ship providing evidence of ownership, destination and cargo, including, for example, the list of crew and passengers, log, register, manifest, and bills of lading.

shirt sleeve diplomacy. Slang term for the handling of international relations with directness and without the usual polite observances of diplomacy. The term is used both in praise, as in the first sense above, and in criticism, as in the latter sense.

shogun. A Japanese title meaning leader of the army, held by the head of the Japanese feudal system. As such, the shogun was the real ruler of Japan, since all the other nobles owed him strict obedience, either directly or indirectly. The first shogun, Yoritomo, was given the title by the imperial government in 1192, and from the beginning he and his successors far overshadowed the emperor. However, they did not completely consolidate their power until the end of the 16th century, when the shogun Nobunaga Oda brought an end to a long period of feudal anarchy. The fifteen shoguns of the house of Tokugawa ruled Japan from 1600 to 1867, when the complex feudal regime was overthrown by the emperor Mutsuhito (Meiji) and the title abolished.

short ballot. A ballot limiting elective office to only the most essential executive and legislative representatives, leaving judicial and lesser administrative posts to be filled by appointment. This plan is an effort to reduce the number of elected offices sufficiently so the voter can become acquainted with the merits of the candidates. It has not been generally accepted in the United States in state and local government.

short session. The second regular session of Congress prior to the ratification of the Lame Duck amendment in 1933. Sessions of Congress opened in December, but since the terms of Congressmen ended on March 4, the second session was thus less than three months long. The first, or long, session, usually ran from December to the following summer. Now the annual sessions start in January, with no regular short sessions.

siege. The maintenance of a continuous attack upon a given territory, city, or fortress.

Siegfried Line. The line of fortifications in western Germany built to balance the French Maginot Line and prevent invasion from the west. Sometimes also called the Westwall. It is often considered that Germany was unable to go to war with either Czechoslovakia or Poland until the practical completion of this line in 1939.

silver certificate. United States paper money issued in denominations of $1 to $1,000 representing like amounts of silver dollars in the United States Treasury, and redeemable in those amounts. They state on the face that they are legal tender for all debts, public and private.

Silver Purchase Act. A law of June 19, 1934 which authorized the domestic and foreign purchase of silver, the issue of silver certificates therefor, and the prohibition of the export of silver. Silver was to be purchased until it reached one-fourth the combined gold and silver stock of the country.

Silver Shirts. The Silver Shirt Legion of America, a fascist organization in the United States along the lines of the early blackshirts in Italy and brownshirts in Germany. It was organized January 31, 1933 by William Dudley Pelley.

sinecure. A public office which requires practically no work.

sine die (SIE-nee DIE-ee). Literally, without day. Used to refer to an adjournment with no day set for reconvening, that is a final adjournment of a convention or a legislative session.

single-member district. A district from which only one member is elected to represent it in a legislative body.

single tax. Usually, a tax on land, advocated as a substitute for the usual variety of taxes. It was suggested that this be levied upon the "economic rent," or value which land receives because of its importance to the community. It was first popularized by the Physiocrats about 1750, and its present prominence is due to the work of Henry George.

sinking fund. An amount set apart

piecemeal over a period of time for the purpose of liquidation of a public debt.

Sinn Fein (shin-fane). Irish nationalist movement largely responsible for the establishment of the Irish Free State in 1922. It dates back to the early 20th century, but grew slowly until the failure of the Easter Rebellion in 1916 and the subsequent British methods of restoring peace and order drove many Irish to accept the policies of Sinn Fein: isolationism in politics and economics, "Ireland for the Irish," including union with the Protestant North, a revival of the Irish (Gaelic) language and of Irish medieval culture. British failure to put down the guerilla fighters of Sinn Fein made them offer the compromise plan embodied in the Free State. Among the leaders of Sinn Fein (which means "we ourselves" in Irish) were Arthur Griffith, Eamon De Valera and Michael Collins.

sit-down strike. A strike in which the workers refuse to work while inside the plant or on the job, that is, by sitting down.

Sitzkrieg. See PHONY WAR.

sixteen-to-one. The ratio of silver to gold in the United States monetary system of 1896, which the Democratic Party proposed to maintain as part of its advocacy of the free coinage of silver. The champion of this program was William Jennings Bryan, who upheld his position as synonymous with this figure by securing and maintaining during his later years at Lincoln, Nebraska, the telephone number 1621.

S. J. Res. Senate Joint Resolution.

Skoda. Czechoslovak munitions company whose chief works are at Brno (Bruenn) and Pilsen. It was one of the leading munitions firms of central and eastern Europe and was controlled by a holding company set up by the French firm of Schneider-Creusot. See SCHNEIDER-CREUSOT.

Skupshtina. (skoop-SHTEE-nah). The parliament of Yugoslavia.

slander. Injurious or defamatory statements made about a person in a non-permanent form, as by the spoken word. See LIBEL.

slate. List of candidates drawn up by a political party.

slave trade. See SLAVERY.

slavery. An institution in which some of the individuals in a community are owned by other individuals as chattels, their labor being completely at the disposal of the owners. Slaves were bought and sold and often became a highly valuable form of property. Many societies in the middle stages of their development established slavery, but in early primitive and nomadic stages it is unknown. Even societies of high culture—such as ancient Greece and Rome—adopted slavery. Modern slavery in America and the colonies in general started when Portuguese, Spanish and particularly English explorers captured black natives in Africa and used and sold them as laborers. This developed into the huge international slave trade, and it has been estimated that between 1680 and 1786 more than two million slaves were carried into the British colonies in America alone. Many humanitarian movements against the slave trade sprang up in the 18th century, one of the most prominent led by Quakers. Slave trade ceased in the French colonies by 1789, was abolished in Denmark in 1802 and by Britain in 1807. The United States forbade the importation of slaves after 1808. At the Congress of Vienna (1815) the European states agreed to abolish the slave trade. Slavery was an important institution in the American southern states, where cotton plantations and the cotton trade were based upon it. Washington freed his slaves in his will; Franklin, John Adams, Madison, and Hamilton opposed slavery, but at the Constitutional Convention Georgia and South Carolina insisted that it should be recognized. All the northern states had abolished slavery by 1804. The struggle for abolition in the rest of the country began in earnest in the 1830's. Among its leading advocates was William Lloyd Garrison whose magazine, the *Liberator,* was founded in 1831. The issue involved, as time went on, not only the humanitarian aspect but also the influence of slavery upon the growing industrialism of the country and upon the interests of the free workers and farmers, especially in the West. The South sought to protect its "peculiar institution" and was willing to go so far as to try to secede from the Union to save it. The Civil War was the result, and though Secession was the immediate cause of the war, slavery lay behind it. As a result the slaves in that part of the South still in rebellion were freed by President Lincoln's Emancipation Proclamation of January 1, 1863 and the rest by the 13th Amendment, ratified in 1865. This was followed by the end of slavery throughout the Western Hemisphere, but slavery survives today in a few isolated regions of Asia and Africa. It existed in Ethiopia though in diminishing numbers of cases until the Italian conquest in 1935. See PEONAGE.

slogan. A word or phrase used to epitomize an issue and to evoke party, or national loyalty.

slum clearance. A project for razing a slum neighborhood and replacing it with some such improvement as a park or a new, modern housing development.

slush fund. A party campaign fund, the size and purposes of which are not necessarily within the law.

small claims court. Courts provided in certain of the United States in which cases involving small amounts may be settled economically and promptly by simple procedure, without the aid of lawyers.

Smaller War Plants Corporation. An emergency war agency set up June 11, 1942 to see that smaller factories were able to contribute their best efforts to defense projects during World War II. It was empowered to extend loans to such firms and to contract with them for war work.

Smith-Hughes Act. A United States federal law of February 23, 1917 establishing a system of Federal aid for vocational education, for example, the teaching of agriculture in high schools.

Smithsonian Institution. A United States government agency set up August 10, 1846 as the result of a gift by James Smithson of England for the diffusion of knowledge in America. It administers the National Museum, the National Collection of Fine Arts, the Bureau of Ethnology, the National Zoological Park, the Astrophysical Observatory and the National Gallery, all in Washington, D. C. or its vicinity. The name is often applied only to the National Museum.

smoke-filled room. A hotel room filled with tobacco smoke, the traditional place to which are ascribed the less savory political deals, especially at political conventions. The negotiations leading to the nomination of Warren G. Harding by the Republicans in 1920 are often cited as a good example.

Smoot-Hawley Tariff. See HAWLEY-SMOOT TARIFF.

smuggle. To import or, less often, to export goods illegally, usually by concealment in an attempt to avoid payment of duties.

snap. Pertaining to a suddenly-held vote or meeting.

soap box. A figurative term for the rostrum from which political figures, usually demagogues, appeal to the masses of the voters.

Sobranje (soh-BRAHN-yeh). The Bulgarian national legislature, a one-chamber body of representatives elected by all men over 21 and by all married women over the same age.

social contract. A term applied by political philosophers to a theory of society and the state which assumes that men lived originally in a "state of nature" where there was no society, no government, no compulsion of any organized variety. For various reasons men decided that by forming a political organization they would be happier and safer. This act was called a social contract, or social compact, and through it man leaves the "state of nature" and forms a state. The most important philosophers who used the "state of nature" and the social contract as the basis for their ideas concerning man, society, the state and government were the Frenchman Jean Jacques Rousseau and the Englishmen, Thomas Hobbes and John Locke. They did not, however, agree on *how* man lived in the "state of nature" and what his reasons were for making a social contract, and consequently their conclusions on government were different. Hobbes believed that life in the "state of nature" was "solitary, poor, nasty, brutish and short." To put an end to this anarchic and war-like condition, men entered into the social contract. Locke believed that the "state of nature" was a condition of peace and rights of life, liberty and property, and that men agreed to form a civil state only because of the common

need of a single known rule for the protection of man's rights. Rousseau felt likewise that the "state of nature" was a carefree condition, but that the state became a necessity with the development of individual inequalities and property. Both stated that men entered the formal agreement known as the social contract, giving up individual, natural rights in order to secure the greater protection of rights which could be rendered by society formed into a civil state. See NATURAL RIGHTS, CONSENT OF THE GOVERNED, POPULAR SOVEREIGNTY.

Social Democratic Party. A German socialist party founded at Gotha in 1875, the model for other parties in other countries with the same or similar names and programs. It advocated the socialization of the means of production by a gradual evolutionary process and grew to be the largest party in Germany, though it never had a majority of the vote. It was a major factor in the Second (Socialist) International and opposed most of the policies of Chancellor Bismarck and William II. It tried unsuccessfully to stem the tide leading to World War I, but during the war it supported the imperial government. With the war's end it was a major factor in the creation and life of the Weimar Republic. While still the strongest party, it lost ground to the left and right extremist parties, and when Hitler came to power it was destroyed along with all the other parties except the Nazis. Following World War II it was revived and showed considerable strength in the first elections under Allied rule.

social insurance. See SOCIAL SECURITY, SOCIALIZED MEDICINE, BEVERIDGE PLAN.

social legislation. In a wide sense all legislation intended to improve the general well-being of a nation and particularly of the lower income groups. It includes measures regulating wages and hours of workers, promoting public health and social security, prohibiting or regulating child labor, establishing and maintaining public education, combatting juvenile delinquency, promoting better housing, etc. See SOCIAL SECURITY, POOR LAWS, CHILD-LABOR LAWS, PUBLIC HEALTH, SOCIALIZED MEDICINE, BEVERIDGE PLAN.

social sciences. Fields of knowledge dealing with the relationships of human beings—economics, history, political science or government, and sociology. Sometimes geography and psychology are included.

social security. A system of provision for compensation against loss of income owing to reasons such as death of the family's provider, illness, accidents, debility, old age and unemployment. It is usually accomplished by a system of compulsory insurance requiring both the employer and the employee to pay a regular sum into a fund administered by the government. In some countries contributions are paid only by the employer, in others only by the employee. Social security is the outcome of modern social philosophy, according to which the government is responsible for the well-being and health of its citizens. Compulsory social or national insurance for medical care and compensation for workers in case of sickness was established in Germany in 1883, in Austria in 1888 and in Britain in 1912. Government pensions for widows, orphans, and old-age pensions at 65 were provided in Britain in 1925. Similar provisions are in force in most European countries. Unemployment insurance (unemployment relief, or "the dole") providing compensation for those who seek work in vain has been in force in Britain since 1911. The first

American unemployment compensation law was passed in Wisconsin in 1932. New York, New Hampshire and California followed suit in 1935. The Federal Social Security Act was signed in August, 1935 and is regarded as one of the main achievements of the Roosevelt administration. It established a federal system of old-age insurance, authorized federal co-operation in establishing and administering state unemployment compensation, and provided federal grants to aid the states in assisting the needy, the aged, the blind and dependent children. Amendments to the Act in 1939 established benefits for the survivors of insured workers. It is administered partly by the states and partly by the Federal Security Agency, which includes the Social Security Board, Public Health Service, Office of Education, Food and Drug Administration, Office of Vocational Rehabilitation, and others. President Truman asked for further extension of social security services in various messages to Congress.

Social Security Act. A law of August 14, 1935 establishing and providing for the national social security system, to be administered by the Social Security Board. It included old-age insurance, unemployment compensation, and aid to the states for the care of the aged, dependent children and the blind. See SOCIAL SECURITY.

Social Security Board. See SOCIAL SECURITY, SOCIAL SECURITY ACT.

socialism. A theory and a movement aiming at a collective organization of the community in the interest of the people, by means of common ownership and control of the means of production (industry, transportation, banking, etc.). Socialism is often identified with communism, because for a long time the followers of Karl Marx (see MARXISM) called themselves socialists. But socialism is much older than Marx and many advocates of socialist systems—such as the Frenchmen Saint-Simon, Fourier, and Louis Blanc and the British Robert Owen, the Fabians and the Guild Socialists, either preceded Marx or differed from his ideas. Today many so-called "socialist" or "social democratic" parties reject the Marxist idea of class struggle, of seizing political power by violent means, and the "dictatorship of the proletariat." Some of them have merged their socialism with Christian belief, forming so-called Christian socialist parties; others have become patriotic socialists, such as President Benes' "National Socialists" in Czechoslovakia (which should not be confused with Hitler's German National Socialist Party, the Nazis having used "socialism" mainly as a catchword to break up the German Social Democrat and Communist Parties). The British Labor Party, the most important moderate socialist party and separated from the Communists by a considerable gap, rejects all totalitarian theories and believes in a gradual development towards a socialist economy within a political democracy which would preserve civil liberties for its citizens. In America Norman Thomas' Socialist Party and the Socialist Parties of France, Italy and Scandinavia are pledged to similar programs.

Opponents of socialism maintain that the socialization of private enterprise would necessarily result in regimentation of all fields of life and would finally produce a totalitarian police-state. See MARXISM, COMMUNISM, BOLSHEVISM, STATE SOCIALISM.

Socialist Party. See SOCIALISM.

Socialist Unity Party. The Sozialistische Einheitspartei, or Social Unity Party, a merger of the Communist and Social Democratic parties in the Russian zone of Germany and the Russian sector of Berlin, which was formed April 22, 1946. Outside Berlin it numbered something over a million members, of which the Communists were a little less than half. In Berlin there were about 80,000 members, only one-fourth of whom were Social Democrats. Throughout Berlin the Social Democratic party continued to function. The new party was a kind of counterpart of the so-called "democratic front" friendly party coalitions sponsored by Russia in the other countries in eastern Europe under Soviet occupation, composed of left-wing parties which would co-operate with the Russians.

socialized medicine. A branch of social security providing medical services and hospitalization on the basis of compulsory insurance. It has been established in many European countries. Opposition to socialized medicine in the United States maintains that it would discontinue the private practice of doctors, make it impossible for patients to choose the doctors they trust most and would end private hospitals. The American Medical Association consequently has opposed its establishment, though many of its individual members have favored it. Voluntary medical insurance of individuals and groups, providing them with medical services and hospitalization, is growing in popularity in America. See SOCIAL SECURITY, PUBLIC HEALTH, BEVERIDGE PLAN.

Soil Conservation and Domestic Allotment Act. The United States federal law passed February 29, 1936 to accomplish the purposes of the Agricultural Adjustment Act (AAA) which had been invalidated by the Supreme Court. It sought to control agricultural production by promoting soil conservation through the voluntary limitation of the soil-depleting crops which were the chief contributors to farm surpluses.

Soil Conservation Service. A branch of the United States Department of Agriculture set up by the Soil Erosion Act of April 27, 1935. Its function is to promote the conservation and intelligent use of both soil and water by research, conservation projects and financial and technical aid to public or private agencies backing such projects.

solicitor. 1. The attorney for the city in many cities and towns in the United States. 2. British attorney to whom a client goes for legal services. If the client needs to go to court he may be represented in the inferior courts by the solicitor but in the higher courts the solicitor must secure for the client a barrister to represent him.

solicitor general. The official in the United States Department of Justice who represents the United States government in court in cases in which it is involved.

Solid Fuels Administration for War. An agency set up April 19, 1943, the administrator of which was the Secretary of the Interior. Its function was to co-ordinate the various government policies in regard to coal and other solid fuels—rationing and prices, industrial needs, transportation, and manpower.

Solid South. States in the South which habitually go Democratic in national elections: Alabama, Arkansas, Florida, Georgia, Louisiana, Mississippi, North Carolina, South Carolina, Tennessee, Texas, Virginia.

sound money. See MONEY.

South Manchurian Railway. That portion of the Chinese Eastern Railway from Changchun (now Hsinking) in central Manchuria south through Mukden to the sea at Port Arthur and Dairen, ceded by Russia to Japan by the Treaty of Portsmouth in 1905 after the Russo-Japanese War. It was on this railroad that the explosion occurred September 18, 1931 which the Japanese used as the pretext for seizing Manchuria and attacking China. The Russo-Chinese Treaty of 1945 merged it with the Chinese Eastern Railway as the Chinese Chanchung Railway, under joint Soviet-Chinese ownership and management.

Southern Slavs. Roughly the Slavic people who compose Yugoslavia— especially the Serbs, Croats, and Slovenes.

Southwest Power Administration. A United States agency set up September 1, 1943 to administer the electrical output of dams in Arkansas, Oklahoma, and Texas, making the power available to war plants and local governmental units.

sovereignty. A term used in international law, constitutional law, and political philosophy meaning the supreme power or governmental authority in a state. In international law sovereignty is generally held to be an essential qualification for full membership in the family of nations. A state which is not "sovereign," or independent from outside domination, is usually denied membership in international organizations. (India, White Russia and the Soviet Ukraine, none of them sovereign but subordinated to central governments in London or Moscow have nevertheless become members of the United Nations.) Mandates, trusteeships, protectorates, colonies, autonomous states and suzerainties are not sovereign states. No state, in fact, is completely free to exercise its sovereignty because the nations of the world have consented to be bound by a vast number of treaties, the general provisions of international law and the obligations of many international organizations. Unwillingness to yield more of this sovereignty for the sake of better co-operation between nations has done much to weaken international law and the prospects of world peace and prosperity.

Constitutional law and political philosophy deal rather with the meaning of sovereignty towards the subjects of a state than its power to conduct international relations. The term was introduced into political theory by Jean Bodin in 1576. Philosophers have defined sovereignty as the highest power in the state which makes and enforces laws and they consider that it is unlimited, and indivisible and inalienable. Sovereign power in a democracy lies with the people itself, who exercise it through representatives. The exercise of this power can be divided between different branches of government such as the executive, the legislative, and the judiciary as in the United States. In a constitutional parliamentary monarchy such as Britain, the British Dominions, Sweden, Norway, Holland, etc., the King is only "sovereign" by name, but sovereignty really resides in the people who exercise it through Parliament. In every constitutional system the rights and powers of the sovereign are strictly limited by the constitution. In absolute monarchies or dictatorships the sovereignty of the monarch or dictator is usually unlimited. Totalitarian states usually boast a constitution but in fact the sovereignty of their leader or leaders is unlimited and they declare that everything they do only expresses "the will of the people." See NATURAL LAW, TOTALITARIANISM, NAZISM, FASCISM, PARLIAMENTARY GOVERNMENT, SEPARATION OF POWERS.

Soviet. 1. Russian word for council, the first revolutionary organization of soldiers and workers in 1917. 2. Later applied to various parts of the Russian government. 3. Used outside Russia as an adjective to describe anything pertaining to communist Russia.

Soviet of Nationalities. See COUNCIL OF NATIONALITIES; SOVIET UNION, CONSTITUTION OF.

Soviet of the Union. See COUNCIL OF THE UNION; SOVIET UNION, CONSTITUTION OF.

soviet republics. The constituent republics which in part make up the Soviet Union. See SOVIET UNION, CONSTITUTION OF.

Soviet Union. The present federal state loosely referred to as Russia. Russia is in fact only a part of the Union, though the dominant part, in which are the fifteen other constituent soviet socialist republics: Armenian, Azerbaijan, Estonian, Georgian, Karelo-Finnish, Kazakh, Kirghiz, Latvian, Lithuanian, Moldavian, Tadzhik, Turkmenian, Ukrainian, Uzbek and White Russian. See SOVIET UNION, CONSTITUTION OF.

Soviet Union, Constitution of. The fundamental law of the Soviet Union, adopted on December 5, 1936. It provides for a federal state of sixteen republics governed by a Supreme Council (or Soviet). This Council consists of two houses: the Council (Soviet) of the Union, elected directly by the people, and the Council (Soviet) of Nationalities, elected by the Supreme Councils of the various republics. The two chambers jointly elect a Presidium or executive committee of 41 members which supervises the work of the cabinet (Council of People's Ministers). The cabinet and the highest judicial body, the Supreme Court, are also selected by the Supreme Council.

Spanish-American War. The war between the United States and Spain in 1898 in which the United States intervened on behalf of the people of Cuba in their struggle to gain their liberty from Spain. By it the United States gained Puerto Rico and the Philippines and a kind of protectorate over Cuba, and became recognized as a great power and one of the leading naval powers.

Spanish Civil War. Internal conflict in Spain from July, 1936 to the end of March, 1939. It began with a revolt of army officers against the established republican government, and ended with victory for the rebels, the extinction of the republic and the establishment of a dictatorship under Francisco Franco. Before it was over the rebels were receiving very important assistance from Italian and German troops, and the government, or Loyalists, as they were called, had been helped by a considerable number of Russians and some Americans and British. See FALANGE ESPAÑOL.

Spartacists. A German left-wing socialist group lead by Karl Liebknecht and Rosa Luxemburg which became the German communist party in December, 1918. The name came from the pseudonym Spartacus, which Liebknecht used when writing pamphlets attacking the war, the government and other Marxist groups. He and Rosa Luxemburg were in the forefront of a mass uprising against the German republican government in Berlin in January, 1919 and when it was put down by force, the two were arrested and murdered by the soldiers who were taking them to jail. After their death the term dropped out of use.

speaker. The title of the presiding officer of the House of Representatives, the House of Commons and various other legislative bodies in the English-speaking world. In Great Britain he becomes a non-party man and is an impartial referee in the debates. In the United States the speaker remains a partisan leader, in fact in years past was the dominant leader of the majority, directing the course of legislation and party policy in the House.

special assessment. A special tax levied against property because it has been benefited by some public improvement such as street paving.

special committee. A temporary committee of a legislative body set up for investigation or study and report on a specific problem.

special district. A unit of government set up to carry out a special function. Examples are sanitary districts, library districts, and mosquito abatement districts.

special legislation. Laws setting up or changing the government of specific municipalities or conferring public utility rights therein. Such legislation is now generally prohibited in state constitutions in the United States so that a state legislature must treat all cities of the same class in the same way.

special session. A session of a legislative body called for a special purpose at a time other than a regular time for convening.

specific duties. Import taxes based on a rate per unit such as so much per pound, per ton, or per yard. See AD VALOREM.

speech of acceptance. Speech in which a candidate, particularly a presidential candidate, accepts his party's nomination. In recent years they have been made at the nominating conventions.

speech from the throne. Speech by the British king to a new parliament. It is prepared by the cabinet and states the new cabinet's policies. In the Dominion Parliaments the speech is read by the Governor-General.

spellbinder. Speaker who holds his

listeners with his oratory rather than with his ideas.

sphere of influence. 1. An area in which an imperialistic power has received, by agreement with one or more other imperialistic powers, the right to exclusive economic exploitation. Political control remains in the hands of the local government. The classic example is the Anglo-Russian agreement of 1907 dividing Persia into a northern sphere for Russia and a southern sphere for Great Britain. 2. An unoccupied colonial area marked out by an imperialistic power for future colonization and annexation, the pretensions for which are conceded by one or more other powers. 3. In a non-technical sense the predominant influence which any great power tends to exert upon the smaller countries which are nearby.

sphere of interest. See SPHERE OF INFLUENCE.

splinter party. Small political party which has split off from a larger party.

split session. A provision found in a few states for a session of a legislative body formally divided into two parts separated by a recess of, for example, a month. In general the last part is devoted almost entirely to passing the bills presented during the first part of the session. The plan is an effort to secure more real consideration for bills and prevent the rushing through of a large number during the last hours of the session.

split ticket. A ballot on which the voter has voted for candidates of more than one party. See STRAIGHT TICKET.

spoils system. An American term for the system in which appointive public offices are considered as spoils to be distributed by the winning party among its faithful members. Until reduced by the extension of civil service after 1883, these jobs included practically all federal administrative

offices. A similar trend has occurred in state and local government.

sponsion. An agreement between representatives who are not fully authorized to conclude such agreement, or one in which authorized representatives exceed their powers. To be binding such an agreement must later be accepted by the parties themselves.

spy. A person who enters and moves about in enemy territory under false pretenses in time of war for the purpose of getting information of military value.

squadrism. The use of bands or squads armed with guns and clubs for the pursuit of economic and political objectives in Italy at the end of World War I. The squads developed most broadly in the areas where socialism was strongest; the ex-soldiers and patriot squads who fought against the socialists were the forerunners of the fascists.

squadristi. Members of Italian squads or armed bands. See SQUADRISM.

squatter. A person who settles on land and farms it without having the legal right to do so. In some cases such action was taken on land privately owned without knowledge or consent of the owner. More often it was on public land for which title might be later secured by fulfilling certain conditions. See POPULAR SOVEREIGNTY.

squatter sovereignty. See POPULAR SOVEREIGNTY.

S. Res. Senate Resolution.

S. S. See SCHUTZSTAFFEL.

Staatenbund (SHTAH-ten-boont). German term for a band or association of states which retain the essentials of their own sovereignty; a confederation.

"Stab in the Back" Speech. Speech of President Franklin D. Roosevelt to the graduating class at the University of Virginia in which he said of Italy's attack on France, "On this tenth day of June, 1940 the hand that held the dagger has struck it into the back of its neighbor." He promised aid to France and preparation of United States forces for defense.

stabilization fund. A fund established to stabilize a currency. In the United States a $2,000,000,000 fund was set up April 30, 1934 for the purpose of stabilizing foreign trade, for foreign dealings in gold and exchange, and for investment in government obligations.

Stahlhelm (SHTAHL-helm). Literally, "steel helmet." A German veterans organization after World War I. It was monarchist in tendency and undermined the republic; it was absorbed into the storm troops in September 1933.

stalwart. 1. The conservative wing of the Republican party during a serious split in the Hayes, Garfield and Arthur administrations (1877-85). 2. Any very dependable party member, especially on the conservative side.

Stalinist. A member of a communist party who believes that Generalissimo Stalin's interpretation of the communist doctrines of Marx and Lenin is the right one. Stalin (1879-) has at least nominally dropped the doctrine of "world-revolution" and believes that a stable, militarily and economically strong Soviet Russia, whose inhabitants are imbued with ardent patriotism, is the best way to serve the ideal of communism. Stalinist communists are usually contrasted with Trotskyite communists and their feuds equal in intensity those between communist and sharply anti-communist groups. See TROTSKYITE, MARXISM, COMMUNISM, WORLD-REVOLUTION, BOLSHEVISM.

stampede. The rush of political followers to a candidate who, it appears, is going to be successful, as at a party nominating convention.

stand. Term used in Great Britain meaning to run for office, as for a seat in the House of Commons.

standpatter. American slang term for a politician who prefers not to change his views, particularly a conservative Republican. Originally used to refer to the Republicans who "stood pat" on their high tariff policy.

standardized examination. An examination for public service so constructed, refined, and tested on persons of known competence that its results offer a dependable ranking, against which may be set the grade of a person taking the examination, with a reasonable assurance that his position in relation to the standard ranking measures his abilities for the position.

standing committee. A permanent committee of a legislative body, set up to handle a certain class of legislation.

Standing Orders of the House of Commons. The manual of procedure of that body.

Star Chamber. A room in Westminister Palace, London, with stars painted on its ceiling, which gave its name to a royal court which sat there. Composed of the king, his council and sometimes additional judges, the court dates from the 14th century, but later assumed arbitrary and despotic powers. It used torture to extract confessions and punished severely, including mutilations. It earned the special hatred of the Puritans under Charles I and was abolished by the Long Parliamant in 1641. The term has been applied since to any arbitrary court.

Star Spangled Banner, The. The national anthem of the United States, designated as such by law on March 3, 1931 though serving in that capacity since 1916 when President Wilson gave it that standing by executive order. The music is that of the old English drinking song, *To Anacreon In Heaven,* and the words were written by Francis Scott Key after watching the British bombardment of Ft. McHenry near Baltimore on the night of September 14, 1814. In the morning Key saw that "the flag was still there."

stare decisis (STAH-ree dee-SIE-sis). The legal doctrine that preceding decisions of the courts are law and thus that legal precedent should be followed in similar cases.

state. A politically organized community which is more or less independent of other states, located permanently in a definite territory. The term in its modern meaning came into use in the 15th and 16th centuries with the dissolution of the all-embracing medieval empire. The state is not identical with the nation, although nowadays we are accustomed to regard the nation-state (that is, a country in which one nation forms a state) as being normal. In a special sense, state means a subdivision of a federal republic, as one of the United States of America. These states, however, are not sovereign and independent and when they ratified the Constitution yielded some of their most important sovereign powers to the federal government. The term state is used in a similar sense in Mexico and Brazil. See SOVEREIGNTY, NATION, NATIONAL, REPUBLIC, STATE RIGHTS, STATISM, TOTALITARIANISM.

state aid. Financial assistance given by the government of one of the United States to a local government or authority, such as a grant to a city or a school district.

state banks. Banking institutions in the United States which operate under charters issued by a state government. They differ from national banks which are chartered by the federal government. The Federal Reserve Act of 1913 secured a higher standard for both state and national banks. By that Act national banks were compelled to become members of the Federal Reserve System, state banks could become members if they desired and could meet set requirements. It is still easier to obtain a charter for a state bank than for a national bank, and control over state banks is usually not too strict. The Banking Act of 1933 requires that all banks submit condition reports to the Comptroller of the Currency.

state church. A religious denomination which is an institution of a state. A state church is subordinated to the political government, which approves its organization, appoints its highest dignitaries and in many cases even controls its doctrines. In exchange the state may give the state church an exclusive position by prohibiting and persecuting all other religious denominations or a privileged position over the other tolerated churches.

The first Christian state church came into existence when the Emperor Constantine recognized Christianity in 313 and formed it into a state institution. The control of the Catholic Church by emperors, which occurred frequently during the late Roman Empire and under the medieval empire, is called "Caesaropapism." The Byzantine emperors in Constantinople completely dominated the Eastern Church, and the Russian Czars after Peter the Great acted as the heads of the Russian Orthodox Church. The Church of England has been a state church since Henry VIII broke with the Pope and placed himself at its head. King and parliament control its organization and appoint its archbishops and bishops. Mohammedanism was the state religion of the Turkish Empire and still is the state religion in present-day Egypt and Iraq. Until the surrender of Japan in 1945, Shintoism was the state religion of that country. The Roman Catholic Church has in many countries been a somewhat modified form of state church, with the state government giving it a privileged position in regard to such matters as education but sharing with the Pope its control over appointments to bishoprics. Spain under the Bourbons and under Franco has been a classic example of such an arrangement. The complete separation of church and state has been a cardinal principle in the United States.

State, Department of. One of the executive departments of the United States government set up July 27, 1789. It was in fact a continuation of the Department of Foreign Affairs existing since 1781 under the Articles of Confederation. Its function is to carry on negotiations and correspondence with foreign countries and suggest policies in the relations of the United States with those countries. It also performs certain domestic functions such as providing for the safekeeping of the great seal, laws and records, and publishing the *Statutes at Large*. The Secretary of State is the ranking member of the cabinet.

state liability. The principle that the state is liable for injury to an individual by an official acting in the line of his duties. This is generally accepted in France and Germany, for example, but not under Anglo-Saxon common law, which assumes that the state (sovereign) cannot be sued. This later view is also held by the governments of the various United States.

state of nature. See SOCIAL CONTRACT.

state of the union. See MESSAGE ON THE STATE OF THE UNION.

state police. Police of one of the United States, where they are usually not much more than state highway police, or the national police in foreign countries such as the Soviet Union.

state socialism. State ownership of the means of production, including industry, transportation, banking, etc., in the interest of a group of or the whole people. State socialism excludes the people from participating directly or through their representatives in the control of the economic system and can easily result in a rigidly controlled dictatorship by government officials and government-appointed industrial and financial managers. See SOCIALISM, MARXISM, COMMUNISM, TROTSKYITE, STALINIST.

state sovereignty. See STATES' RIGHTS.

statelessness. The condition of being without a state or legal nationality. See HEIMATLOS.

state's attorney. Term used in certain of the United States for the prosecuting attorney.

state's evidence. Testimony for the state, particularly by one of the accused in a trial, given in order to mitigate his own punishment.

states' rights. Governmental rights and powers possessed by the states of the United States. They are often invoked by special interest-groups in a state who feel hampered in their activities (economic or social) by the federal government.

In America the various sections of the country have differing economic interests, and this was one of the main reasons for the early conflict between the North and the South. In case the decisions of the federal government were unfavorable to one section, states' rights were invoked. The doctrine of nullification according to which a state has the right to veto (or to resist, or not to co-operate with) federal legislation or executive orders, arose in the early 19th century not only in the Southern States but also in New England. Massachusetts, for instance, refused to furnish troops for the War of 1812. The South was opposed to protective duties, which favored Northern industry but hit the Southern consumer and exporter. John C. Calhoun of South Carolina thereupon developed the doctrine of nullification which asserted that sovereignty lay not with the federal government but with the states and that the former was merely the agents of the associated states. As the states were still sovereign, they were also permitted to withdraw from the association, that is, to secede. This theory was challenged by the North and West and eventually the Civil War ensued. After the war the federal government's power gradually increased and the doctrines of states' rights and nullification seemed dead. But the states' rights argument has been used in questions concerning federal grants-in-aid to states, control over the water reserves of a river basin (the Colorado, Tennessee or Missouri) and similar controversies. Similar conflicts have occurred in other federal states such as Switzerland, Brazil and Canada. Western Australia frequently threatened to secede from the Australian Commonwealth, and the Canadian prairie provinces have been several times seriously dissatisfied with the Ottawa government. See SOVEREIGNTY, POPULAR SOVEREIGNTY, AUTONOMY, SEPARATISM, REGIONALISM.

static policy. A policy which resists change in the existing status quo.

statism. In French *étatisme*. A form of government in which the state, or central government, gradually enlarges its functions and finally controls most fields, such as economics, education, the press, radio, etc. Statism differs, however, from totalitarianism as it does not necessarily base itself on extremist, dynamic social philosophy and a political party rallying marching masses behind the government. It usually occurs in times of grave economic crises, when a strong emergency government is put at the helm of the state. However, such an emergency government usually tries to cling to its emergency powers, and add to them, even after the emergency is over. See STATE, TOTALITARIANISM.

status quo. An existing situation.

status quo ante. The situation existing before a certain event, particularly *status quo ante bellum*, the situation prevailing before the war.

statute. In a general sense any law issued and enforced by a sovereign. In a more technical sense, the term statute in America is confined to an act of a legislature. The signature of the President is necessary for an Act of Congress to become a statute (unless it has been passed over a president's veto). In the states the signature of the Governor has the same function. In Britain an Act of Parliament duly signed by the King becomes a statute. See POSITIVE LAW, SOVEREIGNTY, LAW.

Statutes at Large. The collection of laws and resolutions passed, treaties concluded and proclamations issued during the life of the different Congresses of the United States, published by the State Department.

statute of limitations. Also called limitation of action. A term in Anglo-American law which sets a time limit after which judicial relief cannot be sought in the courts. That is, a lawsuit must be started within a specified time after the occurrence of the act on which it is based.

Statute of Westminster. A law passed by the British parliament December 11, 1931 to legalize the resolutions of the imperial conferences of 1926 and 1930 and outline the legal relations of the parts of the British Commonwealth of Nations. It recognized the equality of Great Britain and the Dominions under the Crown.

statutory. Pertaining to or established by statute.

statutory law. See POSITIVE LAW.

statutory orders. British orders in council issued by the Crown under power granted by parliamentary statute. See ORDER IN COUNCIL.

Stavisky scandal. A financial scandal in France uncovered in December, 1933. Alexander Stavisky, director of the state pawnshop in Bayonne, had promoted the issue of millions of francs worth of worthless bonds. In the discovery of the crime, connections with other officials were uncovered. The affair was of national importance and resulted in part in the resignation of the cabinet. Stavisky fled to Switzerland and allegedly committed suicide.

steam roller. American slang term applied to any techniques, particularly those of a political convention or parliamentary body, by which the group in control pushes through what it wants, crushing all opposition.

steering committee. A committee in a legislative body composed of members of the majority party which facilitates the passage of legislation the party wants passed by managing the legislative machinery and mobilizing the necessary party votes.

sterling. Term applied to British currency, whose principal unit is the pound sterling. The name derives from a German silver coin called the Easterling which was introduced into England in the middle ages. When applied to silver the term also means pure or genuine.

sterling area. The countries whose currencies recently have been at one time or another tied to the British pound sterling; many of them followed Great Britain off the gold standard in 1931. In addition to the various countries of the British Empire, India and the British mandates (Canada is not always included), the other countries that have been included are Norway, Sweden and Denmark, Esthonia and Finland, France, Belgium and the Netherlands, Argentina, Bolivia, Brazil, Colombia and Paraguay, Egypt, Iraq, Iran and Turkey, and Portugal and Japan. More recently there has been a tendency to mean, in addition to the British Empire and India, the independent states and British mandates of the Near and Middle East, Egypt, Palestine, Transjordan, Turkey, Iraq and Iran. These countries particularly agreed during World War II that credits for their exports to Great Britain should be used only for purchases in Britain, and that their balances or credits in other currencies would be traded for British pounds sterling. This gave them only sterling with which to buy abroad, and thus in turn gave the British something of a trade monopoly in the area.

sterling bloc. The countries of the sterling area. See STERLING AREA.

Stern gang. A group of Zionists who advocate and use violence as a means of getting the British out of Palestine. Two of its members murdered Lord Moyne, the British Minister in the Middle East, late in 1944.

Stimson doctrine. The non-recognition theory advanced by Secretary of State Henry L. Stimson in notes to Japan and China on January 7, 1932. The notes stated that the United States did not intend to recognize any situation or agreement which might be brought about by means contrary to the obligations of the Kellogg Pact, or Pact of Paris, that is, by war.

storm troops. The brown shirted organization of the Nazis which furnished the strongarm squads which policed Nazi meetings and broke up those of other parties. The members formed a kind of political army which helped by forceful means to bring the Nazis to power and to keep them there. In German, *Sturmabteilung*.

straddle. 1. An equivocal, ambiguous position taken by a politician or a platform, in the hope of securing the backing of voters both for and against the issue in question. 2. To take such a position.

straight ticket. A vote for all the candidates of, and only the candidates of, a single party. On many party-column ballots such a vote may be cast by placing a single cross in a space at the top of the column.

Straits. The collective term used for the Bosphorus, the Sea of Marmora and the Dardanelles, which form a continuous waterway from the Black Sea to the Mediterranean Sea, dividing southeastern Europe from Asia. For centuries they have been of strategic importance and for a considerable time they were under some kind of international control, but in 1936 by the Montreux Convention Turkey was given the right to fortify the shores, though the passage of warships remained a matter of international agreement.

strategic material. Any raw material of strategic value, that is, of value in the prosecution of a war.

straw vote. An unofficial sample vote used to predict the outcome of a later official vote. Used particularly in recent years to forecast the United States national elections. The validity of such a straw vote depends on the extent to which the sample used in testing accurately reflects a cross-section of the voters.

Strength Through Joy. In German,

Kraft durch Freude. Nazi German workers' organization set up in 1933 to provide the workers with vacation trips, sports events, cultural and educational programs and indoctrination. It was planned in an effort to keep the workers happy and was a substitute for political activity.

Stresa Conference. A conference held at Stresa, Italy, April 11–14, 1935 attended by representatives of France, Great Britain, and Italy. It was agreed that they would continue to seek a security pact like Locarno for eastern Europe, would defend the independence of Austria, would back a treaty for using air forces to suppress aggression, and would stand together in the League of Nations on the matter of German remilitarization.

Stresa front. The combination of France, Great Britain, and Italy, united on the items agreed to at the Stresa Conference. See STRESA CONFERENCE.

strict construction. The literal interpretation of the Constitution, in which the powers of the federal government are considered as limited to those specifically granted in the document.

strike. A strike is the concerted stopping of work by a body of employees usually connected with a dispute between themselves and their employers. Employees by striking attempt to put pressure on the employers to accept or compromise on the terms demanded by the employees. Strikes may also have the purpose of a political demonstration.

A wild-cat strike is a spontaneous strike by a group of workers, or a local labor union that is not properly endorsed by the higher union officials or is in violation of an existing contract. A sit-down strike is a strike in which employees cease working but remain at their posts to make certain that other workers will not be substituted for them. A slow-down strike is a strike in which the workers deliberately reduce their customary rate of production. Picket lines are stationed around the entry to the place of employment during strikes in order (1) to inform those unaware that there is a strike; (2) persuade the workers to join the strike; (3) use moral persuasion or physicial force to prevent others from going to work. Maintenance workers are not regarded by strikers as strike-breakers. Several American states have laws against picketing, some regulate picketing. The U. S. Supreme Court decisions protected it as an exercise of the constitutional right of free speech. Physical violence by pickets is, however, illegal almost everywhere.

In the United States strikes are usually the result of controversies over wages (workers demand their increase or protest against their decrease), union recognition, sympathy with discharged workers or jurisdictional disputes. During a strike the strike committee endeavours to maintain the morale of the strikers through frequent meetings and pays them trade union benefits. Legal right to strike exists practically everywhere except in totalitarian countries. See COLLECTIVE BARGAINING; JURISDICTIONAL DISPUTE; GENERAL STRIKE.

Stuermer, Der. Probably the most fanatical and anti-Semitic of the Nazi newspapers, formerly published in Nuremberg by Julius Streicher.

stuff. See BALLOT BOX STUFFING.

stump. 1. Rostrum from which political speeches are made. Usually, though not always, thought of in connection with speeches by the candidates themselves. The term came from the frequent use of tree stumps for the purpose in the early days. 2. To deliver a series of political speeches on behalf of a candidate or issue during an election campaign.

Sturmabteilung. See STORM TROOPS.

subject. A person who owes allegiance to a state or especially to a sovereign. The term thus covers citizens, who have full rights within a state, and also nationals, who owe allegiance and receive protection without receiving the full privileges of citizenship.

Sublime Porte. The single gate to the palace grounds of the Turkish sultan, hence a title often given to the Turkish Empire or its government.

submarine warfare. The use of the submarine in war created a number of problems, in large part because the submarine was very effective against merchant ships. Ordinarily, because of its own vulnerability, a submarine cannot give such ships the usual warning given by other warships before attack, nor take off the passengers and crew according to the accepted rules of warfare. Numerous attempts were made at various conferences to limit the use of the submarine in war, but they had no apparent effect on Germany, the leading exponent of the use of submarines against merchant vessels.

subpoena. 1. An official summons to appear before a court or legislative body. Penalties are provided for refusal. 2. To summon officially a person to appear before a court or legislative body.

subsidize. To grant public funds to aid in promoting a private undertaking, the development of which is considered to be in the public interest.

subsidy. A grant of public funds to make possible the development of a private enterprise, the development of which is looked upon as being in the public interest.

subsistence homesteads. Homes with sufficient ground about them so that enough food can be raised to aid appreciably in a family's subsistence.

$25,000,000 were appropriated in the National Industrial Recovery Act for such homes for factory workers to reduce their dependence on industrial income.

subsoil jurisdiction. The right of control which a state possesses beneath the surface of the territory and territorial waters over which it exercises jurisdiction. This subsurface control extends down into the earth indefinitely and precludes the control there by any other state. The Anglo-Saxon theory is that private ownership of land similarly carries with it subsoil control; that is, for example, of mining rights, and this idea comes in conflict with a different rule in some countries, as Mexico, that subsoil resources belong to the state and do not follow ownership of the surface of land. See JURISDICTION, MARITIME LAW.

substantive law. That portion of the law which establishes and defines rights. See ADJECTIVE LAW.

subvention. Financial aid or subsidy.

succession. 1. The assumption of an office or rights, after such office or rights are no longer exercised by the person or state which had previously done so. See PARTIAL SUCCESSION, UNIVERSAL SUCCESSION. 2. The order in which persons assume an office if an incumbent cannot exercise that office. See PRESIDENTIAL SUCCESSION, ROYAL SUCCESSION.

Succession States. The new states which were formed from former states after World War I: Finland, Esthonia, Latvia, and Lithuania from Russia; Poland from Austria-Hungary, Germany, and Russia; and Czechoslovakia and Yugoslavia from Austria-Hungary.

Sudetenland. The semi-circular mountain fringe of western Czechoslovakia inhabited by about three million Germans. German irredentist pressure in this area was responsible for a series of crises culminating in the Munich settlement of 1938. See MUNICH ACCORD. After World War II the Czech government began to deport the Germans of the area to Germany.

Suez Canal. The canal between the Mediterranean and Red Seas, begun in 1859 under the direction of Ferdinand De Lesseps and completed in 1869, later enlarged. It is about 100 miles long. It is owned and operated by a private corporation in which the British Government has the largest interest. By the Treaty of Constantinople in 1888 the canal was neutralized by the major European powers.

suffrage. The privilege of voting. Although usually referred to as a right, it is not considered an inherent right in the sense of those in a bill of rights, but rather a right by legal enactment. There are still limitations on this right, the most common one being a minimum age.

suffragette. A woman who actively advocated woman's suffrage before it was generally enacted.

Sugar Act. Law of September 1, 1937 setting up special taxes on sugar and an import quota, and providing benefit payments to American producers for conforming to regulations.

sultan. Title of the ruler in certain Mohammedan countries, most important of which was Turkey. In that country the sultanate, or office of the sultan was abolished in 1922 with the establishment of the Turkish Republic.

summa potestas (SUM-uh poh-TES-tas). The supreme power within a state, that is, the part which rules as opposed to the part which is ruled.

summary. 1. Pertaining to a legal procedure in minor cases stripped of technicalities for the prompt securing of justice. 2. Pertaining to the administrative power to enforce a legal end without a warrant issued by a judge for such action.

sumptuary laws. Laws regulating such things as clothing and personal expenditures. They were designed originally to prohibit the lower classes from imitating the upper classes in their dress, etc. They were common in England from the 14th to 17th centuries, and also in New England, where they formed a part of the "blue laws."

sumptuary tax. A tax on commodities which are considered harmful in some respect, with the purpose of limiting their sale as well as raising revenue, as, for example, taxes on liquors.

Sunni. A member of the majority of Moslems who believe that the succession from Mohammed followed through Abu-Bekr, Omar, Othman, and Ali, who are considered the first four Caliphs. See SHIAH, who believe that Ali was the only legitimate successor.

superpower. A term applied to the greatest of the great powers—the United States, Great Britain, and the Soviet Union.

superstate. An international government with most or all of the attributes of a sovereign state, hence one that would deprive the present states of most of their powers of sovereignty. While it is obvious that such a powerful world organization would be much more able to suppress wars than any international organizations which have been seriously considered, no practical statesman has yet suggested an organization with this much power.

supervisor. The title given in a number of the United States to a member of a county board, usually called a commissioner, and in a few cases to a member of the township trustee board, usually called a trustee.

Supreme Council. See SUPREME SOVIET.

Supreme Court. In the United States the highest tribunal of the federal and most state governments. The federal Supreme Court has nine justices, appointed by the president with the consent of the Senate, and it is a court of appeal from lower federal courts, and from the highest state courts on matters within the federal jurisdiction. It also has original jurisdiction over cases in which a state is a party, or cases involving foreign diplomats and consuls. In some states, Supreme Court judges are elected.

Supreme Court of Judicature. The highest court in the regular British court system. It has two parts, a Court of Appeal and a High Court of Justice. The latter is a trial court with three divisions — Chancery, King's Bench and Probate, Divorce and Admiralty. Appeal may be taken to the Court of Appeal from the High Court of Justice. From the Court of Appeal a case may go to the House of Lords.

Supreme Soviet. The highest organ of the Russian government, primarily a legislative body consisting of two houses, the Soviet, or Council, of the Union, and the Soviet, or Council, of Nationalities.

Supreme War Council. 1. Title of an allied organ of co-operation and control in World Wars I and II. In the former case it was not set up until November 1917. 2. A Japanese advisory council to which important defense problems were referred by the emperor. It included the war and navy ministers and chiefs of staff, field marshals and fleet admirals, and certain specially appointed members.

surgeon general. The title given two United States federal officials, the head of the Public Health Service and the head of the Medical Department of the army.

surplus. Unexpended public monies.

surrogate. Title in some states for a person who performs the functions of a probate judge, that is probating wills, appointing guardians for minors, etc. The word means substitute.

surtax. A special tax added over and above the regular tax as, for example, the additional tax levied on the income tax in the United States.

suspension of arms. Agreement between military commanders for a temporary cessation of hostilities. The object of the agreement is only military and has no political aspects. This term is often used interchangeably with "armistice," though it is usually distinguished as being more local and on a smaller scale.

suspension of hostilities. A temporary cessation of fighting in a war.

suspension of rules. The temporary setting aside of the regular rules regarding the order of business in a parliamentary body to facilitate the passage of a matter of importance. Sometimes such a suspension requires an unusual majority, as two-thirds in the House of Representatives.

suspensive veto. A veto which temporarily prevents a bill from becoming a law and compels its reconsideration and re-passage by the legislative branch, sometimes by only a regular majority.

suzerain. A larger state which controls the foreign relations of a smaller, weaker state. See also VASSAL STATE. Usually in the vassal-suzerain relation only specified powers are enjoyed by the vassal and all residual powers are in the hands of the suzerain. See PROTECTORATE.

swaraj (swuh-RAHJ). Term used in India for complete self-government and independence from Great Britain.

swastika. The hooked cross, the symbol of German nazism. A very ancient design, found in many parts of the world and dating from the Bronze Age on.

sweat shop. The term used, either for a shop or home, where products, usually garments, are made up from stock provided by a contractor. Rates are paid for the work done, not for the time put in, and are very low. Legislation against such production has become general.

swing around the circle. A long speechmaking trip about the country by a presidential candidate.

Sykes-Picot Agreement. An agreement between Sir Mark Sykes for Great Britain and Georges Picot for France of May 16, 1916 outlining a settlement for the Turkish Arab lands. France was to receive the coastal strip of Syria and a sphere of influence east of it; Great Britain was to get lower Mesopotamia and a sphere of influence in upper Mesopotamia; and Palestine was to come under international control.

syndicalism. A revolutionary political movement which attempted to use labor unions to overthrow the state and parliamentary democracy by violence. In France and other Latin countries a distinction is made between revolutionary and reformist syndicalism, but in English-speaking countries only revolutionary syndicalism is meant by the term. Syndicalists played an important part in France and elsewhere in the 1890's and before the first World War, but gradually lost significance in the 1920's. They accepted some Marxist principles but regarded labor unions as the backbone of future society. They were opposed to participation in democratic elections and to attaining political power through the democratic process. Syndicalists were to a certain degree influenced by anarchists in believing that the future society should dispense with the state and with every political government. (Hence the expression: "anarcho-syndicalism.") They envisaged a society in which each industry would be managed by its workers forming so-called "syndicates" and these syndicates would work together harmoniously without any external compulsion. See CRIMINAL SYNDICALISM, MARXISM, SOCIALISM, COMMUNISM, WORLD REVOLUTION, CLASS STRUGGLE.

syndicate. In fascist Italy an organization of employers or employees in a particular industry. See SYNDICALISM.

T

table. To lay a measure on the table, that is, to postpone action on it for the time being.

Tacna-Arica Dispute. The dispute between Chile, Bolivia, and Peru over the ownership of the two provinces of Tacna and Arica. The trouble began when Chile took the provinces in 1884 after a war, promising that their future should be decided by plebiscite in ten years. This vote was not held. Bolivia and Peru tried to get the League of Nations to settle the problem but Chile blocked that. After attempts were made a few years later to arbitrate the dispute and hold a plebiscite, the matter was finally settled through the mediation of the United States in 1929 by giving Arica to Chile and Tacna to Peru.

Taft-Hartley Act. See LABOR-MANAGEMENT RELATIONS ACT, 1947.

Tammany Hall. Democratic political organization in New York City's Manhattan Island. It originated as a patriotic, democratic, fraternal organization in 1789, with branches in the different colonies. Its Indian titles still remain (see SACHEM). The height of its power was reached under Richard Croker in the 1890's.

Tanaka Memorial. A secret memorandum planning Japanese world conquest presented by Premier Tanaka to the emperor July 25, 1927. It advocated a policy of force, mapped the conquest via Manchuria of Mongolia, China, Asia, and Europe, indicated regret at Japan's signing the Nine-Power Treaty, considered war with Russia and the United States inevitable, discussed methods of penetration into Manchuria and Mongolia and the importance of economic controls. It was claimed a forgery by the Japanese when it leaked out in 1929.

tangible property. Immovable property such as land and things which have been made more or less part of the land such as buildings and fixed equipment.

tariff. A schedule, issued by a government, of duties on imported or exported commodities. Export duties virtually disappeared by the 20th century.

Duties on imports, formerly levied

for income, began to serve in the 16th and 17th centuries the task of excluding foreign goods, thereby protecting domestic production, helping to attain a so-called favorable balance of trade and to accumulate money and gold. These duties were called "protective duties," and "prohibitive duties" in cases where they were high enough to exclude certain goods. Protective tariffs have been found most effective in developing the industry of hitherto industrially backward countries. Economic nationalism favored so-called "infant industries." To establish a market for domestic goods it was necessary to keep out or restrict the importation of cheaper or better foreign products. This was the tariff policy of America and Germany in the 19th century. However, this practice has been continued, increasing profits of thoroughly "grown-up" industries both by getting rid of foreign competitors and maintaining a high price level at the same time that costs dropped with quantity production. Opponents of this system say that the consumer foots the bill. Believers in free trade demand that tariffs should be imposed only for revenue, holding that free trade would be beneficial to all in the long run as each nation would concentrate on the production of goods it is best fitted to produce. In 1913 there was a brief tendency toward free trade in the United States, but after World War I there was a reversion to protective duties. Depressions and the policy of "imperial preference" in the British Commonwealth of Nations together with an intense nationalism in Europe favored protective tariffs.

Tariffs have often been so drawn that they discriminated against the products of certain countries, creating international friction. An attempt at reducing such discrimination was the "most-favored-nation" clause, a provision inserted in commercial treaties mutually extending to each party the most favorable concessions granted other states. In the 1930's Cordell Hull inaugurated a United States policy of tariff reduction in the so-called reciprocal trade agreements program. See FREE TRADE, MERCANTILISM, LAISSEZ FAIRE, TAX, RECIPROCAL TRADE AGREEMENTS, QUOTA.

Tariff Commission. A non-partisan commission set up September 8, 1916 by Congress on the recommendation of President Wilson to gather information on tariff matters for the president or Congress. It is still in existence and did much of the work of preparation of the reciprocal trade agreements. The president may change rates on the recommendation of the Commission.

tariff for revenue only. See TARIFF.

tariff war. See TARIFF.

Tasmanian dodge. See CHAIN VOTING. Term used because the practice was allegedly brought from Tasmania.

TASS. (Telegrafnoe Agenstvo Soyusa Sovetskih) Union of Soviet Socialist Republic news agency.

tax. A compulsory money payment levied by the government for any or all of the following purposes: (1) to provide funds intended for the support of the government and for expenditures devoted to the common good (in modern nations taxes are the major source of income of the government); (2) to regulate the economy by using the tax as a barrier or penalty and thus to discourage or limit activities; (3) to redistribute the national income between the various sectors of the economy by giving one sector a smaller tax burden than another.

The most important kinds of taxes are as follows:

direct tax is any tax paid directly to

the government by the taxpayer or his agent.

indirect tax is one which is not paid directly to the government by the taxpayer but is paid indirectly; as, for example, as part of the price of goods bought in a retail store.

progressive tax is one in which the rate becomes larger with increases in the amount to be taxed. Most income taxes thus have higher rates on larger incomes.

regressive tax is one in which the actual rate of taxation decreases as the taxpayer's income increases, even though the nominal rate might be the same for both high income and low income groups. A sales tax on bread, for example, would place a greater burden on the poor than on the rich.

consumption tax is a tax based on the consumption of, or rather expenditure for, an article. It may serve the purpose of limiting consumption of an article, as alchoholic beverages, as well as to provide governmental revenue. Usually it is an indirect tax.

corporation tax is a tax which is paid directly by a corporation, such as undistributed profits tax, excess profits tax, processing tax, etc. Although the tax may be paid by the corporation this does not necessarily mean that the corporation will in all cases bear the burden of the tax. In many cases the tax is passed on to the consumer in the form of higher prices.

excess profits tax is a tax on corporate incomes in excess of a certain return on invested capital or an average normal income. In the United States it was used primarily as a war measure to prevent excessive war profits. In World War II the years 1936–39 served as the base for the average income and most of the time the tax was (after an exemption of $10,000) 95% with a possible 10% refund.

excise tax is a tax levied upon commodities produced within the country where they are consumed. Usually the tax is levied at some point in the production process.

income tax is a tax imposed on income (above a specific exemption) received by an individual. The exemption depends on the status of the individual in regard to dependents, charity contributions, etc. In modern society the income tax is usually progressive.

inheritance tax is a tax on income, wealth, and property which is inherited. It is usually progressive and attempts to prevent the accumulation of wealth from generation to generation by one who has not earned it.

luxury tax is a tax on commodities or services which are considered luxuries rather than necessities.

payroll tax is levied on the payroll of a corporation and is paid as a lump sum by the corporation.

personal property tax is levied on personal possessions such as jewels, silverware, furcoats, pianos, etc.

poll tax is a per capita tax which is usually a fixed amount regardless of income and wealth. In most southern states it has been used as a prerequisite to suffrage and thus, since the Negro or poor white man could not afford the poll tax, it was effective in denying him the right to vote. It has also made possible vote control, when the tax is paid for one individual by another who then dictates how the vote shall be cast.

sales tax is a tax on the selling price of an item. This is a regressive form of taxation.

transaction tax is levied on financial transactions above a given size.

See TARIFF, LAISSEZ FAIRE.

tax colony. An area in which persons establish part-time residences for the purpose of avoiding the higher tax rates on intangibles which prevail in the place in which such persons normally reside.

tax farming. The practice of turning tax collecting over to private persons who are permitted to keep a share of what is collected.

tax commission. A state commission which has the oversight of local taxation and administers the taxation of a non-local nature.

Tax Court of the United States. A kind of court set up in 1924 as the United States Board of Tax Appeals and given its present title by the Revenue Act of 1942. Its function is to settle cases between the Commissioner of Internal Revenue and persons paying processing taxes and taxes on excess profits derived from Army and Navy contracts. Decisions may be appealed to a United States Circuit Court of Appeals or the District of Columbia Court of Appeals and thence to the Supreme Court.

tax dodger. One who knowingly and, for a time, successfully, tries to avoid paying his full taxes.

tax duplicate. The list of taxable real property and its valuation.

tax exempt. Income or property upon which, for some reason or another, as for example, because devoted to educational or religious purposes, the owner does not have to pay the normal taxes.

taxation. The process of imposing upon a person a general contribution to the state to be used for the general governmental expenditures. See TAX.

taxation without representation. A complaint by the American colonies, set forth at the Stamp Act Congress, 1765. They said that Great Britain had no right to tax free Englishmen who could not have a representative voice in the British parliament because they lived in distant colonies rather than in the mother country.

taxing power. The governmental power to levy and collect taxes. It is obviously an essential power as no government can function without funds. It may also be used as a most important means toward other ends for, as the Supreme Court said in McCulloch v. Maryland, the power to tax involves the power to destroy.

Teapot Dome. A United States naval oil reserve transferred to the Interior Department by President Harding in 1921 and thereafter leased by Secretary Albert B. Fall to the oil man, Harry F. Sinclair, president of Mammoth Oil Company without competitive bidding. The Supreme Court affirmed the lower court decision that the lease was fraudulent and void. Sinclair was acquitted of the charge of conspiracy in April, 1928. The phrase Teapot Dome still implies, however, graft in government. See ELK HILLS.

technocracy. A state or government controlled by technology or technologists. Its advocates would do away with present political and economic systems as inadequate to provide the individual with a fair and sufficient share of the results of production, and substitute a system in which money wages are replaced by certificates of energy contributed and costs are figured in terms of shares of energy used in producing a given commodity.

Teheran Conference. A conference of Roosevelt, Stalin, and Churchill held at Teheran, Iran, for four days, concluding December 1, 1943, when the declaration was signed. The declaration expressed the common determination to work together in war and peace; the conclusion of common plans for the destruction of

Germany from east, west and south; the assurance that agreement would make an enduring peace; and the desire for the co-operation of all freedom-loving states, both large and small.

Telecommunications Union. See INTERNATIONAL TELECOMMUNICATIONS UNION.

teller. A person who counts votes or ballots in a parliamentary body or convention.

temperance movement. A movement advocating the prohibition of the sale and consumption of intoxicating beverages. Probably the most active and largest part of this movement has been the Women's Christian Temperance Union.

temporal power. Control based on political allegiance, as opposed to spiritual power wielded by the head of a religious organization.

temporary chairman. A preliminary chairman of a party convention who gives the "keynote" speech and presides until the committees and the permanent organization have been set up. He is usually nominated by the party committee and elected unanimously by the convention.

tender of good offices. An offer by a state not a party to a dispute to transmit suggestions for peaceful settlement, that is, to be a channel for such suggestions without offering any itself. See MEDIATION.

Tennessee Valley Authority. A Federal corporation set up by act of Congress May 18, 1933 to develop the Tennessee River and its tributaries in the interest of navigation, flood-control, and the generation of hydroelectric power. About twenty-five dams have been built providing electricity for local private use and the production of nitrates for agricultural and defense purposes. The Authority is subject in some of its operations to the Federal Power Commission.

tennis cabinet. Name given to the group of close friends and advisers of President Theodore Roosevelt, with some of whom he played tennis.

ten-ten-seven ratio. The approximate ratio of the tonnages of cruisers and smaller vessels reached at the London Naval Conference of 1930. The countries were the United States and Great Britain ten each to about seven for Japan. See LONDON NAVAL CONFERENCE, FIVE-FIVE-THREE RATIO.

tenure. 1. The act of holding office, either during good behavior or until replacement by another appointee in the case of a political appointment. 2. The right which a civil servant has to continue permanently in his post, subject to good behavior, after he has successfully completed a probationary period.

Tenure of Office Act. Title of two laws of 1820 and 1867. The former set the term of certain federal appointees at four years. The second provided that civil appointees should hold office until a subsequent appointment, that the cabinet should serve during the president's term and one extra month, and that suspensions of civil appointees while the Senate was not in session were to be brought before the Senate when it convened. When President Andrew Johnson dismissed Secretary of War E. M. Stanton, Congress impeached Johnson for breaking the 1867 law. Since Stanton had been appointed by President Lincoln, however, it was shown that Johnson had the right to remove him. This law was repealed in 1887.

territorial integrity. The right of a state to maintain its territory intact.

territorial waters. The waters over which is extended the jurisdiction of an adjacent state, such as the seas out to the three-mile limit, certain deep bays and a share of boundary rivers and lakes.

Territories and Island Possessions, Division of. A division of the Interior Department set up May 29, 1933. It administers, supervises, or maintains relations, as the case may be, with Alaska, Hawaii, Puerto Rico, and Jarvis, Baker, Howland, Canton, Enderbury, Virgin, and formerly, the Philippine Islands.

territory. 1. Any piece of land and its adjacent waters over which the jurisdiction of a state may be established. 2. An area inhabited by people that have a dependent status, such as the island possessions of the United States.

terrorist. A person who seeks to gain political ends by intimidation, threats, or acts of violence.

Teschen. A city and district just southeast of the junction of post-World War I Germany, Poland, and Czechoslovakia. As a part of the peace settlement the district was divided between Czechoslovakia and Poland. When Czechoslovakia was involved in the Munich crisis in 1938, Poland seized the Czech portion of the area.

Teutonic Knights. German knights who migrated eastward and settled along the eastern shore of the Baltic Sea during the 13th and 14th centuries. It was their path which Hitler said in *Mein Kampf* should be followed by modern Germany in its expansion to the east.

text. The actual wording, or complete and exact copy of an official document, as, for example, of a treaty.

thalweg (TAHL-vaykh). The middle of the main or navigable channel of a river. This is the customary line which serves as a boundary if the river flows between two countries. This boundary has the obvious advantage of dividing the navigation

facilities of the river and of being likely to change less than any other part of the river as the level rises and falls.

Thanksgiving Day. A legal holiday in the United States set aside by proclamations of the president and governors of the states as a day of giving thanks. For a long time it was the last Thursday in November; now it is by federal law set on the fourth Thursday, though a few states adhere to the last Thursday if there are five Thursdays in the month.

theocracy. A state or government in which the highest government officials are also the chief priests or highest dignitaries in the state religion.

"They Shall Not Pass." (Ils ne passeront pas) French slogan at Verdun in 1916. General Henri Pétain's reply to General de Castenau on being asked if Verdun should be abandoned to the Germans.

third degree. Continued grueling examination of a suspect imposed in the hope of wringing a confession from him.

third house. A term applied to the lobby at a parliamentary body. See LOBBY.

Third International. See INTERNATIONAL.

third party. A political party other than the two main parties in a two party system. The system continues to function as a two party system only so long as such other parties remain of relative insignificance.

Third Reich. Term applied to Germany under Adolf Hitler's Nazi rule, from January, 1933 to May, 1945. The Third Reich, or Third Empire, was supposed to be a continuation of German domination over Europe which according to the Nazis was exemplified in the First Reich (actually the old Holy Roman Empire) and the Second Reich under the rule of the Hohenzollern dynasty (1871–1918). Hitler never made a secret of his expansionist, imperialist, aggressive intentions. When named Chancellor by the senile President von Hindenburg, he set to work to dissolve all opposition and to unite Germany into a strong, totalitarian, militaristic Nazi state. The last free elections in March, 1933 gave the Nazis 44 and the allied Nationalist Party 8 percent of the vote. Thereupon Hitler dissolved the Communist Party and in a dramatic session of the Federal Assembly (Reichstag) virtually abolished the Weimar Republic, investing himself with dictatorial powers. Soon all other parties were dissolved, opposition leaders put in concentration camps and the Nazi state established. The abolition of all democratic institutions, the regimentation of labor unions, industry, agriculture, education, the Protestant Church and cultural institutions followed. The traditional autonomy of the federal states was abolished, the Nazi Party became all-powerful in the Reich, it's uniformed armies, the SA and SS (stormtroopers and élite guard) terrorized everybody and organized a totalitarian state. The Jews were ruthlessly persecuted. Hitler broke the obligations of the Versailles Treaty: i.e. by rearming Germany, remilitarizing the Rhineland, etc. Germany left the League of Nations and began an aggressive foreign policy interrupted by occasional "pacts" with the democracies who tried to "appease" Hitler, but these pacts were never fulfilled. Austria was forcefully annexed in March, 1938, the Czech Sudetenland in October 1938 by the Munich Accord, but this agreement was broken in March 1939, when Hitler occupied the whole of Bohemia and Moravia and marched into Prague, the capital of Czechoslovakia. Poland was the next on the list and Germany's attack against its peaceful eastern neighbor started World War II. Germany was aided by Fascist Italy and militaristic Japan, the other members of the so-called Axis, and by a few small satellites in Europe. By 1942 the Third Reich had conquered everything except Sweden and Switzerland from the English Channel to the Volga and the Caucasus, from the northernmost point of Europe to the Spanish frontier and to Egypt and Turkey, keeping a score of nations under its yoke. On May 1, 1945 Admiral Doenitz declared himself "Fuehrer" (Leader) announcing Hitler's death. A few days later Germany surrendered to the Allies, the Nazi Party was dissolved and the Third Reich came to an end. See NAZISM, FASCISM, TOTALITARIANISM, MILITARISM, IMPERIALISM, WEIMAR REPUBLIC, ARYAN, NORDIC, RACE, ANTI-SEMITISM, WAR CRIMES TRIALS.

Third Republic. The French governmental system from the fall of the Emperor Napoleon III in 1870 to the fall of France in 1940. It continued the republican principles of the First (1793–1804) and Second Republics (1848–51). It's constitution was drawn up in 1875 and provided for a president as head of state and for a bicameral parliament consisting of the Chamber of Deputies and the Senate, freely elected by all adult men. Although the slogans of the Great French Revolution: *Liberté, Égalité, Fraternité* (liberty, equality, fraternity) were still used by the Third Republic, it was in no way a revolutionary system, but essentially a middleclass, democratic parliamentary government, similar in many ways to those in Britain, Sweden, and Belgium. When, after the fall of France Marshal Pétain became Prime Minister, he declared the Third Republic was terminated and established the "French State." After the liberation of France in 1944, de Gaulle restored the laws of the Third Republic but proposed the drafting of a new constitution. In 1945 the people elected a Constituent Assembly, and after the first draft of a constitution was rejected, a second was accepted by the electorate on October 13, 1946, launching the Fourth Republic.

third term. The issue as to whether the president of the United States should serve more than two terms. Prior to the candidacy of Franklin D. Roosevelt in 1940 there had been no third-term candidate for the presidency.

thought control. The imperial Japanese system of hunting out, combatting and punishing ideas considered subversive by the militaristic government, or "dangerous thoughts." It was based on a series of laws, the latest of which were passed in 1925 and 1936.

three-fifths clause. The provision in Article I, Section 2, of the Constitution that slaves should be counted as three-fifths of their number when computing the population of the states for representation in Congress and for direct taxes levied by the federal government. This was one of the constitutional compromises. The southern states wanted to count the slaves for congressional representation and the northern states did not. The three-fifths arrangement resulted.

three-mile limit. The extent of the territorial jurisdiction of a state into the adjacent sea. The rule arose in the 18th century as a result of the theory that a state's jurisdiction should extend over the sea as far as the state could enforce its will, that is, as far as its cannon could shoot, which at that time was considered to be a marine league, or about three miles, usually measured from the low water mark. The rule crystalized to such an extent that the three-mile limit is maintained although the range of coastal guns is now of course much greater.

"Three principles of the people." A translation of a Chinese term made popular by Sun Yat-sen (1866–1925) to describe his political goals. In simplest form they are nationalism, democracy (social, industrial and political), and adequate degree of livelihood. They were to be achieved gradually and by a process of education, both of the leaders and of the people. They have formed the theoretical program of the Kuomintang, or Nationalist Party, but their application has been delayed by the war against Japan and fighting between the Kuomintang and the Communists. See KUOMINTANG.

ticket. A party's list of candidates.

timber-grabbing. The process of illegally buying public timber lands in excess of the maximum acreage permitted to a single individual by collusion with an apparent purchaser.

timocracy. Term for a state, described by Plato (428 BC–348 BC) in his *Republic*, directed by mere men of action for honor and glory, instead of one based on justice or property, for example.

"Tippecanoe and Tyler too." Whig slogan in the United States presidential campaign of 1840. The nickname of "Tippecanoe" was given William Henry Harrison, hero of the Indian battle on the Tippecanoe River in Indiana November 7, 1811. Tyler was the vice-presidential candidate. They were overwhelmingly elected, but Harrison died the month following his inauguration.

tissue ballot. A ballot made of tissue paper so that several deposited at once gave the appearance of one. Use of this fradulent voting went out with the adoption of official ballots.

"To the victors belong the spoils." Statement by William L. Marcy of New York in the Senate in 1832 as the basis for filling federal offices by the followers of Andrew Jackson when Jackson was made president. This practice of looking upon public office as the spoils of political battle has given it the title of the spoils system.

tonnage duty. A tax levied on ships on the basis of their tonnage.

"Too proud to fight." A jibe by his critics at President Wilson for his attitude in the early years of World War I. In a speech in Philadelphia May 10, 1915 he had referred to peace as a leading influence and had said that a man might be too proud to fight and a nation might be so right it did not have to use force to convince others it was right.

Torrens system. A system of land registration providing for a study of titles and claims and the issuing by a court of a certificate of title. Later changes in the title must be put on the register.

Tory. The name of the British Conservative Party before 1832 and still its nickname. Originally Tory was a nickname derived from a Catholic outlaw in Ireland, and was applied in 1677 to those who supported King James II in spite of his Catholic faith. Tories were opposed by Whigs, earlier a nickname for Scottish Presbyterians. In America persons loyal to King George III during the Revolution were called Tories. More recently the term has been used to describe the more extreme American conserva-

tives. See CONSERVATIVE, CONSERVATIVE PARTY, REACTIONARY.

totalitarian. A government which interferes with, affects and regulates every aspect of the life of the individual. This may be done in the interest of one person, of a small group, of a class or of the whole population. A totalitarian government does not tolerate the existence of groups or individuals within its jurisdiction which escape its control and which do not have a definite function in advancing its ends. Consequently totalitarian governments maintain themselves by a highly efficient secret police, various terroristic methods and by the elimination of all criticism and discussion concerning the nature and methods of government and the merits of their leaders. This usually leads to the complete suppression of free speech, free press and free assembly. An essential feature of totalitarianism is a regimented education and indoctrination of the youth from the earliest age in order to achieve a uniform political outlook often resulting in an almost religious fanaticism. The decline of the influence of the churches on individuals and the development of new techniques to mobilize masses of people for political ends have facilitated the emergence of totalitarian systems in the 20th century. The main totalitarian governments of our time have been Nazi Germany, Fascist Italy, and Soviet Russia. The government of Japan, though a ruthless militarist dictatorship, was not able to affect every sphere of the life of its citizens quite so completely. See NAZISM, FASCISM, COMMUNISM, DICTATORSHIP, ABSOLUTISM, COLLECTIVISM.

tourism. Tourist trade. Many of the countries of Europe have found this to be a lucrative source of income and actively promote it by government offices.

town. A small municipality. The New England town includes also the countryside in the vicinity. See SELECTMEN, TOWN MEETING, TOWNSHIP.

town meeting. A popular assembly in which all inhabitants of a town freely participate in the local government. It is one of the few surviving examples of direct democracy (in contrast to representative democracy) and is today still the dominant organ of local government in rural New England. See POPULAR SOVEREIGNTY.

Townsend Plan. In 1934 Dr. F. E. Townsend of California organized Old Age Revolving Pensions, Ltd., to create stabilized prosperity. He planned a Federal sales tax to finance payment of $200 monthly to any citizen over sixty who had never been convicted of a felony, on condition that recipients spend the entire amount within the country and abandon all gainful employment and other income. Local Townsend Clubs were formed to exert political pressure. Although the movement has lost much of its early influence, it still exists as an organization.

township. A subdivision of the county, found chiefly in the Middle West. Some, set up by Congress, are merely bases of land surveys, but usually the township is a unit of local government. Its officials are usually a board of trustees or supervisors and their functions were primarily the care of roads, schools, and the poor, though all of these now tend to be the care of larger units of government.

trade association. An organization of individuals or business firms engaged in a particular industry or trade. They are usually national in scope and devoted to promoting the industry by research, meetings and conventions, and the publication of trade journals, etc. Many are active lobbyists in Congress, state legislatures and local legislative bodies.

trade dollar. A United States silver coin a little larger than the regular silver dollar (420 grains instead of 412.5) struck off between 1873 and 1878 for use in trading in the Far East. Its size was made the same as that of the Mexican dollar which had been in use there for some time.

"Trade follows the flag." An imperialistic axiom used as one of the pretexts for seizing colonies, the idea being that after colonies are set up, trade from the colonizing country then follows.

trade-mark. One or more words or symbols which identify a particular brand of a product. Such a trade-mark is protected from copying by law, so that if a manufacturer produces a superior article another manufacturer cannot market an inferior substitute with the same label.

trade-name. 1. A word or words used as a trade-mark. 2. A word coined by a manufacturer as a name for his product and usually used as a trade-mark.

trade union. An organization of workers set up for the purpose of bettering their wages and other working conditions by means of collective rather than individual bargaining. See COLLECTIVE BARGAINING.

Trades Disputes Act. British law of 1927 making general strikes and picketing unlawful and protecting union members who refused to participate in an unlawful strike. It was passed in reaction to the general strike of 1926. See GENERAL STRIKE.

Trade Union Congress. An association of British trade unions organized in 1868. It has been influential in securing legislation favorable to the working classes and the union movement. It has a General Council, but it does not have the power over its member unions similar to that exercised in the United States by the American Federation of Labor or the Congress of Industrial Organizations. Its early political activity has been taken over by the Labor Party.

transfer of populations. The movement of a minority out of a country to its own national home in an effort to eliminate international friction and irredentism. The most successful case was the exchange of Greeks and Turks carried on under the auspices of the League of Nations in 1923 and after. After World War II other transfers of populations were carried out, particularly of Germans from Poland and Czechoslovakia to Germany.

transit duties. Taxes collected on goods passing through a port or country.

Transocean News Agency. Nazi German official news bureau, for disseminating propaganda. Headed in the United States by Manfred Zapp.

Transylvania. A territory between Hungary and Romania, to both of which it has belonged in recent years. It is inhabited by people of both Hungarian and Romanian ancestry, and has long been a bone of contention between the two countries. Hitler divided it between them, but this was not considered a satisfactory settlement by either country. Following World War II it was given to Romania.

treason. A forceful attack against one's own state or sovereign, or as the United States Constitution says, adhering to the enemies of one's own state or "giving them aid and comfort," (Article III, Section 3).

treasurer. A state or county officer who

receives, is responsible for, and disburses the appropriate public funds.

Treasurer of the United States. An official in the Treasury Department whose function it is to receive and care for the public money in the Treasury and the Federal Reserve Banks.

Treasury Bench. The front bench in the House of Commons, occupied by the cabinet. It is so-called because the treasury is the oldest British department and because the prime minister usually takes the office of First Lord of the Treasury as a cabinet post, it having no real departmental functions, thus leaving him free to co-ordinate the work of the other ministers. Real financial leadership is furnished by the Chancellor of the Exchequer. See CHANCELLOR OF THE EXCHEQUER.

treasury certificate. A short-term note issued by the United States treasury to provide funds until taxes are collected.

Treasury, Department of the. The financial department of the federal government, set up September 2, 1789. It administers the coinage, printing, handling, and borrowing of money, as well as including special functions like the secret service.

treasury note. Note issued by the United States treasury under the Sherman Silver Purchase Act of July 14, 1890, in payment for silver purchased. They have largely been replaced by the silver certificates.

treaty. A term often used for any international agreement. More specifically it is usually applied to international agreements of an important, broad political nature. See CONVENTION.

treaty ports. Several dozen cities in the Far East, particularly in China, in which by treaty foreigners were given the right to reside and carry on business. With certain exceptions foreigners were restricted to the vicinity of these cities, which in time numbered river ports and interior cities as well as sea-ports. These treaty ports were under Chinese jurisdiction in contrast to the areas under foreign administration — the "settlements" and "concessions." American and British special rights in regard to such ports, were renounced in separate treaties with China of January 11, 1943 which ended the extraterritorial rights there of Britain and the United States. See INTERNATIONAL SETTLEMENT, EXTRATERRITORIALITY.

treaty registration. The entering of a treaty on official records, as with the League of Nations. In the latter case treaties were then published.

trial. The process by which a court of law hears and decides cases brought before it. The trial is preceded by various prescribed legal steps such as summons, and due notice. Trials are usually held in public. According to Anglo-American law and to the practice of most democratic countries it is essential that a fair trial should give full opportunity to both sides to present evidence and to argue their case. A trial may be a trial by judge or a trial by judge and jury. See JURY, COMMON LAW, MILITARY LAW.

trial balloon. A suggestion for political action brought forward tentatively to test the direction of the winds of public opinion.

trial by jury. See TRIAL, JURY, COMMON LAW.

trial jury. The group of disinterested people, as part of the trial procedure, who determine the facts in the case. To be distinguished from a grand jury. See GRAND JURY, JURY.

Trianon, Treaty of. The peace treaty with Hungary after World War I, signed June 4, 1920. In addition to a reparations demand and the limitation of the army to 35,000, Hungary lost small bits of territory to Austria and Yugoslavia and large areas to Czechoslovakia and Romania. These areas were largely non-Hungarian, but included many Hungarians nevertheless.

tribunal. A term used for a body which is empowered to hand down decisions, that is, a court or a board of arbitrators.

Tribunal for the Defense of the State. A special Italian fascist court to hear cases of attempts on the king or Mussolini or of attempts to undermine the regime or to bring back political parties. The court was composed of officers of the armed forces and fascist militia and its processes and the execution of its sentences followed the lines of a court martial.

tribune. The rostrum from which a speaker carries on debate in the French Chamber of Deputies. It is in front of, and below, the desk of the president of the chamber.

tributary state. A small weak state which makes payments to a larger, stronger state as evidence of the latter's domination or as a price for its protection. Often the states under suzerainty of the Turkish Empire were designated "vassal, tributary states." See VASSAL STATE.

tribute. A payment given for protection or claimed as of right. See TRIBUTARY STATE.

tricolor. The flag of the French Republic, which has three broad vertical stripes—red, white, and blue.

tripartite. Consisting of three parties or signatories, as a treaty.

Triple Alliance. The military combination of Germany, Austria-Hungary, and Italy, which existed from 1882 to 1914.

Triple Entente. The military relationship of Great Britain, France, and

Russia, which was established by 1914 and which continued until Russia withdrew from World War I in 1917.

Trojan horse. An undermining group or activity set in motion by a state within an enemy or potential enemy state. The term comes from the great wooden horse filled with soldiers which the Greeks left before Troy. The horse was drawn into the city and at night the hidden troops let themselves out, opened the city gates, and let in their returning fellow-Greeks who captured the city.

Trotskyite. Follower of Leon Trotsky (1879–1940), Russian communist leader and organizer of the Red Army. Even before the death of Lenin, the founder of Soviet Russia and head of the Russian Communist Party, Trotsky clashed with Stalin. When Lenin died, Stalin succeeded him and Trotsky gradually lost his leading position in the Party from which he was finally expelled in 1927. From then on he lived in exile and was assassinated in Mexico City in 1940. In exile Trotsky violently attacked Stalin and "Stalinism," which to his mind was a betrayal and perversion of the original ideas of Marx and Lenin. His followers (who are usually dissident members of Communist Parties and are scattered all over the world, but nowhere form sizable groups) believe that Soviet Russia is neither communist nor socialist, but is ruled by an imperialistic, bureaucratic dictatorship. Trotskyites desire a "permanent revolution" and internationalism. In their relentless attacks against the Soviet Union they often join hands with conservatives and capitalists. See STALINIST, MARXISM, COMMUNISM, WORLD REVOLUTION, BOLSHEVISM.

truant officer. An officer of the school board whose function is to compel attendance of school children.

truce. A temporary suspension of hostilities.

Truman Doctrine. A United States policy ennunciated by President Truman on March 12, 1947, that the United States would extend economic and expert assistance to Greece and Turkey and perhaps to other countries in an effort to limit the spread of communism.

trust. 1. A combination of corporations in the same line or allied lines organized for the purpose of controlling prices. 2. A public responsibility or office.

trust buster. One who ardently advocated breaking up trusts. Used especially of Theodore Roosevelt.

trusteeship. The principle that a great power or an international agency should hold a backward area in trust for the inhabitants and not as a colony. The idea implies the progressive development of the territory to ultimate independence. See UNITED NATIONS, TRUSTEESHIP COUNCIL.

Trusteeship Council. An organ of the United Nations whose function is to supervise the administration of trust territories, particularly through reports from the administering states, petitions from the inhabitants, and periodic visits to the trust territories. It is composed of an equal number of states which administer such territories and states which do not, including in one category or the other the five great powers in the United Nations. See UNITED NATIONS, TRUST TERRITORY.

trust territory. Any territory, either former enemy territory, former colony or former mandate, turned over for administration and supervision under the international trusteeship system of the United Nations. The objective of the system is the welfare of the inhabitants, their development toward self-government and the encouragement in such territories of respect for human rights and freedoms.

Turco-Italian War. An imperialistic war by Italy on Turkey. Italy sent an ultimatum to the Turks September 28, 1911 and the war started at once. It ended October 18, 1912 with Italy securing Tripoli and the Dodecanese Islands off the coast of Turkey. She did not entirely pacify the inland tribes in Tripoli, however, until 1929.

tutelage. The relationship of a large guardian or protecting state to a smaller dependent state. The term carries with it the implication that the degree of control by the large state is permanent and that the small state is kept in continued subservience. See TRUSTEESHIP.

T. V. A. See TENNESSEE VALLEY AUTHORITY.

twelve-mile limit. A proposed extension of the three-mile limit which the United States wanted for the enforcement of prohibition. After some negotiation the United States did conclude in 1924 several treaties permitting such extension to a distance of one-hour's sailing.

Twenty-five Points. The Nazi (National Socialist German Workers Party) party program brought out at Munich February 24, 1920. They included demands for the union of all Germans, national equality, abolition of the peace treaties, colonies, exclusion of Jews from citizenship, abolition of unearned income, confiscation of war profits, nationalization of trusts, provisions for old age and a middle class, land reform, a Germanic legal system, better health and education, a national army, a German press, re-

ligious liberty within the limits of the good of the German race, and a strong, centralized government.

twenty-four hour rule. The rule of international law that a belligerent warship may not remain in a neutral port more than twenty-four hours.

Twenty-one Demands. A series of demands presented to China by Japan in 1915. They would have made China a virtual protectorate with all real political, economic, and military control in the hands of Japan.

twisting the lion's tail. Term for an action calculated to exasperate the British.

two-ocean navy. A United States policy of an adequate navy in both the Atlantic and Pacific oceans.

two-party system. The relationship of the political parties in a state where two parties traditionally command the great majority of votes and hence the great majority of representatives in the national legislative bodies, with a result that usually one party or the other commands a clear majority in those bodies. See MULTI-PARTY SYSTEM.

two-power navy. British policy prior to World War I to try to maintain a navy as big as the next two biggest.

two-thirds rule. The rule of the Democratic party, adopted in 1832, that a two-thirds majority was required for a nomination in the national party convention. Abolished in 1936 in favor of a simple majority. See UNIT RULE.

tyrannicide. Assassination of a tyrant.

tyranny. 1. The exercise of absolute and arbitrary power. 2. A government in which such power is exercised.

U

Ual Ual Dispute. A dispute between Italy and Ethiopia resulting from an armed clash by patrols at Ual Ual, near the debated southern Ethiopian-Italian Somaliland frontier December 5, 1934. In spite of Italian objections the matter was turned over to arbitrators, while Mussolini prepared for invasion. The arbitrators unanimously found on September 3, 1935, that blame could be laid on neither side, as each group thought it was on its own territory. This nullified Mussolini's claims, but he invaded anyway a month later.

U.K. See UNITED KINGDOM.

ultimate destination. Term applied to the destination of goods being shipped to a belligerent state, even though they are shipped by way of a neutral state or port. Such goods can be seized by another belligerent power before reaching their first, or neutral, destination if they have the other characteristics of contraband. See CONTINUOUS VOYAGE; CONTRABAND.

ultimatum. The last offer or demand made by a state in an international controversy. If not met, the next step usually has been the beginning of hostilities.

ultra vires. Beyond or exceeding the legal power of a person or agency.

Un-American Activities Committee. See DIES COMMITTEE.

unanimity, rule of. The principle that all states must assent to an inter-national agreement before they are bound by it. This principle flows from the corollary of sovereignty that a state is bound only by its own consent. It is being limited in many international agreements.

unanimous consent. Agreement with no dissenting voice, which is often required for changing the regular order of business of a parliamentary body.

U.N.C.I.O. See SAN FRANCISCO CONFERENCE.

Uncle Sam. Popular name for the United States, apparently arising from the initials U. S. It came into use during the War of 1812. The cartoon characterization is of a tall be-whiskered gentleman with high hat, red and white striped trousers, and a blue starred tailcoat.

unconstitutional. Not in accordance with the Constitution. In the United States the powers of government are set forth in federal and state constitutions. If a person believes a law passed exceeds the powers granted the government, he may take the question to the appropriate court. If his contention is upheld, the law is called unconstitutional and becomes unenforceable.

unconditional surrender. A military capitulation in which the terms are entirely at the disposition of the victorious commander, as opposed to one in which the defeated commander capitulates on certain conditions, such as retaining certain territory.

undeclared war. A war whose beginning is not marked by a formal declaration.

underground. Political opposition groups unable or unwilling to come out in the open are called "underground opposition," "underground parties" or briefly "the underground." Communist parties in countries where their activities were illegal, carried on such organizations. During World War II every German-occupied country developed an underground carrying on illegal leaflet, press, and radio propaganda, passive resistance, hiding people sought by the Germans, and in many cases even organizing armed resistance. The French underground was in constant touch with de Gaulle's "Fighting French" organization in London and later on with General Eisenhower's headquarters. Known as the French Forces of the Interior (FFI) it struck together with the invading American and British troups after V-day following closely orders from Allied headquarters. Belgium, Holland, Norway, Denmark, and other countries also developed effective underground movements. Organized armed resistance was shown by the Polish underground army, by General Mihailovich and Marshal Tito's rival guerilla forces in Yugoslavia, by the EAM in Greece. Underground opposition in wartime is also called "resistance."

underground railway. A system which flourished in the United States before the Civil War by which slaves were helped in escaping from the boundaries of slave territory across free states to Canada. The slaves were usually hidden during the day and then transported farther north during the night. It grew up in opposition to the fugitive slave laws, and was most active during the 1850's.

under-secretary. The person in an administrative department or ministry who ranks immediately below the secretary or minister who is the head of the department. In Great Britain there are two—a parliamentary under-secretary, an assistant who is a member of parliament, and a permanent under-secretary, who is the highest civil servant in the ministry.

undistributed profits tax. A federal tax, instituted in 1937, on corporate profits which were not distributed in the form of dividends.

unearned income. Income received from investments rather than from services. A distinction set up for income tax purposes. See EARNED INCOME.

unearned increment. An increase in the value of property due to some cause other than the efforts or improvements by the owner, such as the building of a new transportation line nearby.

unemployment insurance. See SOCIAL SECURITY, BEVERIDGE PLAN.

U.N.E.S.C.O. See UNITED NATIONS EDUCATIONAL, SCIENTIFIC AND CULTURAL ORGANIZATION.

unfair competition. The use of methods declared legally unfair in business, which would give a person or corporation an advantage over competitors. To ensure free competition in a general sense a large number of conditions have to be present. Legislation has tried from time to time during recent generations to protect free competition from the rise of all-powerful, large-sized business corporations, and from combinations among these intended to restrain trade, but without very much effect. "Unfair competition" nowadays is generally used in a narrow technical sense applying to methods of advertising which willfully deceive the public, for instance by devising trademarks resembling those of other well-known products; publicizing false data as to the excellence of a product, or slanderous information concerning the product of a competitor. See RESTRAINT OF TRADE, LAISSEZ FAIRE.

unicameral. Composed of only one house or chamber. Used in connection with a legislative body. See BICAMERAL.

uniform legislation. State laws which are essentially identical throughout the various United States. There is a national commission appointed by the states which draws up and recommends such laws in fields in which the federal government does not have the power to act but where uniformity in the different states is advisable. Most of the states have adopted the same laws, for example, on negotiable instruments.

unincorporated territories. Territories belonging to the United States looked upon as dependencies but not part of the country itself. The inhabitants cannot claim all the rights of the Constitution, and taxes and jury trials have varied from the practice in the United States. The inhabitants also are nationals rather than citizens of the United States. Such territories include the Philippine Islands (until 1946), Puerto Rico, the Panama Canal Zone, the Virgin Islands, and scattered islands in the Pacific.

union. A combination of two or more states connected by some common tie. See REAL UNION; PERSONAL UNION; CUSTOMS UNION.

Union Calendar. The calendar of the Whole House on the State of the Union in the United States of Representatives. See HOUSE CALENDARS.

Union Central Executive Committee. The executive committee of the Union Congress of Soviets of the U. S. S. R. prior to 1936. This body was omitted from the 1936 constitution, the presidium acting as the executive committee of the new Supreme Council.

Union Congress of Soviets. Supreme governing body of the Soviet Union under the constitution of 1923. See SUPREME SOVIET; SOVIET UNION, CONSTITUTION OF.

Union Council of Commissars. See COUNCIL OF PEOPLE'S MINISTERS; SOVIET UNION, CONSTITUTION OF.

Union of Economic Interests. French union of trade associations.

Union Jack. The British national flag, authorized in 1707 after the union of England, Scotland and Ireland. It contains the English cross of St. George, Scottish cross of St. Andrew and Irish cross of St. Patrick.

Union Now. Organization founded in 1939 favoring a strong international government somewhat on the federal model of the United States to be composed of countries favoring democracy. The principles were originally outlined in a book by the same name by Clarence Streit.

Unionist Party. The British Conservative Party. See CONSERVATIVE PARTY.

unit rule. The former rule of the Democratic national conventions that the votes of the states must all be cast as a unit for one candidate. Exceptions were made after 1912 in cases where the delegates came from districts within the states and the whole rule was dropped in 1940. See also TWO-THIRDS RULE.

unitary government. A government in which the local political units are subordinate subdivisions of the national government and are not more or less independent of it in certain functions, as is the case in a federal system. See also CENTRALIZATION.

Unitas. The name of a new standard

international monetary unit proposed in the American plan presented by Harry D. White of the United States Treasury Department prior to the Bretton Woods agreements.

united front. A union of diverse political parties, elements, or states combined for a purpose, usually to combat a common threat.

United Kingdom. Term for Great Britain, that is, England, Scotland, Wales plus Northern Ireland.

United Mothers of America. A highly nationalistic, ultra-conservative, isolationist organization which developed in the late 1930's.

United Nations. The nations united in fighting the Axis in World War II and the name for the international organization they later formed. On January 1. 1942 the twenty-six nations at war with one or more of the Axis Powers pledged all their resources, no separate armistice or peace, and subscribed to the principles of the Atlantic Charter. At President Franklin D. Roosevelt's suggestion they were officially designated as the United Nations, and the pledge they signed is known as "Declaration by the United Nations." The nations signing were:

Australia	India
Belgium	Luxembourg
Canada	Netherlands
China	New Zealand
Costa Rica	Nicaragua
Cuba	Norway
Czechoslovakia	Panama
Dominican	Poland
Republic	Salvador
Great Britain	South Africa
Greece	Union of Socialist
Guatemala	Soviet Republics
Haiti	United States
Honduras	Yugoslavia

At intervals the Declaration was signed by additional nations. Among them were:

Philippines	Iraq
Mexico	Free French
Ethiopia	Free Danes

Nations who signed the United Nations Charter in addition to the above were:

Argentina	Liberia
Bolivia	Paraguay
Brazil	Peru
Chile	Saudi Arabia
Colombia	Syria
Denmark	Turkey
Ecuador	Uruguay
Egypt	Ukraine
France	Venezuela
Iran	White Russia
Lebanon	

In August, 1946 Afghanistan, Iceland and Sweden were admitted to membership.

See UNITED NATIONS CHARTER.

United Nations Charter. The constitution for the international organization established at the United Nations Conference held at San Francisco April 25–June 26, 1945. It was preceded by, and to a considerable extent was based upon, the drafts for an organization completed at the Dumbarton Oaks Conferences the preceding autumn. The organization in many ways resembles somewhat the structure of the League of Nations. There is a General Assembly, composed of all of the members, which meets annually and in special session to discuss and make recommendations on the whole field of international relations. The Security Council is a smaller body composed of eleven members, and the General Assembly is not permitted to handle questions under discussion by the Security Council. A Secretariat and an International Court of Justice are also provided for in the Charter as well as an Economic and Social Council which has oversight of matters in its special field, and a series of subsidiary organizations which developed later such as U.N.E.S.C.O., F.A.O., and P.I.C.A.O.

The Charter became effective on October 24, 1945 with the deposit of the twenty-ninth instrument of ratification (that of the U.S.S.R.). The United States Secretary of State, James F. Byrnes, then signed the protocol formally attesting that the Charter was in force. The first meeting of the Assembly was held in London in January of 1946 and set up the Security Council and took the preliminary steps in its own organization. The second part of the first session of the Assembly was held in New York in December of 1946 at which it was decided to establish the permanent site of the organization in New York City. See UNITED NATIONS; LEAGUE OF NATIONS; INTERNATIONAL ORGANIZATION; SECURITY COUNCIL; INTERNATIONAL COURT OF JUSTICE; UNITED NATIONS CHARTER (APPENDIX).

United Nations Educational, Scientific and Cultural Organization. One of the specialized international agencies related to the United Nations. Its function is to promote educational and scientific conferences and serve as a kind of international clearing house for educational, scientific and cultural information, ideas and skills, on the assumption that broader international understanding is basic to world peace. Its policy-making body, made up of representatives of all the member states is called the General Conference. Its program is carried out by an Executive Board of nineteen members.

United Nations Interim Commission on Food and Agriculture. A temporary organization of the United Nations to find means of aiding agricultural production and distribution and improving the standards of nutrition, and to set up a permanent organization for handling problems of food

and agriculture. This temporary organization was set up July 15, 1943 pursuant to a resolution of the United Nations Conference on Food and Agriculture at Hot Springs, Virginia, May 18–June 3, 1943.

United Nations Relief and Rehabilitation Administration. The United Nations organization for relief and rehabilitation in liberated areas. Its function was to provide food, clothing, housing, and medical service, to aid in the re-establishment of business and industry, and to handle former prisoners and exiles returning home. It was established November 9, 1943 by an international agreement signed at the White House and terminated in 1947.

United States Census Bureau. See BUREAU OF THE CENSUS.

United States, Constitution of the. The fundamental law of the United States of America. It was drawn up in 1787 after an unsuccessful attempt of the states to organize themselves under the Articles of Confederation. It outlined the framework and powers of the federal government. The framework includes a two house Congress, a president as chief executive, and a supreme and inferior court system, among which are divided various powers. The scope of federal powers is outlined as powers of the Congress, and other powers are reserved to the states and the people. Amendments, of which the first ten are referred to as the bill of rights, have been added. They have the validity of the original document. See AMENDMENT.

United States Court for China. A federal court set up in China in 1906 particularly to hear appeals from the consular courts. Decisions were appealed from it to the Circuit Court of Appeals at San Francisco. See EXTRATERRITORIALITY.

United States Employment Service

United States Employment Service. An employment agency operated by the federal government. It was set up in the Labor Department in 1918, abolished for a time, re-established, placed under the Social Security Board in 1939, and under the War Manpower Commission September 17, 1942.

United States Government Manual. A publication first put out by the Public Inquiries Division of the Special Services Bureau of the Office of War Information. It includes all the federal governmental agencies and bodies with their functions, organization, data on establishment and most important officers.

United States Military Academy. The national college for training army officers located at West Point, New York, established in 1802. A four-year course leads to a commission of second lieutenant in the army. Most of the high army leaders are, and have been, graduates. Qualified young men are recommended by the president, senators and congressmen. Three may come from each congressional district and six from each state at large with others from the territories, District of Columbia, and the Canal Zone. A further 172 may be nominated from the country at large from sons of veterans and certain military schools, and 180 from the regular army.

United States Naval Academy. The national naval college at Annapolis, Maryland, established 1845. A four-year course leads to a commission as ensign in the navy. Four candidates may be named by each senator or representative, with others from the territories, sons of naval officers or men, and from the navy enlisted men.

United States of Europe. A hitherto unsuccessful plan for a regional federation of all the European states. Some advocates would leave out Great Britain and the Soviet Union.

United States Reports. The series of volumes of decisions and opinions of the United States Supreme Court.

United States Shipping Board. See SHIPPING BOARD.

"United we stand, divided we fall." Phrase taken from *The Flag of Our Union*, by George Pope Morris. The idea originally occurred, apparently, in *Liberty Song of 1768* by John Dickinson. State motto adopted by Kentucky in 1792.

Universal Postal Union. An international organization for the facilitation of the transmission of mail from one country to another. It sets common standards of rates and weight, and helps in the settlement of accounts. It was set up by treaty October 9, 1874 with the name General Postal Union, which was changed to the present name in 1878. Its permanent office is the International Bureau of the Universal Postal Union, located at Berne, Switzerland.

universal succession. The case which occurs when a state's existence comes entirely to an end and all the state's territory becomes a part of one or more other states. The other state or states in general assume both the rights and obligations of the extinguished state, with a few exceptions such as those arising from treaties of alliance.

university suffrage. An extra vote given the graduates of British universities for special university members of the House of Commons.

unneutral service. Assistance rendered to a belligerent in a war, as by transporting troops in a vessel belonging to a national of a neutral state. Such assistance invalidates the claim of the owner to receive the treatment normally accorded a neutral vessel.

U.N. See UNITED NATIONS.

unofficial observer. A visitor at an international meeting sent to observe the proceedings by a state which is not officially represented there. The United States was thus represented at a number of sessions of the League of Nations, particularly at meetings of the Council.

U. N. R. R. A. See UNITED NATIONS RELIEF AND REHABILITATION ADMINISTRATION.

Untouchable. One of the 60-odd million outcasts in India. They form a segment of the Hindu religious group but are kept on the outside and cannot participate or associate with the Hindus. The Hindus claim to speak for the Untouchables politically but the latter deny their right to do so.

unwritten constitution. A constitution which is not found in a single formal document but is scattered through a series of laws, such as that of Great Britain.

unwritten law. Customary rules which are considered part of the law but are not included in legislation or constitution. Found chiefly in legal decisions when given the effect of law.

upper house. The chamber in a two-house legislative body which is considered superior to the other for varying reasons, such as tradition, prestige, power, length of term or less susceptibility to direct control by the electorate. In the United States the national and state senates are referred to as upper houses.

Upper Silesia. Iron and coal producing area which was divided between Germany and Poland after a plebiscite in 1921. It lies across the southern end of the pre-1939 German-Polish boundary and is included inside the tentative Polish boundaries an-

nounced at the Potsdam Conference in 1945.

U.S.E.S. See UNITED STATES EMPLOYMENT SERVICE.

U. S. O. United Service Organization. A group of service organizations working together for the welfare of the persons in the armed services in World War II. They were: Jewish Welfare Board, National Catholic Community Service, Salvation Army, Travelers' Aid Association, the Y. M. C. A. and the Y. W. C. A.

U. S. S. R. The Union of Soviet Socialist Republics, loosely referred to as Russia, more correctly called the Soviet Union. See SOVIET UNION; SOVIET UNION, CONSTITUTION OF.

Ustaschi. Croatian terrorist organization under the leadership of Ante Pavelich which developed along Nazi lines as a secret police and exclusive political organization when it came to power in Croatia after the fall of Yugoslavia in April, 1941. It formed the backbone of the puppet kingdom of Croatia proclaimed in May 1941, the titular head of which was one of the Italian princes.

utilitarianism. A political philosophy developed by a group of English liberals in the 19th century, which teaches that a conduct is morally good when it promotes "the greatest good for the greatest number." The best known Utilitarians were Jeremy Bentham, James and John Stuart Mill, the economist David Ricardo and the jurist John Austin. Utilitarians thought that man is ruled by pleasure and pain and that therefore his actions should be guided by the principle of utility, that is to say by trying to avoid pain and by seeking to act in such a way that would result in pleasure. This does not mean selfish or sensuous behavior, but actions or conduct which would give pleasure to the "greatest possible number." In politics Utilitarians formed a group in the British House of Commons called the "philosophical radicals." In economics they continued the school of "classical economics," believing that in the long run well-conceived self-interest promotes common interest. They favored non-interference of the government with economic affairs, the so-called laissez faire. In law, Utilitarians believed in rational, utilitarian legislation and opposed traditional law based on custom, which they considered out of date and often foolish. See RADICAL, LIBERAL, LAISSEZ FAIRE, FREE TRADE.

uti posseditis (YOO-tie poh-si-DIE-tis). The rule of international law that at the end of a war each side keeps such territory as it held at the close of hostilities. It is not universally applied.

Utopia. The name for the ideal society or perfect state as conceived by philosophers, scientists, writers, poets and dreamers. The word was coined from the Greek by Sir Thomas More in 1516 as the name of a distant island where an ideal commonwealth existed. The Greek philosopher Plato in the *Republic*, the English statesman-philosopher Sir Francis Bacon in the *New Atlantis*, Harrington in the *Commonwealth of Oceana*, the Italian Tomasso Campanella in *The City of the Sun*, depicted other "Utopian" societies. Many prophets of socialism indulged in description of ideal societies of the future; noted among them were Fourier, Cabet, Robert Owen and William Morris. Marxists usually call these social reformers "Utopian Socialists." Some more recent examples of "Utopias" are W. H. Hudson: *A Crystal Age;* Bulwer-Lytton: *The Coming Race; or, New Utopia;* Edward Bellamy: *Looking Backward* and *Equality;* H. G. Wells: *A Modern Utopia.*

It is customary to call idealistic plans or projects or goals "utopian" whenever it is asserted that they are much too impracticable ever to be carried out.

V

V. A. The Royal Order of Victoria and Albert.

V. A. See VETERANS' ADMINISTRATION.

Vansittartism. The doctrine that the entire German people share the responsibility for militarism, aggression and war equally with the Nazi regime, and should be treated after World War II on this assumption. Associated with the expressed views of Lord Robert Vansittart, former permanent under-secretary of the British Foreign Office.

vassal state. A state under the suzerainty of another. The suzerain controls the vassal's foreign relations and the vassal has only such rights as specified in the document establishing this relationship. See SUZERAINTY.

V-E Day. The day of victory in Europe in World War II. It was proclaimed by the United States and Great Britain on May 8, 1945 to go into effect at 12:01 A. M. May 9. The Germans signed a military capitulation in Berlin which the Russians considered the formal end of the war in Europe on the afternoon of May 9.

Venezia Giulia. The easternmost province of northern Italy between World War I and World War II. After World War II most of it, though not including the new Free City of Trieste, was given to Yugoslavia.

Vera Cruz incident. The bombardment and capture of the Mexican port of Vera Cruz by United States naval and marine forces in April, 1914. Victoriano Huerta had just seized the Mexican presidency but was not recognized by the United States. Early in 1914 some United States marines were arrested in Tampico, but quickly released and official apologies were made. However, President Wilson insisted that the American flag be given a salute of 21 guns, and when Mexico refused, the fleet was sent to Vera Cruz. The fall of Huerta in July ended the episode. See ABC POWERS.

verdict. The conclusion of the jury on the facts presented to it in a case in court.

Verdun. A French fortress-city at which the Germans attempted to break through the Allied lines in 1916. The Germans launched a tremendous attack in February and they were not driven out of all the important areas around the city until the following December. The French were commanded by General Henri-Philippe Pétain who coined the famous phrase "They shall not pass." (Ils ne passeront pas.)

Versailles Treaty. Allied-German peace treaty signed at Versailles, near Paris, on June 28, 1919. It consisted of 15 parts, and the most important provisions were: I. Covenant of the League of Nations. II. Boundaries of Germany, giving Posen and the Polish Corridor to Poland, Alsace-Lorraine to France, small areas to Belgium. The Saar valley and Danzig were put under the League, and Germany agreed to plebiscites in Upper Silesia, North Schleswig and two other small areas. III. Austrian independence was recognized, the Rhineland demilitarized and the Saar coal mines given to France. IV. Germany's colonies were made mandates of the League. V. Germany was disarmed, her army limited to 100,000 men and her navy to a few old ships, and the General Staff abolished. VII. Emperor William II was to be tried by the five largest Allies. VIII. War guilt was accepted by Germany, and her reparations outlined. XII. The Rhine, Elbe and Oder rivers were put under international control. XIII. The International Labor Organization was established. XIV. The Rhineland was to be occupied by the Allies for 15 years, or longer if Germany defaulted on its obligations under the treaty. The treaty went into force on January 10, 1920 but was not ratified by the United States. Peace between the United States and Germany was effected by the America-German Peace Treaty of 1921.

vested interests. Well-established large-scale economic interests which influence political action in favor of their own good.

Veterans Administration. An independent United States government agency set up July 21, 1930 to consolidate the activities of the government concerning veterans which had been scattered between the Bureau of Pensions, the Veterans Bureau and the National Homes Service. Its function is the administration of benefits to veterans of the armed forces and their dependents, such as pensions, education, vocational rehabilitation, loans, insurance and health service.

veterans' bonus. See BONUS; ADJUSTED COMPENSATION.

veterans' preference. Advantages in employment and promotion in the civil service given to honorably discharged veterans of the armed forces.

veto. 1. The action of a chief executive in refusing to approve legislation passed by the legislative body. In Congress and most of the states the bill becomes a law if passed again by a two-thirds majority, though in some states the majority may be smaller. See ITEM VETO; POCKET VETO; SUSPENSIVE VETO. 2. The right of any of the five great powers to block, by a simple negative vote, action in any procedure, such as the voting in the Security Council, in which passage requires the approval of all of the great powers. This right makes it possible for any great power to block effective action, but the provision was necessary in order to secure the approval of all the great powers for the United Nations. The chief friction on the issue has resulted from the early frequent use of the veto by Russia, and on procedural matters rather than on substantive matters to which the other powers thought its use should be limited.

V for Victory. A sign and slogan used by the Allies in World War II, especially in Great Britain and in Western Europe. Churchill popularized it as a gesture of greeting by

extending only his index and adjacent fingers when he waved to crowds. The Morse code of three dots and a dash was also used.

vice consul. A consular officer, usually of the lowest rank in the regular consular service. See CONSULAR SERVICE.

Victorian Order. See ROYAL VICTORIAN ORDER.

vice-president. The second ranking executive official of the United States, who assumes the presidency if the president dies, is removed, resigns, or becomes unable to discharge his duties. The vice-president is the president of the Senate.

viceroy. The representative of the British king in a colony or other dependent area, as in India.

Vichyite. An adherent of the Vichy regime. See VICHY REGIME.

Vichy regime. The Government of France from June, 1940 until August, 1944 under Marshal Henri-Philippe Pétain as Chief of State. After November, 1942 the real power was in the hands of Pierre Laval as Chief of Government. The name derives from the seat of government, the resort town of Vichy. In the summer of 1940 after the collapse of France, the Nazis divided France into two parts, Occupied (by the Germans) and Unoccupied, or Vichy, France. Less than half the country, in the southeast, was under Vichy control. Marshal Pétain passed a series of acts setting up a corporate state, adjourning Parliament and assuming legislative power. In 1941 economic collaboration with Germany was greatly extended, anti-Jewish laws passed, and the Catholic Church given educational privileges in the schools. Pétain advocated a state paternalism along fascist lines. In 1942, in November, Laval came to power as a Nazi tool and declared that France's future lay with Germany. When the Allies landed in North Africa the same month, the Nazis occupied all of Vichy France. Between that date and the Allied landings in Normandy in June, 1944 French resistance against Vichy and the Nazis grew steadily, and the Vichy regime collapsed in August, 1944 when Pétain and Laval fled to Germany.

Victory tax. A special income tax of 5 per cent (later 3 per cent) added to the United States income tax during World War II.

Vienna, Treaty of. An important international treaty, signed June 9, 1815 reorganizing Europe territorially after the Napoleonic wars. This new European foundation prevailed with minor changes until 1914.

Viet Nam Republic. See INDO-CHINESE FEDERATION.

vigilance committee. An unofficial group of citizens organized for the summary trial of crimes and execution of punishments because the established processes of law and order appear to have become inadequate, notably the San Francisco Vigilance Committee following 1851 during the gold rush.

vigilantes. See VIGILANCE COMMITTEE.

village. 1. The smallest of municipal corporations. 2. A very small town either incorporated or not.

Vilna incident. The seizure of Vilna, the Lithuanian capital, by the Poles on October 9, 1920. Vilna had been the ancient capital and was allotted to Lithuania by the Allies in 1919 as lying east of the Curzon Line. The Poles tried to take it but the League induced them to reach an agreement leaving it to Lithuania. Just before this went into effect, the Poles did seize the city and vicinity. The League again suggested direct settlement but this was unsuccessful. Russia turned the area back to Lithuania in October, 1939.

visa. A permit issued by a country allowing an alien to enter. The permit takes the form of a stamp on the persons passport. See PASSPORT.

viscount. A European title of nobility, originally given to an aide or son of a count or earl. Now merely a recognition of nobility. In Britain viscounts rank between earls and barons in the peerage. See PEERAGE.

viscountess. Wife of a viscount, or a woman inheriting the title in her own right. See VISCOUNT.

visit and search. The right which a belligerent war vessel has to stop and board enemy or neutral merchant ships, to determine the susceptibility of ship and cargo to seizure because of enemy or contraband character. It can also be used as a police measure in times of peace.

vital interests. Those economic and other interests of a state the protection of which the state looks upon as essential to its well-being. See NATIONAL HONOR.

vital statistics. Figures relating to births, deaths, marriages, and cases of illness.

viva voce vote. A voice vote, that is a vote by which the members of a deliberative body respond orally in ayes and noes and the presiding officer determines by the volume of sound which side prevails.

V-J Day. The day, September 1, 1945, on which Japan accepted unconditional surrender in World War II.

V-mail. A system of microfilming and reproducing of correspondence and the transportation of the films by airmail which provided air-mail speed to a volume of mail which could not have been transported by plane. The service was inaugurated for the benefit of those connected with the armed forces serving overseas in World War II. The V stood for victory.

voice vote. See VIVA VOCE VOTE.

void. 1. Of no effect. 2. To make of no effect.

voidable. Pertaining to a thing which may be made of no effect, that is which may be prevented from its normal operation, as for example, a contract made under fraudulent misrepresentation.

Volksturm (FAWLK-shtoorm). The people's army or home guard recruited by Hitler for the defense of Germany during the last months of World War II. It included young boys, old men, and men with minor physical disabilities. They were far from the general German army standards in both ability and morale.

Volstead Act. The law passed October 28, 1919 putting into effect the Prohibition (18th) Amendment and defining as intoxicating liquor any beverage with more alcohol than one-half of one percent. Named for Rep. Andrew J. Volstead of Minnesota.

volunteer. A person who voluntarily enlists in the armed forces.

vote. 1. The process of formally expressing an opinion upon candidates, issues, or questions at an election at the polls, at a political convention, or in a deliberative body. 2. To express one's opinion formally as above.

vote of confidence. A vote of approval by a parliamentary body of the policy of a prime minister or other cabinet member.

voting machine. A machine which registers and adds the votes which are cast by voters in the polls on election day.

Vox Pop. Abbreviation meaning the voice of the people. From an old Latin quotation, *vox populi vox Dei*—the voice of the people is the voice of God.

W

W. A. A. See WAR ASSETS ADMINISTRATION.

Wafd. The Nationalist Party in Egypt. The word means "delegation" and is used because the party grew out of a delegation of Egyptians which, in 1919, was most active in pressing for full national independence.

wage floor. A minimum wage for all industry below which wages are not to fall.

Wagner Act. See the NATIONAL LABOR RELATIONS ACT.

Wailing Wall. A part of the outside face of the retaining wall of the area of the Mosque of the Dome of the Rock, or so-called Mosque of Omar, in Jerusalem, formerly the area of Solomon's temple. The Jews go there to mourn.

Wall Street. A street in lower New York City on which have been located some of the leading financial concerns of the country, hence a term for United States high finance.

Walsh-Healey Act. A law passed in the United States on June 30, 1936 requiring an 8-hour day, 40-hour week, minimum wages, and no child or prison labor on government contracts of over $10,000.

Wal-Wal Dispute. See UAL UAL DISPUTE.

war. 1. A conflict between two states carried on in general under the recognized rules for such conflicts, and including both armed hostilities and the intention to carry on such a conflict. 2. The abnormal non-peaceful relation between two states which are carrying on such a conflict. See LAWS OF WAR.

War Assets Administration. An agency established January 31, 1946 to care for and dispose of surplus government supplies, most of which had been procured in connection with wartime needs but which were not needed after World War II was concluded.

War Between the States. See CIVIL WAR.

war bonds. Government bonds, the proceeds from which are used in the prosecution of a war.

war crimes. Before World War II any acts performed by individuals or bodies of individuals which were against the accepted international law of war. They included (1) acts of war committed by non-combatant people (people not in uniform) or inhabitants of occupied territories; (2) acts forbidden by laws of war such as assassinations, marauding, and treachery in cases where the law of war implies good faith such as keeping a truce, or shooting on emissaries bearing a white flag; and (3) actions not forbidden by the laws of war but punishable under international law such as espionage.

After World War II the planning of a war of aggression, murder, ill-treatment, deportation to slave labor of civilian population, and crimes against humanity were declared war crimes in the Charter of the International Military Tribunal which began in November 1945 to try the chief German war criminals. See WAR CRIMES TRIAL.

war crimes trial. A trial of a person, persons, or organizations accused of war crimes. After World War I Germany was permitted and obliged to try its war criminals in German courts. Only a few were indicted and even fewer were convicted to rather short prison terms. See LEIPSIC TRIALS.

During World War II it became clear that the mass atrocities committed by Germans and Japanese against the population of conquered countries could not go unpunished. In the Summer of 1945, France, Great Britain, the U.S.S.R. and the United States agreed to try the main German war criminals by an international tribunal. The Charter of the International Tribunal was announced on October 19, 1945. The Charter sets a precedent in international practice by dealing with the leaders of an aggressor country not through political measures (such as exile on a distant island), but by trial of leaders, organizers, instigators or accomplices participating in the formulation or execution of the following crimes:

(a) Crimes against peace; plans, preparations, initiating or waging of a war of aggression or a war in violation of international treaties, agreements or assurances, or participation in a common plan or conspiracy of any of the foregoing.

(b) War crimes, namely violations of the laws or customs of war. Such violations shall include, but not be limited to, murder, ill-treatment, or deportation to slave labor, or for any other purposes, of civilian populations of or in occupied territory, murder or ill-treatment of prisoners of war or persons on the sea, killing of hostages, plunder of public and private property, wanton destruction of cities, towns and villages not justifiable by military necessity.

(c) Crimes against humanity, namely murder, extermination, enslavement, deportation and other inhumane acts committed against any civilian population, before or during the war; or persecutions on political, racial or religious grounds in execution of or in connection with any crime within the jurisdiction of the tribunal, whether or not in violation of the domestic law of the country where perpetrated.

The International Military Tribunal opened the war crimes trials at Nuremberg, Germany, on November 20, 1945 indicting 24 Germans and also the following organizations: the German Cabinet, the Leadership of the National Socialist Party, the Elite Guard (SS), the Secret State Police (SD), the Stormtroopers (SA), Gestapo, the German General Staff and High Command collectively and separately. The Tribunal announced its sentences on October 1, 1946. Nineteen of the 24 accused were found guilty, three (Von Papen, Schacht, Fritsche) were innocent, one (Ley) had killed himself and Krupp was unable to stand trial. Of the 19 guilty, 12 were sentenced to death (Goering, who killed himself, Von Ribbentrop, Kaltenbrunner, Keitel, Rosenberg, Frank, Frick, Streicher, Sauckel, Jodl, Seyss-Inquart and Bormann), three received life imprisonment (Hess, Funk, Raeder), four lesser sentences (Von Schirach, Speer, Von Neurath, Doenitz). Of the organizations accused, only the Leadership Corps, SS, SD and Gestapo were found guilty.

Meanwhile military courts of the various Allied powers tried German and Japanese war criminals. Such trials took place in Germany, Italy, Russia and the Philippine Islands. In Japan, 28 leaders were indicted on April 29, 1946 for trial before a tribunal representing 11 nations. The charges were similar to those at Nuremberg, but dated back to 1928.

War crimes trials by so-called People's Courts have been held in Bulgaria, Hungary, Romania, Yugoslavia, Poland, Czechoslovakia, and Finland, sentencing the chief collaborators in these countries to death or long prison terms. In Norway and other countries the leaders who collaborated with the Germans were tried before ordinary courts. In France special tribunals tried collaborators, among others Pierre Laval and Marshal Pétain, heads of the Vichy government. Laval was sentenced to death, Pétain to life imprisonment. See WAR CRIMES, INTERNATIONAL LAW, AGGRESSOR.

War Damage Corporation. A government agency set up to insure property against damage by enemy attacks or by United States defense actions in World War II. It was first set up by the Reconstruction Finance Corporation as the War Insurance Corporation, December 13, 1941. It was transferred from the Federal Loan Agency to the Commerce Department February 24, 1942.

war debts. The debts owed by the Allies to each other after World War I. They were all interrelated with the reparations Germany owed the Allies. Twenty-eight countries were involved in the war debt relations. In 1931 the various nations still owed the United States almost 21 billion dollars, while Germany still owed the Allies more than 25 billion dollars. In June, 1931 President Hoover granted a one year moratorium and in 1932 the Lausanne conference tentatively cancelled most of the reparations owed by Germany to the Allies, which eventually were to go into the United States Treasury. Token payments continued for a while but World War II brought an end to them. Only Finland continued to pay its debts. The example of these difficulties in aiding an ally financially prompted President Franklin D. Roosevelt in 1940 to suggest lend-lease as a way for America to become the "arsenal of democracy" without creating huge debts.

war, declaration of. A statement by a government that a state of war between it and another will be recognized as existing at some time in the near future, or is recognized as having existed since a given time in the recent past, and giving the reasons therefor. As an indication of intention and because of all the new legal relationships and the property and other rights involved, it has usually been considered advisable by belligerents to set thus the exact date for the commencement of these new relationships.

War Department. The second oldest of the executive departments of the United States federal government, established August 7, 1789. Its primary function is to train and maintain the Army, including the development of new weapons and equipment, but it also controls and operates the Panama Canal, has jurisdiction over harbors, piers and wharves, flood control and bridges on navigable streams, power and irrigation developments and other similar duties.

War Finance Corporation. An agency set up April 5, 1918, to provide financial help to war plants and the banks backing them in World War I.

War Food Administration. An over-all food agency in the Department of Agriculture set up March 26, 1943. Its function was to find out military, civil, and export food needs during World War II and make plans to meet them. Under it were such agencies as the Agricultural Adjustment Administration, Commodity Credit Corporation, Farm Security Administration, and offices of distribution, labor, materials, prices and production.

war guilt. Term referring to World War I for which Germany and its allies were held responsible. By Article 231, the so-called war guilt clause, of the Treaty of Versailles the German delegation was made to agree to the statement that Germany and its allies were responsible for the war. The precise degree of responsibility will perhaps never be decided. Some experts point out that the "war guilt clause" made Germany not morally but only legally responsible for the war and was necessary in order to establish a basis for obliging Germany to pay reparations. Hitler and the German nationalists used the "war guilt clause" as a very effective propaganda weapon against the Allied Powers of World War I calling it the "war guilt lie." During World War II the overwhelming majority of the people and leaders of the United Nations were solidly convinced that Germany, Italy and Japan started the war and this question was never a matter of dispute. See AGGRESSOR, WAR CRIMES TRIALS.

war horse. A soldier or politician who is a veteran of many campaigns and still loves the smoke of battle.

war loan. Government loan floated for the purpose of financing a war.

war lord. Term applied particularly to Chinese military leaders who, by force of arms, set up a personal control over part of the country.

War Manpower Commission. An agency in the Office of Emergency Management set up April 18, 1942 whose function was to determine manpower needs in the armed forces, industry, agriculture, etc., and to plan the policies and direct the training and allocation of men for this work.

war potential. The maximum strength of a country in terms of manpower, equipment, industrial plant, and other such relevant factors, which a country can bring to bear in a war effort if all such factors are developed to their highest possible degree.

war powers. Powers which the president exercises in time of war. Most of such powers flow from the fact that the president is the commander-in-chief of the armed forces and as such may not only direct them but can, for example, establish martial law in military areas and set up military governments in occupied territory. See SEPARATION OF POWERS, SOVEREIGNTY, PREROGATIVE.

War Production Board. An office within the Office of Emergency Management set up January 16, 1942 to provide the most efficient use of resources in the production of war materials. Its chief means was the control of allocations and priority ratings of materials.

war rebels. Persons who take up arms against the military government in an area under military occupation.

War Relocation Authority. A government war agency established in the Office of Emergency Management on March 18, 1942 and transferred to the Department of Interior February 16, 1944. Its function was to move out of strategic areas persons who might endanger the national defense by remaining therein. Its chief task was the removal from certain parts of the west coast area of over 100,000 persons of Japanese ancestry. Those of proven loyalty to Japan were placed in a segregation center at Tule Lake, California. This agency also cared for about 1000 European war refugees at Fort Ontario, New York.

War Shipping Administration. The government agency for providing and operating ocean merchant shipping in World War II. It was set up February 7, 1942 in the Office of Emergency Management.

"War to end war." A phrase commonly used at the time to refer to World War I. Usually ascribed to David Lloyd George in 1917.

war, undeclared. See UNDECLARED WAR.

ward. 1. A political subdivision of a city, usually used as single-member election districts for the city council. 2. A person for whom a guardian has been appointed, or occasionally, by analogy a state under mandate or trusteeship.

ward heeler. Political figure who does the small routine jobs for the machine in the ward or other small unit of the organization.

Washington Brigade. One of the units of Americans fighting on the side of the Loyalists in the Spanish Civil War.

Washington Conference. An international conference to discuss naval and Far Eastern questions which met in Washington November 12, 1921. The five great naval powers, the United States, Great Britain, Japan, France, and Italy, agreed principally to limit the number of their large battleships and not to build any for ten years. At the conference were also concluded the Four-Power Treaty and the Nine-Power Treaty. See LONDON NAVAL CONFERENCE OF 1930; FOUR-POWER TREATY; NINE-POWER TREATY.

Washington's Farewell Address. A statement issued by George Washington on September 17, 1796 in which he stated he was not a candidate for the presidency for a third term. He went on to advise the nation to confirm its attachment to liberty and to realize the importance of a united country, being aware of the pitfalls of sectional and party strife. He pointed out the indispensability of religion and morality, education and public credit. In foreign relations he advised a policy of good faith, justice and peace, in the pursuit of which the country should avoid "permanent, inveterate antipathies against particular nations and passionate attachments for others," involvement in European interests in which we are only remotely interested, and permanent alliances—though temporary ones, he conceded, might be necessary.

watchdog of the treasury. Anyone, particularly a legislator, who keeps a close eye on governmental expenditures and opposes governmental extravagance.

watcher. See POLL WATCHER.

"watchful waiting." Phrase used by President Wilson to describe this country's wait-and-see policy toward Mexico during the revolutionary period between 1913 and 1917. It was marked by the Vera Cruz incident in 1914 and the expedition against Francisco Villa in 1916. See VERA CRUZ INCIDENT.

Ways and Means Committee. One of the oldest of the standing committees of the United States House of Representatives, the function of which is to consider all matters relating to the raising of revenue. Since money bills must originate in the House, this is an especially important committee.

Weather Bureau. A United States government agency which forecasts the weather and summarizes weather statistics. It has branches throughout the country and its weather maps are well known. It was set up in the Agriculture Department in 1890 but transferred to the Commerce Department June 30, 1941.

"We have met the enemy and they are ours." Report of Admiral Oliver Hazard Perry after the battle of Lake Erie in which he defeated the British on September 10, 1813. His full report read: "We have met the enemy and they are ours, two ships, two brigs, one schooner and one sloop."

Wehrmacht (VAYR-makht). Term for the collective armed forces of Germany in World War II. The *Oberkommando der Wehrmacht* was set up after the shake-up in the German high command in February, 1938. It was a kind of combination supergeneral staff and defense ministry headed by the chief of staff and directly responsible to Hitler.

Weimar Republic. The political system in Germany from 1919 to 1933. In consequence of defeat in World War I the German Revolution broke out on November 3, 1918 eight days before the Armistice. A series of extremist actions took place throughout Germany which were suppressed by moderate democratic groups. A freely elected National Assembly met at Weimar and drafted the new Republic's constitution which was promulgated in August, 1919. It provided for a president as head of state assisted by a federal ministry with a chancellor at its head. The ministry was responsible to the federal assembly (Reichstag). During the life of the Republic the government was usually based on a coalition between the Social Democrats, Democrats and the Catholic Center Party. It introduced many republican and democratic reforms and succeeded in rehabilitating Germany economically and financially to a considerable degree. It could not, however, ingrain in the German people much democratic or republican fervor during its brief life. The economic depression of 1931 hit Germany very hard and the republican government was placed between two political fires: the strong Communist Party which attacked it from the left and the huge masses of the growing National Socialist Party from the right. The Nazis finally received the aid of monarchists, army leaders, conservatives, big landowners and of many industrialists and bankers, who all feared a "red revolution." President Von Hindenburg made Hitler Chancellor in January, 1933. The last free elections gave the Nazis and the allied Nationalist Party 52 per cent of the vote. Thereupon Hitler dissolved the Communist Party, and the Reichstag, on March 23, 1933 virtually abolished the Weimar Republic, giving dictatorial powers to Hitler, who within a few months dissolved all parties except his own, and established the Nazi "Third Reich." See NAZISM, THIRD REICH, CATHOLIC CENTER PARTY.

Weltanschauung (VELT - ahn - shou-oong). German term for view of the world, the German conception of a world order and the natural position of leadership therein which was the rightful place of the "superior" German nation.

West Point. Popular name for the United States Military Academy at West Point, New York, on the Hudson River about 50 miles above New York City. See UNITED STATES MILITARY ACADEMY.

West Wall. Term used in World War II to refer to both the Siegfried Line at Germany's western frontier and the defensive line the Germans built along the English Channel and the Bay of Biscay prior to the Allied invasion of June 6, 1944. See SIEGFRIED LINE.

western front. The battle lines in western Europe in both World War I and II.

western powers. A collective term used to refer to the great powers which have a common western European democratic cultural heritage—France, Great Britain and the United States.

Western Reserve. A strip of territory in the northeastern corner of Ohio running 120 miles along Lake Erie and inland to a depth of 70 miles at the most. Reserved by Connecticut when it ceded the rest of its western territorial claims to the Confederation in 1786. The land was used for settlement by Connecticut people, the proceeds going to that state. The western portion was further reserved by Connecticut for the benefit of its citizens who suffered losses from British raids along Long Island Sound during the Revolution, and called the Fire Lands. The Reserve was made a part of Ohio Territory in 1800.

Westminister. The area of London including the House of Parliament and many government offices, hence a term used for the whole British government.

Westminister, Statute of. See STATUTE OF WESTMINSTER.

Westphalia, Treaties of. Term given to a series of treaties the last of which were signed at Osnabrueck and Muenster in Westphalia, Germany, October 24, 1648 ending the Thirty Years War. In addition to numerous territorial changes the treaties marked the appearance of independent Switzerland and the United Netherlands, and the growing power of Sweden, France and certain of the German states. The treaties are considered the point of departure for the formation of the subsequent system of national states which has been the characteristic feature of world politics since then.

wet. A person opposed to the prohibition of the manufacture and sale of alcoholic beverages.

Whig. 1. Title of the Liberal Party in England prior to the middle of the 19th century. 2. The patriot group in

America at the time of the Revolution. 3. The anti-Jackson party in the United States which existed from 1832 to 1856.

whip. A party official in a legislative body whose function is to keep the members in line and ready to vote, or to arrange pairs for them in case a vote is suddenly called.

whispering campaign. Circulation of slanderous and derogatory statements against an opposing candidate preceding an election. Such statements are never included in public speeches or printed campaign material but are passed about privately from person to person.

white collar worker. A worker in an office, as opposed to a factory worker, that is, more or less literally a wage earner who can or does wear a white collar while at work.

White House. Residence and office of the president of the United States, located in a sizeable area between the Treasury and State Department buildings at 1600 Pennsylvania Avenue, Washington, D. C. Designed by James Hoban and first used by President John Adams in 1800, expanded in 1824 and renovated in 1902. Offices were added under Presidents Franklin D. Roosevelt and Truman.

white man's burden. The duty (and pleasure) which the white races have felt in extending the blessings of their civilization and economic system to the backward and usually the colored races of the world. The term is the title of a poem by Kipling written in 1899.

White Paper. A committee report presented to the House of Commons, so-called because they are usually bound only in the same white paper used for the text.

white primary. In United States politics a primary election in the South from which Negroes are or have been ex-cluded from voting, on the theory that a party is a private organization and free to bar Negroes from its elections. Since in many southern states the real election choices are made in the Democratic primary, such restrictions on voting in the primary in effect prevent the Negroes from having any real electoral voice. The right to bar Negroes from primaries was denied by the Supreme Court in an important decision in January, 1944 but in practice the restriction is maintained in many communities in the South.

White Russia. Part of western Russia extending from the Polish frontier about halfway to Moscow; its southernmost part was about the same latitude as southern Poland and its northernmost part extended about to the old Latvian-Lithuanian frontier. It forms the White Russian (or Byelorussian) Soviet Socialist Republic, whose capital is Minsk.

White Russian. 1. A native of White Russia. See WHITE RUSSIA. 2. An anti-Bolshevik Russian, distinguished from the "Red" Russians.

Whitehall. Street in London running north from the Houses of Parliament on which a number of government offices are located, hence a term used to refer to the British government.

Whitley Councils. British committees composed of representatives of the employer and employees which consider labor problems. They have been successfully set up also in the civil service where there is a national council and several departmental councils with 50–50 representation from what are called the official side and the staff side. They take their name from J. H. Whitley who proposed the idea in 1916 when Minister of Reconstruction.

Wickersham Commission. A commission under the chairmanship of

George W. Wickersham to study the observance and enforcement of law, appointed by President Hoover in 1929, which reported in 1931. It found particular difficulties resulting from the intrusion of politics into the courts, weakness of enforcement of criminal law, and such factors tending to increase crime as delinquency areas, youth membership in gangs, bad effect of jails, and the economic problems created by the depression.

wildcat banks. State banks which, before the passage of the national bank law of 1863, issued more paper money than they could redeem.

Wilhelmstrasse (VIL-helm-SHTRAH-suh). Street in Berlin on which many government offices were located, hence a term used to refer to the German government, especially the foreign office.

Wilsonian Democracy. The democratic principles of President Woodrow Wilson (1856–1924). As applied to domestic politics they continued in a sense the principles both of Jefferson and Jackson. They consist of a strong belief in liberal democracy, and in the necessity to curtail the excessive power of large industrial and financial corporations as well as of political "bosses." In international politics Wilson's ideas profoundly affected the mentality of the peoples of the whole world during and shortly after World War I. They consisted of a repudiation of American imperialist ambitions and a profound belief in the possibility of establishing such conditions throughout the world as would make it "safe for democracy." The Fourteen Points contain a promise to end secret diplomacy by establishing the practice of "open covenants openly arrived at," the liberation of Germany from oppressive rulers and the repudiation of territorial gains for the victorious Allies,

and mirrored a new spirit of democratic idealism in international politics. The League of Nations was partly Wilson's idea and he had a lion's share in having its Covenant incorporated in the Treaty of Versailles. Wilson was the first American president who tried to carry his democratic and humanitarian principles into international politics. See JACKSONIAN DEMOCRACY, JEFFERSONIAN DEMOCRACY, LIBERALISM, LEAGUE OF NATIONS.

Wilson Line. Line suggested by President Wilson for the northeastern boundary of Italy after World War I. Such a line would have provided Yugoslavia an outlet to the Adriatic at Fiume.

Windsor, House of. The ruling house of Great Britain. Originally called the house of Wettin, which was the family name of Queen Victoria's consort, Prince Albert of Saxe-Coburg. The name was changed to Windsor in 1917. The title duke of Windsor was taken by King Edward VIII following his abdication in December, 1936.

withering away of the state. A socialistic theory that after the capitalists are disposed of and the classless society of the workers is set up, the state, which is merely a tool of the capitalists, will gradually disappear.

withholding tax. An income tax which is turned over to the government by an employer for an employee, and hence is "withheld" from the employee's paycheck. Its use in the United States began on January 1, 1943 in regard to all payrolls. See TAX.

W. L. B. See NATIONAL WAR LABOR BOARD.

W. M. C. See WAR MANPOWER COMMISSION.

Women's Bureau. An agency in the Labor Department set up in 1918 and given its present name June 5, 1920.

Its function is to establish and supervise standards of wages and other working conditions for women in industry.

women's suffrage. The struggle for women's right to vote is only a part of the movement to improve women's position in society and to equalize it as far as possible with that of men. It started in France, Germany and England at the end of the 18th century, led by Olympe de Gouges and Mary Wollstonecraft. They were largely unsuccessful and the movement really got under way only toward the end of the 19th century. In England it was led by the liberal philosopher John Stewart Mill in the 1860's, but Parliament rejected his proposal to enfranchise women. In 1897 the National Union of Women's Suffrage Societies was organized in Britain. These so-called "suffragettes" under the leadership of Emmeline Pankhurst staged mass˙ demonstrations, hunger strikes, etc., attempting to draw attention to their cause by spectacular methods. In 1907 British women were granted the vote in local elections and in 1917 in national elections.

In France women's suffrage was not introduced until recently; the national election of 1945 was the first in which French women went to the polls. Women received the vote in Germany in 1918; in Russia, 1917; Denmark, 1913; Sweden, 1921; Turkey, 1925, and China in 1931. In Japan women's suffrage was introduced in 1945 by General MacArthur. In Italy women received the vote in 1946. In the United States the question of giving women the vote was discussed at the Constitutional Convention but was rejected by a great majority, including Jefferson. Thomas Paine was for women's suffrage. During the 19th century strong movements for women's rights got under way led by Margaret Fuller, Susan B. Anthony and others. Wyoming adopted women's suffrage while still a territory in 1868. Colorado, Utah and Idaho followed suit in the 1890's when Popularism prevailed in the West. President Wilson recommended women's suffrage in 1918 and the Nineteenth Amendment giving women the full vote was ratified by 1920.

workhouse. A place for the detention of persons convicted of minor infractions of the law.

work relief. Financial assistance given to the needy in the form of employment for wages on some public works project such as road-building.

Works Progress Administration. A government agency authorized May 6, 1935 to build useful public works chiefly as a means of providing jobs for the unemployed. Reorganized and placed under the Federal Works Agency July 1, 1939.

World Bank. See BANK FOR INTERNATIONAL SETTLEMENTS.

World Court. See PERMANENT COURT OF INTERNATIONAL JUSTICE.

World Economic Conference. See ECONOMIC CONFERENCE OF 1933.

World Peace Foundation. An organization set up in Boston in 1910 for research and publication of factual material tending to promote world peace. It was founded by Edwin Ginn with an endowment of $1,000,000.

"The world must be made safe for democracy." Often-quoted statement by President Wilson, used in his address to Congress April 2, 1917 asking for a declaration of war against Germany. It became a popular slogan in World War I.

world revolution. The Marxist Communist doctrine, that only a revolution on international scale can bring the world-wide class struggle between the capitalists and the workers to an end, resulting in the "dictatorship of the proletariat" and eventually in world socialism and a classless society. This doctrine, under the influence of Stalin, has been dropped from the communist vocabulary. Although communist parties maintain international contacts even since the dissolution of the Communist International in 1943, they do not aim at a sudden concerted world revolution but rather try to seize political power according to methods adjusted to the particular conditions prevailing in each country. See MARXISM, COMMUNISM, SOCIALISM, BOLSHEVISM, STALINIST, TROTSKYITE, CLASS STRUGGLE, PROLETARIAT.

World War I. The war, July 28, 1914 to November 11, 1918, between the Central Powers (Germany, Austria-Hungary, Turkey and Bulgaria) and the Allied and Associated Powers (at first Great Britain and her Dominions, France, Russia and Japan and later Italy, the United States and a large number of smaller nations). Its causes lay deep in the trends of the nationalism and imperialism on the part of the European peoples on both sides, and in the aristocratic militarism of Germany. The period between 1870 and 1914 had seen the development of two rival alliances, the Triple Alliance of Germany, Austria-Hungary and Italy and the Triple Entente of Great Britain, France and Russia. After the war broke out in Europe, the issue of the freedom of the seas from submarine warfare involved the United States. The immediate issue was the Austrian attack on Serbia, a protégé of Russia, following the murder of the Austrian Archduke Francis Ferdinand by a Serbian terrorist. Russian support of Serbia brought the two alliances into the war, with the exception of Italy which switched to the Allies in 1915.

The main theater of the war was in France, where the Germans tried to break through in 1914 but were stopped at the Marne. After that the fighting settled down to trench warfare, bloody but indecisive. The Russians suffered serious defeats, and the outbreak of the March Revolution in 1917 followed by the Bolshevik October Revolution took Russia out of the war just as the United States was entering it. Italy was won for the Allies by secret promises of territorial gains, but had to be given military aid later in the war. Turkey and Bulgaria were knocked out in October, 1918 and Austria-Hungary on November 3. By that time a final German effort in France had failed, as had her submarine campaign against Britain, and internal revolutions forced the abdication of the Kaiser and the signing of the final Armistice on November 11, 1918.

The immediate results of the war were many and confused. The Treaty of Versailles with Germany included the Covenant of the League of Nations, dismembered the German colonial empire, disarmed Germany and penalized her with immense reparations. Austria-Hungary dissolved into the Austrian Republic and Hungarian Monarchy, as well as the "succession states" of Czechoslovakia and Yugoslavia. An independent Poland was recreated; Turkey was also dismembered, her Arab territory becoming the kingdoms of Iraq and Saudi Arabia, while Syria became a League Mandate of France, and Palestine and Transjordan of Britain. In Europe the economic and social results were catastrophic: revolution and postwar inflation ruined the middle classes, creating the material which fed the new fascist movements; unemployment aided the growth of the extreme left, especially the communists; fear of Bolshevik Russia caused the western powers and Japan to support abortive counter-revolutions there without success. American refusal to enter the League weakened it from the very beginning. See LEAGUE OF NATIONS, SECRET TREATIES, FASCISM, COMMUNISM.

World War II. The war of September 1, 1939 to August 14, 1945 between the Axis powers (Germany, Italy, Japan, and their puppet states) and the United Nations (most of the rest of the world except Spain, Sweden, Eire, Portugal and Switzerland). The immediate cause of the war was Axis—or fascist—aggression, beginning with the Japanese occupation of Manchuria in 1931 and leading up to the German invasion of Poland on September 1, 1939. Behind all this lay the economic instability resulting from World War I, which was intensified by the depression of the 1930's; the cleavage between fascist totalitarianism and democracy and communism; the refusal of powerful groups within the democracies to face the fascist danger, or their acceptance of fascism as an alternative to communism, which permitted the Axis to prepare for the inevitable struggle; distrust of the U.S.S.R. by the democracies, which also permitted the Axis to divide its natural enemies until after the war had begun; and the basic fact that fascism must expand or die.

For the first two years of the war, Germany was overwhelmingly successful. The Nazis overran Poland in 1939; Denmark, Norway, the Netherlands, Belgium and France in 1940; Yugoslavia and Greece in 1941, and in June, 1941 invaded the U.S.S.R., driving to the gates of Moscow that

year and to the Volga and the Caucasus in 1942. Japan entered the war in December 7, 1941 and in six months had conquered the Philippines, Hong Kong, Malaya, Burma, the Dutch and British East Indies and most of New Guinea as well as establishing puppet regimes in Indo-China and Thailand (Siam). While the Japanese were stopped in the Pacific in the summer of 1942, the tide did not turn against the German-Italian armies until November, when the Russians struck back at Stalingrad on the Volga and the British halted a drive for Egypt, and Americans landed in North Africa. From then on the tide flowed steadily in favor of the United Nations. The Germans were driven out of the U.S.S.R. by a succession of massive blows, and then out of the Balkans and Hungary, while the western allies were knocking Italy out of the war and liberating France. By the beginning of 1945 Germany was shattered by aerial attacks and her armies driven inside her own borders, but the Nazis chose "national suicide" in preference to unconditional surrender, and the country had to be conquered district by district and city by city until the High Command had no alternative but to give up and sign armistices on May 8 and 9, 1945. Japan, in the meantime, was meeting a similar fate. American and Australian amphibious operations pushed her steadily back across the Pacific in 1943, reached the Philippines in October, 1944 and Okinawa in the Ryukyus in April, 1945. In other theaters: China refused to accept defeat, Burma was recovered and the road to China re-opened, a beginning was made toward the recovery of the East Indies, and Japan itself was hammered relentlessly from the air and finally from the sea. The final blows came in August, 1945 when the first two atom bombs were dropped on Hiroshima and Nagasaki (August 5 and 8) and the U.S.S.R. entered the war against Japan (August 8). The Japanese surrender was effective on August 14.

During the war the United Nations were welded into an effective fighting unit and their many political and economic differences submerged by the common danger. Their aims were first stated in the Atlantic Charter (August 14, 1941) which was incorporated into the United Nations Declaration, signed by 26 nations on January 1, 1942 and later by 25 others. Their policies, strategy and aims were further expanded and restated at the conferences between the United States, Britain and the U.S.S.R. held at Teheran, Yalta and Potsdam. As put into effect during the war, and under the surrender terms, the most important of these were: (1) the destruction of fascism and fascist parties in the Axis nations and (2) their occupation until such time as they could be trusted to exercise the democratic principle of free elections; (3) the launching of the United Nations organization, whose Charter was written at San Francisco in the spring of 1945; (4) the establishment of democratic regimes in the liberated countries. This last point brought into the open disagreements as to what constituted a "democratic regime."

The terms of unconditional surrender signed by Italy, Germany and Japan varied widely. Italy, which surrendered after Mussolini had been overthrown and the Fascist Party abolished, became a co-belligerent with limited political authority which was expanded as more and more of the country was liberated. Germany, ruined physically and economically, was divided into American, British, Soviet and French zones of occupation, the Nazi party and laws abolished and her factories stripped of the means of manufacturing military equipment. No central government was set up other than a joint Allied commission, and the first elections allowed were those at the lowest level of political organization, the smallest towns. In Japan, the imperial government was continued under the rigid control of Gen. MacArthur as Allied Supreme Commander, who ordered a series of basic political and social reforms including a new constitution, leading eventually to free elections. See UNITED NATIONS, ATLANTIC CHARTER, UNITED NATIONS CHARTER.

W.P.A. See WORKS PROGRESS ADMINISTRATION.

W.P.B. See WAR PRODUCTION BOARD.

wrecker. Russian term for a person who opposes the current regime in Russia and attempts to interfere with its success in either the political or economic spheres.

written constitution. A constitution which is drawn up in a single formal document. See UNWRITTEN CONSTITUTION.

X - Y

xenophobia. Extreme dislike of foreign things and particularly persons.

Yalta Conference. See CRIMEA CONFERENCE.

yeas and nays. A vote in a legislative body in which the members vote separately and the various votes are recorded.

Yellow Book. Name of the French governmental reports of investigating or other committees. See BLUE BOOK.

"yellow-dog" contract. An employer-employee contract in which the latter agrees not to join a labor union; now illegal.

yellow-seal dollar. A dollar bill used by the United States Army as currency for the occupation forces when Italy was invaded. It was a silver certificate on which the regular blue seal was engraved in yellow. The purpose was to provide an occupation currency that would not be directly exchangeable with regular United States currency.

yellow peril. The threat to the white race created by the size of the yellow race. The fact is, however, that in recent years there have been wars within the yellow race as within the white race, rather than a pure racial conflict.

Young Officers. The Japanese Imperial League of Young Officers. A group of army officers in the vanguard of Japanese imperialism, which was responsible for forcing the government to accede to its wishes, often by means of revolt and assassination particularly in February, 1936.

Young Plan. The second major change in the German World War I reparations, drawn up in 1929 and finally agreed to January 20, 1930. It reduced the German reparations to 26½ billion dollars, payable in 60 years, abolished the reparations commission, and provided for the establishment of the Bank for International Settlements. The name came from that of the United States representative, Owen D. Young. See DAWES PLAN.

Young Turks. Revolutionary group in Turkey which took shape prior to 1900 and seized power July 23, 1908. The sultan started a counter-revolution the following April but in a short time the Young Turks were again in control.

yuan. Chinese name for each of five councils established by the Constitution of 1946, and also for the buildings in which they meet. See CHINESE CONSTITUTION OF 1946.

Z

Zentrum (TSEN-troom). See CATHOLIC CENTER PARTY.

Zimmerman Note. A dispatch of January 19, 1917 to the German minister in Mexico from German foreign minister Zimmerman stating that the unrestricted submarine campaign would soon be resumed and that if the United States were then drawn into the war it was the German intention to try to secure an alliance with Mexico, offering certain southwest United States territory as an inducement.

Zionism. The name for the movement to reestablish Palestine as a Jewish national state. It had its origins in Central Europe but its mass support came particularly from Russian and Polish Jews. In a way it continues the traditional longing of the Jews, dispersed all over the world, for the restoration of their homeland. Anti-Semitic movements toward the end of the 19th century helped to spread Zionism. For most European Jews, however, Zionism was alien, as they regarded themselves as Englishmen, Frenchmen and Germans of Jewish religion and such a phrase as the "Jewish nation" was meaningless to them. Thus assimilation, conversion and intermarriage with non-Jews, often split Jewry into two opposing camps. Politically Zionism became organized in 1897 by Theodor Herzl who convoked the first Zionist Congress in Basel, Switzerland. In 1917 Britain, in the famous Balfour Declaration, favored the establishment of "a Jewish national home." It was endorsed by the Allies and included in the Treaty of Sévres (1920). Jewish settlements in Palestine started in the 1880's and increased rapidly after World War I when Palestine became a British mandate. The Arabian population of Palestine has been opposed to the influx of Jews to a varying degree, though many of them profited by a growth in prosperity as Jews established many flourishing agricultural settlements and built a few modern cities, such as Tel Aviv. Arab dissatisfaction resulted in violent outbreaks and revolts. The British sent out a commission of inquiry in 1930 whose recommendations were accepted, resulting in restrictions on Jewish immigration and land purchase in Palestine. This decision was violently attacked by Zionists who demanded unrestricted right of immigration and the creation of a Jewish Commonwealth in Palestine. During World War II illegal entries into Palestine by often desperate and destitute refugees from Nazis were frequent, and were only partly opposed by the British authorities. Arab nationalism has grown rapidly since World War I and has opposed these developments, organizing in many ways to halt further Zionist aspirations. The persecution of Jews in Europe by the Nazis has intensified the demand for Zionism as a solution for European Jews who do not care to return to their homes where only ruins, horrible memories, and little sympathy from the non-Jewish population await them. There are many Zionist groups in America. See NAZISM, ARYANS, ANTI-SEMITISM.

Zollverein (TSAWL-fer-ine). German word for customs union. Beginning in 1818, Prussia developed a customs union of the smaller German states, and by 1854 it included all of them as well as Austria. However, Austro-Prussian rivalry led Prussia to exclude Austria from the union in 1865. After the Seven Weeks War of 1866 in which Prussia finally excluded Austria from Germany, another Zollverein was set up without Austria, but it ended with the foundation of the German empire in 1871. In 1931 the Republic of Germany proposed a Zollverein with the Republic of Austria, but other nations, especially France, feared it might lead to annexation. The World Court, in an advisory opinion, declared it illegal as violating the Austrian loan protocol of 1922.

zoning. Municipal regulations dividing a city into areas each of which is limited to a certain kind of real estate development, such as residential, industrial or retail. The object is the efficient use of land and the protection of property values. Zoning originated in the United States but has been used elsewhere, as in London.

Zveno Group. A Bulgarian pressure group, pro-Russian and pro-Yugoslav, having strong army support and favoring authoritarian measures. It was organized as a party in October, 1943.

APPENDIX I

CHARTER OF THE UNITED NATIONS

We the peoples of the United Nations determined

to save succeeding generations from the scourge of war, which twice in our lifetime has brought untold sorrow to mankind, and

to reaffirm faith in fundamental human rights, in the dignity and worth of the human person, in the equal rights of men and women and of nations large and small, and

to establish conditions under which justice and respect for the obligations arising from treaties and other sources of international law can be maintained, and

to promote social progress and better standards of life in larger freedom,

and for these ends

to practice tolerance and live together in peace with one another as good neighbors, and

to unite our strength to maintain international peace and security, and

to ensure, by the acceptance of principles and the institution of methods, that armed force shall not be used, save in the common interests, and

to employ international machinery for the promotion of the economic and social advancement of all peoples,

have resolved to combine our efforts to accomplish these aims.

Accordingly, our respective Governments, through representatives assembled in the city of San Francisco, who have exhibited their full powers found to be in good and due form, have agreed to the present Charter of the United Nations and do hereby establish an international organization to be known as the United Nations.

CHAPTER I

PURPOSES AND PRINCIPLES

Article 1

The Purposes of the United Nations are:

1. To maintain international peace and security, and to that end: to take effective collective measures for the prevention and removal of threats to the peace, and for the suppression of acts of aggression or other breaches of the

peace, and to bring about by peaceful means, and in conformity with the principles of justice and international law, adjustment or settlement of international disputes or situations which might lead to a breach of the peace;

2. To develop friendly relations among nations based on respect for the principle of equal rights and self-determination of peoples, and to take other appropriate measures to strengthen universal peace;

3. To achieve international co-operation in solving international problems of an economic, social, cultural, or humanitarian character, and in promoting and encouraging respect for human rights and for fundamental freedoms for all without distinction as to race, sex, language, or religion; and

4. To be a center for harmonizing the actions of nations in the attainment of these common ends.

Article 2

The Organization and its Members, in pursuit of the Purposes stated in Article 1, shall act in accordance with the following Principles.

1. The Organization is based on the principle of the sovereign equality of all its Members.

2. All Members, in order to ensure to all of them the rights and benefits resulting from membership, shall fulfill in good faith the obligations assumed by them in accordance with the present Charter.

3. All Members shall settle their international disputes by peaceful means in such a manner that international peace and security, and justice, are not endangered.

4. All Members shall refrain in their international relations from the threat or use of force against the territorial integrity or political independence of any state, or in any other manner inconsistent with the Purposes of the United Nations.

5. All Members shall give the United Nations every assistance in any action it takes in accordance with the present Charter, and shall refrain from giving assistance to any state against which the United Nations is taking preventive or enforcement action.

6. The Organization shall ensure that states which are not Members of the United Nations act in accordance with these Principles so far as may be necessary for the maintenance of international peace and security.

7. Nothing contained in the present Charter shall authorize the United Nations to intervene in matters which are essentially within the domestic jurisdiction of any state or shall require the Members to submit such matters to settlement under the present Charter; but this principle shall not prejudice the application of enforcement measures under Chapter VII.

CHAPTER II

MEMBERSHIP

Article 3

The original Members of the United Nations shall be the states which, having participated in the United Nations Conference on International Organization at San Francisco, or having previously signed the Declaration by United Nations of January 1, 1942, sign the present Charter and ratify it in accordance with Article 110.

Article 4

1. Membership in the United Nations is open to all other peace-loving states which accept the obligations contained in the present Charter and, in the judgment of the Organization, are able and willing to carry out these obligations.

2. The admission of any such state to membership in the United Nations will be effected by a decision of the General Assembly upon the recommendation of the Security Council.

Article 5

A Member of the United Nations against which preventive or enforcement action has been taken by the Security Council may be suspended from the exercise of the rights and privileges of membership by the General Assembly upon the recommendation of the Security Council. The exercise of these rights and privileges may be restored by the Security Council.

Article 6

A Member of the United Nations which has persistently violated the Principles contained in the present Charter may be expelled from the Organization by the General Assembly upon the recommendation of the Security Council.

CHAPTER III

ORGANS

Article 7

1. There are established as the principal organs of the United Nations: a General Assembly, a Security Council, an Economic and Social Council, a Trusteeship Council, an International Court of Justice, and a Secretariat.

2. Such subsidiary organs as may be found necessary may be established in accordance with the present Charter.

Article 8

The United Nations shall place no restrictions on the eligibility of men and women to participate in any capacity and under conditions of equality in its principal and subsidiary organs.

CHAPTER IV

THE GENERAL ASSEMBLY

COMPOSITION

Article 9

1. The General Assembly shall consist of all the Members of the United Nations.

2. Each Member shall have not more than five representatives in the General Assembly.

FUNCTIONS AND POWERS

Article 10

The General Assembly may discuss any questions or any matters within the scope of the present Charter or relating to the powers and functions of any organs provided for in the present Charter, and, except as provided in Article 12, may make recommendations to the Members of the United Nations or to the Security Council or to both on any such questions or matters.

Article 11

1. The General Assembly may consider the general principles of co-operation in the maintenance of international peace and security, including the principles governing disarmament and the regulation of armaments, and may make recommendations with regard to such principles to the Members or to the Security Council or to both.

2. The General Assembly may discuss any questions relating to the maintenance of international peace and security brought before it by any Member of the United Nations, or by the Security Council, or by a state which is not a Member of the United Nations in accordance with Article 35, paragraph 2, and, except as provided in Article 12, may make recommendations with regard to any such questions to the state or states concerned or to the Security Council or to both. Any such question on which action is necessary shall be referred to the Security Council by the General Assembly either before or after discussion.

3. The General Assembly may call the attention of the Security Council to situations which are likely to endanger international peace and security.

4. The powers of the General Assembly set forth in this Article shall not limit the general scope of Article 10.

Article 12

1. While the Security Council is exercising in respect of any dispute or situation the functions assigned to it in the present Charter, the General Assembly

shall not make any recommendation with regard to that dispute or situation unless the Security Council so requests.

2. The Secretary-General, with the consent of the Security Council, shall notify the General Assembly at each session of any matters relative to the maintenance of international peace and security which are being dealt with by the Security Council and shall similarly notify the General Assembly, or the Members of the United Nations if the General Assembly is not in session, immediately the Security Council ceases to deal with such matters.

Article 13

1. The General Assembly shall initiate studies and make recommendations for the purpose of:

a. promoting international co-operation in the political field and encouraging the progressive development of international law and its codification;

b. promoting international co-operation in the economic, social, cultural, educational, and health fields, and assisting in the realization of human rights and fundamental freedoms for all without distinction as to race, sex, language, or religion.

2. The further responsibilities, functions, and powers of the General Assembly with respect to matters mentioned in paragraph 1 (b) above are set forth in Chapters IX and X.

Article 14

Subject to the provisions of Article 12, the General Assembly may recommend measures for the peaceful adjustment of any situation, regardless of origin, which it deems likely to impair the general welfare or friendly relations among nations, including situations resulting from a violation of the provisions of the present Charter setting forth the Purposes and Principles of the United Nations.

Article 15

1. The General Assembly shall receive and consider annual and special reports from the Security Council; these reports shall include an account of the measures that the Security Council has decided upon or taken to maintain international peace and security.

2. The General Assembly shall receive and consider reports from the other organs of the United Nations.

Article 16

The General Assembly shall perform such functions with respect to the international trusteeship system as are assigned to it under Chapters XII and XIII, including the approval of the trusteeship agreements for areas not designated as strategic.

Article 17

1. The General Assembly shall consider and approve the budget of the Organization.

2. The expenses of the Organization shall be borne by the Members as apportioned by the General Assembly.

3. The General Assembly shall consider and approve any financial and budgetary arrangements with specialized agencies referred to in Article 57 and shall examine the administrative budgets of such specialized agencies with a view to making recommendations to the agencies concerned.

VOTING

Article 18

1. Each member of the General Assembly shall have one vote.

2. Decisions of the General Assembly on important questions shall be made by a two-thirds majority of the members present and voting. These questions shall include: recommendations with respect to the maintenance of international peace and security, the election of the non-permanent members of the Security Council, the election of the members of the Economic and Social Council, the election of members of the Trusteeship Council in accordance with paragraph 1 (c) of Article 86, the admission of new Members to the United Nations, the suspension of the rights and privileges of membership, the expulsion of Members, questions relating to the operation of the trusteeship system, and budgetary questions.

3. Decisions on other questions, including the determination of additional categories of questions to be decided by a two-thirds majority, shall be made by a majority of the members present and voting.

Article 19

A Member of the United Nations which is in arrears in the payment of its financial contributions to the Organization shall have no vote in the General Assembly if the amount of its arrears equals or exceeds the amount of the contributions due from it for the preceding two full years. The General Assembly may, nevertheless, permit such a Member to vote if it is satisfied that the failure to pay is due to conditions beyond the control of the Member.

PROCEDURE

Article 20

The General Assembly shall meet in regular annual sessions and in such special sessions as occasion may require. Special sessions shall be convoked by the Secretary-General at the request of the Security Council or of a majority of the Members of the United Nations.

Article 21

The General Assembly shall adopt its own rules of procedure. It shall elect its President for each session.

Article 22

The General Assembly may establish such subsidiary organs as it deems necessary for the performance of its functions.

CHAPTER V

THE SECURITY COUNCIL

COMPOSITION

Article 23

1. The Security Council shall consist of eleven Members of the United Nations. The Republic of China, France, the Union of Soviet Socialist Republics, the United Kingdom of Great Britain and Northern Ireland, and the United States of America shall be permanent members of the Security Council. The General Assembly shall elect six other Members of the United Nations to be nonpermanent members of the Security Council, due regard being specially paid, in the first instance to the contribution of Members of the United Nations to the maintenance of international peace and security and to the other purposes of the Organization, and also to equitable geographical distribution.

2. The non-permanent members of the Security Council shall be elected for a term of two years. In the first election of the non-permanent members, however, three shall be chosen for a term of one year. A retiring member shall not be eligible for immediate re-election.

3. Each member of the Security Council shall have one representative.

FUNCTIONS AND POWERS

Article 24

1. In order to ensure prompt and effective action by the United Nations, its Members confer on the Security Council primary responsibility for the maintenance of international peace and security, and agree that in carrying out its duties under this responsibility the Security Council acts on their behalf.

2. In discharging these duties the Security Council shall act in accordance with the Purposes and Principles of the United Nations. The specific powers granted to the Security Council for the discharge of these duties are laid down in Chapters VI, VII, VIII, and XII.

3. The Security Council shall submit annual and, when necessary, special reports to the General Assembly for its consideration.

Article 25

The Members of the United Nations agree to accept and carry out the decisions of the Security Council in accordance with the present Charter.

Article 26

In order to promote the establishment and maintenance of international peace and security with the least diversion for armaments of the world's human and economic resources, the Security Council shall be responsible for formulating, with the assistance of the Military Staff Committee referred to in Article 47, plans to be submitted to the Members of the United Nations for the establishment of a system for the regulation of armaments.

VOTING

Article 27

1. Each member of the Security Council shall have one vote.
2. Decisions of the Security Council on procedural matters shall be made by an affirmative vote of seven members.
3. Decisions of the Security Council on all other matters shall be made by an affirmative vote of seven members including the concurring votes of the permanent members; provided that, in decisions under Chapter VI, and under paragraph 3 of Article 52, a party to a dispute shall abstain from voting.

PROCEDURE

Article 28

1. The Security Council shall be so organized as to be able to function continuously. Each member of the Security Council shall for this purpose be represented at all times at the seat of the Organization.
2. The Security Council shall hold periodic meetings at which each of its members may, if it so desires, be represented by a member of the government or by some other specially designated representative.
3. The Security Council may hold meetings at such places other than the seat of the Organization as in its judgment will best facilitate its work.

Article 29

The Security Council may establish such subsidiary organs as it deems necessary for the performance of its functions.

Article 30

The Security Council shall adopt its own rules of procedure, including the method of selecting its President.

Article 31

Any Member of the United Nations which is not a member of the Security Council may participate, without vote, in the discussion of any question brought before the Security Council whenever the latter considers that the interests of that Member are specially affected.

Article 32

Any Member of the United Nations which is not a member of the Security Council or any state which is not a Member of the United Nations, if it is a party to a dispute under consideration by the Security Council, shall be invited to participate, without vote, in the discussion relating to the dispute. The Security Council shall lay down such conditions as it deems just for the participation of a state which is not a Member of the United Nations.

CHAPTER VI

PACIFIC SETTLEMENT OF DISPUTES

Article 33

1. The parties to any dispute, the continuance of which is likely to endanger the maintenance of international peace and security, shall, first of all, seek a solution by negotiation, enquiry, mediation, conciliation, arbitration, judicial settlement, resort to regional agencies or arrangements, or other peaceful means of their own choice.
2. The Security Council shall, when it deems necessary, call upon the parties to settle their dispute by such means.

Article 34

The Security Council may investigate any dispute, or any situation which might lead to international friction or give rise to a dispute, in order to determine whether the continuance of the dispute or situation is likely to endanger the maintenance of international peace and security.

Article 35

1. Any Member of the United Nations may bring any dispute, or any situation of the nature referred to in Article 34, to the attention of the Security Council or of the General Assembly.
2. A state which is not a Member of the United Nations may bring to the attention of the Security Council or of the General Assembly any dispute to which it is a party if it accepts in advance, for the purposes of the dispute, the obligations of pacific settlement provided in the present Charter.
3. The proceedings of the General Assembly in respect of matters brought to its attention under this Article will be subject to the provisions of Articles 11 and 12.

Article 36

1. The Security Council may, at any stage of a dispute of the nature referred to in Article 33 or of a situation of like nature, recommend appropriate procedures or methods of adjustment.
2. The Security Council should take into consideration any procedures for the settlement of the dispute which have already been adopted by the parties.

3. In making recommendations under this Article the Security Council should also take into consideration that legal disputes should as a general rule be referred by the parties to the International Court of Justice in accordance with the provisions of the Statute of the Court.

Article 37

1. Should the parties to a dispute of the nature referred to in Article 33 fail to settle it by the means indicated in that Article, they shall refer it to the Security Council.

2. If the Security Council deems that the continuance of the dispute is in fact likely to endanger the maintenance of international peace and security, it shall decide whether to take action under Article 36 or to recommend such terms of settlement as it may consider appropriate.

Article 38

Without prejudice to the provisions of Articles 33 to 37, the Security Council may, if all the parties to any dispute so request, make recommendations to the parties with a view to a pacific settlement of the dispute.

CHAPTER VII

ACTION WITH RESPECT TO THREATS TO THE PEACE, BREACHES OF THE PEACE, AND ACTS OF AGGRESSION

Article 39

The Security Council shall determine the existence of any threat to the peace, breach of the peace, or act of aggression and shall make recommendations, or decide what measures shall be taken in accordance with Articles 41 and 42, to maintain or restore international peace and security.

Article 40

In order to prevent an aggravation of the situation, the Security Council may, before making the recommendations or deciding upon the measures provided for in Article 39, call upon the parties concerned to comply with such provisional measures as it deems necessary or desirable. Such provisional measures shall be without prejudice to the rights, claims, or position of the parties concerned. The Security Council shall duly take account of failure to comply with such provisional measures.

Article 41

The Security Council may decide what measures not involving the use of armed force are to be employed to give effect to its decisions, and it may call upon the Members of the United Nations to apply such measures. These may include complete or partial interruption of economic relations and of rail, sea, air, postal, telegraphic, radio, and other means of communication, and the severance of diplomatic relations.

Article 42

Should the Security Council consider that measures provided for in Article 41 would be inadequate or have proved to be inadequate, it may take such action by air, sea, or land forces as may be necessary to maintain or restore international peace and security. Such action may include demonstrations, blockade, and other operations by air, sea, or land forces of Members of the United Nations.

Article 43

1. All Members of the United Nations, in order to contribute to the maintenance of international peace and security, undertake to make available to the Security Council, on its call and in accordance with a special agreement or agreements, armed forces, assistance, and facilities, including rights of passage, necessary for the purpose of maintaining international peace and security.

2. Such agreement or agreements shall govern the numbers and types of forces, their degree of readiness and general location, and the nature of the facilities and assistance to be provided.

3. The agreement or agreements shall be negotiated as soon as possible on the initiative of the Security Council. They shall be concluded between the Security Council and Members or between the Security Council and groups of Members and shall be subject to ratification by the signatory states in accordance with their respective constitutional processes.

Article 44

When the Security Council has decided to use force it shall, before calling upon a Member not represented on it to provide armed forces in fulfillment of the obligations assumed under Article 43, invite that Member, if the Member so desires, to participate in the decisions of the Security Council concerning the employment of contingents of that Member's armed forces.

Article 45

In order to enable the United Nations to take urgent military measures, Members shall hold immediately available national air-force contingents for combined international enforcement action. The strength and degree of readiness of these contingents and plans for their combined action shall be determined, within the limits laid down in the special agreement or agreements referred to in Article 43, by the Security Council with the assistance of the Military Staff Committee.

Article 46

Plans for the application of armed force shall be made by the Security Council with the assistance of the Military Staff Committee.

Article 47

1. There shall be established a Military Staff Committee to advise and assist the Security Council on all questions relating to the Security Council's military requirements for the maintenance of international peace and security, the employ-ment and command of forces placed at its disposal, the regulation of arma-ments, and possible disarmament.

2. The Military Staff Committee shall consist of the Chiefs of Staff of the permanent members of the Security Council or their representatives. Any Mem-ber of the United Nations not permanently represented on the Committee shall be invited by the Committee to be associated with it when the efficient discharge of the Committee's responsibilities requires the participation of that Member in its work.

3. The Military Staff Committee shall be responsible under the Security Coun-cil for the strategic direction of any armed forces placed at the disposal of the Security Council. Questions relating to the command of such forces shall be worked out subsequently.

4. The Military Staff Committee, with the authorization of the Security Council and after consultation with appropriate regional agencies, may establish regional subcommittees.

Article 48

1. The action required to carry out the decisions of the Security Council for the maintenance of international peace and security shall be taken by all the Members of the United Nations or by some of them, as the Security Council may determine.

2. Such decisions shall be carried out by the Members of the United Nations directly and through their action in the appropriate international agencies of which they are members.

Article 49

The Members of the United Nations shall join in affording mutual assistance in carrying out the measures decided upon by the Security Council.

Article 50

If preventive or enforcement measures against any state are taken by the Security Council, any other state, whether a Member of the United Nations or not, which finds itself confronted with special economic problems arising from the carrying out of those measures shall have the right to consult the Security Council with regard to a solution of those problems.

Article 51

Nothing in the present Charter shall impair the inherent right of individual or collective self-defense if an armed attack occurs against a Member of the United Nations, until the Security Council has taken the measures necessary to maintain international peace and security. Measures taken by Members in the exercise of this right of self-defense shall be immediately reported to the Security Council and shall not in any way affect the authority and responsibility of the Security Council under the present Charter to take at any time such action as it deems necessary in order to maintain or restore international peace and security.

CHAPTER VIII

REGIONAL ARRANGEMENTS

Article 52

1. Nothing in the present Charter precludes the existence of regional arrangements or agencies for dealing with such matters relating to the maintenance of international peace and security as are appropriate for regional action, provided that such arrangements or agencies and their activities are consistent with the Purposes and Principles of the United Nations.
2. The Members of the United Nations entering into such arrangements or constituting such agencies shall make every effort to achieve pacific settlement of local disputes through such regional arrangements or by such regional agencies before referring them to the Security Council.
3. The Security Council shall encourage the development of pacific settlement of local disputes through such regional arrangements or by such regional agencies either on the initiative of the states concerned or by reference from the Security Council.
4. This Article in no way impairs the application of Articles 34 and 35.

Article 53

1. The Security Council shall, where appropriate, utilize such regional arrangements or agencies for enforcement action under its authority. But no enforcement action shall be taken under regional arrangements or by regional agencies without the authorization of the Security Council, with the exception of measures against any enemy state, as defined in paragraph 2 of this Article, provided for pursuant to Article 107 or in regional arrangements directed against renewal of aggressive policy on the part of any such state, until such time as the Organization may, on request of the Governments concerned, be charged with the responsibility for preventing further aggression by such a state.
2. The term enemy state as used in paragraph 1 of this Article applies to any state which during the Second World War has been an enemy of any signatory of the present Charter.

Article 54

The Security Council shall at all times be kept fully informed of activities undertaken or in contemplation under regional arrangements or by regional agencies for the maintenance of international peace and security.

CHAPTER IX

INTERNATIONAL ECONOMIC AND SOCIAL CO-OPERATION

Article 55

With a view to the creation of conditions of stability and well-being which are necessary for peaceful and friendly relations among nations based on respect for the principle of equal rights and self-determination of peoples, the United Nations shall promote:

a. higher standards of living, full employment, and conditions of economic and social progress and development;

b. solutions of international economic, social, health, and related problems; and international cultural and educational co-operation; and

c. universal respect for, and observance of, human rights and fundamental freedoms for all without distinction as to race, sex, language, or religion.

Article 56

All Members pledge themselves to take joint and separate action in co-operation with the Organization for the achievement of the purposes set forth in Article 55.

Article 57

1. The various specialized agencies, established by intergovernmental agreement and having wide international responsibilities, as defined in their basic instruments, in economic, social, cultural, educational, health, and related fields, shall be brought into relationship with the United Nations in accordance with the provisions of Article 63.

2. Such agencies thus brought into relationship with the United Nations are hereinafter referred to as specialized agencies.

Article 58

The Organization shall make recommendations for the co-ordination of the policies and activities of the specialized agencies.

Article 59

The Organization shall, where appropriate, initiate negotiations among the states concerned for the creation of any new specialized agencies required for the accomplishment of the purposes set forth in Article 55.

Article 60

Responsibility for the discharge of the functions of the Organization set forth in this Chapter shall be vested in the General Assembly and, under the authority of the General Assembly, in the Economic and Social Council, which shall have for this purpose the powers set forth in Chapter X.

CHAPTER X

THE ECONOMIC AND SOCIAL COUNCIL

COMPOSITION

Article 61

1. The Economic and Social Council shall consist of eighteen Members of the United Nations elected by the General Assembly.
2. Subject to the provisions of paragraph 3, six members of the Economic and Social Council shall be elected each year for a term of three years. A retiring member shall be eligible for immediate re-election.
3. At the first election, eighteen members of the Economic and Social Council shall be chosen. The term of office of six members so chosen shall expire at the end of one year, and of six other members at the end of two years, in accordance with arrangements made by the General Assembly.
4. Each member of the Economic and Social Council shall have one representative.

FUNCTIONS AND POWERS

Article 62

1. The Economic and Social Council may make or initiate studies and reports with respect to international economic, social, cultural, educational, health, and related matters and may make recommendations with respect to any such matters to the General Assembly, to the Members of the United Nations, and to the specialized agencies concerned.
2. It may make recommendations for the purpose of promoting respect for, and observance of, human rights and fundamental freedoms for all.
3. It may prepare draft conventions for submission to the General Assembly, with respect to matters falling within its competence.
4. It may call, in accordance with the rules prescribed by the United Nations, international conferences on matters falling within its competence.

Article 63

1. The Economic and Social Council may enter into agreements with any of the agencies referred to in Article 57, defining the terms on which the agency concerned shall be brought into relationship with the United Nations. Such agreements shall be subject to approval by the General Assembly.
2. It may co-ordinate the activities of the specialized agencies through consultation with and recommendations to such agencies and through recommendations to the General Assembly and to the Members of the United Nations.

Article 64

1. The Economic and Social Council may take appropriate steps to obtain regular reports from the specialized agencies. It may make arrangements with

the Members of the United Nations and with the specialized agencies to obtain reports on the steps taken to give effect to its own recommendations and to recommendations on matters falling within its competence made by the General Assembly.

2. It may communicate its observations on these reports to the General Assembly.

Article 65

The Economic and Social Council may furnish information to the Security Council and shall assist the Security Council upon its request.

Article 66

1. The Economic and Social Council shall perform such functions as fall within its competence in connection with the carrying out of the recommendations of the General Assembly.

2. It may, with the approval of the General Assembly, perform services at the request of Members of the United Nations and at the request of specialized agencies.

3. It shall perform such other functions as are specified elsewhere in the present Charter or as may be assigned to it by the General Assembly.

VOTING

Article 67

1. Each member of the Economic and Social Council shall have one vote.

2. Decisions of the Economic and Social Council shall be made by a majority of the members present and voting.

PROCEDURE

Article 68

The Economic and Social Council shall set up commissions in economic and social fields and for the promotion of human rights, and such other commissions as may be required for the performance of its functions.

Article 69

The Economic and Social Council shall invite any Member of the United Nations to participate, without vote, in its deliberations on any matter of particular concern to that Member.

Article 70

The Economic and Social Council may make arrangements for representatives of the specialized agencies to participate, without vote, in its deliberations and in those of the commissions established by it, and for its representatives to participate in the deliberations of the specialized agencies.

Article 71

The Economic and Social Council may make suitable arrangements for consultation with non-governmental organizations which are concerned with matters within its competence. Such arrangements may be made with international organizations and, where appropriate, with national organizations after consultation with the Member of the United Nations concerned.

Article 72

1. The Economic and Social Council shall adopt its own rules of procedure, including the method of selecting its President.
2. The Economic and Social Council shall meet as required in accordance with its rules, which shall include provision for the convening of meetings on the request of a majority of its members.

CHAPTER XI

DECLARATION REGARDING NON-SELF-GOVERNING TERRITORIES

Article 73

Members of the United Nations which have or assume responsibilities for the administration of territories whose peoples have not yet attained a full measure of self-government recognize the principle that the interests of the inhabitants of these territories are paramount, and accept as a sacred trust the obligation to promote to the utmost, within the system of international peace and security established by the present Charter, the well-being of the inhabitants of these territories, and, to this end:

a. to ensure, with due respect for the culture of the peoples concerned, their political, economic, social, and educational advancement, their just treatment, and their protection against abuses;

b. to develop self-government, to take due account of the political aspirations of the peoples, and to assist them in the progressive development of their free political institutions, according to the particular circumstances of each territory and its peoples and their varying stages of advancement;

c. to further international peace and security;

d. to promote constructive measures of development, to encourage research, and to co-operate with one another and, when and where appropriate, with specialized international bodies with a view to the practical achievement of the social, economic, and scientific purposes set forth in this Article; and

e. to transmit regularly to the Secretary-General for information purposes, subject to such limitation as security and constitutional considerations may require, statistical and other information of a technical nature relating to economic, social, and educational conditions in the territories for which they are respectively responsible other than those territories to which Chapters XII and XIII apply.

Article 74

Members of the United Nations also agree that their policy in respect of the territories to which this Chapter applies, no less than in respect of their metropolitan areas, must be based on the general principle of good-neighborliness, due account being taken of the interests and well-being of the rest of the world, in social, economic, and commercial matters.

CHAPTER XII

INTERNATIONAL TRUSTEESHIP SYSTEM

Article 75

The United Nations shall establish under its authority an international trusteeship system for the administration and supervision of such territories as may be placed thereunder by subsequent individual agreements. These territories are hereinafter referred to as trust territories.

Article 76

The basic objectives of the trusteeship system, in accordance with the Purposes of the United Nations laid down in Article 1 of the present Charter, shall be:
  a. to further international peace and security;
  b. to promote the political, economic, social, and educational advancement of the inhabitants of the trust territories, and their progressive development towards self-government or independence as may be appropriate to the particular circumstances of each territory and its peoples and the freely expressed wishes of the peoples concerned, and as may be provided by the terms of each trusteeship agreement;
  c. to encourage respect for human rights and for fundamental freedoms for all without distinction as to race, sex, language, or religion, and to encourage recognition of the interdependence of the peoples of the world; and
  d. to ensure equal treatment in social, economic, and commercial matters for all Members of the United Nations and their nationals, and also equal treatment for the latter in the administration of justice, without prejudice to the attainment of the foregoing objectives and subject to the provisions of Article 80.

Article 77

1. The trusteeship system shall apply to such territories in the following categories as may be placed thereunder by means of trusteeship agreements:
  a. territories now held under mandate;
  b. territories which may be detached from enemy states as a result of the Second World War; and

c. territories voluntarily placed under the system by states responsible for their administration.

2. It will be a matter for subsequent agreement as to which territories in the foregoing categories will be brought under the trusteeship system and upon what terms.

Article 78

The trusteeship system shall not apply to territories which have become Members of the United Nations, relationship among which shall be based on respect for the principle of sovereign equality.

Article 79

The terms of trusteeship for each territory to be placed under the trusteeship system, including any alteration or amendment, shall be agreed upon by the states directly concerned, including the mandatory power in the case of territories held under mandate by a Member of the United Nations, and shall be approved as provided for in Articles 83 and 85.

Article 80

1. Except as may be agreed upon in individual trusteeship agreements, made under Articles 77, 79 and 81, placing each territory under the trusteeship system, and until such agreements have been concluded, nothing in this Chapter shall be construed in or of itself to alter in any manner the rights whatsoever of any states or any peoples or the terms of existing international instruments to which Members of the United Nations may respectively be parties.

2. Paragraph 1 of this Article shall not be interpreted as giving grounds for delay or postponement of the negotiation and conclusion of agreements for placing mandated and other territories under the trusteeship system as provided for in Article 77.

Article 81

The trusteeship agreement shall in each case include the terms under which the trust territory will be administered and designate the authority which will exercise the administration of the trust territory. Such authority, hereinafter called the administering authority, may be one or more states or the Organization itself.

Article 82

There may be designated, in any trusteeship agreement, a strategic area or areas which may include part or all of the trust territory to which the agreement applies, without prejudice to any special agreement or agreements made under Article 43.

Article 83

1. All functions of the United Nations relating to strategic areas, including the approval of the terms of the trusteeship agreements and of their alteration or amendment shall be exercised by the Security Council.

2. The basic objectives set forth in Article 76 shall be applicable to the people of each strategic area.

3. The Security Council shall, subject to the provisions of the trusteeship agreements and without prejudice to security considerations, avail itself of the assistance of the Trusteeship Council to perform those functions of the United Nations under the trusteeship system relating to political, economic, social, and educational matters in the strategic areas.

Article 84

It shall be the duty of the administering authority to ensure that the trust territory shall play its part in the maintenance of international peace and security. To this end the administering authority may make use of volunteer forces, facilities, and assistance from the trust territory in carrying out the obligation towards the Security Council undertaken in this regard by the administering authority, as well as for local defense and the maintenance of law and order within the trust territory.

Article 85

1. The functions of the United Nations with regard to trusteeship agreements for all areas not designated as strategic, including the approval of the terms of the trusteeship agreements and of their alteration or amendment, shall be exercised by the General Assembly.

2. The Trusteeship Council, operating under the authority of the General Assembly, shall assist the General Assembly in carrying out these functions.

CHAPTER XIII

THE TRUSTEESHIP COUNCIL

COMPOSITION

Article 86

1. The Trusteeship Council shall consist of the following Members of the United Nations:

a. those Members administering trust territories;

b. such of those Members mentioned by name in Article 23 as are not administering trust territories; and

c. as many other Members elected for three-year terms by the General Assembly as may be necessary to ensure that the total number of members of the Trusteeship Council is equally divided between those Members of the United Nations which administer trust territories and those which do not.

2. Each member of the Trusteeship Council shall designate one specially qualified person to represent it therein.

FUNCTIONS AND POWERS

Article 87

The General Assembly and, under its authority, the Trusteeship Council, in carrying out their functions, may:
  a. consider reports submitted by the administering authority;
  b. accept petitions and examine them in consultation with the administering authority;
  c. provide for periodic visits to the respective trust territories at times agreed upon with the administering authority; and
  d. take these and other actions in conformity with the terms of the trusteeship agreements.

Article 88

The Trusteeship Council shall formulate a questionnaire on the political, economic, social, and educational advancement of the inhabitants of each trust territory, and the administering authority for each trust territory within the competence of the General Assembly shall make an annual report to the General Assembly upon the basis of such questionnaire.

VOTING

Article 89

  1. Each member of the Trusteeship Council shall have one vote.
  2. Decisions of the Trusteeship Council shall be made by a majority of the members present and voting.

PROCEDURE

Article 90

  1. The Trusteeship Council shall adopt its own rules of procedure, including the method of selecting its President.
  2. The Trusteeship Council shall meet as required in accordance with its rules, which shall include provision for the convening of meetings on the request of a majority of its members.

Article 91

The Trusteeship Council shall, when appropriate, avail itself of the assistance of the Economic and Social Council and of the specialized agencies in regard to matters with which they are respectively concerned.

CHAPTER XIV

THE INTERNATIONAL COURT OF JUSTICE

Article 92

The International Court of Justice shall be the principal judicial organ of the United Nations. It shall function in accordance with the annexed Statute, which is based upon the Statute of the Permanent Court of International Justice and forms an integral part of the present Charter.

Article 93

1. All Members of the United Nations are *ipso facto* parties to the Statute of the International Court of Justice.
2. A state which is not a Member of the United Nations may become a party to the Statute of the International Court of Justice on conditions to be determined in each case by the General Assembly upon the recommendation of the Security Council.

Article 94

1. Each Member of the United Nations undertakes to comply with the decision of the International Court of Justice in any case to which it is a party.
2. If any party to a case fails to perform the obligations incumbent upon it under a judgment rendered by the Court, the other party may have recourse to the Security Council, which may, if it deems necessary, make recommendations or decide upon measures to be taken to give effect to the judgment.

Article 95

Nothing in the present Charter shall prevent Members of the United Nations from entrusting the solution of their differences to other tribunals by virtue of agreements already in existence or which may be concluded in the future.

Article 96

1. The General Assembly or the Security Council may request the International Court of Justice to give an advisory opinion on any legal question.
2. Other organs of the United Nations and specialized agencies, which may at any time be so authorized by the General Assembly, may also request advisory opinions of the Court on legal questions arising within the scope of their activities.

CHAPTER XV

THE SECRETARIAT

Article 97

The Secretariat shall comprise a Secretary-General and such staff as the Organization may require. The Secretary-General shall be appointed by the General Assembly upon the recommendation of the Security Council. He shall be the chief administrative officer of the Organization.

Article 98

The Secretary-General shall act in that capacity in all meetings of the General Assembly, of the Security Council, of the Economic and Social Council, and of the Trusteeship Council, and shall perform such other functions as are entrusted to him by these organs. The Secretary-General shall make an annual report to the General Assembly on the work of the Organization.

Article 99

The Secretary-General may bring to the attention of the Security Council any matter which in his opinion may threaten the maintenance of international peace and security.

Article 100

1. In the performance of their duties the Secretary-General and the staff shall not seek or receive instructions from any government or from any other authority external to the Organization. They shall refrain from any action which might reflect on their position as international officials responsible only to the Organization.
2. Each Member of the United Nations undertakes to respect the exclusively international character of the responsibilities of the Secretary-General and the staff and not to seek to influence them in the discharge of their responsibilities.

Article 101

1. The staff shall be appointed by the Secretary-General under regulations established by the General Assembly.
2. Appropriate staffs shall be permanently assigned to the Economic and Social Council, the Trusteeship Council, and, as required, to other organs of the United Nations. These staffs shall form a part of the Secretariat.
3. The paramount consideration in the employment of the staff and in the determination of the conditions of service shall be the necessity of securing the highest standards of efficiency, competence, and integrity. Due regard shall be paid to the importance of recruiting the staff on as wide a geographical basis as possible.

CHAPTER XVI

MISCELLANEOUS PROVISIONS

Article 102

1. Every treaty and every international agreement entered into by any Member of the United Nations after the present Charter comes into force shall as soon as possible be registered with the Secretariat and published by it.
2. No party to any such treaty or international agreement which has not been registered in accordance with the provisions of paragraph 1 of this Article may invoke that treaty or agreement before any organ of the United Nations.

Article 103

In the event of a conflict between the obligations of the Members of the United Nations under the present Charter and their obligations under any other international agreement, their obligations under the present Charter shall prevail.

Article 104

The Organization shall enjoy in the territory of each of its Members such legal capacity as may be necessary for the exercise of its functions and the fulfillment of its purposes.

Article 105

1. The Organization shall enjoy in the territory of each of its Members such privileges and immunities as are necessary for the fulfillment of its purposes.
2. Representatives of the Members of the United Nations and officials of the Organization shall similarly enjoy such privileges and immunities as are necessary for the independent exercise of their functions in connection with the Organization.
3. The General Assembly may make recommendations with a view to determining the details of the application of paragraphs 1 and 2 of this Article or may propose conventions to the Members of the United Nations for this purpose.

CHAPTER XVII

TRANSITIONAL SECURITY ARRANGEMENTS

Article 106

Pending the coming into force of such special agreements referred to in Article 43 as in the opinion of the Security Council enable it to begin the exercise of its responsibilities under Article 42, the parties to the Four-Nation Declaration, signed at Moscow, October 30, 1943, and France, shall, in accordance with the provisions of Paragraph 5 of that Declaration, consult with one another and as occasion requires with other Members of the United Nations with a view to such joint action on behalf of the Organization as may be necessary for the purpose of maintaining international peace and security.

Article 107

Nothing in the present Charter shall invalidate or preclude action, in relation to any state which during the Second World War has been an enemy of any signatory to the present Charter, taken or authorized as a result of that war by the Governments having responsibility for such action.

CHAPTER XVIII

AMENDMENTS

Article 108

Amendments to the present Charter shall come into force for all Members of the United Nations when they have been adopted by a vote of two thirds of the members of the General Assembly and ratified in accordance with their respective constitutional processes by two thirds of the Members of the United Nations, including all the permanent members of the Security Council.

Article 109

1. A General Conference of the Members of the United Nations for the purpose of reviewing the present Charter may be held at a date and place to be fixed by a two-thirds vote of the members of the General Assembly and by a vote of any seven members of the Security Council. Each Member of the United Nations shall have one vote in the conference.

2. Any alteration of the present Charter recommended by a two-thirds vote of the conference shall take effect when ratified in accordance with their respective constitutional processes by two thirds of the Members of the United Nations including all the permanent members of the Security Council.

3. If such a conference has not been held before the tenth annual session of the General Assembly following the coming into force of the present Charter, the proposal to call such a conference shall be placed on the agenda of that session of the General Assembly, and the conference shall be held if so decided by a majority vote of the members of the General Assembly and by a vote of any seven members of the Security Council.

CHAPTER XIX

RATIFICATION AND SIGNATURE

Article 110

1. The present Charter shall be ratified by the signatory states in accordance with their respective constitutional processes.

2. The ratifications shall be deposited with the Government of the United States of America, which shall notify all the signatory states of each deposit as well as the Secretary-General of the Organization when he has been appointed.

3. The present Charter shall come into force upon the deposit of ratifications by the Republic of China, France, the Union of Soviet Socialist Republics, the United Kingdom of Great Britain and Northern Ireland, and the United States of America, and by a majority of the other signatory states. A protocol of the ratifications deposited shall thereupon be drawn up by the Government of the United States of America which shall communicate copies thereof to all the signatory states.

4. The states signatory to the present Charter which ratify it after it has come into force will become original Members of the United Nations on the date of the deposit of their respective ratifications.

Article 111

The present Charter, of which the Chinese, French, Russian, English, and Spanish texts are equally authentic, shall remain deposited in the archives of the Government of the United States of America. Duly certified copies thereof shall be transmitted by that Government to the Governments of the other signatory states.

IN FAITH WHEREOF the representatives of the Governments of the United Nations have signed the present Charter.

DONE at the city of San Francisco the twenty-sixth day of June, one thousand nine hundred and forty-five.

STATUTE OF THE INTERNATIONAL COURT OF JUSTICE

Article 1

THE INTERNATIONAL COURT OF JUSTICE established by the Charter of the United Nations as the principal judicial organ of the United Nations shall be constituted and shall function in accordance with the provisions of the present Statute.

CHAPTER I

ORGANIZATION OF THE COURT

Article 2

The Court shall be composed of a body of independent judges, elected regardless of their nationality from among persons of high moral character, who possess the qualifications required in their respective countries for appointment to the highest judicial offices, or are jurisconsults of recognized competence in international law.

Article 3

1. The Court shall consist of fifteen members, no two of whom may be nationals of the same state.
2. A person who for the purposes of membership in the Court could be regarded as a national of more than one state shall be deemed to be a national of the one in which he ordinarily exercises civil and political rights.

Article 4

1. The members of the Court shall be elected by the General Assembly and by the Security Council from a list of persons nominated by the national groups in the Permanent Court of Arbitration, in accordance with the following provisions.
2. In the case of Members of the United Nations not represented in the Permanent Court of Arbitration, candidates shall be nominated by national groups appointed for this purpose by their governments under the same conditions as those prescribed for members of the Permanent Court of Arbitration by Article 44 of the Convention of The Hague of 1907 for the pacific settlement of international disputes.
3. The conditions under which a state which is a party to the present Statute but is not a Member of the United Nations may participate in electing the members of the Court shall, in the absence of a special agreement, be laid down by the General Assembly upon recommendation of the Security Council.

Article 5

1. At least three months before the date of the election, the Secretary-General of the United Nations shall address a written request to the members of the Permanent Court of Arbitration belonging to the states which are parties to the present Statute, and to the members of the national groups appointed under Article 4, paragraph 2, inviting them to undertake, within a given time, by national groups, the nomination of persons in a position to accept the duties of a member of the Court.
2. No group may nominate more than four persons, not more than two of whom shall be of their own nationality. In no case may the number of candidates nominated by a group be more than double the number of seats to be filled.

Article 6

Before making these nominations, each national group is recommended to consult its highest court of justice, its legal faculties and schools of law, and its national academies and national sections of international academies devoted to the study of law.

Article 7

1. The Secretary-General shall prepare a list in alphabetical order of all the persons thus nominated. Save as provided in Article 12, paragraph 2, these shall be the only persons eligible

2. The Secretary-General shall submit this list to the General Assembly and to the Security Council.

Article 8

The General Assembly and the Security Council shall proceed independently of one another to elect the members of the Court.

Article 9

At every election, the electors shall bear in mind not only that the persons to be elected should individually possess the qualifications required, but also that in the body as a whole the representation of the main forms of civilization and of the principal legal systems of the world should be assured.

Article 10

1. Those candidates who obtain an absolute majority of votes in the General Assembly and in the Security Council shall be considered as elected.
2. Any vote of the Security Council, whether for the election of judges or for the appointment of members of the conference envisaged in Article 12, shall be taken without any distinction between permanent and non-permanent members of the Security Council.
3. In the event of more than one national of the same state obtaining an absolute majority of the votes both of the General Assembly and of the Security Council, the eldest of these only shall be considered as elected.

Article 11

If, after the first meeting held for the purpose of the election, one or more seats remain to be filled, a second and, if necessary, a third meeting shall take place.

Article 12

1. If, after the third meeting, one or more seats still remain unfilled, a joint conference consisting of six members, three appointed by the General Assembly and three by the Security Council, may be formed at any time at the request of either the General Assembly or the Security Council, for the purpose of choosing by the vote of an absolute majority one name for each seat still vacant, to submit to the General Assembly and the Security Council for their respective acceptance.
2. If the joint conference is unanimously agreed upon any person who fulfills the required conditions, he may be included in its list, even though he was not included in the list of nominations referred to in Article 7.
3. If the joint conference is satisfied that it will not be successful in procuring an election, those members of the Court who have already been elected shall, within a period to be fixed by the Security Council, proceed to fill the vacant seats by selection from among those candidates who have obtained votes either in the General Assembly or in the Security Council.
4. In the event of an equality of votes among the judges, the eldest judge shall have a casting vote.

Article 13

1. The members of the Court shall be elected for nine years and may be re-elected; provided, however, that of the judges elected at the first election, the terms of five judges shall expire at the end of three years and the terms of five more judges shall expire at the end of six years.

2. The judges whose terms are to expire at the end of the above-mentioned initial periods of three and six years shall be chosen by lot to be drawn by the Secretary-General immediately after the first election has been completed.

3. The members of the Court shall continue to discharge their duties until their places have been filled. Though replaced, they shall finish any cases which they may have begun.

4. In the case of the resignation of a member of the Court, the resignation shall be addressed to the President of the Court for transmission to the Secretary-General. This last notification makes the place vacant.

Article 14

Vacancies shall be filled by the same method as that laid down for the first election, subject to the following provision: the Secretary-General shall, within one month of the occurrence of the vacancy, proceed to issue the invitations provided for in Article 5, and the date of the election shall be fixed by the Security Council.

Article 15

A member of the Court elected to replace a member whose term of office has not expired shall hold office for the remainder of his predecessor's term.

Article 16

1. No member of the Court may exercise any political or administrative function, or engage in any other occupation of a professional nature.

2. Any doubt on this point shall be settled by the decision of the Court.

Article 17

1. No member of the Court may act as agent, counsel, or advocate in any case.

2. No member may participate in the decision of any case in which he has previously taken part as agent, counsel, or advocate for one of the parties, or as a member of a national or international court, or of a commission of enquiry, or in any other capacity.

3. Any doubt on this point shall be settled by the decision of the Court.

Article 18

1. No member of the Court can be dismissed unless, in the unanimous opinion of the other members, he has ceased to fulfill the required conditions.

2. Formal notification thereof shall be made to the Secretary-General by the Registrar.

3. This notification makes the place vacant.

Article 19

The members of the Court, when engaged on the business of the Court, shall enjoy diplomatic privileges and immunities.

Article 20

Every member of the Court shall, before taking up his duties, make a solemn declaration in open court that he will exercise his powers impartially and conscientiously.

Article 21

1. The Court shall elect its President and Vice-President for three years; they may be re-elected.
2. The Court shall appoint its Registrar and may provide for the appointment of such other officers as may be necessary.

Article 22

1. The seat of the Court shall be established at The Hague. This, however, shall not prevent the Court from sitting and exercising its functions elsewhere whenever the Court considers it desirable.
2. The President and the Registrar shall reside at the seat of the Court.

Article 23

1. The Court shall remain permanently in session, except during the judicial vacations, the dates and duration of which shall be fixed by the Court.
2. Members of the Court are entitled to periodic leave, the dates and duration of which shall be fixed by the Court, having in mind the distance between The Hague and the home of each judge.
3. Members of the Court shall be bound, unless they are on leave or prevented from attending by illness or other serious reasons duly explained to the President, to hold themselves permanently at the disposal of the Court.

Article 24

1. If, for some special reason, a member of the Court considers that he should not take part in the decision of a particular case, he shall so inform the President.
2. If the President considers that for some special reason one of the members of the Court should not sit in a particular case, he shall give him notice accordingly.
3. If in any such case the member of the Court and the President disagree, the matter shall be settled by the decision of the Court.

Article 25

1. The full Court shall sit except when it is expressly provided otherwise in the present Statute.
2. Subject to the condition that the number of judges available to constitute

the Court is not thereby reduced below eleven, the Rules of the Court may provide for allowing one or more judges, according to circumstances and in rotation, to be dispensed from sitting.

3. A quorum of nine judges shall suffice to constitute the Court.

Article 26

1. The Court may from time to time form one or more chambers, composed of three or more judges as the Court may determine, for dealing with particular categories of cases; for example, labor cases and cases relating to transit and communications.

2. The Court may at any time form a chamber for dealing with a particular case. The number of judges to constitute such a chamber shall be determined by the Court with the approval of the parties.

3. Cases shall be heard and determined by the chambers provided for in this Article if the parties so request.

Article 27

A judgment given by any of the chambers provided for in Articles 26 and 29 shall be considered as rendered by the Court.

Article 28

The chambers provided for in Articles 26 and 29 may, with the consent of the parties, sit and exercise their functions elsewhere than at The Hague.

Article 29

With a view to the speedy despatch of business, the Court shall form annually a chamber composed of five judges which, at the request of the parties, may hear and determine cases by summary procedure. In addition, two judges shall be selected for the purpose of replacing judges who find it impossible to sit.

Article 30

1. The Court shall frame rules for carrying out its functions. In particular, it shall lay down rules of procedure.

2. The Rules of the Court may provide for assessors to sit with the Court or with any of its chambers, without the right to vote.

Article 31

1. Judges of the nationality of each of the parties shall retain their right to sit in the case before the Court.

2. If the Court includes upon the Bench a judge of the nationality of one of the parties, any other party may choose a person to sit as judge. Such person shall be chosen preferably from among those persons who have been nominated as candidates as provided in Articles 4 and 5.

3. If the Court includes upon the Bench no judge of the nationality of the

parties, each of these parties may proceed to choose a judge as provided in paragraph 2 of this Article.

4. The provisions of this Article shall apply to the case of Articles 26 and 29. In such cases, the President shall request one or, if necessary, two of the members of the Court forming the chamber to give place to the members of the Court of the nationality of the parties concerned, and, failing such, or if they are unable to be present, to the judges specially chosen by the parties.

5. Should there be several parties in the same interest, they shall, for the purpose of the preceding provisions, be reckoned as one party only. Any doubt upon this point shall be settled by the decision of the Court.

6. Judges chosen as laid down in paragraphs 2, 3, and 4 of this Article shall fulfill the conditions required by Articles 2, 17 (paragraph 2), 20, and 24 of the present Statute. They shall take part in the decision on terms of complete equality with their colleagues.

Article 32

1. Each member of the Court shall receive an annual salary.

2. The President shall receive a special annual allowance.

3. The Vice-President shall receive a special allowance for every day on which he acts as President.

4. The judges chosen under Article 31, other than members of the Court, shall receive compensation for each day on which they exercise their functions.

5. These salaries, allowances, and compensation shall be fixed by the General Assembly. They may not be decreased during the term of office.

6. The salary of the Registrar shall be fixed by the General Assembly on the proposal of the Court.

7. Regulations made by the General Assembly shall fix the conditions under which retirement pensions may be given to members of the Court and to the Registrar, and the conditions under which members of the Court and the Registrar shall have their traveling expenses refunded.

8. The above salaries, allowances, and compensation shall be free of all taxation.

Article 33

The expenses of the Court shall be borne by the United Nations in such a manner as shall be decided by the General Assembly.

CHAPTER II

COMPETENCE OF THE COURT

Article 34

1. Only states may be parties in cases before the Court.

2. The Court, subject to and in conformity with its Rules, may request of public international organizations information relevant to cases before it, and shall receive such information presented by such organizations on their own initiative.

357 **Appendix I: United Nations**

3. Whenever the construction of the constituent instrument of a public international organization or of an international convention adopted thereunder is in question in a case before the Court, the Registrar shall so notify the public international organization concerned and shall communicate to it copies of all the written proceedings.

Article 35

1. The Court shall be open to the states parties to the present Statute.

2. The conditions under which the Court shall be open to other states shall, subject to the special provisions contained in treaties in force, be laid down by the Security Council, but in no case shall such conditions place the parties in a position of inequality before the Court.

3. When a state which is not a Member of the United Nations is a party to a case, the Court shall fix the amount which that party is to contribute towards the expenses of the Court. This provision shall not apply if such state is bearing a share of the expenses of the Court.

Article 36

1. The jurisdiction of the Court comprises all cases which the parties refer to it and all matters specially provided for in the Charter of the United Nations or in treaties and conventions in force.

2. The states parties to the present Statute may at any time declare that they recognize as compulsory *ipso facto* and without special agreement, in relation to any other state accepting the same obligation, the jurisdiction of the Court in all legal disputes concerning:

  a. the interpretation of a treaty;
  b. any question of international law;
  c. the existence of any fact which, if established, would constitute a breach of an international obligation;
  d. the nature or extent of the reparation to be made for the breach of an international obligation.

3. The declarations referred to above may be made unconditionally or on condition of reciprocity on the part of several or certain states, or for a certain time.

4. Such declarations shall be deposited with the Secretary-General of the United Nations, who shall transmit copies thereof to the parties to the Statute and to the Registrar of the Court.

5. Declarations made under Article 36 of the Statute of the Permanent Court of International Justice and which are still in force shall be deemed, as between the parties to the present Statute, to be acceptances of the compulsory jurisdiction of the International Court of Justice for the period which they still have to run and in accordance with their terms.

6. In the event of a dispute as to whether the Court has jurisdiction, the matter shall be settled by the decision of the Court.

Article 37

Whenever a treaty or convention in force provides for reference of a matter to a tribunal to have been instituted by the League of Nations, or to the Permanent Court of International Justice, the matter shall, as between the parties to the present Statute, be referred to the International Court of Justice.

Article 38

1. The Court, whose function is to decide in accordance with international law such disputes as are submitted to it, shall apply:
   a. international conventions, whether general or particular, establishing rules expressly recognized by the contesting states;
   b. international custom, as evidence of a general practice accepted as law;
   c. the general principles of law recognized by civilized nations;
   d. subject to the provisions of Article 59, judicial decisions and the teachings of the most highly qualified publicists of the various nations, as subsidiary means for the determination of rules of law.
2. This provision shall not prejudice the power of the Court to decide a case *ex aequo et bono*, if the parties agree thereto.

CHAPTER III

PROCEDURE

Article 39

1. The official languages of the Court shall be French and English. If the parties agree that the case shall be conducted in French, the judgment shall be delivered in French. If the parties agree that the case shall be conducted in English, the judgment shall be delivered in English.
2. In the absence of an agreement as to which language shall be employed, each party may, in the pleadings, use the language which it prefers; the decision of the Court shall be given in French and English. In this case the Court shall at the same time determine which of the two texts shall be considered as authoritative.
3. The Court shall, at the request of any party, authorize a language other than French or English to be used by that party.

Article 40

1. Cases are brought before the Court, as the case may be, either by the notification of the special agreement or by a written application addressed to the Registrar. In either case the subject of the dispute and the parties shall be indicated.
2. The Registrar shall forthwith communicate the application to all concerned.
3. He shall also notify the Members of the United Nations through the Secretary-General, and also any other states entitled to appear before the Court.

Article 41

1. The Court shall have the power to indicate, if it considers that circumstances so require, any provisional measures which ought to be taken to preserve the respective rights of either party.

2. Pending the final decision, notice of the measures suggested shall forth-with be given to the parties and to the Security Council.

Article 42

1. The parties shall be represented by agents.
2. They may have the assistance of counsel or advocates before the Court.
3. The agents, counsel, and advocates of parties before the Court shall enjoy the privileges and immunities necessary to the independent exercise of their duties.

Article 43

1. The procedure shall consist of two parts: written and oral.
2. The written proceedings shall consist of the communication to the Court and to the parties of memorials, counter-memorials and, if necessary, replies; also all papers and documents in support.
3. These communications shall be made through the Registrar, in the order and within the time fixed by the Court.
4. A certified copy of every document produced by one party shall be communicated to the other party.
5. The oral proceedings shall consist of the hearing by the Court of witnesses, experts, agents, counsel, and advocates.

Article 44

1. For the service of all notices upon persons other than the agents, counsel, and advocates, the Court shall apply direct to the government of the state upon whose territory the notice has to be served.
2. The same provision shall apply whenever steps are to be taken to procure evidence on the spot.

Article 45

The hearing shall be under the control of the President or, if he is unable to preside, of the Vice-President; if neither is able to preside, the senior judge present shall preside.

Article 46

The hearing in Court shall be public, unless the Court shall decide otherwise, or unless the parties demand that the public be not admitted.

Article 47

1. Minutes shall be made at each hearing and signed by the Registrar and the President.
2. These minutes alone shall be authentic.

Article 48

The Court shall make orders for the conduct of the case, shall decide the form and time in which each party must conclude its arguments, and make all arrangements connected with the taking of evidence.

Article 49

The Court may, even before the hearing begins, call upon the agents to produce any document or to supply any explanations. Formal note shall be taken of any refusal.

Article 50

The Court may, at any time, entrust any individual, body, bureau, commission, or other organization that it may select, with the task of carrying out an enquiry or giving an expert opinion.

Article 51

During the hearing any relevant questions are to be put to the witnesses and experts under the conditions laid down by the Court in the rules of procedure referred to in Article 30.

Article 52

After the Court has received the proofs and evidence within the time specified for the purpose, it may refuse to accept any further oral or written evidence that one party may desire to present unless the other side consents.

Article 53

1. Whenever one of the parties does not appear before the Court, or fails to defend its case, the other party may call upon the Court to decide in favor of its claim.
2. The Court must, before doing so, satisfy itself, not only that it has jurisdiction in accordance with Articles 36 and 37, but also that the claim is well founded in fact and law.

Article 54

1. When, subject to the control of the Court, the agents, counsel, and advocates have completed their presentation of the case, the President shall declare the hearing closed.
2. The Court shall withdraw to consider the judgment.
3. The deliberations of the Court shall take place in private and remain secret.

Article 55

1. All questions shall be decided by a majority of the judges present.
2. In the event of an equality of votes, the President or the judge who acts in his place shall have a casting vote.

Article 56

1. The judgment shall state the reasons on which it is based.
2. It shall contain the names of the judges who have taken part in the decision.

Article 57

If the judgment does not represent in whole or in part the unanimous opinion of the judges, any judge shall be entitled to deliver a separate opinion.

Article 58

The judgment shall be signed by the President and by the Registrar. It shall be read in open court, due notice having been given to the agents.

Article 59

The decision of the Court has no binding force except between the parties and in respect of that particular case.

Article 60

The judgment is final and without appeal. In the event of dispute as to the meaning or scope of the judgment, the Court shall construe it upon the request of any party,

Article 61

1. An application for revision of a judgment may be made only when it is based upon the discovery of some fact of such a nature as to be a decisive factor, which fact was, when the judgment was given, unknown to the Court and also to the party claiming revision, always provided that such ignorance was not due to negligence.

2. The proceedings for revision shall be opened by a judgment of the Court expressly recording the existence of the new fact, recognizing that it has such a character as to lay the case open to revision, and declaring the application admissible on this ground.

3. The Court may require previous compliance with the terms of the judgment before it admits proceedings in revision.

4. The application for revision must be made at latest within six months of the discovery of the new fact.

5. No application for revision may be made after the lapse of ten years from the date of the judgment.

Article 62

1. Should a state consider that it has an interest of a legal nature which may be affected by the decision in the case, it may submit a request to the Court to be permitted to intervene.

2. It shall be for the Court to decide upon this request.

Article 63

1. Whenever the construction of a convention to which states other than those concerned in the case are parties is in question, the Registrar shall notify all such states forthwith.

2. Every state so notified has the right to intervene in the proceedings; but if it uses this right, the construction given by the judgment will be equally binding upon it.

Article 64

Unless otherwise decided by the Court, each party shall bear its own costs.

CHAPTER IV

ADVISORY OPINIONS

Article 65

1. The Court may give an advisory opinion on any legal question at the request of whatever body may be authorized by or in accordance with the Charter of the United Nations to make such a request.

2. Questions upon which the advisory opinion of the Court is asked shall be laid before the Court by means of a written request containing an exact statement of the question upon which an opinion is required, and accompanied by all documents likely to throw light upon the question.

Article 66

1. The Registrar shall forthwith give notice of the request for an advisory opinion to all states entitled to appear before the Court.

2. The Registrar shall also, by means of a special and direct communication, notify any state entitled to appear before the Court or international organization considered by the Court, or, should it not be sitting, by the President, as likely to be able to furnish information on the question, that the Court will be prepared to receive, within a time limit to be fixed by the President, written statements, or to hear, at a public sitting to be held for the purpose, oral statements relating to the question.

3. Should any such state entitled to appear before the Court have failed to receive the special communication referred to in paragraph 2 of this Article, such state may express a desire to submit a written statement or to be heard; and the Court will decide.

4. States and organizations having presented written or oral statements or both shall be permitted to comment on the statements made by other states or organizations in the form, to the extent, and within the time limits which the Court, or, should it not be sitting, the President, shall decide in each particular case. Accordingly, the Registrar shall in due time communicate any such written statements to states and organizations having submitted similar statements.

Article 67

The Court shall deliver its advisory opinions in open court, notice having been given to the Secretary-General and to the representatives of Members of the United Nations, of other states and of international organizations immediately concerned.

Article 68

In the exercise of its advisory functions the Court shall further be guided by the provisions of the present Statute which apply in contentious cases to the extent to which it recognizes them to be applicable.

CHAPTER V

AMENDMENT

Article 69

Amendments to the present Statute shall be effected by the same procedure as is provided by the Charter of the United Nations for amendments to that Charter, subject however to any provisions which the General Assembly upon recommendation of the Security Council may adopt concerning the participation of states which are parties to the present Statute but are not Members of the United Nations.

Article 70

The Court shall have power to propose such amendments to the present Statute as it may deem necessary, through written communications to the Secretary-General, for consideration in conformity with the provisions of Article 69.

For China:
Vi-Kyuin Wellington Koo
Wang Chung-Hui
Wei Tao-Ming
Wu Yi-Fang
Li Hwang
Chun-Mai Carson Chang
Tung Pi-Wu
Hu Lin

For the Union of Soviet Socialist Republics:
A. Gromyko
A. Lavrentiev
K. Novikov
S. Tsarapkin
S. Golunsky
S. Krylov
Rodionov

For the United Kingdom of Great Britain and Northern Ireland:
Halifax
Cranborne

For the United States of America:
E. R. Stettinius, Jr.
Cordell Hull
Tom Connally
A. H. Vandenberg

Sol. Bloom
Charles A. Eaton
Harold E. Stassen
Virginia C. Gildersleeve

For France:
J. Paul-Boncour

For Argentina:
M. Cárcano
O. Ibarra G.
Juan Carlos Bassi
A. D. Brunet

For Australia:
F. M. Forde
H. V. Evatt

For the Kingdom of Belgium:
A. E. De Schryver

For Bolivia:
V. Andrade
C. Salamanca F.
E. Arze Q.

For Brazil:
P. Leão Velloso
C. De Freitas Valle
Gen. Estevao Leitao De Carvalho
A. Camillo De Oliveira
Dr. Bertha Lutz

For the Byelorussian Soviet Socialist Republic:
K. Kiselev
A. Zhebrak
V. Pertsev
G. Baidakov
F. Shmygav

For Canada:
W. L. Mackenzie King
Louis S. St. Laurent

For Chile:
Joaquín Fernández F.
Marcial Mora M.
José Maza
Gabriel González
Contreras Labarca
F. Nieto Del Río
E. Alcalde C.
Germán Vergara
Julio Escudero

For Colombia:
Alberto Lleras
Al González Fernández
Eduardo Zuleta Angel
Silvio Villegas
Jesús M. Yepes

For Costa Rica:
Julio Acosta
J. Rafael Oreamuno

For Cuba:
Gmo. Belt
Ernesto Dihigo

For Czechoslovakia:
Jan Masaryk

For Denmark:
Henrik Kauffmann
Hartvig Frisch
E. Husfeldt

For the Dominican Republic:
M. Peña Batlle
Emilio G. Godoy
Gilberto Sánchez Lustrino
T. Franco F.
Minerva Bernardino

For Ecuador:
C. Ponce Enríquez
Galo Plaza
C. Tobar Zaldumbide

For Egypt:
A. Badawi
Ib. Hadi

For El Salvador:
Héctor David Castro
Carlos Leiva, M. D.

For Ethiopia:
Aklilu H.
Ambaye W.
Ephrem T. Medhen

For Greece:
J. A. Sofianopoulos

For Guatemala:
Guillermo Toriello
M. Noriega M.
E. Silva Peña

For Haiti:
Gerard Lescot
A. Liautaud

For Honduras:
Julián R. Cáceres
Marcos Carias Reyes
Virgilio R. Galvez

For India:
A. Ramaswami Mudaliar
V. T. Krishnamachari

For Iran:
Mostafa Adle

For Iraq:
Mohd. Fadhel Jamali

For Lebanon:
W. Naim
A. Yafi
Salem
Charles Malik

For Liberia:
C. L. Simpson
Gabriel L. Dennis

J. Lemuel Gibson
Richard Henries
M. N. Grant

For the Grand Duchy of Luxembourg:
Hugues Le Gallais

For Mexico:
E. Padilla
F. Castillo Nájera
Manuel Tello

For the Kingdom of the Netherlands:
A. Loudon

For New Zealand:
Peter Fraser
C. A. Berendsen

For Nicaragua:
Mariano Argüello
Luis Manuel De Bayle

For the Kingdom of Norway:
Wilhelm Munthe Morgenstierne

For Panama:
Roberto Jiménez

For Paraguay:
Celso R. Velázquez
J. B. Ayala

For Peru:
Manuel C. Gallagher
V. A. Belaunde
Luis Fernán Cisneros

For the Philippine Commonwealth:
Carlos P. Romulo
Francisco A. Delgado

For Poland:
(*to be signed at a later date*)

For Saudi Arabia:
Faisal

For Syria:
F. Al-Khouri
N. Antaki
N. Koudsi

For Turkey:
Hasan Saka
Huseyin Ragip Baydur
Feridun Cemal Erkin

For the Ukrainian Soviet Socialist Republic:
Dm. Manuilsky
Ivan Senin
Alexander Palladin
Mikola Petrovsky

For the Union of South Africa:
J. C. Smuts F.M.

For Uruguay:
José Serrato
Jacobo Varela
Héctor Luisi
Cy. Giambruno
Juan F. Guichón
Héctor Payssé Reyes

For Venezuela:
C. Parra Pérez
Gustavo Herrera
A Machado Hndz.
R. Ernesto López

For Yugoslavia:
Stanoje Simic

APPENDIX II

THE COVENANT OF THE LEAGUE OF NATIONS[1]

with Amendments in Force, June 26, 1945

The High Contracting Parties,

In order to promote international co-operation and to achieve international peace and security

by the acceptance of obligations not to resort to war,

by the prescription of open, just and honourable relations between nations,

by the firm establishment of the understandings of international law as the actual rule of conduct among Governments, and

by the maintenance of justice and a scrupulous respect for all treaty obligations in the dealings of organised peoples with one another,

Agree to this Covenant of the League of Nations.

Article 1

Membership and Withdrawal

1. The original members of the League of Nations shall be those of the Signatories which are named in the Annex to this Covenant and also such of those other States named in the Annex as shall accede without reservation to this Covenant. Such accession shall be effected by a Declaration deposited with the Secretariat within two months of the coming into force of the Covenant. Notice thereof shall be sent to all other Members of the League.

2. Any fully self-governing State, Dominion or Colony not named in the Annex may become a Member of the League if its admission is agreed to by two-thirds of the Assembly, provided that it shall give effective guarantees of its sincere intention to observe its international obligations, and shall accept such regulations as may be prescribed by the League in regard to its military, naval and air forces and armaments.

3. Any Member of the League may, after two years' notice of its intention so to do, withdraw from the League, provided that all its international obligations and all its obligations under this Covenant shall have been fulfilled at the time of its withdrawal.[2]

[1] Entered into force on January 10, 1920. The texts printed in italics indicate the amendments. Article 6 as amended has been in force since August 13, 1924, Articles 12, 13 and 15 as amended since September 26, 1924, and Article 4 as amended since July 29, 1926.

[2] Withdrawals and expulsion from the League listed on p. 377.

Article 2

Executive Organs

The action of the League under this Covenant shall be effected through the instrumentality of an Assembly and of a Council, with a permanent Secretariat.

Article 3

Assembly

1. The Assembly shall consist of Representatives of the Members of the League.
2. The Assembly shall meet at stated intervals and from time to time as occasion may require, at the Seat of the League or at such other place as may be decided upon.
3. The Assembly may deal at its meetings with any matter within the sphere of action of the League or affecting the peace of the world.
4. At meetings of the Assembly each Member of the League shall have one vote, and may have not more than three Representatives.

Article 4

Council

1. The Council shall consist of representatives of the Principal Allied and Associated Powers [United States of America, the British Empire, France, Italy and Japan], together with Representatives of four other Members of the League. These four Members of the League shall be selected by the Assembly from time to time in its discretion. Until the appointment of the Representatives of the four Members of the League first selected by the Assembly, Representatives of Belgium, Brazil, Spain and Greece shall be Members of the Council.
2. With the approval of the majority of the Assembly, the Council may name additional Members of the League, whose Representatives shall always be Members of the Council; the Council with like approval may increase the number of Members of the League to be selected by the Assembly for representation on the Council.
2 *bis. The Assembly shall fix by a two-thirds majority the rules dealing with the election of the non-permanent Members of the Council, and particularly such regulations as relate to their term of office and the conditions of re-eligibility.*
3. The Council shall meet from time to time as occasion may require, and at least once a year, at the Seat of the League, or at such other place as may be decided upon.
4. The Council may deal at its meetings with any matter within the sphere of action of the League or affecting the peace of the world.
5. Any Member of the League not represented on the Council shall be invited to send a Representative to sit as a member at any meeting of the Council during the consideration of matters specially affecting the interests of that Member of the League.
6. At meetings of the Council, each Member of the League represented on the Council shall have one vote, and may have not more than one Representative.

Article 5

Voting and Procedure

1. Except where otherwise expressly provided in this Covenant or by the terms of the present Treaty, decisions at any meeting of the Assembly or of the Council shall require the agreement of all the Members of the League represented at the meeting.

2. All matters of procedure at meetings of the Assembly or of the Council, including the appointment of Committees to investigate particular matters, shall be regulated by the Assembly or by the Council and may be decided by a majority of the Members of the League represented at the meeting.

3. The first meeting of the Assembly and the first meeting of the Council shall be summoned by the President of the United States of America.

Article 6

Secretariat and Expenses

1. The permanent Secretariat shall be established at the Seat of the League. The Secretariat shall comprise a Secretary-General and such secretaries and staff as may be required.

2. The first Secretary-General shall be the person named in the Annex; thereafter the Secretary-General shall be appointed by the Council with the approval of the majority of the Assembly.

3. The secretaries and the staff of the Secretariat shall be appointed by the Secretary-General with the approval of the Council.

4. The Secretary-General shall act in that capacity at all meetings of the Assembly and of the Council.

5. *The expenses of the League shall be borne by the Members of the League in the proportion decided by the Assembly.*

Article 7

Seat, Qualifications of Officials, Immunities

1. The Seat of the League is established at Geneva.

2. The Council may at any time decide that the Seat of the League shall be established elsewhere.

3. All positions under or in connection with the League, including the Secretariat, shall be open equally to men and women.

4. Representatives of the Members of the League and officials of the League when engaged on the business of the League shall enjoy diplomatic privileges and immunities.

5. The buildings and other property occupied by the League or its officials or by Representatives attending its meetings shall be inviolable.

Article 8

Reduction of Armaments

1. The Members of the League recognise that the maintenance of peace requires the reduction of national armaments to the lowest point consistent with national safety and the enforcement by common action of international obligations.

2. The Council, taking account of the geographical situation and circumstances of each State, shall formulate plans for such reduction for the consideration and action of the several Governments.

3. Such plans shall be subject to reconsideration and revision at least every ten years.

4. After these plans shall have been adopted by the several Governments, the limits of armaments therein fixed shall not be exceeded without the concurrence of the Council.

5. The Members of the League agree that the manufacture by private enterprise of munitions and implements of war is open to grave objections. The Council shall advise how the evil effects attendant upon such manufacture can be prevented, due regard being had to the necessities of those Members of the League which are not able to manufacture the munitions and implements of war necessary for their safety.

6. The Members of the League undertake to interchange full and frank information as to the scale of their armaments, their military, naval and air programmes and the condition of such of their industries as are adaptable to war-like purposes.

Article 9

Permanent Military, Naval and Air Commission

A permanent Commission shall be constituted to advise the Council on the execution of the provisions of Articles 1 and 8 and on military, naval and air questions generally.

Article 10

Guaranties Against Aggression

The Members of the League undertake to respect and preserve as against external aggression the territorial integrity and existing political independence of all Members of the League. In case of any such aggression or in case of any threat or danger of such aggression the Council shall advise upon the means by which this obligation shall be fulfilled.

Article 11

Action in Case of War or Threat of War

1. Any war or threat of war, whether immediately affecting any of the Members of the League or not, is hereby declared a matter of concern to the whole League, and the League shall take any action that may be deemed wise and effectual to safeguard the peace of nations. In case any such emergency should

arise, the Secretary-General shall on the request of any Member of the League forthwith summon a meeting of the Council.

2. It is also declared to be the friendly right of each Member of the League to bring to the attention of the Assembly or of the Council any circumstance whatever affecting international relations which threatens to disturb international peace or the good understanding between nations upon which peace depends.

Article 12

Disputes to Be Submitted for Settlement

1. The Members of the League agree that if there should arise between them any dispute likely to lead to a rupture, they will submit the matter either to arbitration *or judicial settlement* or to inquiry by the Council, and they agree in no case to resort to war until three months after the award by the arbitrators *or the judicial decision* or the report by the Council.

2. In any case under this Article the award of the arbitrators *or the judicial decision* shall be made within a reasonable time, and the report of the Council shall be made within six months after the submission of the dispute.

Article 13

Arbitration or Judicial Settlement

1. The Members of the League agree that whenever any dispute shall arise between them which they recognise to be suitable for submission to arbitration *or judicial settlement,* and which can not be satisfactorily settled by diplomacy, they will submit the whole subject-matter to arbitration *or judicial settlement.*

2. Disputes as to the interpretation of a treaty, as to any question of international law, as to the existence of any fact which if established would constitute a breach of any international obligation, or as to the extent and nature of the reparation to be made for any such breach, are declared to be among those which are generally suitable for submission to arbitration *or judicial settlement.*

3. *For the consideration of any such dispute, the court to which the case is referred shall be the Permanent Court of International Justice, established in accordance with Article 14, or any tribunal agreed on by the parties to the dispute or stipulated in any convention existing between them.*

4. The Members of the League agree that they will carry out in full good faith any award *or decision* that may be rendered, and that they will not resort to war against a Member of the League which complies therewith. In the event of any failure to carry out such an award *or decision,* the Council shall propose what steps should be taken to give effect thereto.

Article 14

Permanent Court of International Justice

The Council shall formulate and submit to the Members of the League for adoption plans for the establishment of a Permanent Court of International Justice. The Court shall be competent to hear and determine any dispute of an international character which the parties thereto submit to it. The Court may also give an advisory opinion upon any dispute or question referred to it by the Council or by the Assembly.

Article 15

Disputes Not Submitted to Arbitration or Judicial Settlement

1. If there should arise between Members of the League any dispute likely to lead to a rupture, which is not submitted to arbitration *or judicial settlement* in accordance with Article 13, the Members of the League agree that they will submit the matter to the Council. Any party to the dispute may effect such submission by giving notice of the existence of the dispute to the Secretary-General, who will make all necessary arrangements for a full investigation and consideration thereof.

2. For this purpose the parties to the dispute will communicate to the Secretary-General, as promptly as possible, statements of their case with all the relevant facts and papers, and the Council may forthwith direct the publication thereof.

3. The Council shall endeavour to effect a settlement of the dispute, and, if such efforts are successful, a statement shall be made public giving such facts and explanations regarding the dispute and the terms of settlement thereof as the Council may deem appropriate.

4. If the dispute is not thus settled, the Council either unanimously or by a majority vote shall make and publish a report containing a statement of the facts of the dispute and the recommendations which are deemed just and proper in regard thereto.

5. Any Member of the League represented on the Council may make public a statement of the facts of the dispute and of its conclusions regarding the same.

6. If a report by the Council is unanimously agreed to by the Members thereof other than the Representatives of one or more of the parties to the dispute, the Members of the League agree that they will not go to war with any party to the dispute which complies with the recommendations of the report.

7. If the Council fails to reach a report which is unanimously agreed to by the members thereof, other than the Representatives of one or more of the parties to the dispute, the Members of the League reserve to themselves the right to take such action as they shall consider necessary for the maintenance of right and justice.

8. If the dispute between the parties is claimed by one of them, and is found by the Council, to arise out of a matter which by international law is solely within the domestic jurisdiction of that party, the Council shall so report, and shall make no recommendation as to its settlement.

9. The Council may in any case under this Article refer the dispute to the Assembly. The dispute shall be so referred at the request of either party to the dispute, provided that such request be made within fourteen days after the submission of the dispute to the Council.

10. In any case referred to the Assembly, all the provisions of this Article and of Article 12 relating to the action and powers of the Council shall apply to the action and powers of the Assembly, provided that a report made by the Assembly, if concurred in by the Representatives of those Members of the League

represented on the Council and of a majority of the other Members of the League, exclusive in each case of the Representatives of the parties to the dispute, shall have the same force as a report by the Council concurred in by all the members thereof other than the Representatives of one or more of the parties to the dispute.

Article 16

Sanctions

1. Should any Member of the League resort to war in disregard of its covenants under Articles 12, 13 or 15, it shall *ipso facto* be deemed to have committed an act of war against all other Members of the League, which hereby undertake immediately to subject it to the severance of all trade or financial relations, the prohibition of all intercourse between their nationals and the nationals of the covenant-breaking State, and the prevention of all financial, commercial or personal intercourse between the nationals of the covenant-breaking State and the nationals of any other State, whether a Member of the League or not.

2. It shall be the duty of the Council in such case to recommend to the several Governments concerned what effective military, naval or air force the Members of the League shall severally contribute to the armed forces to be used to protect the covenants of the League.

3. The Members of the League agree, further, that they will mutually support one another in the financial and economic measures which are taken under this Article, in order to minimise the loss and inconvenience resulting from the above measures, and that they will mutually support one another in resisting any special measures aimed at one of their number by the covenant-breaking State, and that they will take the necessary steps to afford passage through their territory to the forces of any of the Members of the League which are co-operating to protect the covenants of the League.

4. Any Member of the League which has violated any covenant of the League may be declared to be no longer a Member of the League by a vote of the Council concurred in by the Representatives of all the other members of the League represented thereon.

Article 17

Disputes Involving Non-Members

1. In the event of a dispute between a Member of the League and a State which is not a Member of the League, or between States not Members of the League, the State or States not Members of the League shall be invited to accept the obligations of membership in the League for the purposes of such dispute, upon such conditions as the Council may deem just. If such invitation is accepted, the provisions of Articles 12 to 16 inclusive shall be applied with such modifications as may be deemed necessary by the Council.

2. Upon such invitation being given the Council shall immediately institute

an inquiry into the circumstances of the dispute and recommend such action as may seem best and most effectual in the circumstances.

3. If a State so invited shall refuse to accept the obligations of membership in the League for the purposes of such dispute, and shall resort to war against a Member of the League, the provisions of Article 16 shall be applicable as against the State taking such action.

4. If both parties to the dispute when so invited refuse to accept the obligations of Membership in the League for the purposes of such dispute, the Council may take such measures and make such recommendations as will prevent hostilities and will result in the settlement of the dispute.

Article 18

Registration and Publication of Treaties

Every treaty or international engagement entered into hereafter by any Member of the League shall be forthwith registered with the Secretariat and shall as soon as possible be published by it. No such treaty or international engagement shall be binding until so registered.

Article 19

Review of Treaties

The Assembly may from time to time advise the reconsideration by Members of the League of treaties which have become inapplicable and the consideration of international conditions whose continuance might endanger the peace of the world.

Article 20

Abrogation of Inconsistent Obligations

1. The Members of the League severally agree that this Covenant is accepted as abrogating all obligations or understandings *inter se* which are inconsistent with the terms thereof, and solemnly undertake that they will not hereafter enter into any engagements inconsistent with the terms thereof.

2. In case any Member of the League shall, before becoming a Member of the League, have undertaken any obligations inconsistent with the terms of this Covenant, it shall be the duty of such Member to take immediate steps to procure its release from such obligations.

Article 21

Engagements that Remain Valid

Nothing in this Covenant shall be deemed to affect the validity of international engagements, such as treaties of arbitration or regional understandings like the Monroe doctrine, for securing the maintenance of peace.

Article 22

Mandate System

1. To those colonies and territories which as a consequence of the late war have ceased to be under the sovereignty of the States which formerly governed them and which are inhabited by peoples not yet able to stand by themselves under the strenuous conditions of the modern world, there should be applied the principle that the well-being and development of such peoples form a sacred trust of civilisation and that securities for the performance of this trust should be embodied in this Covenant.

2. The best method of giving practical effect to this principle is that the tutelage of such peoples should be entrusted to advanced nations who by reason of their resources, their experience or their geographical position can best undertake this responsibility, and who are willing to accept it, and that this tutelage should be exercised by them as Mandatories on behalf of the League.

3. The character of the mandate must differ according to the stage of the development of the people, the geographical situation of the territory, its economic conditions and other similar circumstances.

4. Certain communities formerly belonging to the Turkish Empire have reached a stage of development where their existence as independent nations can be provisionally recognised subject to the rendering of administrative advice and assistance by a Mandatory until such time as they are able to stand alone. The wishes of these communities must be a principal consideration in the selection of the Mandatory.

5. Other peoples, especially those of Central Africa, are at such a stage that the Mandatory must be responsible for the administration of the territory under conditions which will guarantee freedom of conscience and religion, subject only to the maintenance of public order and morals, the prohibition of abuses such as the slave trade, the arms traffic and the liquor traffic, and the prevention of the establishment of fortifications or military and naval bases and of military training of the natives for other than police purposes and the defence of territory, and will also secure equal opportunities for the trade and commerce of other Members of the League.

6. There are territories, such as South-West Africa and certain of the South Pacific Islands which owing to the sparseness of their population or their small size or their remoteness from the centres of civilisation or their geographical contiguity to the territory of the Mandatory, and other circumstances, can be best administered under the laws of the Mandatory as integral portions of its territory, subject to the safeguards above mentioned in the interests of the indigenous population.

7. In every case of mandate, the Mandatory shall render to the Council an annual report in reference to the territory committed to its charge.

8. The degree of authority, control, or administration to be exercised by the Mandatory shall, if not previously agreed upon by the Members of the League, be explicitly defined in each case by the Council.

9. A permanent Commission shall be constituted to receive and examine the annual reports of the Mandatories and to advise the Council on all matters relating to the observance of the mandates.

Article 23

Social and Other Activities

Subject to and in accordance with the provisions of international conventions existing or hereafter to be agreed upon, the Members of the League:

(a) will endeavour to secure and maintain fair and humane conditions of labour for men, women, and children, both in their own countries and in all countries to which their commercial and industrial relations extend and for that purpose will establish and maintain the necessary international organisations;

(b) undertake to secure just treatment of the native inhabitants of territories under their control;

(c) will entrust the League with the general supervision over the execution of agreements with regard to traffic in women and children, and the traffic in opium and other dangerous drugs;

(d) will entrust the League with the general supervision of the trade in arms and ammunition with the countries in which the control of this traffic is necessary in the common interest;

(e) will make provision to secure and maintain freedom of communications and of transit and equitable treatment for the commerce of all Members of the League. In this connection, the special necessities of the regions devastated during the war of 1914–1918 shall be borne in mind;

(f) will endeavour to take steps in matters of international concern for the prevention and control of disease.

Article 24

International Bureaus

1. There shall be placed under the direction of the League all international bureaux already established by general treaties if the parties to such treaties consent. All such international bureaux and all commissions for the regulation of matters of international interest hereafter constituted shall be placed under the direction of the League.

2. In all matters of international interest which are regulated by general conventions but which are not placed under the control of international bureaux or commissions, the Secretariat of the League shall, subject to the consent of the Council and if desired by the parties, collect and distribute all relevant information and shall render any other assistance which may be necessary or desirable.

3. The Council may include as part of the expenses of the Secretariat the expenses of any bureau or commission which is placed under the direction of the League.

Article 25

Promotion of Red Cross and Health

The Members of the League agree to encourage and promote the establishment and co-operation of duly authorised voluntary national Red Cross organisations having as purposes the improvement of health, the prevention of disease and the mitigation of suffering throughout the world.

Article 26

Amendments

1. Amendments to this Covenant will take effect when ratified by the Members of the League whose Representatives compose the Council and by a majority of the Members of the League whose Representatives compose the Assembly.

2. No such amendment shall bind any Member of the League which signifies its dissent therefrom, but in that case it shall cease to be a Member of the League.

ANNEX

I. Original Members of the League of Nations, Signatories of the Treaty of Peace

*United States of America
Belgium
Bolivia
Brazil
British Empire
  Canada
  Australia
  South Africa
  New Zealand
  India
China
Cuba
†Ecuador
France
Greece
Guatemala
Haiti

*Hedjaz
Honduras
Italy
Japan
Liberia
Nicaragua
Panama
Peru
Poland
Portugal
Roumania
Serb-Croat-Slovene State [Yugoslavia]
Siam
Czecho-Slovakia
Uruguay

States invited to accede to the Covenant

Argentine Republic
Chile
Colombia
Denmark
Netherlands
Norway
Paraguay

Persia [Iran]
Salvador
Spain
Sweden
Switzerland
Venezuela

* Never accepted membership by ratification of treaty of peace.
† Did not accept membership by ratification of treaty of peace, but was admitted in 1934.

II. First Secretary-General of the League of Nations
The Honorable Sir James Eric Drummond, K.C.M.G., C.B.[1]

States Admitted to Membership

Afghanistan	Sept. 27, 1934	Germany	Sept. 8, 1926
Albania	Dec. 17, 1920	Hungary	Sept. 18, 1922
Austria[2]	Dec. 15, 1920	Iraq	Oct. 3, 1932
Bulgaria	Dec. 16, 1920	Irish Free State[3]	Sept. 10, 1923
Costa Rica	Dec. 16, 1920	Latvia	Sept. 22, 1921
Dominican Republic	Sept. 29, 1924	Lithuania	Sept. 22, 1921
Ecuador	Sept. 28, 1934	Luxemburg	Dec. 16, 1920
Egypt	May 26, 1937	Mexico	Sept. 12, 1931
Estonia	Sept. 22, 1921	Turkey	July 18, 1932
Ethiopia	Sept. 28, 1923	Union of Soviet	
Finland	Dec. 16, 1920	Socialist Republics[4]	Sept. 18, 1934

Withdrawals and Expulsion from Membership in the League of Nations

Country	Notification of Withdrawal	Ceased to be a Member
Austria[2]		
Brazil	June 14, 1926	June 13, 1928
Chile	June 2, 1938	June 1, 1940
Costa Rica	Dec. 24, 1924	Jan. 1, 1927
Germany	Oct. 21, 1933	Oct. 20, 1935
Guatemala	May 26, 1936	May 25, 1938
Honduras	July 10, 1936	July 9, 1938
Hungary	Apr. 11, 1939	Apr. 10, 1941
Italy	Dec. 11, 1937	Dec. 10, 1939
Japan	Mar. 27, 1933	Mar. 26, 1935
Nicaragua	June 27, 1936	June 26, 1938
Paraguay	Feb. 24, 1937	Feb. 23, 1939
Peru	Apr. 8, 1939	Apr. 8, 1941
Roumania	July 11, 1940	July 10, 1942
Salvador	Aug. 10, 1937	Aug. 9, 1939
Spain	May 9, 1939	May 8, 1941
Union of Soviet Socialist Republics		Dec. 14, 1939
Venezuela	July 11, 1938	July 10, 1940

[1] Served until June 30, 1933; succeeded by Joseph Avenol, who resigned in July, 1940, after which Sean Lester of Ireland became Acting Secretary-General.

[2] The German Government informed the League on March 18, 1938, that Austria ceased to be a member owing to the joining of Austria with the Reich.

[3] The new constitution, which became effective December 29, 1937, designates the Gaelic name "Eire" for Ireland.

[4] Expelled from membership on December 14, 1939.

Members of the League of Nations, June 26, 1945

Afghanistan	Eire (Ireland)	New Zealand
Albania	Estonia	Norway
Argentina	Ethiopia	Panama
Australia	Finland	Poland
Belgium	France[1]	Portugal
Bolivia	Greece	South Africa
Bulgaria	Haiti	Sweden
Canada	India	Switzerland
China	Iran (Persia)	Thailand (Siam)
Colombia	Iraq	Turkey
Cuba	Latvia	United Kingdom of
Czechoslovakia	Liberia	Great Britain and
Denmark	Lithuania	Northern Ireland
Dominican Republic	Luxemburg	Uruguay
Ecuador	Mexico	Yugoslavia
Egypt	Netherlands	

[1] Admiral Darlan sent a telegram of withdrawal on April 19, 1941. General de Gaulle on April 16, 1943, in a telegram to the Secretary-General declared that the notification "made under foreign pressure can have no effect and that consequently France continues to be a member of the League."